The Canada Among Nations Series

Canada Among Nations 1998: Leadership and Dialogue, edited by
Fen Osler Hampson and Maureen Appel Molot
019-541406-3

Canada Among Nations 1999: A Big League Player?, edited by
Fen Osler Hampson, Michael Hart, and Martin Rudner
019-541458-6

Canada Among Nations 2000: Vanishing Borders, edited by
Maureen Appel Molot and Fen Osler Hampson
019-541540-X

Canada Among Nations 2001: The Axworthy Legacy, edited by
Fen Osler Hampson, Norman Hillmer, and Maureen Appel Molot
019-541677-8

Canada Among Nations 2002: A Fading Power, edited by
Norman Hillmer and Maureen Appel Molot
019-541791-7

Canada Among Nations 2003: Coping with the American Colossus,
edited by David Carment, Fen Osler Hampson, Norman Hillmer
0-19-541924-3

CANADA AMONG NATIONS 2003

Coping with the American Colossus

Edited by
David Carment, Fen Osler Hampson,
and Norman Hillmer

OXFORD
UNIVERSITY PRESS

OXFORD
UNIVERSITY PRESS

70 Wynford Drive, Don Mills, Ontario M3C 1J9
www.oup.com/ca

Oxford University Press is a department of the University of Oxford.
It furthers the University's objective of excellence in research, scholarship,
and education by publishing worldwide in

Oxford   New York

Auckland   Bangkok   Buenos Aires   Cape Town   Chennai
Dar es Salaam   Delhi   Hong Kong   Istanbul   Karachi   Kolkata
Kuala Lumpur   Madrid   Melbourne   Mexico City   Mumbai   Nairobi
São Paulo   Shanghai   Taipei   Tokyo   Toronto

Oxford is a trade mark of Oxford University Press
in the UK and in certain other countries

Published in Canada
by Oxford University Press

Copyright © Oxford University Press Canada 2003

The moral rights of the author have been asserted

Database right Oxford University Press (maker)

First published 2003

The National Library of Canada has catalogued this publication as follows:
Canada among nations
Annual.
1984-
Produced by the Norman Paterson School of International Affairs at Carleton University.
Publisher varies.
Includes bibliographical references.
ISSN 0832-0683
ISBN 0-19-541924-3 (2003 edition)

1. Canada—Foreign relations—1945- —Periodicals. 2. Canada—Politics and government—
1984- —Periodicals. 3. Canada—Politics and government—1980-84—Periodicals.
I. Norman Paterson School of International Affairs

FC242.C345   327.71   C86-031285-2 rev
F1034.2.C36

1 2 3 4 - 06 05 04 03

This book is printed on permanent (acid-free) paper ∞.
Printed in Canada

CONTENTS

CONTRIBUTORS

Stephen Azzi is a policy officer at the Department of National Defence.

David Bercuson is Director of the Centre for Military and Strategic Studies at the University of Calgary.

Brian Buckley is a retired foreign service officer and teaches news media at The Norman Paterson School of International Affairs at Carleton University.

Anthony Campbell is President of the Canadian Association for Security and Intelligence Studies.

David Carment is an Associate Professor at The Norman Paterson School of International Affairs, Carleton University, Director of the Centre for Security and Defence Studies, and Principal Investigator of the Country Indicators for Foreign Policy Project.

Grant Dawson is a doctoral candidate in the History Department at Carleton University.

Drew Fagan is editorial page editor of the *Globe and Mail*.

Tamara Feick is a graduate student in Canadian Studies at Carleton University and an analyst at the Department of Canadian Heritage.

Robert R. Fowler is Canada's Ambassador to Italy and the Prime Minister's Personal Representative for Africa.

Allan Gotlieb is Chairman of the Donner Canadian Foundation, the Ontario Heritage Foundation, Sotheby's Canada Inc., a senior adviser to the law firm Stikeman Elliott, and was Canadian Ambassador to the United States, 1981–9.

Fen Hampson is a Professor and Director of The Norman Paterson School of International Affairs, Carleton University.

Frank P. Harvey is Director of the Centre for Foreign Policy Studies and Professor of International Relations in the Department of Political Science at Dalhousie University.

Norman Hillmer is Professor of History and International Affairs at Carleton University.

Steven Langdon is Director of African Programs at the Parliamentary Centre, Ottawa, and Conjunct Professor of International Development Studies at Trent University.

Dwight N. Mason is a senior associate at the Center for Strategic and International Studies in Washington. He was the Chairman of the US Section of the Permanent Joint Board on Defence, Canada–United States, from 1994 to 2002.

Mark F. Proudman is a doctoral student in Modern History at Oxford and a contributor to the *National Post*.

Elizabeth Riddell-Dixon is a Professor of International Relations in the Department of Political Science at the University of Western Ontario.

Mira Sucharov is an Assistant Professor in the Department of Political Science at Carleton University.

Christopher Waddell holds the Carty Chair in Business and Financial Journalism at the School of Journalism and Communications at Carleton University.

Inger Weibust is an Assistant Professor at The Norman Paterson School of International Affairs, Carleton University.

ABBREVIATIONS

AAP	Africa Action Plan
APR	Personal Representative for Africa
AU	African Union
AWACS	Airborne Warning and Control System
BMD	ballistic missile defence
BMEWS	Ballistic Missile Early Warning System
CBC	Canadian Broadcasting Corporation
CBC	Conference Board of Canada
CCA	Canadian Conference of the Arts
CCCE	Canadian Council of Chief Executives
CCRA	Canada Customs and Revenue Agency
CF	Canadian Forces
CIA	Central Intelligence Agency (US)
CIDA	Canadian International Development Agency
CP	Canadian Press
CRTC	Canadian Radio-television and Telecommunications Commission
CROP	Centre de Recherche sur l'Opinion Publique
CSE	Communications Security Establishment
CSIS	Canadian Security and Intelligence Service
DEW	Distant Early Warning
DFAIT	Department of Foreign Affairs and International Trade
DND	Department of National Defence
DOD	Department of Defense (US)
ECOWAS	Economic Community of West African States
EU	European Union
FAST	Free and Secure Trade
FBI	Federal Bureau of Investigation (US)
FBIS	Foreign Broadcast Information Service
FDA	Food and Drug Administration (US)
FEMA	Federal Emergency Management Agency (US)
FTA	Canada–US Free Trade Agreement
GATS	General Agreement on Trade in Services
GATT	General Agreement on Tariffs and Trade
GDP	gross domestic product
HIPC	highly indebted poor countries
HUMINT	Human Intelligence

ICBM	intercontinental ballistic missile
ICC	International Criminal Court
IMF	International Monetary Fund
IMINT	Imagery Intelligence
INCD	International Network for Cultural Diversity
INCP	International Network on Cultural Policy
INS	Immigration and Naturalization Service (US)
ISAF	International Security Assistance Force (Afghanistan)
ITARs	International Traffic in Arms Regulations (US)
JEEMM	Joint Energy and Environment Ministers' Meeting
JIDA	Juxtapose Integrated Development Association (Ghana)
KFOR	Kosovo Force
LDCs	least-developed countries
LORAN	long-range navigation
MAD	mutually assured destruction
MAP	Millennium African Plan
MCC	Military Co-operation Committee
NACD	nuclear non-proliferation, arms control, and disarmament
NAFTA	North American Free Trade Agreement
NAMU	North American monetary unit
NATO	North Atlantic Treaty Organization
NDP	New Democratic Party
NEPAD	New Partnership for Africa's Development
NGO	non-governmental organization
NORAD	North American Aerospace Defence Command
NORTHCOM	Northern Command (US)
NSA	National Security Agency (US)
NSS	National Security Strategy (US)
OAU	Organization of African Unity
OAS	Organization of American States
OCIPEP	Office for Critical Infrastructure Protection and Emergency Preparedness
ODA	official development assistance
OECD	Organization for Economic Co-operation and Development
OPEC	Organization of Petroleum Exporting Countries
OSSINT	Open Source Intelligence

PCO	Privy Council Office
PJBD	Permanent Joint Board on Defence
PLO	Palestine Liberation Organization
PRSP	Poverty Reduction Strategy Paper
RCAF	Royal Canadian Air Force
RCI	Radio Canada International
RCMP	Royal Canadian Mounted Police
RWG	working group on refugees
SAC	Strategic Air Command
SAGIT	Sectoral Advisory Group on International Trade
SFOR	Stabilization Force (NATO, Bosnia-Herzegovina)
SHIRBRIG	Stand-by High Readiness Brigade
SIGINT	Signals Intelligence
SLBM	submarine-launched ballistic missile
UNESCO	United Nations Educational, Scientific and Cultural Organization
UNDP	United Nations Development Program
UNICEF	United Nations International Children's Emergency Fund/ United Nations Children's Fund
UNMOVIC	United Nations Monitoring, Verification and Inspection Commission
UNSCOM	United Nations Special Commission
USTR	United States Trade Representative
VCR	Voluntary Challenge and Registry
WMD	weapons of mass destruction
WSSD	World Summit on Sustainable Development
WTO	World Trade Organization

Preface

Our subject is Canada's complex relationship with the United States. Just three years ago, when *Canada Among Nations* presented its last examination of Canadian-American relations, *Vanishing Borders*, the US economy was experiencing the longest uninterrupted period of growth and expansion in the post-World War II era. Canadians peeked enviously across the border at booming American incomes, productivity, and hopes for the future. But now the US struggles, running up sizable deficits while political leaders in Ottawa hold to balanced budgets and increase government expenditure on health, education, and defence. In 2001, the Canadian economy grew by 1.5 per cent, and it surged by 3.3 per cent in 2002. Canada's job-creation numbers continue to surprise the most hardened skeptics. Even the Canadian dollar is moving out of the doldrums in response to growing investor confidence and rising interest rates. Canada sports one of the best economic performances among the G-7 industrial countries.

Yet Canadians are experienced pessimists, and with some reason. The echoes of a weakening US economy are already reverberating north of the border. The Canadian economy is slowing, too, with the rate of growth, at 1.2 per cent for the first quarter of 2003, less than had been expected. Protectionist impulses are increasing in the United States, with the potential to jeopardize Canadian trade, which

is more concentrated in the American market than ever before. The
American share of Canada's exports has risen from 73 per cent to 87 ✗
per cent since the signing of the Canada–US Free Trade Agreement
in 1988.

The essays in this volume concentrate on the impact of Canada's
relationship with the American colossus on a wide range of fronts:
economic, diplomatic, political, cultural, military/security, and global.
The international security environment changed dramatically with
the 11 September 2001 terrorist attacks on the World Trade Center in
New York and the Pentagon in Arlington, Virginia. Washington's
responses—the intervention in Afghanistan, conflict with Iraq, anti-
insurgent forces in the Philippines, a global crackdown on Al-Qaeda
ring leaders, Tom Ridge's Department of Homeland Security, and a
series of major initiatives to secure the US/Canada/Mexico borders—
signal a government in Washington with a revolutionary conception
of the American national interest. Like many of America's traditional
allies, Canada is concerned about American military power and the
long-term consequences of President George W. Bush's war against
terrorism. Unlike Britain, France, or Germany, whose economic and
political fortunes are tied to the European Union, Canada's trade
dependence on the United States and vulnerability to US pressure
give this country less latitude to express its views and chart an
autonomous course. The events of 11 September fundamentally
altered the context and dynamic of the Canada-US relationship.

The Canadian diplomatic tradition has been to react where and
when necessary, and to meet new risks and dangers with caution and
creativity, one step at a time. Canada's officials have been effective
crisis managers, but in the world's emergencies of 2003 too much
improvisation may ultimately take the country in directions it is
unprepared to go. Unless Canada develops its own clear sense of
what it wants out of the Canada–US relationship and a well-defined
strategy for achieving its goals, it is possible that policies on a whole
range of issues will increasingly be driven by Washington's agenda
and interests. But growing ties with the US can translate into opportunity. Canadians are apt to forget how important their country is to
the United States. Wise leadership will chart a course for Canada into
the twenty-first century that rediscovers the fine balance between
autonomy and interdependence.

We have again benefited from the support of Laura Macleod and
Mark Piel and the fine editorial team, led by Phyllis Wilson, at Oxford

University Press. Maureen Molot's experience and counsel were invaluable. Richard Tallman rooted out errors and inconsistencies. Janet Doherty organized the authors' workshop in December 2002 and frequently organized the editors as well. David Perdue provided valuable research assistance and ensured a smooth line of communication between editors and contributors. Vivian Cummins superbly proofread the final typescript. For their crucial support in the production of the volume, we thank Allan Maslove, the Dean of Carleton University's Faculty of Public Affairs and Management, and the Centre for Security and Defence Studies at Carleton.

This is the nineteenth volume in the *Canada Among Nations* series of The Norman Paterson School of International Affairs, and this is the nineteenth time we have relied utterly on Brenda Sutherland's administrative acumen. With humour, skepticism, and an infallible sense of timing, she guided the manuscript to completion under the tightest of deadlines. We dedicate this volume to her with respect, affection, and gratitude.

David Carment
Fen Osler Hampson
Norman Hillmer

11 March 2003
Ottawa, Ontario

1

Introduction: Is Canada Now Irrelevant?

NORMAN HILLMER, DAVID CARMENT,
AND FEN OSLER HAMPSON

Talk of war and empire is everywhere. In the 2000 presidential campaign, George W. Bush promised a humble United States, mindful of
its own business and respectful of others, but the terrorist attacks of
11 September 2001 transformed him into a war leader. Those attacks,
Michael Ignatieff has argued, unleashed 'an exercise in imperialism.
This may come as a shock to Americans, who don't like to think
of their country as an empire. But what else can you call America's
legions of soldiers, spooks and Special Forces straddling the globe?'
(Ignatieff, 2002: 28). As we write in early March 2003, President Bush
fights his war on terror on several fronts, at home and in Afghanistan,
the Philippines, Pakistan, and Yemen. He is on the edge, too, of
opening another front in Iraq, which stands accused of links with
Osama bin Laden's Al-Qaeda as well as ambitions to launch weapons
of mass destruction and build even more lethal ones. North Korea,
far more dangerous than any other external threat because its nuclear
weapons capability is real, is left to one side, despite its official

standing in Bush's axis-of-evil club. War in Asia would be unthinkable. There is a limit even to the power of the American empire.

EMPIRE: 'GET USED TO IT'

War and empire, as practised in President Bush's Washington, have presented the international community with a daunting challenge: how to cope with an American colossus awakened from a deep sleep of domestic tranquility and economic good times, and absolutely determined to have its own way in the world. In one sense, the problem is a familiar one, and one with which Canadians have more than a passing acquaintance. The colossal weight of the United States is hardly news. French journalist and politician J.J. Servan-Schreiber used precisely that terminology in the mid-1960s to describe 'not classic imperialism' but 'an overflow of power' deriving from the sheer size and smack of the American economy and the dynamism of American society (Servan-Schreiber, 1969: x, 69–71).

Nor is there anything novel in the assertion that Americans, one way or another, are empire-builders. At about the same time that Servan-Schreiber was enjoying blockbuster sales, Michael Ignatieff's uncle, George Grant, published a hugely popular polemic, *Lament for a Nation*, about the defeat of a Canadian nationalism no longer able or willing to cope with the American imperial colossus.

In his *American Empire*, Boston University's Andrew J. Bacevich traces the imperial impulses in recent US foreign policy. Combining the administrations of Presidents George H.W. Bush, Bill Clinton, and George Bush the younger under a single rubric, he argues that the 'purpose is to preserve and, where both feasible and conducive to US interests, to expand an American imperium. Central to this strategy is a commitment to global openness—removing barriers that inhibit the movement of goods, capital, ideas and people. Its ultimate objective is the creation of an open and integrated international order based on the principles of democratic capitalism, with the United States as the ultimate guarantor of order and enforcer of norms.' Different drummers, same drum, says Bacevich of the transition from Clinton to another Bush. 'Like it or not, America today *is* Rome' (Bacevich, 2002: 3, 223–4, 244).

Still, something is different. George W. Bush's America is angry, unsubtle, and insecure. The style, Secretary of State Colin Powell apart, is all strut and swagger, the tone one of 'piety' and 'triumphal arrogance' (Miller, 2003: AR 13). 'The Bush folks are big on attitude, weak on strategy and terrible at diplomacy', complained Tom Friedman in the *New York Times*. And there is the President himself, because the new US diplomacy is difficult to separate from the leader who is its inspiration and personification. Describing Bush as he visited Europe last year, a *Guardian* columnist noted that he looked a bit like a character from an Oscar Wilde novel, 'one of those middle-aged mediocrities, who have no enemies, but are thoroughly disliked by their friends' (Younge, 2002: 17). A 'moron', blurted the communications director of one of those friends, the Canadian Prime Minister (Fife and Alberts, 2002: A13). Françoise Ducros was dismissed for her slip, but so slowly and reluctantly that it reinforced the impression of a Jean Chrétien government that held the same view of President Bush.

Bush is a mediocrity perhaps. He is no intellectual, certainly. But he is a believer, solid in his messianic convictions and firmly in control of his administration (Woodward, 2002: 106). He is easy to underestimate. He will not be shaken, and that, for those who worry, is the most worrying aspect of all about Bushism.

Members of the Bush team, understandably enough, shy away from admitting that they are in the business of empire, but the imperial shout is very much in vogue (Lapham, 2003: 7; Dowd, 2003a: A23). 'The American Empire', announced a red-white-and-blue cover of the *New York Times Magazine* on 5 January 2003, complete with a bit of mellow advice, neatly tucked away in brackets at the bottom of the page, 'Get Used to It' (Ignatieff, 2003). Underlying George Bush's powerful speech to the US Congress, nine days after 11 September, was the claim that the United States had the right to defend itself and 'defend freedom' wherever it deemed necessary. The 'war' (a word unfashionable in the Bill Clinton 1990s, but back in the American strategic lexicon with a vengeance) on terror was to be an all-out campaign, with no room for ambiguity. The President who said he wanted to preside over a modest country gave the world a blunt ultimatum on 20 September, and he has repeated it dozens of times since: 'Either you are with us or you are with the terrorists' (Bacevich, 2002: 225–32).

In Bush's efforts to disarm and oust Saddam Hussein, the US sought the hearts and armies of old allies and new friends for an attack on Iraq. The response was uneven. Tony Blair's British government saluted loyally, and so did Australia. Eight European nations, including Spain and Italy, signed an open letter of support, and the 10 Vilnius nations of eastern Europe did the same. But many others, including the French and the Germans, made their reservations known and happily gathered up political and diplomatic capital from their disagreement. The governments of Russia, China, Mexico, the Gulf states, South Africa, Turkey, and Canada, among others, voiced their concern about the American strategy. Publics dissented everywhere, letting it be known that unless it was a UN war they wanted no part in it (AFP, 2002). 'American imperialism used to be a fiction of the far-left imagination', the *Guardian* reported in an article on European opinion, 'now it is an uncomfortable fact of life' (Bunting, 2003: 13). The President of the United States did not waver, and issued a new threat. As the *New York Times* put it, 'President Bush did not say, You're with us or against us. He said something far more shrewd: Either you're with us, or you're irrelevant' (Schememann, 2003: WK 1).

The admonition of irrelevance has a particular resonance for America's northern neighbour. It has become conventional wisdom to think of Canada as a vulnerable country in international decline, so dependent on the United States that what little room there was for manoeuvre exists no more (Molot and Hillmer, 2002: 6–7). The media are jammed with commentators and experts saying just that. Canadians, writes veteran observer Richard Gwyn, have become 'invisible' and 'irrelevant' on the international stage (Gwyn, 2003: A13). Historian Michael Bliss has gone so far as to propose that Canada consider joining the United States (Bliss, 2003: A14), a strategy reminiscent of late nineteenth-century annexation movements that sought to tie a struggling Canada to a brilliantly shining United States. Yet Canadians have always married their admiration for the US with a stubborn skepticism towards the American experiment, particularly when the White House is in the grip of those thought to be warmongering Republican ideologues like Ronald Reagan or Bush Two. What to do, then? How to become or stay relevant? Is relevance, defined by President Bush, relevant for Canada and Canadians?

THE BUSH DOCTRINE

Canada and the world at large are witnessing a major new assertion of US 'hard' power and influence. The Bush administration has made it abundantly clear that it will not permit its allies or international institutions to stand in the way of the projection and use of that power when real or imagined vital security interests are threatened. The President's National Security Strategy (NSS), promulgated one year after 11 September, proceeds from the assumption that the United States is in a position of unparalleled military strength, political influence, and economic power. It identifies America's main threat as failing states and discounts deterrence and containment as ineffective in a world of amorphous and ill-defined terrorist networks (*Economist*, 2002). The threats in the world are so dangerous that the US should 'not hesitate to act alone, if necessary, to exercise our right of self-defense by acting preemptively' (NSS, 2002: 6). The strategy also states that the US aims to create a new world order that favours democracy and defeats terror at the same time.

Only recently has it been accepted in policy circles that state failures are the single biggest predicament facing the world today, and the NSS document is laudable in recognizing the importance of addressing state failure as an immense structural and global problem that is unlikely to go away in the short run. Many states in the world have failed, are failing, or will fail, largely because the support they received from one or both of the superpowers as proxy allies during the Cold War withered away after the fall of the Berlin Wall. As a result, many weak states were left on their own to live or die or find some existence between the two. The list of failing states is extensive and growing, and all regions of the world are affected by the multiple consequences of these failures: state failures serve as the breeding ground for extremist groups, and most contemporary wars are fought either within nation-states or between states and non-state actors. Few wars pit one nation-state against another. One legacy of the Cold War is that many governments are less readily prepared to wage a conventional war against non-state actors, which are moving targets because they depend on highly decentralized structures that are semi-autonomous and can act and survive on their own.

Bush's National Security Strategy recognizes that conventional approaches to developing a US security policy are inadequate to the task. These traditional approaches can be defined as interest-based or capacity-based. An interest-based strategy is inherently state-based and incapable of addressing faraway and imprecise problems, such as terrorism, that are apparently unrelated to a narrowly defined national interest. A capacity-based approach emphasizing the pursuit of national security policy within existing capabilities is even less applicable because US capabilities and resources now outstrip anything that an adversary could or would want to develop. The NSS suggests a third way based on threat assessment. The US is manifestly in danger both at home and abroad. The Bush strategy is to establish a safe and secure homeland while countering threats, manifest or emergent, from abroad.

None of this is easy or straightforward. In the immediate aftermath of 11 September, media reports indicated that primary countries harbouring terrorists included Afghanistan, Sudan, and Algeria. However, dismantling the Al-Qaeda network now involves intelligence and law enforcement efforts in the over 30 countries where the terrorist gang is believed to have cells. There is also the danger that emphasis will be placed on immediate military solutions to terrorist threats, while the long-term prevention of emergent threats is given a lesser priority. As a consequence, the American penchant for making foreign militaries preferred partners of co-operation in the war against terrorism may undermine delicate civil-military relations in countries such as Pakistan, the Philippines, and Colombia. The implications for countries with fragile or emerging democracies are serious. Hard-won civilian control will be compromised. In other cases, dictators will seize the opportunity thrown up by the Western shift of focus to the fight against terrorism. They might return to old, dictatorial ways, similar to those seen in the Cold War era. Hard-earned progress towards democracy, economic growth, and regional integration could be lost.

James Wolfensohn of the World Bank, as well as others who recognize these problems, has called for attention to the root causes of terrorism and state failure, including poverty, political marginalization, and inequality. To be sure, the Bush government's efforts to address threats abroad do take other forms beyond military intervention. Continuities in US foreign policy exist, including training for armies and police forces trying to deal with terrorism, such as in the Philippines, Pakistan, and Yemen; enhanced American participation in multilateral aid programs, where aid is increasingly tied to 'good governance' by recipient countries; and the pursuit of 'integration', which has the US directing many of its policies towards helping countries to join the international flow of trade and finance. As the world's first 'hyperpower', the US will continue to act firmly within the international system—promoting global public goods, encouraging a world economy, sustaining co-operative relationships with the world's principal powers, curbing rogue states, and helping failed states.

But discontinuities are also notable. The Bush National Security Strategy points to three significant changes in US foreign policy. First, it marks a shift towards military pre-emption to address potential security problems, as opposed to imminent threats. Second, with its emphasis on American-centric norms of appropriate state behaviour, the Bush strategy constitutes a revival of ideological differences, based primarily on democratic principles as defined by the US, as a means to differentiate clearly between allies and enemies. Third, with the wars on Saddam Hussein and Osama bin Laden at centre stage, the current strategy emphasizes the superficial construction of international politics based on personality, the demonizing of individual leaders rather than a more critical and deeper assessment of national and international problems.

The often-argued assumption that US foreign policy is somehow guided by a choice between unilateralism and multilateralism is also troubling. International politics has never been a simple choice of one over the other. Current problems such as human rights, regional conflicts, and terrorism, as well as larger dilemmas such as the growing power and wealth disparities in the world, do not lend themselves to such simple dichotomous analytical frameworks.

A much more significant concern is whether the US is an 'assertive hegemon' or a 'multilateral leader'. Both terms do not deny American power and importance, but they differ in their interpretation of intent. An assertive hegemon is imposing and blind to the interests of its allies; its emergence results in counterbalancing by regional blocs. Multilateral leadership is a more benign interpretation of American power, suggesting a hyperpower sensitive to and cognizant of the needs and interests of allies and a willingness to work through institutions. Gains on all sides are expected and lead to ongoing co-operation and reciprocity.

Critics who accuse the US of hegemonic ambitions call the war on terrorism a 'war without end' that will 'provide a breeding ground for the terrorism the war aims to eliminate' (Light, 2002). Others say the necessity to have allies, intelligence-sharing, and use of foreign airspace and facilities has made the US more multilateralist than ever, adding that, in Dumbrell's words, 'the US under Bush is committed to a new mixture of unilateralism and multilateralism—defined and pursued almost entirely on America's terms' (Dumbrell, 2002). Whether the US is in what EU foreign policy commissioner Chris Patten calls 'unilateralist overdrive' (ibid.) may be debatable. What is clear is that traditional US allies are clearly uncomfortable with America's stance. America's relationships with its friends are strained, and the institutions that once held them together are deteriorating under the Bush Doctrine. Can the US hold onto a unilateralist foreign policy and its friends at the same time?

PRE-EMPTION OR PREVENTION?

Disconcertingly for its allies, the Bushites claim the right of preemption. In fact, the Bush administration often uses the terms 'preemptive' and 'preventive' interchangeably, though these terms have vastly different meanings, logic, and policy implications. Traditionally, 'pre-emptive' action refers to times when states react to an imminent threat of attack. For example, when Egyptian and Syrian forces mobilized on Israel's borders in 1967, the threat was obvious and immediate, and Israel felt justified in pre-emptively attacking those forces. While pre-emptive attacks refer to military action taken in the face of an imminent threat, 'preventive' action usually refers to responding to high-risk situations before they become violent or, in the face of violent conflict, deterring further escalation through limited force and threats to use force.

New in the Bush policy is the application of a 'preventive' doctrine not only to global terrorists but to undesirable state behaviour as well, such as in the case of armed intervention in Iraq. This innovation in foreign policy could have the potential of encouraging other states to follow suit (for example, the Russians in Chechnya) under the protective cover of the Bush canon. The emerging parameters, targets, and approach of the war on terrorism could represent a dangerous 'free licence' for alliance members to attack a range of groups that oppose the state for sound reasons. Attacks on legitimate political expression could spawn a reckless backlash, with uncertain but doubtless substantial consequences.

As John Ikenberry (2002: 45) points out, the critical inconsistency inherent in the new US strategy is that it has the potential to make sovereignty more absolute for the United States even as it becomes more conditional for countries that challenge American standards of internal and external behaviour. By eschewing a multilateral approach aimed at maintaining a global balance of power through containment and deterrence while building order around personalized political relations, the United States may be weakening essential ties with its allies and placing itself in a more insecure and hostile world as a result. In essence, efforts by the US to strengthen its security through 'cowboy diplomacy' could reverse decades of coalition-building and developing international institutions. Marginal states on the threshold of breakdown, such as Egypt, Saudi Arabia, and Indonesia, could find themselves abandoned and even weaker.

US initiatives to build European support for its war against terrorism have centred on the North Atlantic Treaty Organization's push eastward into Central Asia and the Baltics and the encouragement of its members to spend more on defence and to enhance their collective military capabilities. The Iraq issue has divided Europe, and the Germans and French, joined by the Russians, have reacted to American coalition-building for war with a coalition of their own. The Franco-Russian-German declaration of 5 March 2003 against Bush's rush to a military engagement with Saddam Hussein was, in the hyperbole of one journalist, possibly 'the loudest "No!" shouted across the Atlantic in a half century or more' (Tyler, 2003).

The French and German governments remain friendly to the United States, if George Bush will let them. Many European governments are US-boosters, even over Iraq. That issue has torn the European Union asunder—so much for the EU as a rival centre of strength to the US. Beyond Europe, no great alliances are in the making. Russia, China, and India are likely to side with the United States on a great many global issues; Beijing and Moscow have been working hard to build stronger ties with Washington. The complex relationships between Russia, China, and India, furthermore, make co-operation among them unlikely (De Roquefeuil, 2002).

Yet there can be no doubting the Bush administration's rough-and-tumble international conduct on a range of issues on which it would brook no compromise. The US withdrew from the Kyoto Protocol on the environment. It damned the International Criminal Court. It rejected suggested new enforcement provisions for the Biological and Toxin Weapons Convention. It refused to send the comprehensive test-ban treaty to the US Senate a second time for ratification. It decreased funding for nuclear arms control and raised the possibility of designing and testing a new generation of nuclear bombs. So there is a context for the complaints and alarms of the community of nations about American foreign policy and for the polls that find, for example, that a majority of Europeans (55 per cent) believe that the US is itself partly to blame for 11 September (AFP, 2002).

THREATS, 'REAL, IMMEDIATE, HERE'

In Canada, where similar doubts and concerns are rife, anti-Americanism is enjoying one of its recurrent seasons. The Bushites are a rich target for criticism, a tough breed of 'swaggering and contemptuous' ally-adversaries, to adopt the words of an American career diplomat who resigned in early 2003 to protest against the administration's policies (Krugman, 2003). Those 'damn Americans.
I hate those bastards', Liberal parliamentarian Carolyn Parrish scowled as President Bush inched closer to an Iraq war, making it clear that her feelings of animosity centred on the government in Washington. Her colleague Colleen Beaumier had met sympathetically with the Iraqi leadership in late 2002, winning her the nickname 'Baghdad Beaumier' (Fagan, 2003: F2). 'When even the Canadians, normally drearily polite, get colorfully steamed at us, we know the rest of the world is apoplectic', wrote an American commentator (Kristof, 2003). Added another, 'We are scared of the world now, and the world is scared of us' (Dowd, 2003b: WK13)

Richard Gwyn's argument about Canada's irrelevance suggests that anti-Americanism might be an expensive luxury after 11 September. Up until then, it was possible for Canada to parade as the world's great multilateralist, a stance pleasing to a national ego proud of being un-American, while in fact living an existence as a resolutely North American country, increasingly dependent economically and militarily on the United States. The terrorist attacks made the Americans no longer tolerant of lax Canadian security and military policies. A choice must be made, Gwyn believes, between standing 'with the US at its time of need' with the attendant compromise on 'some cherished Canadian values' or standing apart, 'provided we're prepared to pay the economic and diplomatic price. . . . The one thing we cannot do is continue to pretend to ourselves that we can eat our cake and have it.' That would be 'reckless irresponsibility . . . when the conditions that made it possible to maintain the hypocrisy no longer exist' (Gwyn, 2003: A13).

The North American agenda is shaped by international terrorism. Reports by both the US Central Intelligence Agency (CIA) and the Canadian Security and Intelligence Service (CSIS) have underlined the need for a common and tighter security approach, at least on the home front. In March 2002 George Tenet, the CIA director, testified before Congress that terrorism is the most pressing threat to the United States and thus to North America. CSIS concludes that another attack by Islamic extremists remains very likely, drawing attention to the fact that many of Canada's security preoccupations originate abroad, making it imperative to identify and understand overseas developments that could become 'homeland issues' for Canada. A senior Canadian intelligence agent, Michael Kelly, has stated that the threat to Canada 'is real, it's immediate, it's here' (Stern, 2002).

Washington's interest in Canada and the border is unmistakable, and sometimes uncomfortably so for Canadians. The administration has, through a variety of private and public channels, been pressing Ottawa hard to spend more on defence. The Chrétien government, after a long and willful neglect of the military, surrendered an $800 million annual increase for the armed forces in the 2003 budget, to the mild applause of American critics. A Planning Group Agreement of December 2002 arranges for the development of Canadian-American contingency plans to meet a terrorist attack or national disaster (DND, 2002), while US Northern Command, established 1 October 2002, has military operations in the United States, Mexico, and Canada within its jurisdiction (Priest, 2003: 38). American and Canadian officials signed, on 12 December 2002, a comprehensive Smart Border agreement designed to improve security and screening along the border while not impeding the free flow of legitimate goods and people. The Bush administration has also put in place entry visa requirements for Canadian landed immigrants amid continuing accusations, notably from New York Senator Hillary Rodham Clinton, that Canada is a terrorist haven. As of 1 March 2003, the new Department of Homeland Security unleashed a bewildering security bureaucracy, which was bound to create border lineups, difficulties for business, and fewer admissions to the United States from Canada (Segal, 2003: A15).

More is doubtless coming. The US seems intent on a common North American security zone covering land, air, sea, and even outer space. There is likely to be continuing pressure to keep Canadian energy markets open and to strengthen North American energy security in the face of continued vulnerability to disruptions in oil and gas exports from the Middle East, the Persian Gulf, Latin America, and Africa. In the effort to control the flow of illegal immigrants and refugees, the demand is growing for a harmonization of American-

Canadian policies and perhaps even a move in the direction of a common, EU-style customs and immigration zone. Will the 'smart border' prevent a rupture of the Canada–US frontier in the event of future terrorist attacks in the United States? Will the United States government be convinced that Canada has done everything possible if it is discovered that the terrorists came from the north? If Canada is a grudging partner (or no partner at all) in future US-led 'coalitions of the willing'—or what might better be called 'coalitions of the conscripted'—will the White House rush to Canada's defence when Congress demands that the northern border be closed or tightened?

THE FUSION OF ECONOMICS AND SECURITY

With the attacks on the World Trade Center and the Pentagon, Canada–US relations may be entering an era of 'forced linkage' and the fusion of economics and security. The US looks northward, worried about its physical security more than ever before, and embarks on a widespread series of measures to secure its territorial space. The American response to 11 September dramatically demonstrated that Washington will close its borders and stop all traffic if it feels sufficiently threatened. American politicians like Senator Clinton, rightly or wrongly, continue to express concerns about whether their borders are sufficiently protected. An open border—and the relatively free mobility of goods, services, and people across that border—was not very long ago taken for granted. This concept is now hostage to US national security interests and a domestic debate, much of it highly partisan, about how best to keep Americans secure. President Bush has turned a hard face towards the world. He has threatened Mexico with reprisals if it does not support the US over Iraq, saying that 'there will be a certain sense of discipline' if his southern neighbour or other allies oppose him (Krugman, 2003). Perhaps that was careless and inadvertent chatter, perhaps not.

The history of Canadian-American relations has been remarkably free of linkage, the practice of making threats and tying policy performance in one area to another. Canada has pursued its policies without fearing reprisals or sanctions from its neighbour when priorities clashed. The two countries shared values, interests, and goals during the long darkness of the Cold War and into the 1990s. They placed a premium on keeping economic and security policies separate, and the border open for business. Cross-border trade and investment flourished, and the relationship remained on an even keel despite the irritations and controversies of the moment. Historian Greg Donaghy's fine book, *Tolerant Allies: Canada and the United States, 1963–1968*, depicts an alliance constantly negotiated and renegotiated by mature governments:

> Between 1963 and 1968 the Liberal government adopted diplomatic and military postures that acknowledged the diminished Soviet threat, European recovery, and growing domestic demands for a Canadian approach to the world. It undertook this task carefully, with due regard for Washington's strategic interests in North Atlantic solidarity and continuing bilateral arrangements for continental defense. The United States generally accepted Ottawa's evolutionary approach and realistically amended its expectations for Canadian policy. (Donaghy, 2002: 178)

The fusing of economics and security in Canada–US relations—a direct consequence of the US war against terrorism and other security threats in Asia and the Middle East—has occurred with such speed and such a sense of urgency that the dimensions and seriousness of the problem are not as yet fully appreciated. Canada has entered front and square into the American political consciousness because of US concerns about how to manage its borders and reduce its vulnerability to a wide range of internal and external security threats. As the United States looks across its northern border, sometimes glaringly, Canada can react defensively, fuelling American fears, or it can engage the United States, putting forward initiatives of its own and demonstrating that Canada is a strong and reliable ally. The first option probably exposes Canada to ever greater American pressure and might force it to accept decisions that are not of its own making. The second holds out the hope and possibility of setting the agenda or at least influencing the terms of the debate.

The pressures for the deeper integration of North America are inescapable. Formal institutions may be required to facilitate the rapidly expanding flows of goods, services, capital, and even labour, and to accommodate the post-11 September United States. A number of ideas are in the air, aiming at a Canada–US 'strategic framework' linking the American homeland security requirements to Canada's economic security imperative (Fagan, 2003: F2). Allan Gotlieb, the former Ambassador to the United States, calls in this volume for a 'grand bargain' to establish a North American community designed for the continental context but taking inspiration from the European Union. 'It must be bold', he wrote in the *National Post*, 'it must come from Canada and be espoused at the highest level. It must be comprehensive so as to allow trade-offs and broad constituencies to come into play. It must address the US agenda as well as ours. Incrementalism won't work' (Gotlieb, 2003: A14).

It might be necessary to reinvent Canadian conceptions of 'sovereignty' and the understanding of what it is to be 'Canadian' in a world where some walls are coming down while others are apparently being erected or resurrected. In recent years, through such initiatives as the International Criminal Court and the International Commission on State Sovereignty, Canadians have led the charge to redefine international conceptual and legal meanings of sovereignty in failed and ailing states where human rights are routinely trampled. Something need not be lost if new institutional relationships are devised to manage and define the North American relationship. Nor is it inevitable that Canada will weaken or lose its international influence if it embraces a continental agenda and develops a new relationship with Washington. It is at least arguable that the Mulroney government's close alignment to the US from 1984–93 gave Canada unparalleled weight in Washington, translating into economic benefits and global significance. In a unipolar world, access to the most powerful state could elevate international standing, especially if others perceive that Canada has credibility and clout where it counts.

TOLERANT ALLIES STILL

The portrait of difficulty and discord is easily overdrawn. The irritation was admittedly all too evident on the face of US National Security Adviser Condoleezza Rice when she watched Chrétien declare victory for the United States in Iraq on an American political talk show in early March 2003 (ABC News, 2003), long before either George Bush or Saddam Hussein would have admitted it was so. The Prime Minister is seen in Bush's Washington as an old-guard political hack—hence his nickname, 'Dino', for dinosaur—weak on defence, easy on would-be terrorists in Canada or clamouring to enter it, and no Brian Mulroney in his devotion to American causes. On the first anniversary of 11 September, Chrétien's commentary, linking the terrorist attacks to the gap between rich and poor countries (Alberts, 2002: A1) rather than to the bile of anti-American thugs, were extensively reported in the US, and extensively resented. So, too, were the remarks by Ducros and Parrish, members of Team Chrétien.

The Chrétien policy on Iraq infuriated critics at home and in the United States as it zigged and zagged its way through the crisis. But it was clear, in the Prime Minister's murky way. He thought Saddam an ogre who must be disarmed. In line with its long-standing multi-lateralist impulses, Canada supported the United Nations in efforts to bring Iraq to heel and was prepared to fight in order to enforce UN resolutions demanding Saddam's compliance if the world body sanctioned it. Canada did not lust after 'regime change' (Lindgren, 2003: A1) or want a war outside the auspices of the UN, but its overall support for the United States was solid. The coverage of his major foreign policy speech in Chicago, on 13 February 2003, emphasized that support (Aduroja, 2003: 1, 6; Chrétien, 2003).

Canada, furthermore, at about the same time put a resolution before the UN that 'gave Iraq a firm deadline and clear benchmarks to meet if it wants to avoid war' (Knox and Sallot, 2003: A11; Alberts, 2003: A12). There were meanwhile two Canadian frigates patrolling the Gulf of Oman as part of the war on terror, and a destroyer went on its way to the same mission after the embarrassing crash of its Sea King helicopter. A Canadian commodore was put in charge of coalition forces in the Persian Gulf, and 25 Canadian Forces officers were assisting the US military in Qatar. A battle group and brigade headquarters of peacekeepers were assigned to Afghanistan, easing the US burden there (Blanchfield, 2003: A1). And all this took place against the background of a public opinion twitchy about Bush and 83 per cent against war with Iraq if it does not carry the UN seal of approval. Half of the Quebecers polled opposed a war with or without the UN (*Economist*, 2003: 26; Brean, 2003: A2).

Relations between the two governments are strained. That cannot be refuted after US Secretary of State Colin Powell suggested to his Canadian counterpart, Bill Graham, that the government ought to put on display some of the persistently friendly (and, Powell said, effective) diplomacy of Chrétien's hated rival, Mulroney (Fife, 2002: A5). The confusion over Iraq, and there is confusion, does not help because it gives, at the very least, the impression of a government that is irresolute on the great issue of the day, and one at the heart of US policy. Perhaps deliberately, the Prime Minister emphasizes one aspect of his thinking the first day and another a second day, and refuses to commit categorically to participation in an American-led coalition that is not under the banner of the UN.

Relations between the two countries are nevertheless strong. They are not in a state of crisis. After 11 September, Canada moved quickly to assuage American fears that it was a terrorist nest, and a major effort has been underway since to harmonize customs and immigration policies, prepare for awful contingencies, share intelligence, and facilitate cross-border traffic in people, goods, and services. At the bureaucratic and inter-agency level, Canadian and American officials continue to work closely together to reduce continental vulnerabilities to various internal and external threats. There would be, it is true enough, obvious benefits to the long-term strategic planning and guidance that has been absent in the Chrétien decade, and Paul Martin, the Prime Minister's almost certain successor, has pledged to provide them (Fife, 2003: A6).

Canada remains as internationally relevant as a secondary power can be. Its activist diplomacy in trying to bridge the gaps at the UN over Iraq in February-March 2003 demonstrated that. Nor is the issue Canada's relevance to President Bush's America. He will be in office one more year, or five, but not forever. Canada's dependence on the United States is well-known and documented, but 'it is well to remember that the two countries are interdependent. If that had been missed in a Washington intoxicated by Mexican President Vicente Fox or pleased by their new acquisition, Tony Blair, 11 September brought the fact back home. Those eagle eyes are fixed intently upon Canada now, and we look back with nostalgia at the days when they were ignoring us and we were bleating about it' (Hillmer, 2002). Canada is America's leading trading partner in terms of exports and imports, and the largest global supplier to the US of oil, gas, electricity, uranium, and motor vehicles. Five American states send more than 50 per cent of their exports to Canada, and 33 more have Canada as their leading market (Molot, 2002). Canada is relevant to the US because it needs a stable, secure northern partner in order to feel prosperous and safe.

NOTE

The Social Sciences and Humanities Research Council supported research for this chapter, and officials from a number of government departments granted us interviews. Susan B. Whitney discovered a number of pertinent references and smoothed our prose. We also express our gratitude to Stephen Azzi, Maria

Babbage, Robert Bothwell, J. Michael Cole, Greg Donaghy, Michael Hillmer, Hector M. Mackenzie, and Ryan Shackleton.

REFERENCES

ABC News. 2003. 'This Week with George Stephanopoulos', 9 Mar., videotape.

Aduroja, Grace. 2003. 'Canadian Leader Urges US to Seek UN Backing on Iraq', *Chicago Tribune*, 14 Feb., 1, 6.

Agence France Presse (AFP). 2002. 'US Foreign Policy Partly to Blame for 9/11: Poll', 4 Sept.

Alberts, Sheldon. 2002. 'PM Under Fire for "Shocking" Remarks', *National Post*, 13 Sept., A1, A7.

———. 2003. 'Saddam Should Have Weeks, Not Months: Chrétien', *National Post*, 25 Feb., A12.

Bacevich, Andrew J. 2002. *American Empire: The Realities and Consequences of US Diplomacy*. Cambridge, Mass.: Harvard University Press.

Blanchfield, Mike. 2003. 'Troops Bound for Afghanistan', *Ottawa Citizen*, 13 Feb., A1, A14.

Bliss, Michael. 2003. 'The Multicultural North American Hotel', *National Post*, 15 Jan., A14.

Brean, Joseph. 2003. 'UN Approval Key to Canadian Support for War', *National Post*, 10 Mar., A2.

Bunting, Madeleine. 2003. 'Beginning of the End', *Guardian Weekly*, 6–12 Feb., 13.

Canada. 2002. *Canadian Security Intelligence Service 2001 Public Report*, 6 June.

Chrétien, Jean. 2003. 'Notes for an Address by Prime Minister Jean Chretien to the Chicago Council on Foreign Relations', 13 Feb.

De Roquefeuil, Christophe. 2002. 'Foreign policy attracts new interest in US', Agence France Presse, 26 Aug.

Department of National Defence (DND). 2002. 'Canada and the US Enhance Security Cooperation', News Release, NR-02.079, 9 Dec.

Donaghy, Greg. 2002. *Tolerant Allies: Canada and the United States 1963–1968*. Montreal and Kingston: McGill-Queen's University Press.

Dowd, Maureen. 2003a. 'What Would Genghis Do?', *New York Times*, 5 Mar., A23.

———. 2003b. 'The Xanax Cowboy', *New York Times*, 9 Mar., WK13.

Dumbrell, John. 2002. 'Unilateralism and "America First"? President George W. Bush's Foreign Policy', *Political Quarterly* 73, 3: 279–87.

Economist, The. 2002. 'Unprecedented Power, Colliding Ambitions', 26 Sept.

———. 2003. 'We'll help, but um . . . ah . . .', 15 Feb., 26

Fagan, Drew. 2003. 'Working for the Yankee Dollar—Like It or Not', *Globe and Mail*, 8 Mar., F2.

Fife, Robert. 2002. 'Powell Hints Mulroney's Style Worked Better', *National Post*, 25 Nov., A5.

———. 2003. 'Martin Would Seek Closer Ties to US', *National Post*, 5 Mar., A6.

——— and Sheldon Alberts. 2002. 'PM Calls Bush Friend, "Not Moron"', *National Post*, 22 Nov., A1, A13.

Friedman, Thomas L. 2003. 'Tell The Truth', *New York Times*, 19 Feb., A25.

Gotlieb, Allan. 2003. 'A Grand Bargain with the US', *National Post*, 5 Mar., A14.

Grant, George M. 1970. *Lament for a Nation: The Defeat of Canadian Nationalism.* Toronto: McClelland & Stewart. Reprint of 1965 edition, with a new introduction.

Gwyn, Richard. 2003. 'Our Foreign Policy Making Us Invisible', *Toronto Star*, 23 Feb., A13.

Hillmer, Norman. 2002. 'Iraq: Canada's War', a paper presented to The Norman Paterson School of International Affairs Roundtable on Iraq, 1 Nov.

Ignatieff, Michael. 2002. 'Nation-Building Lite', *The New York Times Magazine*, 26 July, 26–31, 54, 56, 58.

———. 2003. 'The Burden', *The New York Times Magazine*, 5 Jan., 22–7, 50, 53–4.

Ikenberry, G. John. 2002. 'America's Imperial Ambition', *Foreign Affairs* 81, 5: 44–60.

Knox, Paul, and Jeff Sallot. 2003. 'Canada's Low-Key Quarterback at the UN', *Globe and Mail*, 7 Mar., A1, A11.

Kristof, Nicholas D. 2003. 'Losses, Before Bullets Fly', *New York Times*, 7 Mar. Available at: <http://www.nytimes.com/2003/03/07/opinion/07KRIS.html?th>.

Krugman, Paul. 2003. 'Let Them Hate as Long as They Fear', *New York Times*, 7 Mar. Available at: <http://www.nytimes.com/2003/03/07/opinion/07KRUG.html?th>.

Lapham, Lewis H. 2003. 'Notebook: Light in the Window', *Harper's Magazine* (Mar.): 7–9.

Light, Margot. 2002. 'The Response to 11.9 and the Lessons of History', *International Relations* 16, 2: 275–80.

Lindgren, April. 2003. 'PM Opposes Removing Saddam', *National Post*, 1 Mar., A1, A18.

Miller, Arthur. 2003. 'Looking for the Conscience', *New York Times*, 23 Feb., AR 1, 13.

Molot, Maureen Appel. 2002. 'The Trade-Security Nexus: Canada–US Economic Relations at the Beginning of the 21st Century', *American Review of Canadian Studies*, forthcoming.

——— and Norman Hillmer. 2002. 'The Diplomacy of Decline', in Norman Hillmer and Maureen Appel Molot, eds, *Canada Among Nations 2002: A Fading Power.* Toronto: Oxford University Press, 1–33.

NSS. 2002. 'The National Security Strategy of the United States of America'. Available at: <http://www.whitehouse.gov/nsc/nss.html>.

Priest, Dana. 2003. *The Mission: Waging War and Keeping Peace with America's Military.* New York: W.W. Norton.

Schememann, Serge. 2003. 'America's War Train Is Leaving the Station', *New York Times*, 2 Feb., WK 1, 4.

Segal, Heather. 2003. 'Welcome to the Border', *Globe and Mail*, 7 Mar., A15.

Servan-Schreiber, J.J. 1969. *The American Challenge.* New York: Avon Books.

Stern, Leonard. 2002. 'Canada Faces "Real" Terrorism Threat', *National Post*, 8 Mar.

Tenet, George. 2002. 'Worldwide Threat—Converging Dangers in a Post 9/11 World', testimony before the Senate Armed Services Committee, 19 Mar.

Tyler, Patrick E. 2003. 'A Deepening Fissure', *New York Times*, 6 Mar. Available at: <www.nytimes.com/2003/03/06/international/europe/06ASSE.html?th>.

Woodward, Bob. 2002. *Bush at War.* New York: Simon and Schuster.

Younge, Gary. 2002. 'Do As We Say, Not As We Do', *Guardian*, 27 May, 17.

2

Foremost Partner: The Conduct of Canada–US Relations

Perhaps the best way to understand a country's foreign policy is to look at how it actually behaves on the international plane. Lester B. Pearson, Canada's Foreign Minister a half-century ago, was once asked, 'What is Canada's foreign policy?' 'Ask me in December', he replied, 'when I can look back at what Canada has done in the course of the year. Then I'll describe Canada's foreign policy for you.' The story may be apocryphal. But it is in some respects an accurate representation of Canada's approach to foreign policy. While we have always proclaimed our core belief in the United Nations, world organizations, and multilateralism, there has been a great deal of the ad hoc in the way we conduct our activities in the international sphere.

Ever since Canada began to act independently of its status as a dominion in the British Empire, the United States has been our most important foreign partner. Although our dependency on the United States has grown steadily deeper since World War II, Canada rarely set out to formulate its foreign policy vis-à-vis that country. Perhaps the most ambitious review of Canadian foreign policy ever undertaken was by Pierre Elliott Trudeau's government in 1970. *Foreign Policy for Canadians* was a comprehensive attempt to analyze our foreign relations. It consisted of six volumes. The first did not specifically address the question of what should be our foreign policy vis-à-vis the United States. Nor did any of the other five. The study had hexagons, goals, values, objectives, and many prescriptions, but no attempt was made to prescribe strategies for dealing with our foremost partner.

Not long after, in the wake of the 'Nixon shock' of 1971 when the US placed a surcharge on our exports to them, Mitchell Sharp, the Secretary of State for External Affairs, sought to address the gap. In 1972 in an article in *International Perspectives* (a departmental magazine), he announced 'The Third Option' for dealing with the United States. Canada would not accept the status quo, nor seek further integration with the US, but would seek to diversify our relations with countries other than the US and strengthen the instruments of our economic development in the domestic sphere. In this way it was hoped that Canada could reduce its economic dependency on the US. 'Contractual links' were established with the European Community and Japan in 1976 to facilitate increased trade.

Contrary to widespread belief, Pierre Elliott Trudeau, the cabinet, and the Canadian bureaucratic establishment tried consistently throughout Trudeau's mandate to advance the 'Third Option'. But the results were dismal. When the policy was announced, Canada's exports to the United States were in the neighbourhood of 65 per cent of our total. Twelve years later, when the Prime Minister took his walk in the snow, our exports to the US were heading towards 80 per cent. Moreover, at the very end of its mandate, the Trudeau government was trying to negotiate sectoral free trade agreements with the United States, Third Option notwithstanding.

Canada's unwillingness to articulate its foreign policy towards the United States was reflected in a singular characteristic of the bilateral relationship. Its management was overwhelmingly ad hoc and remained so even as conflicts and problems mushroomed. It is true that, in different decades, various attempts were made to set up some machinery or procedures to address disputes in joint cabinet committees in the 1960s; consultative mechanisms on energy in the 1970s and on communications and trucking in the 1980s; quarterly foreign ministers' meetings and annual summits in the same decade; structured consultative arrangements and dumping and countervail dispute-settlement procedures under the Canada–US Free Trade Agreement (FTA); and commissions under the North American Free Trade Agreement (NAFTA) to address environmental issues. With the exceptions of the International Joint Commission, established in 1909 to address North American boundary water issues (often neglected) and the Permanent Joint Board on Defence set up during World War II (of diminishing importance), few of these institutions or procedures had traction.

There were less than a handful of third-party arbitrations in the period of our independence. The most ambitious effort Canada ever made at joint resource management, the East Coast Fisheries Agreement, was disdained by the US Senate. In the grand scheme of things, the world's largest bilateral economic and trading relationship was managed without the assistance of bilateral institutions, binational tribunals, and formal procedures.

Until the Free Trade Agreement, the rules governing the two-way trading relationship were defined exclusively (the Auto Pact and defence production excepted) by multilateral arrangements. Viewed from the perspective of the past two decades when our bilateral relationship has been scarred by major trade disputes across the entire spectrum of our economy (the long-festering softwood lumber issue, wheat, groundfish, lobsters, hogs and frozen pork, potatoes, film, broadcasting, cultural policies, shingles and shakes, steel, and almost anything that comes out of the ground), one might well ask how Canada got through so many years of economic conflict without greater harm to the relationship.

The answer is the Cold War. During most of this period, the US sought to prevent economic disputes from undermining its greater political interests. In the titanic struggle against the USSR, the US was able to find ways to ensure that economic competition and conflict with its allies did not weaken or destabilize the Western alliance. In the later stages of the Cold War, this became less true. In a meeting of the Bilderberg Conference in Europe in the mid-1980s, a powerful Democratic Senator from Texas, Lloyd Bentsen, startled his audience by warning them that the days were over when the US would subordinate its geopolitical goals to its economic interests.

Nevertheless, for several decades the Americans managed to keep a lid on economic conflict with its allies. Several factors helped them achieve this. During the first quarter-century after the end of World War II, the era of the Imperial Presidency, Congress was far from the free-for-all it would become after the damage done the presidency by the Vietnam War and the Watergate scandal. The bosses of both houses of Congress (for example, Speaker Sam Rayburn and Senate Majority Leader Lyndon Johnson) exercised powerful control over the legislative bodies responsible for external trade. Hence, special interests did not have the political clout on Capitol Hill that they have today. Moreover, the labour unions and the Democratic Party favoured free trade.

The number of trade disputes, particularly with Canada, were few and far between. During Arnold Heeney's two terms as Canadian Ambassador in Washington during the 1950s and the 1960s, he had no economic disputes to address. In his memoirs, there is nothing on the subject, which I found astonishing when I took up my responsibilities in Washington in the early 1980s. This was a time of growing recession in the United States and great concerns about declining US economic power.

Nevertheless, there were still remnants of the earlier era. When I called for the first time on the Secretary of Agriculture, I informed him that I was simply making a courtesy call, since there were no significant agricultural issues on my agenda. But as the US economy struggled and slowed in the 1980s and as recently minted trade legislation in Congress made it much easier for special interests to harass foreign competition (section 201 and 301 actions and others), Canada–US trade disputes mushroomed. While trade between us has more than doubled since the FTA, and Canada has made substantial use of binational panels (far greater than ever anticipated), the number and seriousness of trade disputes have remained high, the mode of settling them relatively primitive, and the cost to the relationship substantial.

Much of the difficulty in resolving trade disputes arises from deeper trends in both of our democracies. The role of regions, special interests, pressure groups, and local lobbies makes the political process more and more responsive to the power and influence of parochial forces. Trade conflicts arise when democratic jurisdictions on opposite sides of the border adopt conflicting policies. It is true that this is less likely to occur in the growing high-tech sectors of our two economies, but the resource sector remains of huge importance to Canada. Such conflicts might arise with regard to virtually any product—raspberries, apples, potatoes, lobsters, potash, lumber, to cite concrete examples. It is often impossible for a democratically elected government to back off the support of a domestic interest, no matter how local or small, in order to meet a foreign one. Within a national jurisdiction, the mechanisms are in place—in Parliament, Congress, the courts—to work out compromises, adjudicate, over-rule, or override particular interests. But on the international level, when sovereign jurisdictions are parties to the dispute, there are often no such mechanisms. Even if the World Trade Organization is involved, as with the General Agreement on Tariffs and Trade (GATT) in earlier years, the disputes often remain unresolved or fester or escalate as calls for retaliation mount.

The core belief in Ottawa since World War II has been that when conflicts arise they should be resolved by diplomatic means. The view in official circles in Canada has always been that this policy serves us reasonably well. While it was true that disputes could remain unresolved for many years, even several decades (for example, the Garrison Diversion, the Skagit Dam), Canada could expect to get a fair hearing from the US administration and in most instances acceptable solutions were worked out over time.

But as special interests and protectionist forces in Congress made resort to diplomatic channels less and less effective, Ottawa decided to break new ground. It moved decisively to a wider strategy. In the 1980s we decided to engage in direct lobbying of key players in both the Senate and the House of Representatives. We also decided to resort to public diplomacy and public relations to reinforce our diplomatic efforts.

When I took up my assignment as Ambassador to Washington, it was still the general practice for the Ambassador and the Embassy staff to avoid lobbying the Hill. For the Embassy, Congress had always been off limits. With Ottawa's full support, the Ambassador in particular, supported by select members of the Embassy, began to engage in strenuous lobbying efforts. To the annoyance of some of the tradionalists in Ottawa, I would often refer to myself as Canada's chief lobbyist. We backed our efforts by a program of public diplomacy orchestrated by the Ambassador and his staff. For the first time, we actually spent money on public relations and all of our consulates were harnessed to the same task. Lobbying went from forbidden territory to a central focus of our diplomatic effort.

In order to be more effective in Washington, many Canadians are now advocating that we should conduct more aggressive public campaigns in the United States. Americans, we hear over and over again, know so little about Canada, not even that we take over one-fifth of all US exports. The business community and media are virtually united in calling for more aggressive public relations campaigns and lobbying on the part of Canada.

There is reason to be skeptical about how successful such efforts can be. Canadians have no domestic political (i.e., ethnic) lobby in the United States, Americans of Canadian origin do not vote with any Canadian agenda in mind, and Canada does not contribute campaign funds. The way we can be most effective is to align ourselves with US domestic interests that favour policies similar to our own. Thus we need to be making constantly shifting alliances, depending on the issue of the moment, with special US interests.

Yet it is very difficult to play effectively in domestic political games. One can make a noise, but noise is not synonymous with results. In the United States there is often resentment of foreign lobbying. Direct involvement in the US political process can backfire, as many foreign countries know, and as I know from personal experience in advocating acid rain controls. Necessary as it is to make such efforts in select situations, it is defeatist to believe that this is the best way to protect our interests in the United States.

Are there ways, other than lobbying and persuasion, that can help Canada win its battles in the American arena? For many years Canadian officials and political scientists have debated whether 'linkage' could enhance our clout and give us leverage. The idea behind linkage is that Canada should negotiate with the United States in such a way as to connect two, or more, different disputes. We should say to the Americans, when we are the *demandeur*, that unless they accept our position in a particular matter of dispute, we would not accede to their demands in the other. If the Americans want something from us badly enough in the second area of dispute, they might accede to our position in the first.

Canadian diplomats have long taken the position that linkage is not in Canada's best interest. Each area of contention being difficult enough in itself to resolve, connecting one dispute to another would complicate the negotiation and inhibit solutions. Another difficulty in linkage is that governments have to be ready to subordinate the interests of one group of voters or region to another, always difficult if not impossible in a democracy. During the comprehensive fishery negotiations initiated by Prime Minister Trudeau and President Carter,

Canada made a major effort to link the negotiations of east coast issues with west coast ones. This proved politically impossible and the linkage with the west coast was dropped.

Some Canadians are now urging that we should link forest products and our energy exports. Energy is close to the heart of America's national security concerns. We should tell the Yanks, 'lift tariffs on our softwood lumber or we will restrict our energy exports to you.' The problem with this strategy is that it could easily lead to Canadians being injured by our own actions. Canada has vigorously pursued energy markets in the United States for generations because they generate wealth for Canadians. If the linkage was unsuccessful, Canada would end up with two damaged industrial sectors rather than one.

Another restraining factor for Canada has been the belief that in the battle of linkages, the US being the bigger power, it could easily outlink Canada. Worse, Congress, with its lack of discipline and susceptibility to pressure groups, might be attracted to the practice. It would not take much encouragement. When, during the Trudeau years, Canada refused to change its restrictive practices on border broadcasting, Congress passed a law, at the behest of the industry, making American convention expenses spent in Canada non tax-deductible. Because Canada did not retreat on border broadcasting, the linkage did not work for the US, but the Canadian tourist industry suffered heavily as a result of the linkage.

Nevertheless, the state of our relations with the United States is not always irrelevant in the settlement of disputes. Canadian diplomats in Washington have always been convinced that goodwill counts for something, although it is very difficult to quantify. Canada's stance on security and defence issues is treated with great importance in the White House. There are grounds to believe that our willingness to address security issues high on the agenda of the United States could have a bearing on how a President would deal with an unrelated issue such as steel quotas. Although the President has limited discretionary power in respect of trade, he is still by far the most powerful single player in the US system. It is only common sense to recognize that raw geopolitical factors can sometimes have a bearing on the White House's sensitivity to Canadian complaints. There is no linkage on the part of the United States, but in the real world everything, broadly speaking, is linked.

There are still other reasons why ad hoc diplomacy is unlikely to yield satisfactory results for Canada, even when backed by lobbying and public advocacy. Narrow lobbies are very effective on the Hill; the narrower or more specific the interest the more deadly it can be. A powerful senator or congressman can easily be beholden to a special interest. Senator George Mitchell, the liberal Democrat from Maine, voted against the Free Trade Agreement thanks to the muscle of a couple of hundred potato growers in his state. Because of senatorial courtesy, congressional procedures and practices, and the power of committee and subcommittee chairs, a single legislator can block a proposal favoured by a foreign power even if it has the support of the administration. US domestic interests easily trump foreign powers and will do so every time. Experience in Washington teaches that, in the US domestic process, a foreign power is just another special interest and not a very special one at that. When a foreign power plays in the US domestic political game, the playing field, to borrow a beloved American expression, is not level and never will be.

Hence the most basic question of Canadian foreign policy remains: what can Canada do to better protect its interest in the United States? In the new security environment following the World Trade Center attack in September 2001, the need to find an answer to this question is the single most important issue facing the country.

In the event of more terrorist strikes in the US, huge border disruptions and threats to Canada's economic security must again be anticipated, notwithstanding the success of the Manley-Ridge 'Smart Border' Accord of December 2001. In coping with such threats to the functioning of the integrated North American market, the skills of Canadian negotiators will once again be of paramount importance. Lobbying and public relations may help, but reliance on traditional ad hoc responses to issues of this magnitude places Canada in a deeply precarious position.

There are many signs that Canadians are not burying their heads in the sand. Since the events of 11 September 2001, there has been an explosion of proposals about what Canada should do to place our economic security on a more sure footing. Many are pouring out of the Canadian business community. The Canadian Council of Chief Executives has proposed that we should 'reinvent this notion of the border'. In academe, imaginative proposals are being made for 'a new strategic framework' that could maintain existing sovereignties by linking physical security, defence, and greater North America economic security. Few days go by without new ideas for deepening NAFTA being explored in university conferences and think-tanks.

It is no surprise that virtually all of these ideas come from north of the border. They are also almost all coming from the private sector, media, and the academy. The Canadian government has announced a foreign policy review of sorts, rather more of a tepid limited public consultation than an independent review. However, the Canadian government, provincial governments, the Liberal Party, pretenders to the Liberal throne, and even ex-politicians have not given much evidence of broad new thinking. With 85 per cent of our exports going south, the Smart Border Accord was an intelligent, well-executed attempt to alleviate the choking up of the border, but there is little evidence of new grand strategies now being debated in the official corridors of power.

There are lessons to be learned from the Canadian–US Free Trade Agreement. For many years the idea of a free trade agreement was in the wind, but it was always obvious that the idea would have to come from Canada, not the United States. This did not mean that the US national interest would not be served by such an accord. Prime Minister Brian Mulroney's broad-gauged initiative triggered a course of action that changed the rules between us dramatically in respect of trade in goods, services, and investment. Notwithstanding enormous opposition on the Hill, innovative new binational procedures for countervail and dumping were agreed upon. Changes of this magnitude could never have been achieved incrementally, nor under the modest initiatives of Pierre Elliott Trudeau, because they could not have come close to attracting sufficient political support in the United States.

There are six essential elements in achieving a new and more secure basis for the conduct of Canada–US relations:

1. Both the vision and initiative must come from Canada. There is an absolute requirement for Canadian political leadership.
2. The scope of the initiative must be comprehensive. It must be broad enough to marginalize specific lobbies and interests and must provide ample room for trade-offs and deal-making. If the initiative is narrowly defined, it will be stillborn.
3. The initiative must address the US as well as the Canadian agenda. Otherwise it will, once again, be stillborn. It is surprising that so obvious a point should often be overlooked in Canadian debates.
4. There must be recognition that the US agenda is national security. Since the events of 11 September 2001, the world is

more fraught with vulnerability for Canada than the United States, given our asymmetrical dependency, but it also presents new opportunities. Never before have security issues placed higher on the US agenda—higher even than during World War II and the Vietnam War because, for the first time in history, there is the perception in the US, correct, as it turns out, that their homeland security is at stake.

5. There must be a recognition that the time is right to consider the possibility of striking a grand bargain in which issues of economic security and homeland security are brought together and resolved in such a way as to elicit broad political support in both countries.

6. We must recognize that the objective of such negotiations would be the creation of a community of law, which substitutes the rule of law for political discretion and arbitrary action. After all, the US Congress is the force behind most trade harassment. By creating a regime of law, important new restraints are placed on unpredictable and discriminatory legislative initiatives that the administration is often not in the position to resist. Building on the FTA and NAFTA, such a community need not fall into the category of being a free trade zone, common or single market, or customs union or any other category. This community of law could be uniquely designed to meet the North American context.

In summary, it is possible to envisage the negotiation of a comprehensive agreement establishing a common set of laws favouring the movement of people, services, and goods within a joint Canada–US space. It could also establish a common perimeter surrounding the space, with common criteria for entering and moving within the space. There could also be a common external tariff for the two countries with regard to goods entering the space. Common regulatory standards or reciprocal recognition of each other's standards could be adopted to avoid duplication.

Of particular importance would be the abolition of trade dispute actions—anti-dumping and countervail actions—against each other and reliance, as the European Community has done, on common competition and anti-trust laws, possibly but not necessarily administered by a single tribunal. This was a primary goal Canada set out to achieve, but failed to gain, in the free trade negotiations with the

United States. Prime Minister Mulroney, as well as the principal negotiators, made it abundantly clear that this was a top priority for
Canada, a goal that was at the very heart of the rationale for seeking
a free trade area with the US. Far from seeing the abolition of our
independent resolution of trade disputes as reducing our sovereignty,
we saw it as an important step in enhancing it. Had we succeeded,
we would have been liberated from seemingly endless assaults on
our softwood lumber and other products as well.

Nor would a common perimeter restrain Canadian sovereignty over
its immigration policy. A common security fence would require close
cohesion in all areas related to enforcement action and intelligence,
but it would not entail restricting our sovereign ability to determine
the rules in all the basic areas of our immigration policy. Canada
would maintain control over policies governing how many immigrants
it would take annually, where they come from, what would be the size
of the independent class and what qualifications were needed, what
people would be included in the family class and who should be
included. As for refugees, both countries acknowledge and accept the
same basic international definitions and legal obligations.

As to Canada contributing far more to the joint defence of our
perimeter, this again could hardly contribute to the diminution of our
sovereignty. We have long participated in joint arrangements with the
US for our common defence in North America and elsewhere. If we
do more, we increase our voice and influence and participate more
in decision-making. If we do less, we diminish our sovereignty, a
strange position for Canadian nationalists to advocate.

In the European movement towards a continent-wide common
space, the impetus has been to create a larger and deeper community of law. While political union has always been a goal since the
movement was launched after World War II, the driving force in
Europe has been towards economic integration. The purpose of the
European Community was never to achieve a new nationality to
replace the older ones, but a common set of rules, supported by common institutions, that would facilitate the free movement of people,
goods, and services.

Absolutely crucial to the entire concept is that what was being created was an open community, open to other states that wanted to
become part of the common space and were prepared to accept its
governing rules. The European Community is therefore not aimed at
the creation of a new nationality but a new community of law.

Although it is growing on a regional basis, the concept is not necessarily constrained by the notion of the region.

Canadian political scientists seem never to tire of pointing out why the European experience is not relevant to North America. They are right in emphasizing the overwhelming dominance of a single power in North America, as distinct from Europe, and that, for this reason alone, Canadians are not seeking any form of political confederation, or common political or economic institutions, or a common currency. If common institutions were established, a Canadian voice, it is said, would barely be heard. This is probably correct, but nevertheless the European experience is profoundly relevant to Canada's aspirations.

The creation of a community of law in North America could well be similar to the European experience in a number of ways. First and foremost, the North American space would be open to accession by other states within the region that are willing to accept the rules. Mexico is an obvious example. It would, as in the European Community, make the border irrelevant insofar as the movement of goods, services, and people are concerned. It would, like the Community, rely on competition policy and anti-trust legislation rather than on retrograde trade remedy laws in each jurisdiction. Again, as in Europe, a common customs tariff at the boundary would avoid endless definitional and other squabbles about rules of origin and the like. Finally, there would be common rules, or reciprocal recognition of laws, with regard to most regulatory requirements, whether these are health-related, environmental, nutritional, or whatever.

Would such a community of law require common institutions? The answer is probably no. There would seem to be no compelling reason to go down the European route in regard to establishing political bodies. A community of laws should not require joint legislatures or other joint political institutions, nor for the most part would it require common adjudicatory tribunals. In a few areas, joint institutions might help the smooth functioning of the common economic and security space, such as with regard to competition policy. Even then there is no compelling reason to believe that there need be some political super-architecture. Perhaps this might come in time, but perhaps it might not. Canadians would be free to judge their national interest then as now.

Canadian critics of any new initiative to build a more integrated North American community often bring forward two objections. The first, of course, is the sovereignty argument and its variants. Such a community, they maintain, would force Canada to harmonize most of its laws with the US. Moreover, Canada would have to do all the harmonizing, not the US. The same criticism was launched at the time of the Free Trade Agreement; Canadians were warned it would be the end of medicare and unemployment insurance. This proved to be false. Yes, there would be more harmonization of rules relating to commerce and the flow of goods and services, but the reality is that with or without building a broader legal community, Canadians are going to have to conform their rules to those of their largest customer if that is the cost of keeping that market open. After two decades of conflict, Canada is coming closer today than ever to moving to a US market-based system in the harvesting of our forests. We have a much better prospect of receiving a quid pro quo for harmonization if it is part of a larger negotiation rather than a series of ad hoc compromises on our part.

Second, Canadian advocates of maintaining the status quo often assert that the Americans would not be interested in an agreement for deeper integration with Canada. Others say that the integration will happen anyway, so why speed it up with an agreement. Some allege that the US would not even be interested in a joint federation. Even if they were, it is argued, specific economic interests would have enough clout to prevent any negotiation from being successful. Neither history nor common sense supports so negative an assessment. Special interests are, it is true, effective in blocking incremental or ad hoc change that would be to their disadvantage, but they are far less influential in a major negotiation when there is a grand panoply of issues and interests in play. The experience of negotiating the FTA and NAFTA demonstrates this reality.

An even more important reality is that, in the areas of national defence, national security, energy security, and the movement of people into the United States, there are great American interests at stake. They stand at the summit of the concerns of the American people. At this historic conjuncture, Canada has the leverage to shape our destiny in a manner that will enhance prosperity and security without significant loss of sovereignty.

Canada has cards and now is the time to play them. There probably has never been a better moment to do so. But if there is no game, what good are cards?

3

Beyond NAFTA: Towards Deeper Economic Integration

DREW FAGAN

Retired politicians tend to want to relive their victories. But former Prime Minister Brian Mulroney and former President George H.W. Bush have a particular inclination for celebrating free trade milestones.

In mid-1999 they spoke at a Montreal conference marking the tenth anniversary of the Canada–US Free Trade Agreement, which began on 1 January 1989. Mulroney, who staked re-election on the pact, was joined by Canada's negotiators, and they all hailed the impact of the FTA.

Bush's presence was somewhat incongruous. As Ronald Reagan's vice-president, he wasn't directly involved in the FTA. It went into effect three weeks before he became President. But many allies played key roles, especially James Baker III. He joined the FTA negotiations in the last 72 hours and relived that at the conference, which was a time for reminiscences. Bush and Mulroney even sat for a joint interview (Cohen and McIlroy, 1999).

But for these two leaders, once was not enough. In December 2002 they got together for another landmark. If the tenth anniversary of the FTA was marked late, Mulroney and Bush seemed pleased to mark the tenth anniversary of the North American Free Trade Agreement early. They were joined at a Washington conference by former Mexican President Carlos Salinas de Gortari, who counts NAFTA as his greatest accomplishment.

The trilateral pact had gone into effect not quite nine years earlier, on 1 January 1994. Only Salinas was still his nation's leader then. By that time Jean Chrétien and Bill Clinton—who both criticized the text negotiated by their opponents—were in office. The Washington event, as a result, was timed to the tenth anniversary of the signing of NAFTA, which preceded legislative approval. Salinas, in particular, praised the world's first free trade agreement between developing and developed countries. It marked, he suggested, a parting of the ways for Mexico.

So it was for Canada, as well. NAFTA was less important for this country than the Canada–US pact. But together they marked a turning point after almost 150 years of debate on economic relations with the United States. This debate preceded Canadian Confederation. The 1854 Reciprocity Treaty was abrogated by Washington in 1866, after the Civil War—one more reason why John A. Macdonald brought the Canadian colonies together in Confederation. Largely in response to Washington's cold shoulder, he proceeded in 1879 with a 'National Policy' to build indigenous industry.

Canada and the United States would enter into two free trade negotiations before the FTA. In 1911, Wilfrid Laurier lost an election after concluding a trade pact; his credibility was damaged when the speaker of the US House of Representatives suggested annexation would result. In 1948, William Lyon Mackenzie King refused, at the last minute, to approve a similar agreement secretly negotiated at his behest. He feared Laurier's fate.

Canada waited another 40 years for free trade; it would be the first such agreement signed by Washington with a foreign country. The FTA went beyond the traditional aim of such pacts—to eliminate tariff barriers—not only by phasing out tariffs over 10 years (with some exceptions, especially for agriculture), but by including terms on services, energy, investment, and government procurement. Its provisions to help solve trade disputes, while clearly a step forward, were criticized for not adequately blunting protectionist US trade powers.

Years later, the effect of the agreement is substantial.

This chapter will examine the impact that free trade has had on Canada and outline the questions this raises for the country. The term 'continentalism' is being used with growing frequency in a North American context to describe the deepening interrelationship of the Canadian and American economies, and, increasingly, that of Mexico. The integration of the nations of Europe may even provide some limited context for what could develop in North America. Integration here is barrelling ahead on an ad hoc basis now, whereas in Europe it was more closely controlled at the political level. Still, the options just entering the public discourse concerning what Canada might consider regarding cross-border ties suggest that the process needs to be channelled politically to ensure it works in Canada's interest. That would be a strong exercise of Canadian sovereignty.

Canada is the most open of the three North American economies. Exports of goods and services accounted for 46 per cent of gross domestic product in 2000, an increase from 28 per cent 10 years earlier and 21 per cent in 1970. Import growth has followed a similar pattern. (Exports of US goods and services are almost double the level when free trade took effect, but still represent just 13 per cent of GDP.)

Bilateral merchandise trade totalled $569 billion in 2001, an increase of 185 per cent over 1990 levels. A full 83 per cent of Canada's exports now flow to the United States, as compared to 71 per cent when the FTA took effect, and the figure is roughly 90 per cent for Ontario. (As well, about 60 per cent of two-way trade is intra-corporate, a reflection of close investment and ownership ties.)

By the end of the 1990s, eight of the 10 provinces (save for Nova Scotia and Prince Edward Island) were trading more internationally than interprovincially. In fact, Canada's total international trade was more than double interprovincial trade. This trend is particularly striking among the country's core producers. In 2000, almost two-thirds of Canada's industrial output was sold directly into the United States, more than triple the percentage in 1989. The domestic marketplace now purchases less than 30 per cent of Canada's industrial output.[1]

The growing integration of the Canadian and US economies has been evident in other ways. There is closer co-ordination of capital markets, and a major increase in portfolio and direct investment, including mergers and acquisitions. (Canadian investment in the United States has grown by 150 per cent since 1990, slightly more than the increase in the other direction.) The cross-border flow of business people, an issue that NAFTA dealt with only tangentially, has grown as well.

The extraordinary reorientation of the Canadian economy—from east-west to north-south lines—is particularly notable to Donald Macdonald, who presided over a 1985 Royal Commission that advocated free trade. He now believes—with much justification—that another Royal Commission would be advisable, to examine this galloping process of continental integration in a high-profile manner that would involve experts and average citizens alike. As Macdonald has said: 'The free-trade agreement was far more successful than I would have contemplated. It really was dramatic' (Fagan, 2002b).

And yet, this very success has led to growing concern within Canada about the creeping growth of continentalization. In some ways, this may be like searching for the cloud in the silver lining. Free trade is viewed widely as a key step in the economic modernization of the country, which included the Bank of Canada's assault on inflation in the early 1990s and the attack by the federal and provincial governments on the fiscal deficit in the mid-1990s. Free trade eased the impact of restructuring. It accelerated the transformation of the private-sector economy from resources to knowledge-based industries, which, whether domestic or foreign-owned, are often specialized producers with global mandates. Indeed, free trade is now paying dividends as part of a virtuous circle of lower taxes, smaller government, and growing private-sector productivity, leading to rising living standards after a decade of stagnation, particularly vis-à-vis the United States.

But there is now a strange dichotomy at the core of the open borders issue, as greater attention is turned to the option of additional forms of integration. Such steps would make the Canada–US border less economically intrusive and, it is hoped, provide stronger guarantees of access to the US marketplace and further incentives for offshore investors to locate in Canada. But they might, as well, lead Canada more tightly into the US orbit, with potentially profound impacts on this country's ability to maintain distinct social and fiscal policies or even an independent foreign policy.

Despite the success of free trade, disquieting signs of lagging economic performance remain. Canada's share of foreign direct investment in North America has fallen in half since 1985, as the dynamic American economy continues to attract funds from offshore and

Mexico's attractiveness as a manufacturing location grows (Harris, 2001). This is one reason why the Conference Board of Canada recently suggested the gap between US and Canadian per capita income could double to $12,000 over the next decade (CBC, 2002).

Academic studies still suggest that US-bound exports, while rising at a significantly faster pace than economic growth, remain lower than what might be possible if government hurdles to cross-border trade were no greater than those affecting internal trade.[2] While these figures suggest the need for greater integration, concerns remain that the Canadian economy, while benefiting from improved access to the rich US market, has become even more vulnerable to the self-interest of the United States.

The imbalance in economic relations is primarily a consequence of the huge disparity in size between the two countries, resulting in a striking lack of mutual dependence. Canada is the largest trading partner of the US, purchasing 21 per cent of American exports. But Canada still buys only about 2.5 per cent of all US GDP, whereas the United States buys no less than 38 per cent of Canadian GDP.

The very success of free trade has led many to question why open border arrangements should be frozen with a deal that was hardly as sweeping as opponents and supporters of the FTA suggested in 1988, especially when compared with the profound economic integration underway in Europe.

Michael Kergin, Canada's Ambassador to the United States, has estimated that non-tariff barriers increase the cost of shipping a product across the border by about 5 per cent of the final invoice price and more than 10 per cent for some trade-sensitive industries—a reflection, in part, of the burden of meeting the paperwork requirements of customs services (Kergin, 2001). This process was largely unaffected by free trade, but the cost often is as high as the tariffs eliminated by the trade pact. Indeed, these costs may be a key reason why Canada is not getting its share of North American investment. 'There is a very real doubt on the part of investors about investing in Canada, given the reality of the border', concluded the Conference Board of Canada (CBC, 2002: 95).

Regulatory differences between the two countries, continuing restrictions on foreign investment, remaining tariff barriers in some sensitive industries, domestic preferences for some government procurement—these have all been suggested as potential steps for building on NAFTA. As well, continuing high-profile trade battles, especially over softwood lumber exports, have led some Canadian officials to argue that it may be time again to press for a step-by-step elimination of anti-dumping and countervail investigations, even though more than 95 per cent of Canadian exports to the United States are not subject to any complaints that could lead to sanctions.

This potential agenda, which has come to be identified with the moniker 'NAFTA-plus', had been gaining attention prior to the 11 September 2001 terrorist attacks. Mexican President Vicente Fox, in trips to Washington and Ottawa before taking office in December 2000, had suggested that the three countries begin work on what might, within roughly 20 years, amount to a common market, involving the free movement of goods, services, investment, and people (the so-called four freedoms). Mulroney suggested similar arrangements, although he differed with Fox by eschewing the idea of a common currency.

But it was 11 September that gave the issue gargantuan impetus, and convinced many Canadians—especially in the business community—that Ottawa had to become more active in trying to shape the Canada–US relationship. The terrorist attacks temporarily shut the border (the lineup of trucks stretched 36 kilometres on 13 September 2001 to cross the Ambassador Bridge between Windsor and Detroit, which handles more trade than between the United States and any other country, and one-quarter of all Canada–US trade) (Hart and Dymond, 2001; Beatty, 2002). Quiet integration suddenly became a very public issue, amid fears that US security concerns would lead to a prolonged slow-down, or even shut-down, of a border that had become Canada's economic lifeline.

Some Ottawa officials responsible for bilateral relations had warned of this vulnerability for years, noting—even without taking into account security concerns—that border infrastructure was not keeping pace with the demands of growing trade. After 11 September, the Liberal government paid notice. Within months, Deputy Prime Minister John Manley had negotiated with Homeland Security Director Tom Ridge a 30-point Smart Border Accord designed largely by Canadian bureaucrats.

The pact laid out technology programs to speed the cross-border flow of low-risk commerce, especially intra-company trade common in the integrated auto industry in eastern Michigan and southwestern Ontario that operates a cross-border 'just-in-time' delivery system. The pact also increased some bilateral security efforts at the border and other entry points, such as ports on each coast.

More recently, the calls for a NAFTA-plus agenda have grown louder. Manley and Industry Minister Allan Rock have both talked vaguely about building on the trilateral agreement to eliminate further barriers to Canada–US commerce. Bank of Canada Governor David Dodge has mused about opening up the border to the freer flow of labour (Beauchesne, 2002). International Trade Minister Pierre Pettigrew has been more specific, suggesting a six-part agenda to deepen overall Canada–US economic ties. It includes: increasing Canada's share of overall US imports beyond the present 19 per cent; boosting two-way investment flows, particularly so Canada draws in more US capital than the $42 billion in 2001; and improving regulatory co-operation in areas such as civil aviation safety and biosecurity. His list also includes a broad goal to 'eliminate the border as an impediment to trade, investment and business development' (Pettigrew, 2002).

This last objective, in fact, was one of the key topics at the Washington conference attended by the three former North American leaders. The forward-looking event in Washington, with less of the Montreal conference's nostalgic air, focused on the next steps towards closer North American ties. Free trade is now viewed as just a stepping stone to deeper integration (something Mulroney and Bush hardly considered 15 years ago). Even Washington, intent as it is on fighting terrorism, is starting to pay some attention.

In the fall of 2002, the Canadian government quietly suggested a NAFTA-plus agenda to the Bush administration that was similar to some of the ideas floated publicly by Pettigrew. The proposal, entitled 'Securing Growth: Beyond the Border Accord', was aimed clearly, as reflected in the title, at building on the close relationship between Manley and Ridge (Fagan, 2002c; Fagan, 2003). Just two pages in length, it contemplated the widespread co-ordination of government regulations in the testing, inspection, and labelling of goods so as to eliminate impediments to trade. It suggested reviewing the complex rules established under NAFTA for determining whether goods qualify for duty-free trade and overhauling the burdensome paperwork involved in cross-border business trips, especially in services industries. The proposal also highlighted a need for improved infrastructure co-ordination, greater joint efforts at combatting telemarketing fraud, and better co-ordination towards safeguarding the environment, possibly under the auspices of the International Joint Commission (which was the first bilateral institution involving Canada and the United States, formed in 1909).

The paper received a cautiously positive response from Bush administration officials, predicated on Mexico having some involvement and that nothing would require congressional approval. The objective seemed to be to launch a new phase of cross-border co-ordination, but to do so in a manner that did not draw major public attention. As Pettigrew said, Ottawa did not currently have 'an appetite' for grander schemes approaching common market arrangements, or especially the radical suggestion of a joint currency or Canadian adoption of the US dollar. He suggested, instead, that consideration might be given to a sectoral customs union for the highly integrated steel industry, in which the two countries would co-ordinate their trade policies vis-à-vis other nations and eliminate the possibility of trade actions among themselves in steel products.

In this sense, critics pointed out, Canada generally was seeking to replicate the 1965 Auto Pact. But the federal government also sought to interest Washington in industry-specific initiatives in 1983, with little success. Given how difficult it can be to build support in the United States for narrow objectives, such proposals might have no more chance of winning the interest of President George W. Bush's administration than they did with the Reagan administration two decades earlier.

As trade analysts Michael Hart and Bill Dymond argue: 'In order to gain appreciable support in the United States, a bilateral initiative must be sufficiently broad and creative to capture the imagination of leading US political figures . . . It will require Canada to come to grips with some difficult issues' (Hart and Dymond, 2001: 19).

In 1985, that creative proposal was to negotiate a free trade agreement. Now, the creative proposal might be a customs union, or a common market, or a mix of aspects of each. Or, as a widely noticed paper by the C.D. Howe Institute suggested, a 'strategic bargain' in which measures aimed at closer economic co-ordination would be mixed with increased security co-ordination in areas such as defence and immigration (Dobson, 2002; CCCE, 2003).

The security aspect—such as improved joint intelligence and policing—is the key goal of the United States in the aftermath of 11 September. For this reason, in particular, the US government is planning a sweeping system to record all those who enter and exit the country. This could have a substantial impact at the Canada–US border by increasing the transaction costs for companies. Canada is fighting this measure and considering ways to co-ordinate security efforts with the United States. Ottawa's goal likely will be to convince Washington that physical security and economic security are inextricably linked.

The European Union provides some basis for considering the path forward in North America, although there are as many differences between the continents in terms of the rationale and circumstances of closer integration as there might be potential similarities. The EU began life in 1951 as the European Coal and Steel Community, a sectoral agreement involving six nations. It became a full-fledged customs union in 1957 with the Treaty of Rome, and it evolved into a common market including the free movement of citizens after the Single European Act of 1987. Along the way, the number of countries expanded to 15 (another 10 are now being considered for membership) and a series of common institutions was established, including a significant 'cohesion' fund aimed at improving living standards in the EU's poorer countries. Monetary union, negotiated under the 1992 Maastricht Treaty, took a decade to bring into force; 12 of the 15 nations discarded their currencies for the euro on 1 January 2002. A European constitution setting out the basis for further integration is currently being negotiated.

This step-by-step approach is being examined by those studying North American integration. Yet, to what extent does it provide useful guidance? European integration was a politically motivated movement, aimed at ensuring that the bloodshed of two world wars would not be repeated. European nations, as a result, were willing to consider joint arrangements, including a European Parliament. Some analysts have suggested that preliminary steps could be taken towards similar institutions here (Pastor, 2001). But the more common view is that this would be anathema to both Canada and the United States; Americans guard their sovereignty jealously, and Canadians would be fearful of being overwhelmed by the United States in joint decision-making bodies such as a legislature with even limited powers. While the terrorist attacks of 11 September added a key security aspect to the bilateral relationship, they have not provided the same impetus as war did to the post-1945 integration movement in Europe.

Furthermore, the very different compositions of the two continents are striking. The United States is dominant in North America, representing almost 90 per cent of continental GDP. Some Europeans feared that Germany would dominate the EU, even when it represents only about 25 per cent of European GDP. Still, Germany dwarfs its

Benelux neighbours in terms roughly similar to Canada–US comparisons. In 1960, West Germany had reached a degree of economic integration with Belgium and Luxembourg, in trade and investment terms, that Canada and the United States did not reach until 1990 (Hufbauer and Schott, 1998: 39). But, unlike in Europe, Canada–US integration has accelerated since then without corresponding changes in the underlying economic framework. What are the options, then, beyond free trade?

A customs union is the next stage in economic integration after a free trade area. While a free trade zone eliminates tariffs between the participating countries, a customs union takes the further step of applying a common tariff to all other countries. The benefit to a nation like Canada, which does most of its trade with the United States, would involve the simplification of procedures at the Canada–US border. In order to qualify for duty-free trade under NAFTA, companies must comply with rules of origin set out to check that their goods are produced primarily in North America. (For example, to be subject to NAFTA's zero-tariff arrangements, 62.5 per cent of an automobile must be made in North America.) The rules themselves can be Byzantine; an annex to NAFTA devotes about 200 pages to rules of origin specifications. Paperwork required to ship goods can run to more than 10 pages (Mirus, 2001: 51).

In a customs union, however, imports into the trade zone face the same tariffs anywhere, so rules of origin need no longer apply. Regardless of where an item entered North America and cleared customs, it could be shipped within the continent without further regulatory oversight. This would speed the flow of legitimate commerce and free up resources to focus on more critical issues such as cross-border security.

The downside of a customs union is that it would be more difficult for Canada to apply an independent trade policy with a country like Cuba, which is subject to an embargo with the United States but has open trading arrangements with Canada. The United States has imposed embargoes on other countries as well, particularly in the Middle East, that Canada sometimes has not completely followed. These distinct policies might be put at risk if Canada and the United States went so far as to form a joint team at World Trade Organization negotiations. (The European Union operates as one entity at the WTO.) As well, the power disparity between the two countries would ensure that trade policy was more likely to be set in Washington than Ottawa.

Yet, third-country tariffs now applied by Canada and the United States generally are similar, with a small number of key exceptions such as agricultural products and trucks. In effect, Canada and the United States have moved on an ad hoc basis towards an informal customs union in significant ways, but the current arrangement offers few of the cost advantages that a customs union brings in terms of reduced border bureaucracy.

Almost 40 per cent of Canadian and US tariff lines are within one percentage point of each other. Even a unilateral step by Ottawa to harmonize tariffs at US levels, which tend to be slightly lower, would affect only 20 per cent of Canada's overall trade with countries other than the United States and Mexico.[3] However, the costs of the rules of origin system have been estimated in at least one academic study to be substantial—up to 2–3 per cent of GDP.[4]

'More worrisome for Canada and Mexico is the fact that the existence of rules of origin creates uncertainty for potential investors', concludes economist Richard Harris in a study for the federal Industry Department's North American Linkages project. 'Economic objectives would best be served by achieving a customs union, while demands for national sovereignty are more consistent with the independence in trade policy that [free trade] offers. In reality, of course, there is a trade-off between these objectives' (Harris, 2001: 11). The House of Commons Foreign Affairs and International Trade Committee, after extensive hearings on such trade-offs, concluded in a report released in December 2002 that the federal government should 'initiate a detailed review of the advantages and disadvantages of the concept [of a customs union] in the North American context' (Chase and Sallot, 2002).

A common market is the third form of economic integration, and involves the free movement of people in addition to goods, services, and capital. Increasing labour mobility, according to testimony before the Commons committee, could provide income growth by increasing economic efficiency.

NAFTA included some provisions on labour mobility, especially the temporary migration of business persons under the TN-1 (Free Trade Professional Work Visa) program. But it included nothing close to the guarantees for Europeans under the Schengen agreement that allows citizens of EU countries to work freely in other member countries. Only about 2 per cent of EU citizens have taken advantage of this, a reflection of language and cultural barriers across the EU that are, excepting Quebec, largely absent between Canada and the United States. 'I would certainly support getting rid of all this stuff at the borders', Mulroney said. 'Why would you and I have trouble crossing the border . . . when Germans can whip into France and Ireland and Spain with no trouble at all?' (Clark, 2000).

Indeed, the small Canadian economy has placed the country's citizens in an unenviable position. Among the major industrialized nations, Canadians may have the least economic opportunity in terms of the size of the marketplace in which they work. Europeans have the right to work anywhere within the EU. Americans have the right to work anywhere in a nation with a population approaching 300 million. Canadians' employment opportunities, at least those granted by right of citizenship, are limited to what is available in a nation with a population barely greater than 30 million. That is a stunted vista for Canadians and is damaging, as well, to the Canadian economy.

Services trade is growing at a faster rate than goods trade, adding to the necessity of allowing open travel to assist customers on both a short-term and longer-term basis. Multinational corporations routinely seek to move senior staff between countries. In each case, the continuing restrictions on North American labour mobility may be, as with rules of origin requirements, a disincentive for international companies to invest in Canada to supply the entire continental market.

In a sense, labour mobility would be nothing new for Canada. Canada's prolonged rejection of free trade is well-trod history, but the open border arrangements for labour that applied until the United States imposed restrictions during the 1920s are less well known. A century ago, one in five Canadians lived in the United States. Canadian emigration outpaced immigration in every decade between 1860 and 1900—a reflection of the higher standard of living in the United States and the opportunities there. American officials even had offices in Canada to facilitate the trip south. Immigration outpaced emigration (largely to the US) in all but one decade in the twentieth century, lately by a factor of roughly four to one. From 1851 to 1996, total immigration to Canada was 14.6 million; total emigration was 8.5 million (Industry Canada, 2001).

Today, however, the free flow of labour would benefit workers and companies on both sides of the border, easing corporate efforts to hire specialists. Industry Canada has undertaken studies of the implications of an open labour market, suggesting that the impact would not be increased brain drain—a matter of much public concern in Canada in recent years—but 'brain circulation', in which skilled workers could significantly expand their horizons without the artificial constraints imposed by the border (ibid.).

Under NAFTA, certain classes of skilled workers, such as nurses, are already quite mobile. But their ability to relocate remains largely dependent on the existence of tight labour markets. The EU experience suggests, however, that a common Canada–US labour market would provide benefits in the form of increased competition and productivity.

The fourth form of integration is monetary or economic union, with greater co-ordination of fiscal policies—and especially the adoption of a common currency. This is the least likely option, at least in the foreseeable future. This is also the step that has elicited the most commentary in Canada, largely because of the symbolic importance and sovereignty implications of giving up the Canadian currency in favour of dollarization (adoption of the US dollar) or a common currency, which some advocates have dubbed the amero or NAMU (North American monetary unit). The debate often has seemed to come in waves, usually timed to declines in the value of the Canadian dollar vis-à-vis the US currency.

Even David Dodge of the Bank of Canada has refused to rule out the possibility that Canada and the United States might eventually use the same currency, although he discounts this possibility 'as far into the future as I can see' (Globe and Mail, 2002). As Dodge also has pointed out, the Canadian and American economies—despite their close ties—remain distinctly different and, thus, Canada benefits from the flexibility of being able to control its own monetary policy.

The Canadian economy is less dependent on natural resources than a generation ago, but commodities production remains about 10 times as important to Canada as to the United States. Raw materials still account for about one-third of gross export revenues, a key reason why the Canadian dollar is still viewed internationally as a resource-based currency. The United States, however, is a major net importer of natural resources (Murray, 1999). Bank of Canada studies have suggested that the slide in the Canadian dollar's value over the last 30 years (apart from the surge from 1986 to 1991 caused by a high interest-rate policy) can be attributed largely to the steadily declining value of international commodities, as well as lower productivity improvements compared to the United States and a slight variance in long-term inflation trends (Robson and Laider, 2002).

Advocates of a common currency, such as Canadian economists Tom Courchene and Herbert Grubel (as well as Nobel Prize-winner Robert Mundell, who teaches in the United States), maintain that its adoption would hold a number of benefits. It would reduce transaction costs and boost bilateral trade, by as much as 30 per cent, according to some studies. It would essentially provide a cold bath for Canadian companies that have become less competitive (by not purchasing expensive new technologies offshore) and leaned on the currency's low value to increase sales abroad.

But there are significant differences in the degree of Canada–US policy co-ordination that would be required to institute a common currency, particularly when compared to customs union or even open labour market arrangements. As noted above, the two countries already maintain similar external tariff rates. Even advocates of a common currency admit there is little likelihood of the US government agreeing to any kind of joint institutions to run a common currency, such as adding a thirteenth seat to the Federal Reserve to accommodate a Canadian representative.

These definitions of ever-deeper forms of economic integration may be, all the same, less useful to politicians than they are to academics. The European process leading to economic union didn't follow precisely the cut-and-dried stages set out above, nor would North American integration. In fact, a myriad of other cross-border issues on this continent don't fit easily into these categories. But they represent significant impediments to smooth economic relations, and are now being examined more closely by federal officials.

Ottawa is reviewing the regulations imposed by federal departments with the aims of reducing the burden on business. This much was specified in the Speech from the Throne in September 2002. But an internal government report goes further, suggesting that 'our interconnections . . . particularly with the US' mean more effort must be made to co-ordinate regulatory oversight with Washington. The study indicates that Canada must counter the false presumption that regulations must be made in Canada, rather than arising out of joint oversight. A common approach could involve 'harmonized' standards or—and this is Ottawa's preference—the 'joint recognition of standards'.[5]

For example, Ottawa is beginning consultations with the US Food and Drug Administration to determine whether ways can be found to improve the co-ordination of drug approvals, beyond existing channels for the simple exchange of information. Federal officials question whether progress can be made in this area, given public sensitivity about drug safety. But they are more confident of establishing other joint efforts, including the testing of medical devices and chemicals, and establishing common nutritional standards for foods. More than 200 food producers operating in Canada, many of them multinationals, now have to reformulate their production runs, often at significant expense, just to comply with different nutritional labelling required in the two countries. Other areas now being examined by Ottawa include joint safety standards for road and rail transportation.[6]

As the December 2002 report of the House of Commons Standing Committee suggests, Ottawa should examine 'how Canada can move towards more regulatory equivalency within an integrated North American economy and society (being mindful not to create competitive disadvantages)'. To be sure, Canada—as the much smaller economic partner—would be more likely to move towards the US standard than vice versa in those circumstances where harmonization might be deemed appropriate. But Ottawa's primary goal would be to identify areas where regulations already are similar but in which there is little co-ordination, and thus to reduce private-sector costs and regulatory expenses on both sides of the border.

There are reasons to think that the high-profile trade disputes between Canada and the United States, now involving particularly softwood and wheat, may become less common in the future. Trade disputes occur most often in sectors where the products have reached maturity or are at an even later stage in the product cycle, and these frequently involve American industries that are no longer competitive because they have been protected for years, even decades. Those are the sectors—agriculture, in particular—that were excluded from NAFTA's zero-tariff provisions.

But the United States is a leading free-trader in sectors in which the product cycle is in an earlier stage. Trade disputes with Canada are rare in the so-called new economy—high-technology and services industries that are largely continental in scope. There are no trade disputes over computer components. Nor are there such disputes in the auto and auto parts industries—the most integrated in trade and investment terms of the major North American industrial sectors.

All the same, existing NAFTA provisions concerning anti-dumping and countervail investigations remain flawed. A watered-down version of Canada's demand for an exemption from US trade law was put in place, involving a binational dispute settlement process. But, as Canada has experienced in the softwood lumber case, even that compromise can be skewed in favour of US producers through further changes in US laws.

Customs union or common market arrangements generally include the eradication of trade remedy laws, on the basis that the countries involved are part of a common economic space. Competition law usually takes its place. But the US Congress has traditionally been unwilling to relinquish its authority to oversee protectionist measures, evident recently during the Bush administration's drive for trade promotion authority. This remains a significant hurdle to any future bilateral effort towards deeper economic integration.

Nonetheless, interim steps could be taken to reduce the number of trade actions involving Canada and the United States, and such stress might eventually lead towards more substantial reform. The level of dumping and subsidization required to impose tariffs could be raised to more than 'de minimis' levels, for example. And a joint team could be appointed by Washington and Ottawa to analyze the findings of each country's trade authorities. They would not have decision-making power, but they could be the next stage in the process towards establishing a permanent binational court (Macrory, 2002).

According to some estimates, as much as 45 per cent of the Canadian economy remains protected, to varying degrees, from foreign competition. Some sectors are politically sensitive, such as cultural industries, and Ottawa would be loath to lift foreign ownership restrictions, even alongside the continued existence of Canadian content regulations. Other sectors, however, appear ripe for reform. A report for the federal government by industry analyst Debra Ward, released in September 2002, suggested that Ottawa consider new Canada–US airline negotiations, building on the 1995 Open Skies agreement. This would include the implementation of cabotage, in which Canadian-based airlines would be allowed to fly between American cities instead of servicing solely domestic and Canada–US routes (rights that also would be granted in equivalent fashion to US airlines) (Fitzpatrick, 2002). As well, certain industries—especially telecommunications and cable—have been lobbying for more liberal foreign investment rules in order to gain access to international capital markets. This may also become an issue for the banking industry, which is now embroiled again in pressing for domestic mergers.

The border accord signed by Manley and Ridge likely was only the first step towards easing the routine customs clearance of shipments and business people. Programs like Nexus and Customs Self-Assessment, in which individuals and companies apply for security clearance and receive faster treatment at customs, may be applied along the entire Canada–US border in 2003.

Still, infrastructure investment has lagged in many ways. Until 11 September, the US Customs Service employed the same number of guards at the Canada–US border as in 1980, although trade had increased exponentially (Beatty, 2002: 40). The Canadian government introduced a five-year border infrastructure program worth $1.2 billion in its 2001 budget. The US government has increased its funding as well.

But in the eyes of many analysts there have been insufficient steps towards transportation and infrastructure co-ordination, especially by road but also by rail and air. As the Commons committee report argues: 'Given the volume of Canada–US/NAFTA trade, an efficient and cost-effective transportation system over our shared border is needed.'

It is a matter of some dismay in Mexico that Vincente Fox's call for the three North American nations to begin work on a long-term plan towards a common market has been met with little enthusiasm. President George W. Bush was noncommittal, at best, when they first met. Prime Minister Jean Chrétien acted no differently. And since 11 September, even the meagre advances Fox sought in terms of improved border treatment of migrants have made little progress. Similarly, Fox's hopes for the establishment of nascent trilateral organizations have been met with silence. Mexican officials conceive of closer integration as a process leading, to some extent, to European-style institutions (Fagan, 2002a). That is not the thinking in Ottawa among those officials now studying new continental concepts. Instead, a path forward likely would involve a two-step process, in which Canada–US negotiations cleared the way eventually for trilateral action and then would lead to the establishment of minimal permanent institutions.

This was, after all, the path undertaken regarding free trade: the FTA was expanded to include Mexico five years later. And this was the process undertaken after 11 September regarding the border accord. Initially, Mexico sought to make this process a trilateral negotiation. But Canadian officials were convinced that this would prove unwieldy and significantly delay progress at the Canada–US border, which deals with trade more than migration, unlike the Mexico–US border. Mexican officials insist that an opportunity was lost. But they signed their own border deal with the Bush administration some months after the Smart Border accord was completed, and many of the terms to speed trade across the Rio Grande were based on terms won by Ottawa.

This, again, is likely to be the model for any future negotiations. Mexico's different level of development ensures that its integration will come more slowly. As Chris Sands, director of the Canada Project at the Center for Strategic and International Studies, noted at a conference in November 2001, all countries could negotiate common goals, but policy convergence on those goals would proceed on separate schedules for developed and developing countries. This would permit Canada and the United States to proceed on important issues bilaterally, while allowing Mexico to converge at a slower, mutually agreed pace.

And what is the likelihood of such an agenda? Fox's grand scheme was met with a frosty reception, but the leaders of the three countries have made a general commitment to pursue closer ties. At the Summit of the Americas in Quebec City in April 2001, Bush, Chrétien, and Fox recognized that 'patterns of co-operation—by governments, business and other members of civil society—are building a new sense of community among us.' They pledged to 'promote our mutual economic interest' and 'examine options to further strengthen our North American partnership'.

Sentiment only, perhaps. But those words bore a greater resemblance to the goals laid out by the advocates of European union in the 1950s—'to lay the foundations of an ever-closer union among the peoples of Europe'—than they did to the pinched preamble to NAFTA, which set out a limited vision to 'reduce distortions to trade' and 'enhance the competitiveness of firms'.

At a meeting of Asia-Pacific leaders in Mexico in October 2002, Fox again suggested a grand vision to Bush and Chrétien and was rebuffed again, but not as completely as the first time he tried. Whereas there was little appetite for new negotiations in Washington and Ottawa two years earlier, this time Chrétien proposed that the three leaders consider a NAFTA-plus agenda when they meet in 2003. As he said, 'Perhaps the time has come to pause and look at where we're going' (Dawson, 2002). Although Bush did not address this issue publicly, some American officials have suggested that the US administration might be willing to consider such options, especially if the examination of closer economic ties is mixed with a discussion of closer security co-ordination.

In any case, it is expected that integration will be an issue during the Liberal leadership race to succeed Prime Minister Chrétien. How close does Canada want to get to the United States, especially in the post-11 September environment of heightened fears of terrorist attack? What is the best mix of policies to maintain an open Canada–US border in times of great insecurity? And to what extent will the United States ultimately focus on continental issues when its mindset is often far away—in Afghanistan, or Iraq, or North Korea?

The public, for the most part, does not appear ideologically opposed to an agenda of closer continental ties. Polls have revealed that citizens of Canada, the United States, and Mexico generally have an open mind about closer economic co-ordination (and greater security co-operation), just so long as those do not also involve radical steps towards increased political integration or even political union.

Extensive polling undertaken by Ottawa-based Ekos Research Associates found that support in Canada for free trade is at its highest level since the negotiations with the United States began in 1985 and that NAFTA remains fairly popular in the United States and Mexico. Almost two-thirds of Canadians and Americans also support deeper forms of economic integration, especially an open labour market (though, not surprisingly, that support plummets when considering open labour flows involving Mexico).[7] Another poll found that two-thirds of Canadians want the Liberal government to foster closer economic ties with the United States, while only 5 per cent were adamantly opposed (Fife, 2002). 'The rather surprising conclusion is that the people of North America are way ahead of their leaders', says US academic Robert Pastor. Perhaps; yet governments may slowly be coming around to consideration of the options now being placed before them.

Certainly, the Canadian government will not be able to avoid grappling with continentalization. Two decades ago, Canada took the lead in proposing a free trade agreement with the United States aimed at building the Canadian economy in the face of US protectionism, and several years later Canada signed on to NAFTA. Now, Canada is again in the midst of a vital challenge, and an opportunity, regarding its place on the continent, forged by the events of 11 September.

Economic security has become linked with physical security, and a means must be found that better protects both. Outdated views of what constitutes sovereignty need to be re-examined. Canada and the United States, which share similar values and interests, also have come to share a common economic space. Recognizing that, and nurturing it, means considering the continent anew.

NOTES

1. Many of these statistics come from the December 2002 report of the House of Commons Standing Committee on Foreign Affairs and International Trade. The figures on Canada's core producers are cited in speeches by Jayson Myers, chief economist at the Canadian Manufacturers and Exporters.
2. John Helliwell and John McCallum have estimated that the propensity for trade between provinces still remains many times higher than that for trade between provinces and states, once having accounted for size of market and transportation distances.
3. Cited at the Public Policy Forum conference 'Managing Our Border with the United States', 28–9 Nov. 2001. Also mentioned in testimony to Commons committee by University of Alberta business professor Barry Scholnick.
4. Ph.D. thesis by A. Appiah, cited by Harris (2001: 11).
5. Draft, unreleased report by the Department of Foreign Affairs and International Trade's External Advisory Committee, dated 10 Oct. 2002.
6. Based on October 2002 interviews by the author with senior DFAIT officials.
7. The Ekos polling provided the statistical basis for a day-long conference, 'Rethinking North American Integration', organized by the Public Policy Forum, 5 June 2002, Toronto.

REFERENCES

Beatty, Perrin. 2002. 'Canada in North America: Isolation or Integration', in Peter Hakim and Robert E. Litan, eds, *The Future of North American Integration*. Washington: Brookings Institution Press.

Beauchesne, Eric. 2002. 'Dodge wants new free trade deal', *National Post*, 24 Oct., A1.

Canadian Council of Chief Executives (CCCE). 2003. *Security and Prosperity: The Dynamics of a New Canada–United States Partnership in North America*, Jan.

Chambers, Edward J., and Peter H. Smith, eds. 2002. *NAFTA in the New Millennium*. Edmonton: University of Alberta Press.

Chase, Steven, and Jeff Sallot. 2002. 'MPs draft report suggests tighter ties with U.S., Mexico', *Globe and Mail*, 6 Nov., A1.

Clark, Campbell. 2000. 'Get rid of border posts, says Mulroney', *Globe and Mail*, 6 Sept., A1.

Cohen, Andrew, and Anne McIlroy. 1999. 'On the Ties that Bind', *Globe and Mail*, 7 June, A1.

Conference Board of Canada (CBC). 2002. *Performance and Potential 2002–03: Canada 2010: Challenges and Choices at Home and Abroad*, Oct.

D'Aquino, Thomas Paul, and David Stewart-Patterson. 2001. *Northern Edge: How Canadians Can Triumph in the Global Economy*. Toronto: Stoddart.

Dawson, Anne. 2002. 'PM wants to take fresh look at NAFTA', *National Post*, 28 Oct., A1.

Dobson, Wendy. 2002. 'Shaping the Future of the North American Economic Space', *C.D. Howe Institute Commentary*. Toronto: C.D. Howe Institute.

Doern, G. Bruce, and Brian W. Tomlin. 1991. *Faith and Fear: The Free Trade Story*. Toronto: Stoddart.

Fagan, Drew. 2002a. 'Continental integration complicated, to Mexico's dismay', *Globe and Mail*, 4 Mar., B8.

———. 2002b. 'Donald Macdonald: Royal Commission Anew', *Globe and Mail*, 11 Apr., B16.

———. 2002c. 'What Canada must do to crack the U.S. market', *Globe and Mail*, 5 Nov., A17

———. 2003. 'Is it time for a summit?', *Globe and Mail*, 14 Jan., A15.

Fife, Robert. 2002. '66% favour stronger ties to U.S.', *National Post*, 21 Oct., A1.

Fitzpatrick, Peter. 2002. 'Give U.S. airlines freer rein: report', *National Post*, 27 Sept., A1.

Globe and Mail. 2002. 'Dodge Discounts Call to Embrace U.S. Dollar,' 7 Oct., B3.

Hakim, Peter, and Robert E. Litan, eds. 2002. *The Future of North American Integration*. Washington: Brookings Institution Press.

Hart, Michael. 2002. *A Trading Nation: Canadian Trade Policy from Colonialism to Globalization*. Vancouver: University of British Columbia Press.

——— and William Dymond. 2001. *Common Borders, Shared Destinies: Canada, the United States and Deepening Integration*. Ottawa: Centre for Trade Policy and Law, Carleton University.

Harris, Richard. 2001. 'North American Economic Integration: Issues and Research Agenda', Industry Canada Discussion Paper Number 10, Apr.

House of Commons Standing Committee on Foreign Affairs and International Trade. 2002. *Partners in North America: Advancing Canada's Relations with the United States and Mexico*.

Hufbauer, Gary C., and Jeffrey J. Schott. 1998. *North American Economic Integration: 25 Years Backward and Forward*. Ottawa: Industry Canada Research Publications Program.

Industry Canada. 2001. 'The Consequences of Increased Labour Mobility within an Integrating North America'.

Kergin, Michael. 2001. 'The Canada–U.S. Border: Moving to the Fast Lane', speech to American Association of Exporters and Importers, New York, 21 May. Available at: <http://www.canadianembassy.org/ambassador/speeches-en.asp>.

Macrory, Patrick. 2002. 'NAFTA Chapter 19: A Successful Experiment in International Trade Dispute Resolution', *C.D. Howe Institute Commentary*. Toronto: C.D. Howe Institute.

Mintz, Jack M. 2001. *Most Favoured Nation: Building a Framework for Smart Economic Policy*. Toronto: C.D. Howe Institute.

Mirus, Rolf. 2001. 'After Sept. 11: A Canada–U.S. Customs Union', *Policy Options* (Nov.).

Murray, John. 1999. *Why Canada Needs a Flexible Exchange Rate*. Bank of Canada Working Paper 99–12.

Pastor, Robert A. 2001. *Toward a North American Community: Lessons from the Old World for the New*. Washington: Institute for International Economics.

Pettigrew, Pierre. 2002. Speech to Canadian-American Business Council, Toronto, 16 Oct.

Ramirez, Bruno. 2001. *Crossing the 49th Parallel: Migration from Canada to the United States, 1900–1930*. Ithaca, NY: Cornell University Press.

Robson, William B.P., and David Laidler. 2002. 'No Small Change: The Awkward Economics and Politics of North American Monetary Integration', *C.D. Howe Institute Commentary*. Toronto: C.D. Howe Institute.

4

Erasing the Line: Rebuilding Economic and Trade Relations after 11 September

CHRISTOPHER WADDELL

The winds gently blew the gigantic Stars and Stripes and Maple Leaf flags hanging on the side of the Ambassador Bridge, as Prime Minister Jean Chrétien and US President George Bush stepped onto a stage on the morning of 9 September 2002.

Beneath the flags on the Detroit side of the St Clair River, the two leaders had just watched over the shoulders of shirt-sleeved US Customs officers as they demonstrated two new procedures designed to speed trucks and people across the Canada–US border.

Now the leaders were speaking in front of a sea of faces of Canadian and American customs and police officers. It was a photo-friendly backdrop for a message about enforcement and co-operation.

'We are trying to help people cross borders as quickly as possible', the President told the assembled crowd that consisted mostly of officials of the two governments and the media.

Canada had wrestled with the border issue for the previous year, since 11 September 2001, and desperately needed co-operation from the United States to keep the border open. It is the lynchpin of the Canadian economy. Long lines of trucks and lengthy delays at border crossings and airports undermined the just-in-time economy that now dominated Canada's trade relations with the United States as a by-product of their 1989 Free Trade Agreement.

In the United States, it was all security and no economics. Enforcement at the border, always a concern on the US side, drove every decision after 11 September. For Canada, winning co-operation on economic issues meant proving it could be serious about enforcing security.

The Bush-Chrétien ceremony in Detroit was the symbolic end to a year of intense negotiations between Canada and the United States that implemented a 'Smart Border' agreement to work more closely on both economic and security issues. It tied the countries even more closely together than under the original Canada-United States Free Trade Agreement (FTA) and its successor, the North American Free Trade Agreement (NAFTA). It may also set the stage for discussions about even closer ties in the future.

This chapter examines how Canada and the United States responded to the security demands and economic disruptions after 11 September at the border between the two countries. It outlines the process the two countries developed to work together to address the border issues they jointly faced and explains how and why that process may have limited applicability to other aspects of Canada–US trade and general relations. In that respect it touches on but does not go into detail about the prospects for further North American economic integration. Instead, the chapter suggests that potential difficulties remain, and these could threaten the durability of the agreement the two countries reached to modernize the border for the movement of goods and people. Such difficulties could delay or set back any attempt to bring Canada, the United States, and Mexico into closer integration as one economic unit.

Canada's post-11 September goal was to make the Canada–US border virtually invisible for legitimate trade and travel—the $1 billion worth of goods and 500,000 people that cross the border every day. At the border, the American reaction to 11 September threatened to negate everything Canada had done since the two countries started free trade on 1 January 1989. Crossing the border suddenly meant huge delays as every document was analyzed closely, people were questioned at great length, and anything at all suspicious or out of the ordinary was frequently rejected and turned back. A process that had always taken just minutes now took hours for both individuals and trucks carrying goods. The lineups stretched for kilometres.

Free trade had meant companies could locate in Canada and sell into the US without worrying about problems getting their goods across the border. The Canadian government feared that more permanent border delays would quickly translate into businesses leaving Canada for the US or refusing to establish or expand operations in Canada to serve the US market. Canada believed the risks to investment were too great to stand by and do nothing.

It was more than slightly ironic that a Liberal government in Canada was suddenly so anxious to agree to arrangements that would move a large step closer to eliminating the border for daily commerce. Only 14 years earlier, the Liberals had campaigned against free trade with a doomsday election advertisement showing a hand erasing the Canada–United States border. Free trade would be the ultimate surrender of Canadian independence, the Liberals told Canadians then. Without that border, Canada would become the fifty-first state.

But that was then, and a lot had changed since the 1988 election. Commerce grew tremendously between the two countries—so much so that Canada and the US began talks about easing border restrictions in the late 1990s. That process meandered along and as 2001 began, bureaucrats in both capitals worked on border-related issues but with no political interest or pressure driving them to decisions on either side.

Initially it appeared unlikely that the arrival of George W. Bush in the White House in January with a Republican administration would break that stalemate. For the first time in more than a decade and a half, there were not like-minded governments across the border. After the closeness of first the Mulroney government with the Reagan and Bush administrations and then the cordial Chrétien-Clinton match, this would be something different. Now a liberal government in Ottawa would face a conservative one in Washington, and Canadian officials approached that prospect with trepidation. The fear was that those different political philosophies, plus the new President's Texas roots and close links to Mexico, meant the new Bush administration's economic attention would turn south at the expense of the north.

It took several months and the Quebec City Summit of the Americas before that Canadian concern started to ease. President Bush and Prime Minister Chrétien met for the first time over a friendly lunch in Washington early in 2001. Politicians to the core, they joked and swapped political war stories. Next was Quebec City in April, where Canada did everything to make the new President comfortable at his first international meeting. Trade problems with Canada were not ignored, as Chrétien ensured that PEI potatoes were on the dinner menu. He then joked about it at a news conference to draw attention to US trade restrictions on Canadian potatoes—a high-publicity dispute that was resolved not long after.

As spring turned to summer, fears the relationship would be very tense slowly faded. Even with a new dispute on softwood lumber looming as the US industry launched countervailing duty and anti-dumping complaints against Canadian producers, there was a sense in the Canadian government that the broader trade and economic relationship would not produce crises.

Then came 11 September. The border was never completely closed although all air links were severed for several days. Traffic at border points came to almost a dead stop. Hourly and daily updates on the length of lineups went to Ottawa from the main crossing points for trucking at Lacolle, Quebec, Fort Erie and Windsor in Ontario, and Douglas, BC. The clampdown on border crossings was a huge shock to Canadian governments, businesses, and communities. It was even more of a shock to find that, as the days passed, there was no sign of an easing in delays. The threat of more attacks meant that the US placed national security ahead of economic concerns, and that meant checking everything and everyone moving into the US. Suddenly all the border issues the two governments had worked on slowly in the backrooms in the preceding years became critically important. Canada had to ensure procedures at the border had not changed forever.

The two weeks after 11 September were filled with questions in Washington and Ottawa. Would there be more attacks? How had the terrorists entered the United States? What about widely reported statements some had come from Nova Scotia to Maine? Was 11 September a successful version of what Ahmed Ressam tried but failed to do when he was caught trying to enter the US from Canada at Port Angeles, Washington, in the dying days of 1999, intent on a millennium bomb attack on Los Angeles International Airport?

The attacks of 11 September radically changed American perceptions of the threat posed to US security by the Canadian border. For
the previous 50 years, the threat had been airborne—either bombers
or missiles from the Soviet Union travelling over Canada. In those
years Canada and the US responded with the Mid-Canada Line and
the Distant Early Warning (DEW) line as radar defence systems and
the North American Aerospace Defence Command (NORAD). No one
thought the land border was a threat, just as no one thought individuals could travel into the US and hijack aircraft to crash them into
city centres.

On 12 September the world's longest undefended border became,
in the eyes of the US media, government, and general public, a wide-
open door through which terrorists could flood. Unlike the Mexican
border it was virtually unmanned, heightening the American sense of
vulnerability to more attacks. The reporting and re-reporting of false
suggestions that the 11 September attackers came through Canada to
the US made it more difficult for Canada to argue that the border should
return to pre-11 September conditions. Individual Canadian cabinet
ministers responsible for transport, customs, immigration, and security
all tried and in some cases did arrange meetings with their US counterparts to talk about common security issues. But there was no co-
ordination on the Canadian side and not much in talking in Washington.

Worried that the US had many more critical preoccupations,
Canadian Ambassador Michael Kirgin waited a day or two after 11
September, then called Andrew Card, President Bush's chief of staff.
In a return call Card agreed the border disruptions needed to be
addressed, but the border crossings were still hopelessly congested.

The Canada–US border was not the only one where problems
were building. On 20 September, Foreign Affairs Minister John
Manley arrived in Washington for an emergency meeting of the
Organization of American States called by the US. At that meeting
Mexican Foreign Minister Jorge Castaneda raised privately with
Canada the possibility of a trilateral approach to border issues as
Mexico faced identical problems after 11 September with its US border. Canada quickly brushed off those suggestions from its NAFTA
partner. Facing a serious economic threat, Canada chose bilateral
action over any faith in a multilateral approach. The Canadian government had no interest in Canada–US trade getting lumped in with
chronic disputes about Mexican migration to the US. Canada
promised only to keep the Mexicans informed of how it dealt with

the US on the northern border. Viewing the post-11 September borders as a great opportunity for North American co-operation, a pet project of President Vicente Fox, the Mexicans were greatly disappointed by the Canadian reaction.

The same day he rejected Mexico's overtures, Manley met with US Secretary of State Colin Powell. Powell, who was preoccupied with the global aftermath of the terrorist attacks, noted that the night before in a speech to Congress the President had announced the creation of an Office of Homeland Security under the direction of Pennsylvania Governor Tom Ridge. Powell suggested Manley direct his concerns to Ridge.

Three days later, Prime Minister Chrétien was in Washington for his first post-11 September meeting with the President. The two agreed their governments needed to ensure the border would not become a permanent obstacle to trade. As Manley had become head of a hastily created ad hoc cabinet committee on public security and anti-terrorism, he was the logical choice to take charge of the border for Canada.

During the succeeding year the Manley-Ridge connection would be the crucial element in changing the border. They were an interesting pair. Canada was fortunate that President Bush had chosen a governor of a northern border state to oversee homeland security. The situation might have been much different had the President selected a governor of New Mexico or Arizona, with little knowledge of Canada or Canada–US trade relations, to take on the problem of border security for the United States.

In the past Ridge had travelled to Canada, had participated in Great Lakes governors' and premiers' events, and knew first-hand of the importance to the US of trade with Canada. He even shared some of Manley's interests in education and technology and had participated with Manley in one of the first Internet signings of an official document. They also had similar low-key personalities. All of these commonalities clicked when they began talking for the first time in October. It would be the start of a close relationship and the political impetus for changing the border.

The President and Prime Minister had pointed to the need to get the border open and working again, but the US remained preoccupied with other terrorist issues. These included anthrax attacks, the war against Al-Qaeda, building a coalition of nations willing to send troops to Afghanistan, and the regular threats of new terrorist attacks against the US mainland. By early October 2001, the two different perceptions of the border began to solidify. For Canada the border after 11 September remained all about economics and the movement of goods and people essential to the country's prosperity. For the US, it was all about security and preventing new terrorist attacks from road, rail, sea, and air. If Canada wanted any guarantee of access on the economic front, it would have to address the US security concerns with both actions and money.

Canada had to persuade the Bush administration that economic security and national security were mutually reinforceable. Making progress on one would also mean making progress on the other, and lockstep progress could result in the easing of border restrictions. Canada had to demonstrate that it would treat US security concerns seriously, again with the legacy of Ahmed Ressam using Canada as a base for his planned attack hanging over Ottawa's moves.

The business community in Canada had been quick to recognize the risk that border delays posed. It formed a coalition at the start of October to advocate secure trade and efficient borders, began talking publicly about border problems, and commissioned a study of the impact of border delays after 11 September. From the start it called for the Canadian government to initiate action on solving border problems, not just respond to actions taken by the US.

By mid-October the Liberal government had put together a small task force of bureaucrats based in the Privy Council Office to co-ordinate a new approach to border discussions with the United States. The objective was to ensure uninterrupted movement across the border of goods and people involved in legitimate business. If the border was no longer a hurdle, the argument went, then it would not discourage investors. The Canadian government believed that secure and speedy access to the US would mean companies could locate in Canada without fear of their trade being disrupted.

After all, that was the original objective of the Free Trade Agreement—to make Canada a desirable location for new investment and expansion to sell into the US market. More than a decade of free trade had tied the countries much more closely together than ever before. The reaction to the attack on 11 September in an instant undermined all that. The lengthy delays had to be eliminated, the Canadian government believed, before they became institutionalized in the name of increasing US security.

Several things were quickly obvious. This time the northern tier of US states that border on Canada were quiet. In the past they had often supported Canada on border issues as they recognized the economic advantages to themselves of the quick flow of people and goods back and forth between the two countries. This time, though, they quickly concluded that arguing economic concerns—if these in any way compromised security—had no public support in the United States, so they did not bother to make the case.

That left it to Canada. The Canadian government departments involved in the border—Solicitor General, Justice, Transport, Canada Customs and Revenue Agency, and Citizenship and Immigration—each had its own relationship with its US counterpart—Customs, Transportation, the FBI, and the Immigration and Naturalization Service. Canadian cabinet ministers, their deputies, and senior civil servants all accepted that there needed to be co-ordination in how Canada dealt with the border, but none of them wanted to give up their individual links to Washington. However, because any new agreement required trade-offs, it needed to be negotiated centrally rather than department by department. Since the late September Bush-Chrétien meeting, Canadian officials had been dealing on border matters through the US Embassy in Ottawa, which co-ordinated issues initially through the State Department in Washington. By November, the Office of Homeland Security had taken over and became the key player in lining up US government agencies to address cross-border issues with Canada.

Working with the embassy, the Privy Council task force decided the best approach would be to try to write a 'smart borders' declaration. It would consolidate the principal ideas that had emerged from two years of discussions between Canada and the United States on easing border problems, modified to address the new security concerns of the US. There would also need to be a commitment to increase infrastructure spending to support those changes.

By early November, Ridge and Manley agreed they would meet to discuss the issues in mid-December, which provided a deadline for officials from the two governments to reach a deal. On 12 December 2001 Manley and Ridge met in Ottawa and signed a 'Smart Border' declaration that included a 30-point action plan. It was the result of two months of give and take between the two governments and laid out a program that would keep officials in the two countries busy for the next six months. It was a work plan in which each country had made some concessions to the other, stepping back in areas each had long resisted.

In general, the US pushed for measures that would enhance its security. Canada pushed for guarantees for the quick movement of goods and people through the border. The United States pressed Canada successfully into concessions on some of the 30 points. For instance, it wanted biometric identifiers such as eye iris scans or other high-tech identification tools included in travel documents. Canada did not see that as essential but ultimately agreed, rationalizing changing its position by suggesting biometrics was the way of the future in identification. Similarly, Washington wanted Canada to adopt US visa requirements for entry to Canada, but here Canada agreed only to conduct a joint review as the two countries had different lists of the nations whose citizens required visas to travel to Canada or the US. That left for the future a contentious decision about whether to let the US effectively set visa policies for Canada. As an interim step the two countries agreed to share among officials working at Canadian and US visa offices around the world their 'lookout' lists of individuals who posed a possible threat.

For air travel, the US also wanted Canadian airlines to share passenger lists in advance of flights and retain the lists afterward. Again Canada conceded, shelving any concerns about privacy. That raised the subsequent ire of Canada's Privacy Commissioner, who attacked the retention of lists after flights as unnecessary archiving of personal information about individuals that undercut privacy. The two countries also agreed to set up joint passenger analysis units at international airports to share examination and verification of travel documents of people arriving in either country.

Canada also won some concessions from the US administration. The NEXUS program at Sarnia-Port Huron, Michigan, suspended on 11 September, was resumed. It allowed frequent cross-border travellers to apply for security clearance and obtain identification cards that could include biometric indicators to allow them to cross the border and bypass lineups simply by showing their card. The US also agreed to expand NEXUS to crossing points all along the border and resumed customs and immigration clearance in Canadian airports of US-bound passengers—a procedure that had been suspended after 11 September.

The most important accomplishment for Canada was agreement to establish complementary systems for processing commercial goods crossing the border. Tied to that was a plan to process trucks away from the border. Known as the Free and Secure Trade (FAST) program, trucks would be cleared at their point of loading and transponders in each vehicle would file shipping documents to border officials electronically as the truck approached the crossing. As the President and Prime Minister observed first hand, the trucks would then be waved through reserved lanes at the crossing point and on their way in seconds. Once implemented, this plan would make it so that truckers no longer would have to stop and show customs documents that had to be checked and stamped before entry, nor would there be the risk of further delay for cargo inspections.

Canada argued that as both countries accept self-reporting by corporations and individuals of their income and expenses for tax purposes, that same approach should apply to reporting the contents of cross-border shipments. There was no need to stop and confirm at the border the contents of vehicles operated by regular transborder shippers such as the automobile industry.

This was a major victory for Canada as the US had been dragging its feet on the matter for years. The US government was never interested in moving enforcement away from the border. It seemed out of the question after 11 September. Yet Washington ultimately agreed. The US administration realized it needed to focus on security priorities, and that much of the cross-border movement of goods and people was not and never would pose a threat. It would therefore be better to concentrate resources on identifying and dealing with potential risks rather than spreading surveillance thinly across the full range of people and goods travelling between the two countries. At the same time, Canada backed down on its past opposition to sharing customs data, putting aside long-standing fears that the US could use such information for commercial advantage or trade actions if the US government decided to share shipment data gathered at the border with US industries and corporations.

Consistent with the US view of the border as a line of defence, Washington was keen on such points as integrated border and marine enforcement teams to work together examining goods crossing borders and entering ports by container. The US also pushed to integrate intelligence and fingerprint databases of the two countries. Canada and the US also agreed to work together to remove deportees, pass counter-terrorism legislation, and freeze terrorist assets.

The rest of the 30 points in the new border protocol came not through trade-offs but as a result of broad general agreement by both countries on issues that were less contentious. They included everything from refugee and asylum processing, a safe third-country agreement to handle refugee claims, and having overseas immigration officers working together with compatible immigration databases to establish a single joint border station for both countries rather than two separate stations in remote locations. They also agreed to improve roads and access at border crossings.

The two months of negotiations were just the starting point and the December 2001 announcement was simply an agreement-in-principle. Two important matters remained outstanding. First, the two countries had to turn the idea into reality, with direction from Ridge and Manley proving crucial to that stage of the process. Then came the longer-term challenge that will take years to determine—whether the two countries will respect the agreement and carry through on the changes they negotiated.

After the breakfast that launched the action plan on 12 December 2001, the two politicians told their officials they wanted regularly updated progress reports on the implementation of the 30 points. Each of the points was given a colour code. Green would signify good movement towards implementation. Yellow would still mean movement but not fast enough towards a plan for implementation. The problems were coloured red and they would ultimately go to Manley and Ridge for solutions. The two would meet or talk every six weeks and expected to hear at every meeting how much closer the two countries had moved towards implementing the 30 points. That kept the pressure on officials from the two countries to compromise and reach deals. The individual departments—Citizenship and Immigration Canada with INS, Transport Canada with Transportation, CCRA with US Customs—handled that work. It was all overseen in Canada by the same Privy Council group that pulled together the 30 points. In Washington the Office of Homeland Security established a Canada desk staffed with a group whose job it was to stickhandle problems through the various US agencies that handle border issues.

When the department-to-department meetings could not produce agreement on how to implement elements of the plan, the central co-ordinators would look for trade-offs across departments and agencies. They would then make recommendations to Manley and Ridge. The two ministers would make the final decisions. On the Canadian side, the cabinet was briefed regularly on Manley-Ridge sessions, but only issues that needed formal cabinet approval were outlined in detail.

The colour codes were effective shorthand to show general progress, but they did not distinguish between disagreements that were easy to solve and those that developed into more serious disputes. For example, it proved relatively easy to work out a timetable for expanding the NEXUS system to additional border crossings, but the issue of cross-border passenger clearance at Canadian airports was much thornier.

One lengthy dispute revolved around US Customs and Immigration clearance of passengers at Canadian airports. How would a traveller's rights under Canada's Charter of Rights and Freedoms be protected when a US official working in a Canadian airport wanted to detain someone being questioned in the clearance area? It soon became a sovereignty question, as Canada did not want any of its officials in the US Customs and Immigration clearance areas. The two countries finally agreed that the RCMP would always station an officer in the vicinity to be available on three minutes' notice to handle any detentions in Canada while respecting Charter rights. Much of the work after December 2001 involved sorting out such specifics to implement the 30 points.

By late June considerable progress had been made when Manley and Ridge met at Niagara Falls to settle some details, paving the way for Chrétien and Bush to meet in Detroit in September. At the end of their Niagara Falls session, the two released a progress report on implementing the 30 points. While work was far from finished, a lot had been accomplished. In less than a year Canada and the United States had taken a major step towards even closer economic integration—not eliminating the border yet, but approaching that point for much of the commerce and people who cross it regularly.

There were five reasons why the two countries reached agreement quickly on the 'Smart Border' details.

First and foremost, the terrorist attacks had revealed to the US its vulnerability to the movement of people and goods across the Canadian border. It desperately needed to address that security threat but it could not do so by itself. It needed Canada's help. Senior officials in the US administration realized that and so were prepared to listen to proposals from Canada and strike a deal, but only if the final agreement benefited the US by increasing security measures at that border.

Second, there had been a lot of work done on border issues in the years and months before 11 September that the two governments revived and moved forward quickly in October and November 2001.

Third, the US realized it also needed an open border for its own economy, and was prepared to work for that providing it was not at the expense of security. Normal traffic could not be delayed to meet US security concerns without doing considerable damage to both the Canadian and US economies. Free trade had already brought sufficient integration that a suddenly closed border would have had serious economic repercussions. Canadian industry was quick to launch a high-visibility lobbying campaign in late September 2001, pressing the Canadian government to act. US businesses were quieter, although those in industries directly affected, such as automobiles, were making their concerns known to the Bush administration.

Fourth, that industry pressure had an impact at the top. Both President Bush and Prime Minister Chrétien indicated as early as their 24 September 2001 meeting that they wanted action to ease border congestion. Canada backed that up with a five-year $7 billion security program announced in the December 2001 budget that would increase spending on policing and intelligence, improve screening of people arriving in Canada, and provide better emergency preparedness, more funding for the Canadian military, and significant border infrastructure traffic improvements for road and rail. It helped demonstrate to the US that Canada was serious about improving security. With the stamp of approval from the two leaders, their officials on both sides of the border had the authority to proceed quickly.

Fifth, Ridge and Manley were the lynchpins, sharing a vision of how the border should work for the benefit of both countries and exerting constant pressure on their bureaucracies to keep the process moving to ensure agreements that could lead to implementation. Just as Ridge on the US side was crucial to the success of the Smart Border exercise, so was Manley important in Canada. He was on the conservative side of the governing Liberal Party and sympathetic to the United States, and he had considerable influence within the Canadian government. Had the job been given to a left-wing member of the Liberal government with its tradition of anti-Americanism, an agreement would have been much more difficult to reach.

To some senior officials in the Canadian government, the Smart Border negotiations became about more than just ensuring the border would remain open. They believed the experience and approach could be applied to solving broader trade disputes and could even be the basis for reopening NAFTA and moving to greater Canada–US integration. They argue that the process is an excellent example of how the two countries could work together to address a critical issue in a way that meets both their interests. That remains just a theory, for the co-operative spirit of the Smart Border agreement has not extended to the broader Canada–US economic relationship. While the two countries were implementing the Smart Border declaration, US trade actions proceeded against the same commodity that had been in dispute for a decade and a half—softwood lumber.

When Prime Minister Chrétien met President Bush at an international summit in Mexico in late March 2001—days before an existing softwood agreement between the two nations expired—the Canadian government thought that the President agreed to find a solution that would avoid new anti-dumping and subsidy investigations. Canada had already failed in attempts in early 2001 to promote the idea of appointing two envoys to find a long-term solution to US complaints that Canada's forest practices amounted to subsidies for Canadian lumber exporters selling into the US market. But the new President did not keep his pledge. In early April 2001 the US lumber industry filed a petition alleging subsidies in Canada. That led to a preliminary determination of injury to US producers and a preliminary determination of subsidy a month before 11 September 2001.

In the succeeding year, as Canada and the US worked closely to solve their border problems, the case against Canadian softwood producers ground on, producing a final determination of subsidy in March 2002 and injury claim two months later. Over that year Canada launched a series of actions against the US under NAFTA and also with the World Trade Organization in an effort to overturn the US rulings. It was business as usual on trade sanctions, and there are mixed views even within the Canadian government as to whether relief can ever be expected.

Some point to the auto industry and note that prior to the 1965 Canada–US Auto Pact there had been a series of trade complaints against Canada. That only ended when the industry rationalized across the border and started producing the same vehicles for Canada and the US, not separate plants and products for each country. Once the industry structured its operations on a continental rather than national basis, pressure for US trade sanctions ended.

The lumber industry will go that way too, argue those who point to increasing cross-border ownership and the activities of companies like Weyerhaeuser, based in Washington state but now with major forest product operations in both countries. In late 2002, it began a public campaign for an end to the softwood lumber dispute. Supporting that campaign in the US was a new organization headed by former US Ambassador to Canada and Michigan Governor James Blanchard and former US Trade Representative Bill Brock. The US–Canada Partnership for Growth, a US lobby group financed by some of the $20 million Canada provided to its lumber industry for advocacy work in the United States, also called for an end to the dispute, arguing it hurt US consumers.

An integrated industry may ease some pressures but demand for action on Canadian lumber has always been centred on producers in the US Southeast with no links to Canada. To date they are not integrated and have no interest in backing down from protecting their own markets.

Some Canadian trade officials argue that the frustration on lumber and continuing disputes over the Canadian Wheat Board and US agricultural subsidies mean the time has come for a new process for dealing with the United States on trade and economic issues. New negotiations based on the Smart Borders approach might lead to a deal that could end some of the cross-border trade problems that remain 13 years after the FTA and a decade after NAFTA. NAFTA's tenth anniversary next year might provide an opportunity, the officials believe, to resolve some outstanding issues. The idea has supporters but there would first need to be changes to the current economic and diplomatic environment in North America.

First, Canada and the United States must address Mexico's alienation. After dismissing Mexican involvement in September 2001, Canada did keep Mexico informed during the Smart Border negotiations in the fall of 2001. Canadian officials even flew to Mexico City in mid-November to brief the Mexican government on what was happening. Partly as a result, Mexico completed its own 22-point border agreement with the US in March 2002, but little has been done to implement that agreement. The US has no interest in allowing Mexico to take on some of the surveillance and enforcement of the movement of people that Canada provides for the US on the northern border. Easing travel for Mexicans into the US is out of the question.

By the fall of 2002, no one in Canada argued, as they did in early 2001, that President Bush's Texas origins and links to Mexican President Vicente Fox would mean the US and Mexico would draw closer together economically at the expense of the US–Canada relationship. Ultimately, a market of 100 million people will overwhelm a market of 31 million for the US in terms of commerce, but that remains some years into the future. US security concerns had overwhelmed President Fox's dream of making progress on the migration issue. Relations are now cool at best between Presidents Bush and Fox and there is no longer much talk of Mexico's efforts under President Fox to increase its influence in the United States.

That could give Canada an opportunity to consolidate further its integration with the United States. Perhaps the Smart Border could be the first step towards something else—open borders with free movements of goods and people inside a common perimeter like the European Union? A customs union between the two countries? A new NAFTA that solves problems all three partners have with the relationship after a decade?

In many ways the Smart Border approach in Ottawa duplicated the way the government of Canada negotiated the original Free Trade Agreement with the US. In both cases Canada gained American attention and influenced joint trade and economic policy by being first with ideas, by crystallizing its objectives, and then by finding a way to persuade the US administration that it is in Washington's best interest to deal with the issues as well. In both cases a small central group did the work in Ottawa, and these officials had the influence within the Canadian government to negotiate, finding the pressure points in the US administration and pushing whatever buttons were needed, regardless of rules and protocol, to get a desired outcome. On the Canadian side, in the autumn of 2001 there was also a private-sector advocacy group and campaign pushing for action on easing border congestion and simplifying rules, just as the Canadian private sector played a vocal and influential role as advocate for free trade in the late 1980s.

It works, so some argue that should be the process to address future Canada–US relations on trade. Whether a new Canada–US trade arrangement should be small steps beyond what is presently there or a grand bargain that examines the extent of Canada–US relations on every level, not just trade and economics, the process itself seems unlikely to eliminate the old worries and arguments that came up during the first FTA debate about Canada's independence and sovereignty. The process of determining what Canada would concede and what it would get in return for restructuring its whole relationship with the US would force those broader questions back into the political limelight.

In September 2002, speaking in Banff, Alberta, US Ambassador Paul Cellucci suggested it was time to consider broadening NAFTA to ensure there would be no more trade disputes in areas such as softwood lumber, wheat, and cultural industries. However, he added a crucial caveat—solve the existing disputes in these areas first and then talk about ensuring they cannot happen again. Doing that could take a long time. Canada responded a month later when Deputy Prime Minister John Manley suggested an interest in 'broadening or deepening' NAFTA if it meant addressing such issues as US ability to use countervailing duties and anti-dumping provisions against imports from Canada. He described the objective as taking care of unfinished business. That same week the Governor of the Bank of Canada, David Dodge, suggested to the House of Commons Finance Committee that any renegotiation of NAFTA should consider labour mobility as an important objective. At the same time, the Trade Minister, Pierre Pettigrew, while talking about making progress in NAFTA working groups, dismissed suggestions Canada could be headed for a customs union or common market with the US or as part of NAFTA.

Any debate about reopening NAFTA or doing anything else to promote more economic integration with the US would take place in a very different environment from that of the original free trade talks in the 1980s or the NAFTA negotiations in the early 1990s. An Ekos Research study of opinion in the three NAFTA countries released in June 2002 found 72 per cent support among Canadians for free trade among the three countries, rising to 78 per cent support for Canada–US free trade. That was a huge change from the roughly 30 per cent of Canadians who supported NAFTA a decade earlier. As well, 63 per cent of Canadians thought Canadians and Americans should be able to work in either country while 50 per cent thought that same approach to labour mobility should cover the three NAFTA countries. A separate poll by Environics Research and CROP in October 2002 found almost two-thirds of those Canadians polled believing that free trade should be expanded to include labour.

This level of public support may explain why Canadian officials continue to work behind the scenes on what they describe as NAFTA-plus. These are amendments and changes to the original NAFTA agreement that would make cross-border commerce flow more smoothly and bring the three economies—but really Canada and the United States—into even closer alignment. Its goals are to eliminate duplication, improve mobility for business people, and fix problems with rules of origin that NAFTA countries use in deciding which imports to their country can then be trans-shipped to another NAFTA country duty-free. At a deeper level, supporters of NAFTA-plus talk about harmonizing regulations.

One of the issues most frequently mentioned for harmonization is pharmaceutical approvals. It is superficially attractive in the face of the duplication produced by the Federal Drug Administration (FDA) in the US and Health Canada in Canada, both of which test and usually approve the same drugs. However, some substantive questions remain. Harmonization with rules in the United States means only one thing for Canada—accepting US rules. In the case of pharmaceuticals this would involve accepting FDA approval as binding on Canada. In practical terms, it would amount to an end to independent Canadian drug testing and approvals. Ultimately, the US Congress controls the FDA, which would mean Canada accepting pharmaceutical decisions controlled by the US Congress, which itself is open to the lobbying and pressures of the US political system. Put in that light, it is potentially a much different and more contentious issue than simply eliminating duplication and making trade more efficient. It is an example, though, of some of the broader issues that lie behind the superficially simple goal of eliminating duplication.

What may be missing is a tough-minded assessment of how such a NAFTA-plus negotiation might proceed. Unlike the European Union, with several countries of roughly the same population and influence, the NAFTA relationship includes only three countries, with one much more powerful than the other two.

The Smart Border process worked to produce an agreement because Canada used its leverage in negotiations. That may have been a one-time opportunity thanks to a convergence of circumstances. The United States had no real interest in slowing commercial cross-border traffic and was desperate to increase border security. Canada's co-operation made that possible and Canada gained something in return.

The same is simply not true for the issues involved in NAFTA-plus, such as harmonization of regulations. While both countries may want harmonized regulations and standards, it is not the same as having a 'smart border'. The US does not want harmonization badly enough to negotiate. That means Canada and Mexico would adopt US rules and regulations. There is no reason why the US would change any of its rules, regulations, or procedures to adapt to Canadian or Mexican standards. Politically and practically, a process where all the concessions and adapting go only one way is a much tougher sell in Canada, let alone in Mexico, than the give and take of the Smart Border negotiation. It is not impossible, but it is much more difficult, even with the strong support for freer trade found in public opinion polls, than the dry language of eliminating duplication suggests.

Of course, any reopening of NAFTA immediately raises a broader question. What would the US want or what might Canada have to offer to make reopening or modifying NAFTA of interest to Washington? At the moment that interest does not exist. Security is still the issue, not NAFTA. Beyond that, it is hard to see any advantage the United States might gain by forgoing its ability to use trade remedy legislation to protect its producers. Canada does launch trade actions against US goods, but in absolute terms US actions damage Canada's economy more than Canadian actions hurt the United States, which suggests there is no point in pushing anything forward in the near future.

In addition, the relationship among the NAFTA partners also suggests that now may not be the time for any action. Mexico is upset there has been no progress with the US on migration questions and Canada's choice of a bilateral deal with the US instead of NAFTA multilateralism did not help relations among the three trading partners. The climate must improve first if the idea of changing NAFTA is to gather any steam.

The continuing US emphasis on security was obvious when Manley met Ridge in Washington in early December 2002 to mark the first anniversary of their agreement. At the end of that two-day session, they released a one-year status report on implementing the Smart Border declaration. Focusing on some of the 30 points, the two politicians confirmed that FAST lanes would open at Windsor, Sarnia, Fort Erie, and Queenston in Ontario, Lacolle, Quebec, and Douglas, BC, before year-end. The NEXUS system for regular border crossers already in operation at Sarnia and Douglas, BC, would expand to Windsor, Fort Erie, Queenston, and Niagara Falls in the first half of 2003 and to all other high-volume border crossings before year-end. A version of NEXUS for air travellers would begin a trial in Montreal and Ottawa in the spring of 2003.

The two countries agreed to study joint or shared border facilities at four locations in New Brunswick, two in Quebec, two in Manitoba, two in Saskatchewan, and two in British Columbia. At the same time, the two countries began joint customs operations focused on another security threat—container traffic arriving at seaports in both countries. Canadian customs officials began working in Newark, NJ, and Seattle, checking containers ultimately destined for Canada. US Customs started doing the same for US-bound containers arriving in Halifax, Montreal, and Vancouver. That was part of a broader effort underway to harmonize customs procedures for goods entering either country by truck, rail, ship, or aircraft.

The border had changed dramatically in the course of a year but significant issues remained. The treatment of rail cars remained one contentious question. The US wanted to X-ray rail cars individually at the borders, a plan that could cause huge disruption of transborder rail traffic. Canada has argued that rail cars should be treated the same way the two countries had agreed to treat truck shipments under the FAST program, by conducting inspections at rail yards, where the trains are assembled, rather than tearing trains apart at the border, where there are no facilities to do that.

Containers coming into North American ports also remained a major security issue into 2003. Inspection and enforcement had only scratched the surface of the potential problem, and Congress continues to press for tougher inspections of more containers entering the United States. Only a minuscule percentage of those arriving in the US are presently inspected. The US wants much greater assurance that the contents of containers pose no threat and is prepared to pay an economic price in the slower movement of goods in order to inspect more containers more closely. Canada has no quick answer for that and the result could slow container traffic considerably.

In all of this, the most important issue for Canada has become Washington's plan to track the entry and exit of all people into and out of the United States. Anti-terrorism legislation passed by Congress gives the administration two years to introduce such a system for the Canada–US border. This could quickly bring a permanent return to the slowdowns of the immediate post-11 September period.

Starting 1 January 2005, the US administration must collect, record, and retain information on every individual who enters or leaves the United States by land, sea, or air. In extraordinary cases fingerprinting and biometric identification may be used to determine identities and deal with potential risks. Having to catalogue 200 million movements across the Canada–US border annually is a massively expensive and complicated proposition for Washington to undertake—perhaps more massive than those who legislated the system realized. The likely result will be some sort of compromise between the two countries to modify the application of this congressional order.

American willingness to proceed with such dramatic proposals for the Canada–US border, however, is a sign of the hold security has on border issues even 15 months after 11 September. That will continue to shape how the Smart Border agreement is implemented. In fact, in early 2003, despite the success of the agreement, considerable doubt remains about how that implementation will take place and fears have grown that there will be backtracking on agreements already reached. Many Americans remain nervous about handing responsibility for US security over to anyone else, including Canadians. In the crunch, the US attitude will likely be to do it by itself, and that could yet undermine much of the basis of a 'smart border'.

As well, the focus within the Department of Homeland Security remains on the physical security of the United States, with the need for economic security, as argued by Canada, not nearly as important. As the department is formed and develops, physical security will hold the upper hand over economic issues for a long time to come. Ridge's presence may moderate that but he will not be there forever and his successor may not look as favourably upon Canada and its concerns.

Underlying all this remains the question: what happens if there is another terrorist attack? Border procedures are changing but a fresh terrorist attack in either country would undoubtedly prompt the United States to react as it did after 11 September and block land, sea, and air access to its territory. Despite the Smart Border accord, no one really knows how quickly or even if the Canada–US border would reopen using the NEXUS and FAST systems after another attack. In addition, there could easily be pressure after another attack to reverse the changes made during the past year. These are the central challenges even those involved in the negotiations hope they never have to address. Only another crisis will test the strength of the Canada–US Smart Border commitment.

Canada and the United States keep talking, exploring the possibility that the newly established approach may have broader application in relations between the two nations. The Manley-Ridge process will continue, too, although Manley's future in the position will depend on the views of Chrétien's successor as Prime Minister.

In the United States, the Republican success in mid-term elections in November 2002 makes a second Bush term more likely. If that happens then some time after 2004, with a new Prime Minister in Canada, there could be interest in both countries in reopening NAFTA in one way or another to address various concerns.

At that point, energy or water could be on the minds of the United States. If the US persists with its entry-exit controls, Canada would then have to decide whether more US access to its natural resources is a suitable or acceptable inducement to persuade the US to eliminate those new and economically harmful procedures on the Canada–US border, to address existing problems with NAFTA, or to take other steps towards even closer integration of the North American economy.

Fifteen years after that free trade election, Canada and its Liberal government will soon have to decide how aggressively to keep erasing the line.

REFERENCES

Associated Press. 2002. 'Business group urges streamlining NY border security checks', 16 Sept.

Chase, Steven. 2002. 'Ottawa open to broadening NAFTA', *Globe and Mail*, 25 Oct.

———. 2002. 'Pettigrew rejects idea of reopening NAFTA', *Globe and Mail*, 26 Oct.

Chrétien, Jean. 2002. 'Address by the Prime Minister on the occasion of the Canada–US border summit', Detroit, 9 Sept.

Dawson, Anne. 2002. 'Pettigrew confirms push to add labour to NAFTA', *National Post*, 26 Oct.

Department of Foreign Affairs. 2001. The Canada–US Smart Border Declaration, Ottawa, 12 Dec.

———. 2002. Progress report on the Smart Border Declaration, news release, Niagara Falls, Ont., 28 June.

Dobson, Wendy. 2002. 'Shaping the Future of the North American Economic Space: A Framework for Action', *C.D. Howe Institute Commentary*, Apr.

Ekos Research. 2002. 'Rethinking North American Integration', June.

———. 2002. '11 September in Hindsight: Recovery and Resolve', An opinion poll conducted for the Canadian Broadcasting Corp. and the *Toronto Star*, 11 Sept.

Fagan, Drew. 2002. 'What Canada must do to crack the US market', *Globe and Mail*, 5 Nov.

Government of Canada. 2002. Prime Minister Chrétien, President Bush release Joint Statement on Canada–US Border co-operation, news release, Detroit, 9 Sept.

———. 2002. $300-million Canada–Ontario investment at Windsor gateway, news release, Windsor, Ont., 25 Sept.

————. Safety and Security for Canadians. Available at: <http://canada.gc.ca/wire/2001/09/110901-US_e.html>.

————. Canada and the United States: A Strong Partnership. Available at: <http://www.dfait-maeci.gc.ca/can-am/menu-en.asp>.

Jack, Ian. 2002. 'Ottawa sees closer NAFTA ties', *Financial Post*, 25 Oct.

Manley, John. 2002. Speech to the Canadian-American Business Council, Washington, 27 Sept.

McCabe, Aileen. 2002. 'Canada losing credibility with the US', *Ottawa Citizen*, 28 Sept.

McKenna, Barrie. 2002. 'The long arm of the new US security agency will reach far into our sphere', *Globe and Mail*, 26 Nov.

May, Kathryn, and Robert Sibley. 2002. 'The New Canadian: Proud, confident and free', *Ottawa Citizen*, 2 Nov.

Pettigrew, Pierre. 2002. Speech to the Diplomatic Forum, Halifax, 18 Oct.

Public Policy Forum. 2002. *Rethinking North American Integration: Report from the PPF/Ekos Conference*, 18 June.

Ramirez, Rogelio. 2002. 'Mexico: NAFTA and the Prospects for North American Integration', *C.D. Howe Institute Commentary*, Nov.

Russo, Robert. 2002. 'US wants extensive info on every Canadian: Manley sees border parking lots', Canadian Press, 6 Dec.

The Economist. 2002. 'Washington's mega merger', 21 Nov.

Weiner, Tim, and Ginger Thompson. 2002. 'Mexico struggles for the attention of a preoccupied US', *New York Times*, 15 Oct.

5

The News and the Neighbours: The Media and Canada–US Relations

BRIAN BUCKLEY

This chapter explores the place of the Canadian news media in the Canada–US relationship. Three major theses are advanced: that the media as political actors are plural; that their impact on the bilateral relationship varies with the functions they perform; and that technological and economic factors are steadily reshaping and redistributing core media roles. Our exploration begins with an overview of Canadian news organizations, moves on to consider their political roles and narratives in the bilateral relationship, and then considers how and where their effects are likely to manifest themselves. As the discussion would be incomplete without at least a sketch of American public perceptions of Canada, we will also examine briefly views from 'south of the line'. The chapter concludes with a few general policy observations.

THE NEWS MEDIA IN CANADA

The press has long been recognized as a potent factor in foreign and domestic affairs. In recent years interest in the subject has grown, as has a tendency to treat the media as a single unitary phenomenon, usually synonymous with television. While the unitary approach has its place when the media are considered as a social institution, it is of little value when we examine them as political actors. In Canada, as in every other industrialized democracy, the news media differ in structure, interest, role, and impact. Crowding them all into the same tent—no matter how commodious—oversimplifies a highly complex reality and abrades important textural differences.

We will take 'news' to mean the organized production of information and comment about contemporary events intended to explain their significance to a mass audience. While our focus is on the three most widely available news distribution systems in Canada—newspapers, radio, and television—we will also look briefly at the Internet. Although almost anything that permits the transmission of information from one consciousness to another is in a sense a news medium, even our constrained set embraces a vast sweep of activity.

Newspapers

Over 100 newspapers—in English or in French—collectively sell slightly in excess of five million copies a day (Canadian Newspaper Association, 2002). Although the number and circulation of dailies have declined over the years, the rate has slowed and perhaps halted. Newspapers remain a very significant element in the total mix of Canadian media. In size, the dailies range from the *Toronto Star*, with a circulation of over 450,000 copies, to the *Daily Bulletin* of Kimberly, British Columbia, with its tiny, and no doubt committed, readership of 1,905. Canadians are devoted newspaper readers; 56 per cent of adults polled recently reported reading a paper on an average weekday, and 82 per cent had read a paper within the past week (Newspaper Audience Databank, 2002).

Virtually without exception, Canadian daily newspapers are commercial, for-profit enterprises. The press must be able to sell its product if it is to operate at all. Historically, this has not been onerous; newspapers in Canada have long been profitable enterprises and most continue to do well. Nonetheless, the business dimension remains important in Canada's press.

The focus of Canada's daily press in unabashedly local and regional. The cleavage between English- and French-language papers is long-standing and pervasive. Even within each linguistic family, however, localism prevails. In English Canada only the *Globe and Mail* and the *National Post* claim a national readership. While both publish local editions in cities across the country, they remain heavily dependent on their Toronto area readers. Overwhelmingly, English-speaking readers rely on locally produced, locally oriented dailies. In French Canada no newspaper even claims a pan-Canadian readership.

Canada's daily press is marked by high ownership concentration. In 2001, of the country's 102 dailies, 95 were owned by 11 ownership groups. In terms of circulation, one-quarter of all Canadian dailies—roughly those with a circulation of 60,000 or more—produce about three-quarters of all copies sold. In 2001, these 25 largest papers were owned by just seven groups.

A related matter is the quasi-monopolistic position of many newspapers in their local markets. In many cities that once witnessed competition among several papers, only one has survived, often becoming a local institution. One mid-1990s survey found that, among 90 cities with dailies, only 13 had two or more papers. Allowing for differing linguistic markets and common ownership, significant competition existed in only eight cities (Siegel, 1996: 123). Much the same set of sources underpins a great deal of the international and national coverage provided by Canadian dailies. While there are exceptions, most dailies serve largely as retail outlets on matters judged of less than immediate interest to local readers. Canadian papers have long depended on Canadian Press (CP), Canada's 80-year-old co-operative news agency, for much of their Canadian material. An analysis in the mid-1990s found that 84 per cent of the stories carried by the morning papers surveyed, and 74 per cent of those in the afternoon papers, originated with CP's own staff (ibid., 195). The dailies generate even less of their international coverage. Their cadre of foreign correspondents—never numerous—shrank in the 1990s and remains small. In 1995 a majority of editors surveyed reported CP as their most important source of international news (Lee and Soderlund, 1999). Long criticized for overreliance on American wire services for international news, CP at the time employed the grand total of two foreign correspondents (in Washington and London) on its own.

Whatever their particularities, Canada's dailies remain influential. Newspaper readers tend to be better educated and more affluent than the broader Canadian public, implying higher levels of political activity and opinion leadership. Moreover, the papers themselves often serve as the base of the information pyramid, thereby influencing the type and content of the offerings of other news media. Finally, through their continued dominance of CP, Canada's dailies have a substantial impact on the management, policies, and personnel of a key source for all Canadian media.

Radio

In contemporary Canada virtually all citizens enjoy access to radio programming in English, French, or one of a host of other languages. Although radio resembles the press in its maturity and market saturation, the differences are also important. As Peter Desbarats (1996: 31) notes, public ownership has played a major role in both radio and television virtually since their inception. In addition, all broadcasting is nationally regulated, through the Canadian Radio-television and Telecommunications Commission (CRTC).

Radio receivers are plentiful, cheap, and ubiquitous. They are also well used. Although the rate of radio listening has remained steady for some years, it has stabilized at a high level. Canadian listeners devoted 22 hours per week to their radios in 2000, about the same as in 1995. Moreover, while the percentage of radio listeners has declined slightly, in 2000 it still stood at an impressive 93.2 per cent of the population over the age of 12 years (CRTC, 2001: 2).

Given the general theme of this book, it is worth recalling that Canada's publicly owned radio (and later television) networks were the product of earlier efforts to cope with a colossus. The explosive growth of radio after World War I—every bit as dramatic as the Internet phenomenon of our time—meant that by the late 1920s the only service available across much of the country was that provided by powerful American transmitters. Driven by concerns that Canadian voices were being drowned out, the 1928 Aird Commission led to a national regulatory framework, Canada's first public broadcaster, and the 1932 Canadian Radio Broadcasting Act. For Graham Spry, an influential proponent of public broadcasting, the issue was 'whether Canada is to establish a [radio] chain . . . owned and operated and controlled by Canadians, or whether it is to be owned and operated by commercial organizations, associated or controlled by American interests? The question is the State or the United States?' (quoted in Nolan, 2001: 90)

Despite the importance of Canada's public broadcaster in shaping our distinctive, mixed regime, most radio broadcasting—about 80 per cent of 'total hours tuned' in 2000—is provided by the country's 500 privately owned radio stations. Nonetheless, CBC/Radio Canada (AM and FM) audiences remain numerous and loyal. As in the print sector, ownership is concentrated and becoming more so. The top 10 radio ownership groups now operate over half of all radio stations in the country, a sharp and rapid rise, and account for over 70 per cent of all revenues accruing to private radio.

As a news medium, radio in Canada has seen its role shrink substantially from its dominance immediately after World War II. As a source for coverage of international and national events, radio for years has ranked well behind both television and newspapers and the gap continues to widen. Like the daily press, much of Canadian radio has a sharply local focus. Privately owned stations are usually directed towards specific, carefully differentiated, local markets. Further, as a medium radio has migrated steadily towards entertainment. The number of AM stations—the traditional radio news broadcasters—has declined, even as the number of FM stations has grown substantially. Radio listening, as Arthur Siegel, notes 'is often a secondary activity. We listen to radio while driving, picnicking, doing housework or home repairs, and even on the job' (Siegel, 1996; 162). It is this flexibility that has assured radio a continuing role in the Canadian information world. We may no longer rely on radio for in-depth analysis of world events; many of us, however, will first hear of those events on our radios.

Important differences exist between private radio and the publicly owned networks of CBC/Radio Canada. The latter currently operates four commercial-free national radio networks, two in English and two in French (AM and FM), and offers programming in eight Aboriginal languages. According to CBC/Radio Canada, some 40 per cent of Canadians over the age of 12 report using its radio services in any given month (CBC/Radio Canada, 2001–2002: 12). For Canada's public broadcaster, news and current events have long been a central part of its raison d'être and were confirmed as such in the 1970s and 1980s as the pressure from television intensified. The private radio stations, in contrast, have largely abandoned the collection of anything other than purely local news, and depend heavily on others for their national and international coverage. The public radio networks also give greater priority to identifiably Canadian, cross-cultural programming. Interestingly, their reach is both national and international. A significant American audience, much of it in the northern-tier states, tunes in regularly to the CBC and does so quite consistently. In addition, Canada's international short-wave radio broadcaster, Radio Canada International (RCI), forms part of the publicly owned radio system. RCI currently offers programming in eight languages and is available worldwide. It reports a direct weekly audience of three million and an indirect, possibly larger one through its several hundred partnership agreements with foreign broadcasters and via the Internet.

Television

In Canada, the policy and regulatory framework within which television came to maturity was largely that established to deal with radio. As a news medium television began to make itself felt in the late 1950s and by the early 1980s had become the pre-eminent source. Curiously, communications scholars generally rate television well behind newspapers in terms of its information content. Some go so far as to dismiss television news as 'junk food journalism' and 'entertainment, period'. Despite such views, the Canadian public continues to place great trust in television as its chief news source. In 1998 some 60 per cent of Canadians reported using television 'a great deal' to follow the news, against 46 per cent for daily newspapers and 37 per cent for radio (Angus Reid Group, 1998: 15). Dominance of the information world by television, however, may have peaked. Canadians' overall use of the medium is in gradual decline, dropping some 7 per cent between 1995 and 2000 (CRTC, 2001: 24). Interestingly, the decline occurred just as the volume of programming and number of channels were expanding. Similarly, Canadian advertisers may be losing their enthusiasm for the medium. While television continues to account for the lion's share of the $7.6 billion annually spent on media advertising, in relative terms it has also experienced a small but significant decline.

In contrast to radio, and apart from the US programming that appears on Canadian television, CRTC data show that American TV is widely watched in English-speaking Canada, accounting for a quarter of all viewing (and 6–7 per cent in Quebec). Although this share remained virtually constant throughout the period 1993–2000, major shifts took place away from conventional network TV towards specialty and pay-per-view programming, including two all-news channels. With the share of such services around 25 per cent in English Canada (and almost 20 per cent in Quebec) and rising fast, the days when watching one or two national networks offered a shared national experience are well behind us.

As with radio, private television broadcasters long ago displaced CBC/Radio Canada from its once dominant place. The latter, by 2000, ranked third in English Canada (after CTV and Global) and second in Quebec (after TVA) in terms of the combined viewing share of its conventional and specialty services. Although CBC/Radio Canada continues to fight the trend, it has not secured for its television services the broad public support its radio programming enjoys. Public television in Canada, however, remains significantly different from its private-sector competitors, notably in the area of news and current affairs. CBC/Radio Canada maintains that it is the largest single news organization in Canada, with a television or radio reporting capacity in nearly 70 locations across the country, employing 'over 800 people in different journalistic functions, in Canada and abroad' (CBC/Radio Canada, 2001–2: 22).

Although all English-Canadian television networks carry a considerable volume of foreign—predominantly American—shows, the phenomenon is least evident in the 'news and other information' programming category. By CRTC standards, most such broadcasting qualifies as Canadian programming. While most news and current affairs broadcasting, in final form, is prepared and delivered by Canadians, the 'upstream' Canadian contribution, in terms of gathering the material, is much weaker.

As we have seen, CP, a central source of international news for Canadian retail media outlets, has almost no independent international news-gathering capacity of its own and has long depended heavily on the international—largely American—wire services. Although Canadian electronic media do better than the country's newspapers in international news-gathering, this in itself is a very modest achievement. One Canadian journalist recently calculated that there were fewer than 30 full-time Canadian reporters—English and French, television, radio, and print combined—overseas. In contrast, the *New York Times* alone maintains approximately 40 foreign correspondents abroad. As of 2001, 'No Canadian media [were] permanently based in Australia, eastern Europe, Japan, Korea, the

Middle East outside Jerusalem, or South America. The entire continent of Africa [was] covered by one Canadian correspondent based
in the Ivory Coast' (Halton, 2001: 502). The United States, however,
is well covered by Canadian standards, with Washington and New
York hosting the largest single groups of Canadian journalists abroad.

The Internet

The rise of the Internet as a news medium appears to have come
chiefly at the expense of television. Declines in the number of weekly
television viewers and advertising revenue correspond closely with
Canadians' growing use of the Internet. Moreover, the impact is particularly marked with respect to news and current affairs. By 1998
almost 10 per cent of adult Canadians were using the Internet 'a great
deal' as a news source, notably for information on international
events. Internet users were significantly better educated, younger,
and more affluent than the population at large. The percentage of
Canadian households with personal computers has continued to
grow sharply, from about 50 per cent in 1998 to 63 per cent in early
2001. Expanding Internet access, as well as the youth, education, and
wealth of Internet users, suggests that they will continue to grow
sharply in numbers and political influence.

Canada's major media providers are, of course, fully aware of
these developments. All have established their own on-line news services and are integrating them into their more traditional operations.
It bears note, however, that in examining the political roles of the
news media in Canadian society, the Internet must increasingly be
taken into account.

The Canadian electorate and media, particularly in English Canada,
are thoroughly exposed to American media operating through channels that range from the major wire services, to US origin material
carried by Canadian media outlets, to the spillover influence of US
media accessed directly by Canadian viewers. American influence,
however, is neither uniform nor constant. It is probably greatest in
general international coverage and filler material and least felt on
Canadian domestic events, which are adequately covered by CP and
CBC/Radio Canada, and bilateral Canada–US matters, on which a
Canadian press corps in the United States can offer an alternative
account. By the same token, the American presence in the international information world is such that information and opinion of
American origin are bound to influence Canadian public perceptions

of virtually any international matter that arises. The truism that Canadians see the world through American eyes remains valid, except paradoxically with respect to the Canada–US relationship.

POLITICAL POWERS OF THE MEDIA

Representative democracy requires a 'virtual public space' in which citizens may apprehend, assess, and agree on their common affairs. It is precisely here, in establishing and maintaining our public space, that the news media play an irreplaceable role in all democratic systems. It is a role, moreover, with several dimensions. Arthur Siegel, in his thoughtful analysis (Siegel, 1996: 21–3), identifies five power sources of the Canadian media. They are summarized below.

1. *The provision of information.* The media monitor social and political developments, providing a large and steady stream of information and commentary. In doing so they alert the public to potential hazards, both national and international, and prepare it for the challenges that lie ahead.

2. *Political linkage.* As direct contact between ruler and ruled long ago became impractical, and the role of party declined, the media are now the chief link between government and the electorate. Rational choices by the electorate presuppose the availability of relevant information and its scrutiny in public debate. The media are now the chief means through which these essential services are provided.

3. *Agenda-setting.* The news, however, is more than a tickertape flowing ceaselessly past our glazed eyes. The world of events is far too vast and complex to be fully captured. Selection is inescapable in the newsmaking process, as is the use of frames and narratives to make sense of events. In determining some developments to be 'newsworthy', the media also label them as worthy of public attention. Equally important is the marginalization of matters that the media decide to ignore.

4. *Editorial offerings.* The media provide context and explanation as well as information. News is as much about meaning as it is about fact. The lines between information, comment, and recommendation are often blurred. In making the news meaningful and relevant the media also provide support for a particular world view.

5. *Influencing political actors.* By virtue of whom they cover and how they do it, the media confer status on political aspirants —and remove it as well. The relationship is reciprocal. As the politician seeks to use the media to amplify and transmit his/her messages, so the news organizations rely on political figures for accounts of what is newsworthy.

The theoretical powers of the media, though extensive, are not unconstrained. Political impact depends on the media's presumed capacity to mould and to mobilize public opinion. While some such capacity exists, simple stimulus-response models are clearly insufficient. Since the French Revolution, totalitarian regimes have tried to use public information channels to reshape their subjects in line with their ideologies, usually with limited success. The process by which media offerings are taken up and transformed into those broadly held opinions that governments find it necessary to heed is complex and only partially understood. Public opinion is no single, homogeneous factor. In foreign affairs, at least three publics—mass, intermediate, and attentive—can be distinguished (Holsti, 1995: 260–5). Not all media hold equal appeal for all levels of public opinion. Indeed, the sharp differences in educational level, affluence, age, and other characteristics of their audiences make clear that the news media have differential impacts on public opinion at large. The roles of public opinion will also differ, often sharply so, in the near and in the medium term, in peace and in war.

Other constraints exist. Thus, the media report but they do not act. In Greek mythology the prophetess Cassandra was punished by having her predictions, despite their accuracy, always fall on deaf ears. Unless the media are able to move other social actors—government, opposition party, advocacy group, irate citizen—they, too, suffer Cassandra's fate. Further, the media rarely speak with one voice. News stales quickly. Given the competitive operating environment, unrelenting need for novelty, and resource limitations, very few news organizations can afford the luxury of focusing for very long on a single subject. In Western societies the expectations and the sensibilities of consumers also establish limits. The media may be free to publish unpalatable truths, but they do so at their own risk. Nor should the symbiosis between those who produce the news and those who provide their information be overlooked. The relationship between source and journalist is in itself an important boundary to the newsmaking process.

Beyond these theoretical considerations, the Canadian media are subject to other influences that bear on their relevance to policy-making, particularly to the Canada–US policy-making process. Canadians as a people, French- and English-speaking, are fundamentally well disposed to the United States: witness the spontaneous outpourings of support and solidarity following the terrorist attacks of 11 September. This does not mean that Canadians wish to join the US, or to emulate it. By and large, however, Canadians get along well with Americans; they possess a well-founded and sophisticated appreciation of the importance of the United States to Canada and do not wish to see it jeopardized. A Canadian medium that consistently challenged or upset this fundamental view likely would be given short shrift by its audience.

The convergence phenomenon is bringing a growing number of private-sector media outlets under the control of corporations that are themselves partisans of a free-market, right-of-centre political philosophy. 'Market pressures', comments Dan Halton on the North American press, 'have created a competitive media environment increasingly characterized by the intrusion of commercial interests into newsroom decisions. Self-censorship of newsworthy stories that may be damaging to the financial interests of news organizations has become a significant issue in media organizations' (Halton, 2001: 505). As several Canadian media corporations themselves have significant stakes abroad, the environment provides stony soil for a grounded, coherent critique of free-market principles or of their most powerful champion.

To judge from the limited investment that private-sector Canadian media make in their own capacity to gather and interpret international news, they evidently feel no great need to play a role in the policy-making process. The Canada–US relationship is the only major foreign policy sector where this may be challenged, though even here the media role as policy initiator is slight. A comparison of major Canadian newspaper coverage of foreign policy matters in 1982 and 1992 found that an already dubious role in 1982 had eroded still further 10 years later. Although the press tended to criticize more frequently than it supported government policy, in the great majority of instances it chose to offer no opinion for or against. The study concluded that 'the Canadian press seems destined to remain, as we found it in 1982 and 1992, "an uncertain intellectual force in the definition and interpretation of Canadian foreign policy"'

(Burton et al., 1995: 69). Little has changed since that conclusion was drafted.

Finally, Canadian media dependence on predominantly American sources ensures that simply through routine news operations US accounts will secure wide and largely uncritical exposure in Canada. A study of North American television accounts of the American intervention in Panama (Soderlund et al., 1994) found that, in part because of their use of the same sources, coverage by Canada's CBC and CTV differed little from that of American networks—despite the very different policies of Washington and Ottawa, and the CBC's ostensibly greater devotion to news and current events.

MAINSTREAM NARRATIVES

The news media available to Canadians are numerous, varied, and well developed, fulfilling key roles in Canada's democracy and providing vast flows of information and comment on current affairs. Despite occasional criticism Canadians appear generally content with the quality and the quantity of the information available to them. One recent poll (Leger Marketing, Apr. 2002: 7) found that almost 80 per cent of respondents considered that the information in the media was either superior or of equal value to that presented 10 years ago. From a comparative perspective, freedom of the press is well entrenched in theory and in practice in Canada. The Canadian Charter of Rights and Freedoms explicitly protects 'freedom of the press and other media of communication'. In a recent global survey of press freedom, an international advocacy group (Reporters Without Borders, 2002) ranked Canada fifth among the 139 countries examined, best among the G-8 states.

Yet the substantive diversity of the information and opinion provided is open to question. The range of philosophic orientations of Canada's main news organizations is quite narrow. The type of consistently left-of-centre approach found in Britain's *The Guardian*, for example, is conspicuous for its absence. Other distinctive orientations fare no better. History and ownership concentration (and perhaps audience expectations) have produced a situation in which the dominant political stance of Canada's private media is a rather unreflective free-market approach to the world. The Canadian media do criticize governments and their policies and do so to considerable effect. Much of the effort, however, is from the same point of departure. Such philosophic variety as is provided—and the informed, critical comment that it permits—depends heavily on a small number of columnists and commentators.

There are several recurring narratives in media treatment of the bilateral relationship. The following comments are limited to the English-language media as space and time limitations preclude the separate analysis that the French press deserves. The comments are also largely impressionistic, because the topic has attracted little rigorous study. Nonetheless, the themes described here appear to contribute to the shape and tenor of the broad information flow on which Canadians depend.

Our American Cousins
Frequently encountered in Canadian media coverage is the notion that the Canada–US tie is analogous to a family relationship. While the approach is valid in that both countries clearly belong to the 'West', the cousinly theme gives rise to some curious beliefs in Canadian media accounts. Thus, differences between the two countries are seen as somehow unnatural or aberrant. Issues that do arise are framed as stemming less from divergent interests or values than from ignorance, incompetence, or ill will in Ottawa or Washington. The upshot is an adolescent quality that frequently attaches to Canadian media coverage. For one American observer formerly stationed in Canada (DePalma, 2002), two of the more prominent characteristics of Canadian media, and public, discourse on the bilateral relationship are its immaturity and its tendency to moralize.

Canada and the United States are deeply rooted liberal democratic states whose interests and values frequently, though not invariably, coincide. The relationship is largely governed by considerations of complex interdependency, though the reality of the great asymmetries in power can never be entirely excluded. Reducing this multifaceted and intricate relationship to a two-dimensional stereotypical analogy does little to encourage a better understanding of it or of events relevant to it.

The Navel of the Universe
Canadian news media seem fascinated to the point of intoxication by events in the US. Certainly, they use vast amounts of American-origin filler material. The papers and the airwaves regularly carry generous accounts of bizarre happenings to obscure individuals in distant

American localities with no clear connection to Canada. Perhaps because of the volume, accessibility, and low cost of American material, some Canadian media outlets do a better job covering events in the US than in other Canadian provinces. Even respecting events that meet conventional criteria of newsworthiness, Canadian coverage of US stories appears exaggerated. While Canadian audiences may well be more interested in events in the US than elsewhere, the reactions of the Canadian news media often seem to be simple reflexive responses to the locale of the story. Repeated endlessly, this automatic attribution of significance to American-origin stories devalues events occurring elsewhere, including elsewhere in this country.

The Elephant and the Mouse
Media accounts regularly privilege disparities in size and power in covering the US and Canada. While many aspects of the United States are exceptional, the other half of the narrative—the miniaturization of Canada—is more fantasy than analysis.

Consider two of those liturgical phrases often embodied in the narrative: our 'small population base' and all those Canadians eking out a frail existence along 'a narrow band within a hundred miles of the border'. Although Canada remains a sparsely populated land by global standards, we ceased having a small population quite some time ago. In 2000, Canada ranked thirty-fourth in the world by population, larger than over 80 per cent of the membership of the United Nations. Second, while most Canadians do live close to their southern border, ignored in the narrative is the reality that they often comprise the only sizable settlements on either side of the line. Apart from the Great Lakes and the Pacific coast areas, most of the larger urban centres along the Canada–US border are in Canada. If a relationship existed between population density and political absorption, much of the northern tier of the US would have packed its Winnebagos and trekked north some time ago.

A more realistic narrative would recognize that Canada is now one of the oldest continuously democratic states in the world; that it has a solid track record of success at home and abroad; that it has developed through the years, with its more powerful continental neighbour, a wide range of mechanisms to address shared concerns; and that it has usually held its own in straight bilateral negotiations on matters ranging from boundary waters to trade relations. While each of these propositions is easily documented from the historical record, none can be readily accommodated within 'the elephant and mouse' narrative.

Although Canadians use and support their media vigorously, neither use nor support is unqualified. According to one recent poll (Leger Marketing, Apr. 2002: 3–4), a strong majority (61 per cent) of Canadians do not see the media as providers of unbiased information, and skepticism increases as education and income rise. An equally strong majority (62 per cent) are critical of excessive sensationalism in the news. Credibility, the *sine qua non* of every mass medium in the information age, is by no means something that Canadian news outlets can take for granted. In the Canada–US context, in which a sophisticated Canadian public takes a strategic approach towards bilateral matters, oversimplification, dramatization, and outmoded frames in coverage can only limit the potential contribution of the news media to the policy-making process.

PROBABLE EFFECTS

Before examining what the effects of the news media are likely to be in the Canada–US relationship, it may be helpful to provide an assessment of the strengths and weaknesses of the Canadian news media. In a world in which hundreds of millions of people have access only to such information as their rulers consider appropriate, it bears reflection that the problems and deficiencies of the Canadian news media are very much second-order concerns.

Canadian news media are numerous, providing a dense and richly textured information environment to virtually all citizens. They are also diverse. Despite concerns over ownership concentration, the differing means of available mass communication, the presence of publicly and privately owned organizations, and the availability of American media all ensure a strong measure of diversity in the information mix. Technological sophistication is another manifest strength. The country has often pioneered in communications technology and the media have been among the major beneficiaries. Moreover, by global standards the news media are well endowed financially and materially, and thereby enjoy substantial autonomy. In addition, professional standards are good, thanks in part to the several schools of journalism in operation across the country. Finally, and perhaps most importantly, freedom of the press is solidly entrenched and well defended in Canada.

Even in Camelot North, however, rain sometimes does fall. The local/regional focus of most Canadian news organizations limits their national impact. Within the electronic press, the public broadcaster probably does a better job of broadening the focus, but it, too, must heed internal Canadian sensitivities, notably the linguistic division. In addition, the pseudo-monopolistic position that many newspapers enjoy locally encourages a tendency to be all things to all people and to avoid controversial stances. A related concern is the absence of competing political philosophies among the major private media out-lets and their owners. A local focus and the dominance in many of business over journalism norms mean that relatively low priority is assigned to news not immediately pertinent to local clients. Publicly owned media provide a partial offset, and of all foreign regions the US enjoys by far the greatest attention. Nonetheless, relative to national and international developments, most privately owned media organizations have only a modest independent news-gathering capa-bility and a limited in-house analytical ability. Compounding a ten-dency to rely on others is the dominant role of international—mainly American—wire services as foreign news sources.

The influence of the news media depends upon themselves and upon others. One analyst (Seib, 1997: 150) explains their role on a given issue in terms of a sliding scale. The more unified, articulate, and confident the political leadership, the less likely the media are to play a role beyond the simple provision of information and com-ment. Their place in the Canada–US relationship will be closely affected by the quality of the Canadian leadership directing our half of the process. In addition, news media tend to rally round the flag during international crises—at least in the short run—and to soften or dilute their scrutiny of governmental policies. Here lies a second imponderable. If the bilateral relationship unfolds against a tense international backdrop, the prospects of the media differing sharply from their chief sources—and their audiences—are much reduced.

Although forecasting is an uncertain business, particularly in cir-cumstances of such complexity, a few thoughts are worth advancing. While the media will remain, as they have long been, a potent factor in the Canadian political process, their importance will continue to depend on traditional sources of influence rather than on a major, newly acquired capacity. They are likely to serve as powerful tools that various other players seek to use for their own ends, rather than as an autonomous agent in the policy-making process. Some rebalancing among their specific functions is already underway. In the provision of political information television, newspapers, and radio will continue to fulfill an essential role. Given the dominance television has achieved as the most trusted news source, it will exercise great influence over political actors. That said, the media role in maintaining linkage seems to be declining. While they continue to shape public perceptions of leaders and policies, the reliance of politicians on opinion polling suggests that they see in them a more reliable means of interpreting public opinion than the editorial pages that they once scrutinized. The growing use of the Internet by the attentive public also suggests that Net-based sources, as well as newspapers with their greater depth and detail, will play relatively more active roles in agenda-setting in Canada–US matters, as well as contributing, through their editorial offerings, directly to the policy process.

Even as individual media increase their capacity, the collective media impact on agenda-setting is likely to decline. The days when the national news provided Canadians with a shared national experience are long gone. Competition, diversity, and a commitment to novelty mean concentrated media campaigns obliging governments to act are likely to be ever more rare. Even so, if the media show only a limited capacity to determine what is important, their capacity to determine what is unimportant should not be underestimated.

The media role in shaping, as distinct from setting, the political agenda warrants comment. Bilaterally, the distinction is best understood as encouraging longer-term policy orientations rather than adopting more immediate, specific policies. The many and varied ways in which the US influences the information environment in general, and the Canadian environment in particular, suggest that American concerns and their implications for Canada will figure prominently in public policy debate in this country. The osmosis is such that it is often difficult to determine where American preoccupations end and Canadian concerns begin. Historians may eventually determine that global climate change in the end proved a greater threat to our well-being than the entire international terrorism phenomenon. But American preoccupation with the latter, mediated through multiple information channels, virtually guarantees that it will have the greater impact on Canadian policy.

Media capacity to complicate relations should not be ignored. The news media provide services essential in a democracy by furnishing citizens with information and opinion, by holding governments to account, by amplifying the messages of the articulate (and muffling the incoherent), and by augmenting, and reducing, the credibility of political leaders. They also have a considerable capacity to embarrass leaders and complicate their dealings with others. A clumsy or thoughtless public observation, an ill-tempered or mean-spirited remark, can easily become grist for the bilateral mill. Such is the informality of North America as a whole, and the transparency and ubiquity of the news media, that such material easily passes through the filters that older, more formal, and more distant relationships use to screen them out.

SOUTH OF THE LINE

Americans at large have a generally positive opinion of Canada and Canadians. While the depth and reach of the perception may be debated, its reality is clear. 'When most Americans think of Canada', writes Anthony DePalma, 'they feel warm and generous toward the country' (DePalma, 2001: 256). Polls carried out on the first anniversary of the 11 September terrorist attacks in the US (Harrisinteractive, 2002; Leger Marketing, Sept. 2002) emphasize the point. When the American people are asked which foreign countries they most like and trust, Canada ranks very near, if not at, the top. There is a broad and long-standing reservoir of good will towards Canada on the part of the American population at large. Very little of this favourable situation, however, owes anything at all to the American news media. Serious studies of US media portrayals of Canada and Canadian issues are very rare, a finding that speaks volumes on its own. The conclusions of the few that exist are generally consistent and will surprise no Canadian analyst.

Quantitative coverage of Canada by the American media has long been scant and shows little sign of changing. In contrast to Canadian news organizations, which maintain a high percentage of their foreign reporting capacity in the US, the American press is underrepresented in Canada. A Canadian assignment is not seen as a particularly valuable career move, and few American journalists develop expertise in Canadian affairs. As Bernard Gwertzman of the *New York Times* once remarked, 'the hardest part of my job is to get a guy up there' (quoted in Flournoy et al., 1992: 15). By any measure, US dealings with Canada comprise one of the most important relationships—perhaps the most important—that Washington maintains. In matters ranging from North American defence, through trade, investment, and tourism, to shared environmental problems, the two countries have an unrivalled capacity to affect each other's tangible interests. Despite their importance, the American news media are content to pass over such matters in silence. One study of television coverage in the period 1972–81 found that 'of the 50 most frequently mentioned nations in US TV network coverage . . . Canada tied with Switzerland for 19th place' (Barton, 1990: xx). During the period 1981–89, coverage of Canada apparently decreased (Gonzenbach et al., 1992). More recently, two observers noted: 'Perhaps the most surprising findings, however, are those about coverage of Canada. The country that we share a border with, that has been a close ally and is our biggest trading partner, gets relatively little attention in our media' (Husselbee and Stempel, 1997: 591). While some exceptions to the pattern exist, the conviction of Canadians that their country is largely ignored in the American media is well grounded.

The quality of American coverage of Canada has also attracted critical comment. One American academic studied the coverage of Canadian foreign relations provided over two years by major television networks and the American prestige press. As a control, he also examined coverage of Canada derived from what was then known as the Foreign Broadcast Information Service (FBIS), a CIA mechanism that monitors foreign media output across the world. To his surprise, he found that the FBIS offered better coverage of Canadian affairs than the major networks and quality press. 'The irony residing in our finding [is] that information routinely classified as propaganda', he observed, 'gathered by American intelligence via FBIS reports is perhaps more useful to internationally tuned citizens than international affairs coverage by the mainstream American press, [and this] should not be overlooked' (Barton, 1990: 143).

The problem, the analyst found, lay in the manner in which the facts were forced to fit into established American media frames:

> The American press examples reviewed here, in both network television and prestige print forms, are aggressively ethnocentric, offering the public forum comparatively few opportunities to understand and evaluate specific Canadian/American issues in the context of the larger international community. This news is largely unconnected to and uninformed by international political discourse about Canada's international role. The appeals are framed for a highly generalized, apolitical audience perspective that is locked into a domestic world view. (Ibid., 144)

Others have voiced similar concerns. As a study of the 1995 Quebec referendum, the only event in years to attract significant American media attention, concluded: 'In this one instance, US media discovered Canada, but there is little indication that the awareness continued. We wonder if anything less than a threat of secession of a major province and the subsequent break-up of the country can make US media aware of Canada' (Husselbee and Stempel, 1997: 599).

In fairness, the ethnocentrism of the US media is hardly unique. Nor is it remarkable that the US media should approach Canadian events through the prism of US interests. Moreover, the bilateral significance of the American media should not be underestimated. The news—and of equal or greater importance, the entertainment—media will have some long-term impact on American public attitudes. If an account is repeated often enough—the porosity of the Canadian border to terrorists or low defence spending—to enter into the American folk memory, it certainly can act to diminish public goodwill and complicate the management of the issue. That said, American media roles in bilateral dealings seem unlikely to extend beyond the following: (1) as channels of American information and opinion to the Canadian electorate that allow it to test and compare policy stances of the Canadian government; (2) as one of several contributors to the shaping of short- and long-term American mass opinion on bilateral matters; (3) as the voice of conventional wisdom in setting the boundaries imposed by American mass opinion within which viable American policy options must lie.

IMPLICATIONS FOR POLICY

Let us look first at the Canadian half of the equation:

1. The Canadian news media will continue to provide basic political information, to confer recognition and legitimacy, and to act as external auditors of the manner and the substance of the Canada–US relationship.
2. The roles of policy dialogue participant and of provider of political linkage appear to be migrating away from the traditional news media, towards a small number of respected columnists, opinion polling firms, and think-tanks and NGOs with developed Internet capability.

3. Media powers to amplify the messages of confident and persuasive leaders are as real as ever. By the same token, inconsistency, incompetence, and division will be detected even more quickly than in the past.

4. Except on issues of immediate local concern, few Canadian news media are likely to mount a major intellectual challenge to established policies or policy initiatives.

5. The Canadian electorate has sophisticated, strategic expectations from Canada's most important foreign relationship. News media, and governments, that fail to act within these bounds should expect to pay a price.

As to the role of the American news media:

1. Their power, ubiquity, and easy availability to Canadians imply that they need always be taken into account by Canadian policy-makers, particularly in shaping mass American opinion towards Canada and Canadian interests.

2. At the same time, 'active defence' seems the most appropriate Canadian stance. Errors of fact and opinion need to be promptly and vigorously rebutted, but efforts to use the US media to transmit Canadian messages are unlikely to bear fruit. American news values, audience expectations, and resource limitations make them an unlikely partner in the policy process.

3. In contrast, the wire services, the workhorses in the collection of international news and its dissemination by retail media outlets on both sides of the border, might offer opportunities to project a clearer Canadian voice.

4. Canada's strongest and most effective ally in the US is the generalized goodwill that a great many ordinary Americans bear towards their neighbour to the north. The origins and the extent of the sentiment may be a little fuzzy but its presence is clear. A strategic Canadian approach to the US media would incorporate as a central aim the maintenance and expansion of that fund of goodwill.

One final, more general observation has been made by others but deserves to be made again. The greatest challenge before Canadians in our dealings with the US is to develop a more mature appreciation of our strengths, along with our weaknesses. 'A strong, self-confident Canada', argues Andrew Cohen, 'will not care if we are not noticed in Washington . . . if we are confident that we are a good neighbour at home and a good ally abroad, pursuing our agenda as a warrior, peacekeeper, humanitarian, and diplomat, true to ourselves' (Cohen, 2002: 47). As a prescription for a positive and productive relationship with the colossus, Cohen's words have much to recommend them. The vigorous and effective pursuit of the roles he identifies can be greatly aided, or impeded, by the news media. In the end, however, what matters most is what we think of ourselves and how we act on that vision.

REFERENCES

Angus Reid Group. 1998. 'Canadians and the News Media', Mar. Available at: <www.cric.ca>. Accessed Oct. 2002.

Barton, R.L. 1990. *Ties that Blind in Canadian/American Relations: Politics of News Discourse*. Hillsdale, NJ: Lawrence Erlebaum Associates.

Burton, B.C., W.C. Soderlund, and T.A. Keenleyside. 1995. 'The Press and Canadian Foreign Policy: A Re-examination Ten Years On', *Canadian Foreign Policy* 3, 2: 51–69.

CBC/Radio Canada. 2002. 'Annual Report 2001–2002'. Available at: <www.cbc.radio-canada.ca>. Accessed Oct. 2002.

Canadian Newspaper Association (CAN). 2002. Available at: <www.can-acj.ca>. Accessed Oct. 2002.

———. 2002. 'Online Guide to Canadian Newspapers'. Available at: <www.can-ajc.ca>. Accessed Oct. 2002.

Canadian Radio-television and Telecommunications Commission (CRTC). 2002. 'Broadcast Policy Monitoring Report 2001', 2. Available at: <www.crtc.gc.ca>. Accessed Oct. 2002.

Cohen, Andrew. 2002. 'Canadian-American Relations: Does Canada Matter in Washington? Does It Matter If Canada Doesn't Matter?', in Norman Hillmer and Maureen Appel Molot, eds, *Canada Among Nations 2002: A Fading Power*. Toronto: Oxford University Press, 34–48.

DePalma, Anthony. 2001. *Here: A Biography of the New American Continent*. Toronto: Harcourt Brace.

———. 2002. Telephone interview, 20 Dec.

Desbarats, Peter. 1996. *Guide to Canadian News Media*, 2nd edn. Toronto: Harcourt Brace.

Flournoy, D., D. Mason, R. Nanney, and G.H. Stempel III. 1991. 'Media Images of Canada: U.S. Media Coverage of Canadian Issues and U.S. Awareness of Those Issues'. Ohio Journalism Monograph. Athens: Ohio University.

Gonzenbach, W.J., M.D. Arant, and R.L. Stevenson. 1992. 'The World of US Network Television News: Eighteen Years of International and Foreign News Coverage', *Gazette* 50: 53-72.

Halton, Dan. 2001. 'International News in the North American Media', *International Journal* 56, 3: 499-518.

Harrisinteractive. 2002. 'Britain, Canada, Australia and Israel Now Top List (of 25 Countries) Most Widely Seen as Close Allies', Sept. Available at: <www.harris interactive.com>. Accessed Oct. 2002.

Holsti, K.J. 1995. *International Relations: A Framework for Analysis*, 7th edn. Englewood Cliffs, NJ: Prentice-Hall.

Husselbee, L.P., and G.H. Stempel III. 1997. 'Contrast in U.S. Media Coverage of Two Major Canadian Elections', *Journalism and Mass Communication Quarterly* 74, 3: 591–601.

Lee, M.F., and W.C. Soderlund. 1999. 'International Reporting in Canadian Newspapers: Results of a Survey of Daily Newspaper Editors', *Canadian Journal of Communication* 24: 243–59.

Leger Marketing. Apr. 2002. 'Canadians and the Media'. Available at: <www.circ.ca>. Accessed Oct. 2002.

———. Sept. 2002. 'How Americans Feel About Canada'. Available at: <www.circ.ca>. Accessed Oct. 2002.

Newspaper Audience Databank. 2002. 'NADBank 2002 Interim Study Released', press release, 6 Sept. Available at: <www.can-acj.ca>. Accessed Oct. 2002.

Nolan, M. 1986. *Foundations: Alan Plaunt and the Early Days of CBC Radio*. Montreal and Toronto: CBC Enterprises.

Reporters Without Borders. 2002. 'Reporters Without Borders is publishing the First Worldwide Press Freedom Index', Oct. Available at: <www.rsf.fr/article>. Accessed Oct. 2002.

Seib, Philip. 1997. *Headline Diplomacy: How News Coverage Affects Foreign Policy*. Westport, Conn.: Praeger.

Siegel, Arthur. 1996. *Politics and the Media in Canada*, 2nd edn. Toronto: McGraw-Hill Ryerson.

Soderlund, W.C., R.C. Wagenberg, and I.C. Pemberton. 1994. 'Cheerleader or Critic? Television News Coverage in Canada and the United States of the U.S. Invasion of Panama', *Canadian Journal of Political Science* 27, 3: 581–604.

6

Coping with the Cultural Colossus: Canada and the International Instrument on Cultural Diversity

STEPHEN AZZI AND TAMARA FEICK

Canada has long struggled to find a solution to the culture-trade quandary, the challenge of maintaining cultural policies without violating international trade agreements that generally work from the principle that governments should not favour domestic products over imports. In the mid-1990s the United States used the legal mechanisms of the World Trade Organization (WTO) to force Canada to repeal its policies in support of Canadian magazines. This defeat jarred the Canadian government, resulting in a fundamental reorientation of the country's approach to cultural trade questions. No longer did Canada take a defensive and inward looking position. The government—and in particular Sheila Copps, Minister of Canadian Heritage—pursued an active, multilateral approach, leading a group of like-minded countries in an effort to define a new international regime on trade in culture.

The Canadian government is at the forefront of an effort to shift the focus in the international discussion of cultural trade. The debate in the past had been concerned largely with trade agreements and liberalized trade; the language had been that of open versus closed markets, of free trade versus protectionism. Cultural policy, as a result, had assumed a defensive and reactive role. Determined to be positive and active, the Canadian government shifted its emphasis from trying to insert cultural exemptions in trade agreements to creating a new international accord that would recognize the importance of cultural diversity and the right of governments to enact measures to protect it. The original goals of Canadian cultural policy remain, but now Canada is enlisting allies in an effort to find a multilateral solution to the conflict between cultural policy and trade obligations.

CULTURAL POLICY IN A CHANGING ENVIRONMENT

The support of domestic culture is an established element of the Canadian political tradition. The first measures to protect Canadian magazines were introduced in 1931. In 1932, the forerunner of the state-owned Canadian Broadcasting Corporation (CBC) was founded. The board now known as the Canadian Radio-television and Telecommunications Commission (CRTC) began to oversee broadcasting in 1958, imposing Canadian content quotas for television in 1961 and for radio in 1971. In 1967, the government created the Canadian Film Development Corporation, now Telefilm Canada, to provide funding for Canadian feature films.

The stated purpose of these policies has remained remarkably consistent over the years: Canadian independence 'would be nothing but an empty shell without a vigorous and distinctive cultural life'. These words are from the 1951 report of the Massey Commission, but could just as easily have come from Heritage Minister Sheila Copps, who has argued that the purpose of cultural policy is to resist absorption by the United States (Royal Commission, 1951: 18; Copps, 1999: 41). For the Canadian government, state intervention is necessary to prevent cultural assimilation. Political activist Graham Spry's oft-quoted line about the choice for Canadian radio—'The State or the United States'—reflects government policy today as much as when he said it in 1931. As Copps said recently, 'It is a fact of life in Canada that the government has to intervene' (Copps, 1999: 41).

Despite the government's attempts to prevent foreign domination of popular culture in Canada, foreigners provide 95 per cent of feature films shown in Canada, 86 per cent of prime-time English-language television drama, 84 per cent of retail music sales, and 83 per cent of the newsstand magazine market (Rabinovitch, 1998: 30). This situation is not merely a reflection of consumer choice. The economics of culture make it difficult to produce distinctly Canadian products. The cost of purchasing the rights to broadcast an American television program in Canada, for example, has variously been estimated at 3 to 10 per cent of the total production costs (Ritchie, 1997: 218; Mandate Review Committee, 1996: 196). A Canadian program of comparable quality, furthermore, cannot be produced at one-tenth the cost of its American counterpart. Similar rules apply for other cultural products. The choice for Canadian producers, in the words of trade negotiator Gordon Ritchie, is to 'sell to the American mass market by completely de-Canadianizing the work, or try to speak to a Canadian reality—and go broke in the process' (Ritchie, 1997: 218). To offset the economies of scale in the culture industries, the federal government has created subsidies, quotas, tax incentives, and other policies to assist domestic producers.

The American government has opposed efforts to preserve and promote Canadian culture for almost as long as Canada has been pursuing these goals. The American position has been based on a mix of interests and ideology. Efforts to encourage Canadian culture come at the expense of wealthy, powerful American publishers and producers, with all their capacity to lobby the government. Washington provides a receptive audience. In the language of the American government, television, motion pictures, music, and magazines are not culture, but 'communications' or 'entertainment'. Washington has argued that culture is not special, that it is simply another industry, and that other countries have used culture 'as an excuse to take commercial advantage of the United States', to quote a US trade representative (Spicer, 1997). Trade disputes in this area differ little from discussions over softwood lumber, steel, or dairy products. Television 'is just another appliance—a toaster with pictures', according to Mark Fowler, head of the US Federal Communications Commission from 1981 to 1987 (*Economist*, 1996).

American officials have argued that its neighbour's approach to culture violates its international trade obligations, particularly the General Agreement on Tariffs and Trade (GATT).[1] The agreement (in both the original 1947 and the revised 1994 versions) deals with the provision of physical products, including cultural goods such as magazines. Its two main principles are that countries should treat all GATT members equally (most-favoured-nation treatment) and should not favour domestic producers over foreign ones (national treatment). The agreement contains two cultural exemptions: one to allow quotas requiring screening of domestic motion pictures and one to protect artistic, historical, and archaeological treasures. All other cultural products have been subjected to the terms of the GATT from the beginning. Several countries tried to expand the cinema exemption to cover other forms of popular culture, but the United States consistently and successfully opposed these efforts. Though the American government believed that some Canadian cultural policies violated the agreement, it never lodged a formal challenge with the GATT secretariat.

Nor did the United States retaliate under the terms of the Free Trade Agreement with Canada, which was negotiated in 1987. Cultural goods were exempted from the agreement, meaning that Canada could continue to support domestic culture. The United States, however, retained the right to respond by implementing 'measures of equivalent commercial effect' against Canada. These articles were replicated in the North American Free Trade Agreement (NAFTA) signed by Canada, the United States, and Mexico in 1992. In essence, nothing had changed: Canada could maintain its cultural policies, but the United States could retaliate. Though retaliation was always possible, American officials have never taken advantage of this clause in the agreements.

The real change in cultural trade relations between Canada and the United States came with the formation of the WTO, which came into existence on 1 January 1995. The WTO replaced the GATT secretariat as a permanent organization to administer the GATT and other trade agreements, including the General Agreement on Trade in Services (GATS), which was signed in 1995. In contrast to the GATT, GATS gave member countries the right to opt in or out of particular provisions for specified sectors. Canada, for instance, chose not to make commitments dealing with audiovisual services. Thus, under the current international trade regime, countries may protect culture when it is a service (under GATS), but not when it is a good (under GATT), a distinction that is seldom easy to make.

The birth of the WTO provided an incentive for the United States to file formal complaints against Canada. The new organization has a more effective dispute resolution system than that of the now-dissolved GATT secretariat, dubbed the 'General Agreement to Talk and Talk' because of its inability to settle disputes. The WTO, by comparison, offered the opportunity for a quick and binding resolution to American grievances. WTO members have the right to a hearing in front of a tribunal, whose rulings are quicker and more binding than those under the old system. As a result, the United States began to defend its interests more forcefully, taking disputes to the WTO and threatening retaliation against Canada for measures that violated the GATT agreement.

The new American approach also reflected the changing nature of the country's economic interests. Trade has been growing in importance, accounting for 26 per cent of American GDP in 2000, up from 11 per cent in 1970 (USTR, 2002: annex I). At the same time, American merchandise exports are falling relative to other products, particularly technology and popular culture. In 1998 US corporations earned $36.8 billion (US) in royalties and licensing fees from audiovisual services, software, copyright payments, and other similar sources (Crane, 1999). Entertainment is now the largest export of the United States (UNDP, 1999: 33). American cultural products are increasingly available in a wide array of languages, making them accessible to a large portion of the world's population. *Reader's Digest*, to take a notable example, now publishes in 19 languages (Garten, 1998).

At the same time, media convergence has increased the clout of a few corporations—the largest being AOL Time-Warner, Walt Disney, and Viacom, conglomerates that depend increasingly on the international market. They have used their growing influence to push the American government to defend their interests abroad. The effectiveness of Jack Valenti, the charming and politically astute head of the Motion Picture Association of America, seems to grow as it becomes easier for him to convince American leaders that their personal political future and the country's economic interests lie in opening markets to American films. The words of former American trade negotiator William Merkin summarize the situation well: 'The U.S. is not in a position either politically or from a commercial perspective to grant any nation carte blanche to restrict our access in . . . the entertainment sector, which is an important earner for the U.S.' (Tamburri, 1998).

THE MAGAZINE CASE

The turning point in Canada's cultural trade relations with the United States came in the mid-1990s. Canadian law since 1965 had tried to limit split-run magazines, foreign periodicals with content from the foreign parent edition but with advertising sold specifically for the Canadian market (Azzi, 1999: 519). The purpose was to limit the ability of foreigners to compete with Canadian publishers for advertising revenues. In January 1993, *Sports Illustrated*, a Time-Warner publication, announced that it would begin publishing a Canadian split-run edition in April. *Sports Illustrated Canada* would be produced in New York City and sent electronically to a printing plant in Richmond Hill, Ontario.[2] The existing policy, which rested in part on a law that prevented the importing of split-runs from abroad, would be circumvented: no physical product was crossing the border, only an electronic signal.

Fearing that other American periodicals would follow suit, the government amended the Excise Tax Act, imposing an 80 per cent tax on the advertising revenues of split-run publications. *Time* and *Reader's Digest* (both of which had been established in Canada since 1943), but not *Sports Illustrated*, were exempted from the measure. The new legislation did not violate Canada's international obligations, argued the government. Advertising was not a good but a service, and Canada had not made any commitments under GATS related to advertising. Moreover, the measures dealt with all split-runs regardless of the owner's nationality, and did not, therefore, discriminate against foreigners.

United States Trade Representative (USTR) Mickey Kantor made it clear that he would pursue this issue as a test case to serve as a warning to other countries. 'We want to say this to the world—this is not to be tolerated', he insisted. 'We want the same access to others' markets that others enjoy to this market and we're going to continue to push for that in every available form' (Magder, 1998: 35). In March 1996, Kantor's office announced that it would use the WTO's dispute settlement process to challenge four measures promoting the Canadian magazine industry: the law preventing the importation of split-runs printed abroad; the advertising tax on the publishers of split-runs; Canada Post's differential postal rates; and the government's magazine postal subsidy. On 14 March 1997, a WTO dispute settlement panel ruled that three of the four measures violated the GATT, siding with Canada only on the issue of the postal subsidy. Both countries appealed the decision to a WTO appellate body, which, on 30 June 1997, ruled in favour of the United States on all four issues. Though advertising was a service, it was tied to a good (the magazine) and was therefore subject to GATT rules. The WTO had struck down not only the new 80 per cent tax on advertising revenues, but also other long-standing measures, including the 1965 ban on the import of split-runs printed abroad. Canadian magazine policy had, in the opinion of the dispute settlement panel and the appellate body, violated the GATT agreement for more than 30 years. Kantor's replacement as USTR, Charlene Barshefsky, hailed the American victory: 'This case makes clear that WTO rules prevent governments from using "culture" as a pretense for discriminating against imports' (USTR, 1997). On the Canadian side, the ruling was a shock. In the words of communications scholar Ted Magder, it was 'the most dramatic single blow ever levelled against Canadian cultural policy' (Magder, 1998: 49).

Initially, the Canadian government responded with bravado. Insisting that Ottawa would not back down, the government introduced a bill in October 1998 to ban foreign publishers from selling advertising intended for the Canadian market, with an exemption for *Time, Reader's Digest,* and *Sports Illustrated.* Because the measure dealt solely with the selling of advertising, a service, the Canadian government argued that it was not subject to the GATT. Barshefsky responded that Canada had merely substituted 'one form of protectionism for another' and had ignored 'both the letter and the spirit of WTO rules' (USTR, 1998). American officials threatened to retaliate should the bill pass, announcing that they would apply tariffs to several Canadian products, including steel, an important export from the Hamilton area, home to Heritage Minister Copps. Anger on the Canadian side was barely concealed. Trade Minister Sergio Marchi said that the United States was 'absolutely indifferent to our national interest', while expecting other countries to 'genuflect' to American interests (Taber, 1999).

Canada found that it had little choice but to make concessions to the United States. On 26 May 1999, the two countries reached a compromise. Advertisers would be allowed to claim a tax deduction for only 50 per cent of the value of advertising in magazines with less than 80 per cent original editorial content (i.e., the total non-advertising content). Advertising in magazines with 80 per cent or more original material would receive a full tax deduction. Split-runs published abroad would be permitted to have 12 per cent advertising directed at the Canadian market, increasing in stages to 18 per cent after three years. In addition, the Canadian government would provide cash subsidies to domestic publishers through the Canadian Magazine Fund. After one year, the government's 25 per cent ownership limit on Canadian magazines would be removed. For its part, the United States agreed not to challenge these measures through the WTO and not to retaliate against Canada, as it can under the NAFTA agreement. Either side could terminate this agreement with 90 days' notice, which meant that the United States might still take the dispute to the World Trade Organization or retaliate, so long as it gives advance warning. Though Canada had conceded more than the United States, the compromise showed some flexibility on the American side and was the first time the American government had recognized the principle that a country could enact measures to pre-serve local culture, even if they came at the expense of American producers (Pearlstein, 1999).

Canadian officials were dismayed at this outcome. The country's trade obligations, it now seemed, posed a significant threat to cul-tural policy. Canada would have to find a way to ensure that it could continue to achieve its goals in the cultural field while respecting its international agreements. Before the magazine case was even settled, the Canadian government began the search for a new international regime, one that would allow it to support domestic culture.

A NEW APPROACH

Cultural diversity became the new rallying cry and Canada became a leader in the drive for its international recognition. Canada could lay claim to certain advantages. Affluent and technologically advanced, with a long-standing commitment to multilateralism, Canada has many of the strengths necessary to head such a campaign. Its knowl-edge and expertise in the area of cultural diversity come from being a multicultural and officially bilingual country, one that has long con-sidered diversity a part of official policy. Canada has almost a cen-tury of experience in cultural policy and has been dealing with the impact of American culture for longer than any other country.

Canada's work to obtain international recognition of the impor-tance of cultural diversity began at a time when the subject was receiving increasing attention around the world. UNESCO had appointed former UN Secretary-General Javier Pérez de Cuéllar to chair the World Commission on Culture and Development. Its 1995 report, *Our Creative Diversity*, raised awareness about cultural issues in a global world and gave prominence to the notion of cultural diversity. The origin of the term can be traced to the negotiation of the 1992 Convention on Biological Diversity, which was based on the idea that the planet's well-being required the survival of a large, diverse number of species. From this concept came the related argument that the existence of a large number of diverse cultures is necessary for continued innovation, for development, and for democracy, in short, for the world's intellectual health. There is no agreement on the meaning of the term 'cultural diversity', which is not surprising given that 'culture' is one of the most complicated words in the English language. At the risk of oversimplifying, it can be defined as the world's broad range of cultural expression, cultural communities, viewpoints, and lifestyles.

The World Commission's report provided a starting point for discussion at UNESCO's Intergovernmental Conference on Cultural Policies for Development, a meeting of culture ministers in Stockholm in March and April 1998. This was the first time in 16 years that UNESCO's culture ministers had met. Concerned about threats to cultural diversity, the conference called for cultural goods and services to be treated differently from other products. Canada's Sheila Copps had gone to Stockholm looking for kindred spirits and found that many of her counterparts also wanted a place where common concerns could coalesce. She began to establish herself as an international leader of the cultural diversity campaign.

At Copps's invitation, 20 culture ministers met in Ottawa in June 1998 and formed the International Network on Cultural Policy (INCP). The group did not include a representative of the United States, which has no cabinet minister responsible for cultural matters. The Americans asked if they could send a trade representative, a request that Canada denied (Cobb, 1998). The Canadian government was insistent that this would be an organization of culture ministers, not a trade forum; as a result, the United States has not been a member of the network, though the American government has been invited to send observers to INCP meetings and has often done so. An informal organization, it works by operational consensus rather than recorded votes, allowing it to make rapid progress. The INCP now has some 50 member countries from all parts of the globe, with strong support from Canada, Switzerland, Sweden, Greece, South Africa, France, Croatia, and Mexico, to name only a few. It is led by a steering committee (called the 'contact group') that consists of 10 countries, including Canada. Canada chairs the Working Group on Cultural Diversity and Globalization and hosts the network's permanent liaison office, which is situated in the Department of Canadian Heritage in Gatineau (formerly Hull), Quebec. Canada also plays a leading role in a parallel NGO with a name almost identical to the network of ministers: the International Network for Cultural Diversity (INCD). Originally called the World Coalition for Cultural Diversity, the network was founded in 1999 and is now composed of more than 300 organizations representing over 50 countries, including the United States. The Canadian Conference of the Arts (CCA) was instrumental in creating the INCD and houses its secretariat.

Canada provided the key proposal in the cultural diversity campaign with the February 1999 report of the Cultural Industries Sectoral Advisory Group on International Trade (SAGIT), a body established by the Minister of International Trade. With 16 representatives from the cultural industries and the worlds of law, accounting, and the academy, it was chaired by Ken Stein, senior vice-president of Shaw Communications and a former official with the now-defunct Department of Communications. The group's report, *Canadian Culture in a Global World*, argued that the purpose of Canadian cultural policy should be to 'Ensure that Canadian cultural content is available to Canadians—*without limiting their access to foreign cultural products*' (SAGIT, 1999: 3). The report rejected the idea that Canadian cultural trade policy should focus on seeking a cultural exemption to international trade agreements. Instead, it recommended that Canada take the lead in negotiating a new international instrument: a legally binding treaty, convention, or protocol that would allow countries to pursue their own cultural policies without facing the threat of retaliation from trading partners. The authors were vague, not suggesting any specific wording and not saying where the instrument should be housed—that is, which international organization should administer it. Nevertheless, their key recommendation was soon endorsed by the Commons Committee on Foreign Affairs and International Trade and by the Committee on Heritage. On 19 October 1999, cabinet accepted the recommendation, a decision that Prime Minister Jean Chrétien announced in a 3 November speech and that was confirmed in the government's 15 November formal response to the report of the Foreign Affairs Committee (Schoffield, 1999; Chrétien, 1999; DFAIT, 1999: 23). The idea gained the enthusiastic support of many cultural organizations, particularly those representing Canadian writers, publishers, composers, actors, broadcasters, film and television producers, and visual artists.

Though it has often differed with Canadian Heritage in its approach to cultural policy, International Trade clearly supports the instrument. In the Doha round of trade negotiations, Canada has announced that it will not make any commitments on cultural matters under GATS until an international agreement on culture is established. A recently leaked memorandum drafted by officials from Finance, Industry, and Foreign Affairs and International Trade called for Canada to compromise in upcoming trade negotiations in 'certain service sectors', but the document stipulated that there can be no concessions on culture. The government must protect Canadian cultural policy, and do so through an international agreement (Sallot, 2002). When discussing the instrument in public, International Trade Minister Pierre Pettigrew's enthusiasm is evident, and it is an issue he raises in meetings with other trade ministers (Pettigrew, 2002a; Pettigrew, 2002b). While there is still a gap between Heritage and International Trade, both departments are working together for its realization.

The INCP accepted the idea for the instrument at its September 2001 meeting in Lucerne and set out to draft an agreement. The task was entrusted to the Working Group on Cultural Diversity and Globalization, which was given two years to prepare a text for the instrument and asked to submit a draft at the next year's meeting. A first draft of the text was presented to the ministers in October 2002 when they met in Cape Town, where they agreed to make the instrument a high priority and directed the working group to continue to develop the draft text, with particular attention to the rights and obligations of governments and the needs of developing countries.

THE DRAFT TEXT

The draft text of the instrument remains vague, although it does provide a starting point for discussion. The document's goal is to ensure that states are able to pursue the cultural policies they deem appropriate. The draft is based on the principles that 'Market forces alone cannot guarantee the maintenance and promotion of diverse cultural expressions and of cultural diversity' and that 'Public policy, developed in partnership with civil society and the private sector [is] of a vital importance in realizing the objectives' of the instrument. The draft broadly outlines policy areas viewed as appropriate, such as financial support, public institutions, and measures to provide space for domestic cultural products, but does not yet say specifically what policies will and will not be acceptable.

The most developed section of the draft deals with dispute resolution, a reflection of the importance of creating a binding document. The authors propose two options. Under the first, either party to a dispute may request the formation of a 'committee of experts' after a period of consultation. The governing council would have to approve the committee's decision, either by unanimous vote or by consensus, before it would become binding. This is essentially the same slow and ineffective process abandoned by the international trade regime at the end of 1994. The second option is similar to the mechanism in the Convention on Biological Diversity. Members may at any time indicate that they are willing to allow disputes to go to a three-member arbitration tribunal or the International Court of Justice for a binding decision. If both parties to a dispute have not accepted the same or any procedure, an effort will be made to settle the dispute through conciliation. A weakness of this procedure is that it involves a third party, reducing both its efficiency and the authority of the instrument's administrative body.

GOVERNANCE

The instrument will require an organization to administer it. No consensus exists within the Canadian government over where the instrument should be housed. UNESCO, which has its home in Paris, is the first choice of the French government, and in Cape Town culture ministers indicated a preference for having UNESCO provide the administrative framework. As the only large international organization with a specific mandate to deal with culture, it would seem to be a natural choice. Its membership includes many developing countries and its staff is familiar with the relevant issues, having recently issued a Universal Declaration on Cultural Diversity. In February 2003, INCP representatives met with UNESCO's director general, Koichiro Matsuura, who agreed to begin developing the instrument within that organization, subject to the approval of the General Conference at its October 2003 meeting.

The recent announcement that the United States is seeking to rejoin UNESCO has to some extent altered this discussion. The American government pulled out of UNESCO in 1984, complaining about corruption and mismanagement in the organization and expressing concern about the organization's work towards a new world information and communication order, which American officials saw as a threat to a free press and the free market. After the events of 11 September 2001, the American administration and Congress have indicated a desire to rejoin UNESCO because, in the words of President George W. Bush, the 'organization has been reformed' and American membership will be 'a symbol of our commitment to human dignity' (Bush, 2002). Negotiations are underway and the return of the United States is expected by October 2003. The American presence at UNESCO offers the opportunity to include the United States in the negotiation of the instrument, but the NGO network has expressed concern that the US might 'influence negatively . . . the creation and implementation of an instrument for cultural diversity', watering down the terms of the agreement and then refusing to sign it (INCD, 2002).

Though UNESCO is the option the culture ministers prefer, there are some difficulties in this choice. Any instrument must be enforceable, meaning that it must take priority over trade agreements to be effective. Yet UNESCO has no authority to override trade agreements and has little influence at the WTO. In addition, because trade negotiations are currently underway, ministers have agreed that the instrument must be adopted by 2005. UNESCO, however, is renowned for being slow and bureaucratic.

Another option would be the WTO itself, the body responsible for the very trade agreements that have created so many of the recent cultural trade disputes. Culture ministers have expressed little interest in having the WTO as the instrument's administrative body (INCP, 2002d). The instrument is supposed to provide a cultural point of view in the culture-trade quandary, but the WTO is not known for its expertise in or sensitivity to cultural issues. Indeed, the instrument and the WTO have objectives and principles that often conflict. Basing the instrument in the WTO would, in the view of the INCP, subject it to primarily commercial considerations. Moreover, members of the European Union—many of whom are members of the INCP—cannot make individual commitments under the WTO since multilateral trade negotiations are the sole prerogative of the EU itself.

For the culture ministers, the option of a stand-alone instrument, one not affiliated with any existing organization, offers the advantage of preserving the instrument's intent and allowing the agreement to be implemented quickly. The instrument would be drawn up by those states most committed to its goals. Yet, an independent agreement without institutional sponsorship and a critical mass of signatories would be more likely to fail. A stand-alone instrument is also an expensive option, and many of the signatories could not afford to provide the necessary financial support for the creation of a new bureaucracy. The establishment of an independent mechanism, however, does not prevent it from becoming part of an existing international organization in the future.

THE CHALLENGES AHEAD

The creation of a legally binding agreement with an effective dispute resolution mechanism will be an arduous task. To have any real impact—to respond to the challenges the instrument seeks to address—it must be legally binding and enforceable. It requires a link to Canada's trade obligations, meaning that it must have force at the WTO. The instrument, furthermore, needs precise definitions. The term 'culture' is so broad that it can be used to cover virtually the entire human experience. If there are no fixed definitions, if countries are allowed to invoke 'culture' to justify policies that would otherwise violate trade agreements, it is unlikely that many countries would be willing to sign on—certainly not the United States, the largest exporter of cultural products in the world, whose support is essential. The instrument will not work if the United States is not brought under its aegis. As Pettigrew has acknowledged, without the United States, 'it would be an instrument that would not have much teeth or significance' (Monchuk, 2001). A cultural diversity agreement, however, is not in the best interests of the United States and is not consistent with American ideology, which tends to see cultural policy as infringing on the freedom of the individual. The participation of the United States is crucial, but not likely.

INCP countries are apt to be successful if they can provide an incentive for the United States to agree to a cultural diversity instrument. Perhaps the only route is for them to hold up future trade negotiations. There is a precedent for this. In the final stage of the Uruguay Round of the GATT in 1993, disputes over culture could not be resolved. The United States called for trade liberalization in audiovisual services, but France, Canada, and several other countries argued instead for a 'cultural exemption'. At that time the protagonists agreed to postpone the discussion until the next round. Similarly, in 1998, France—with Canada's assistance—killed the proposed Multilateral Agreement on Investment largely because of issues surrounding culture. The current round of trade negotiations, the Doha Round, began in November 2001 and is scheduled to conclude by 1 January 2005. Few countries have indicated a willingness to make concessions on audiovisual services.[3] The European Union has said it will ensure that its members maintain the power to 'define and implement their cultural and audiovisual policies for the purpose of preserving their cultural diversity' (European Commission, 2002). Canada has refused to make further commitments on cultural matters until the instrument comes into force (WTO, 2001).

A standoff on trade in cultural products may well be the only way to win American acceptance of a cultural diversity agreement. The United States is not rigidly opposed to cultural policy. By negotiating a settlement to the magazine dispute with Canada and by applying to rejoin UNESCO, it has shown some willingness to compromise. But American agreement will only come if there is overwhelming support from the international community and a willingness to insist on an instrument during trade negotiations. It is far from clear whether the will is there. Considerable and growing support for an international instrument exists, with the INCP having almost 50 member countries. Still, the signatures of even these countries are far from assured. The culture ministers are enthusiastic, but many of them hold low or middle-level positions in their respective cabinets and may find that they cannot convince their own governments. Because of the overlapping nature of the issues and the agreement's impact on areas other than culture, it may be difficult for them to obtain backing at home.

CONCLUSION

Canada has led the campaign for the International Instrument on Cultural Diversity. Not only did the country first propose the idea, it convened and hosted the founding meeting of the International Network on Cultural Policy, serves on the network's steering committee, houses the secretariat, and is a member of the committee drafting the agreement's text. The proposed instrument brings together several enduring traditions in Canadian public policy. Canada has used cultural policy to offset the domestic impact of American popular culture, and Canadian foreign policy has been similarly concerned with the overpowering influence of the United States. As the Canadian and American economies become more integrated, and as the two countries pull closer together in military and foreign affairs, cultural policy might well be taking on an increased importance. In many areas, Canadian officials have employed multilateralism as a tool to offset American dominance. Through the instrument, two emblems of Canadian policy—multilateralism and concern about American culture—have met; whether they have been reconciled is still to be seen.

Multilateralism has not always been a perfect solution to Canada's problems. Several of Canada's recent multilateral forays—the Kyoto Accord on the environment, the International Criminal Court, and the Ottawa Convention on Anti-Personnel Landmines—were only limited successes because of the failure to bring the United States on board. Similarly, a cultural diversity agreement will have to include the United States for it to be more than a limited success. Herein lies the paradox of the International Instrument on Cultural Diversity. Canada has pursued it primarily as a way to prevent American cultural domination, but the agreement will only meet its objectives with the participation of the United States.

NOTES

Stephen Azzi is a policy officer with the Department of National Defence, and Tamara Feick is an analyst with the Department of Canadian Heritage, working part-time. The views expressed in this article are entirely their own, and do not necessarily reflect those of either department.

1. When in 1956 Canada announced a short-lived 20 per cent tax on the advertising revenues of foreign magazines, Washington argued that the measure violated the General Agreement on Tariffs and Trade (DFAIT, 2002: 257). In 1961, the United States claimed that the GATT agreement prevented content restrictions on television programming and asked the organization to clarify the matter (Carmody, 1999: 258–9). The American government also accused Canada of violating the trade agreement with the more extensive and longer-lasting magazine policy introduced in 1965 (Azzi, 1999: 512–14). In the early 1970s, the US complained about television and film subsidies in more than 20 countries, including Canada. The US was troubled by a decision of the CRTC in the 1970s to require cable companies to replace American advertisements with Canadian ones on American channels when a program was also being telecast simultaneously on a Canadian network (Berlin, 1990).

2. As Keith Acheson and Christopher Maule have noted, *Time*'s Canadian split-run edition had been produced this way since 1986, but had provoked no government reaction (Acheson and Maule, 2001: 469).
3. A 1998 World Trade Organization background note showed that only 19 of the organization's more than 130 members had made specific commitments in audiovisual services (WTO, 1998).

REFERENCES

In the course of their research, the authors undertook interviews with government officials.

Acheson, Keith, and Christopher Maule. 1997. 'Canada's Cultural Policies: You Can't Have It Both Ways', *Canadian Foreign Policy* 4, 3 (Winter): 65–81.

———. 1999. *Much Ado About Culture: North American Trade Disputes*. Ann Arbor: University of Michigan Press.

———. 2001. 'No Bite, No Bark: The Mystery of Magazine Policy', *American Review of Canadian Studies* 31, 3 (Autumn): 467–81.

Azzi, Stephen. 1999. 'Magazines and the Canadian Dream: The Struggle to Protect Canadian Periodicals', *International Journal* 54, 3 (Summer): 502–23.

Barlow, Maude. 2000. 'Coca-Cola Culture: Can National Cultures Survive Globalization?', *Canadian Perspectives* (Fall): 8–10.

———. 2001. 'The Global Monoculture: "Free Trade" versus Culture and Democracy', *Earth Island Journal* 16, 3 (Fall). Available at: <www.globalpolicy.org/globaliz/cultural/2001/1001mono.htm>.

Beaudoin, Louise. 2002. 'Il Nous Faut un Kyoto de la Culture', *Le Devoir*, 20 Sept., A9.

Berlin, Barry. 1990. *The American Trojan Horse: U.S. Television Confronts Canadian Economic and Cultural Nationalism*. New York: Greenwood Press.

Bernier, Ivan. 1997. 'Opening Markets and Protecting Culture: A Challenging Equation', *Forces: Economic, Social and Cultural Quarterly* no. 117: 84–7.

———. 2002. 'Establishing A New Instrument on Cultural Diversity', lecture at the Korean National Press Centre.

——— and Hélène Ruiz Fabri. 2002. *Evaluation of the Legal Feasibility of an International Instrument Governing Cultural Diversity*. Quebec: Group de travail franco-québécois sur la diversité culturelle.

Browne, Dennis, ed. 1998. *The Culture/Trade Quandary: Canada's Policy Options*. Ottawa: Centre for Trade Policy and Law.

Brunet, Alain. 2002. 'L'autre Sheila Copps', *La Presse*, 12 Oct., B4.

Bush, George W. 2002. 'President's Remarks at the United Nations General Assembly', 12 Sept. Available at: <www.whitehouse.gov/news/releases/2002/09/20020912-1.html>.

Carmody, Chi. 1999. 'When "Cultural Identity Was Not at Issue": Thinking about Canada—Certain Measures Concerning Periodicals', *Law and Policy in International Business* 30, 2 (Winter): 231–320.

Chrétien, Jean. 1999. Speech to the joint plenary session of the Americas Business Forum and Free Trade of the Americas Ministerial Meeting, Toronto, 3 Nov. Available at: <www.americascanada.org/eventabf/fileview-e.asp?file=9>.

Clarkson, Stephen. 2002. *Uncle Sam and Us: Globalization, Neoconservatism, and the Canadian State*. Toronto: University of Toronto Press.

Cobb, Chris. 1998. 'Canada Hosts International Summit of Culture Ministers, but the U.S. Is not Invited', *Hamilton Spectator*, 12 June, D7.

Copps, Sheila. 1999. 'Canadian Cultural Policy in a Global Economy', *Canadian Business Economics* 7, 3 (Oct.): 40–3.

Crane, David. 1999. 'Real Test of WTO Will Be Cultural Agreement', *Toronto Star*, 2 Dec.

Cultural Industries Sectoral Advisory Group on International Trade (SAGIT). 1999. *Canadian Culture in a Global World: New Strategies for Culture and Trade*. Ottawa: DFAIT.

———. 2002. *An International Agreement on Cultural Diversity: A Model for Discussion*. Ottawa: DFAIT.

Curzi, Pierre, Jack Stoddart, and Robert Pilon. 2001. 'Coalition for Cultural Diversity: Position'. Available at: <www.cdc-ccd.org/Anglais/Liensenanglais/who_we_are/Coal_position_eng.pdf>.

Department of Canadian Heritage. 2002. *Canadian Content in the 21st Century: A Discussion Paper about Canadian Content in Film and Television Productions*. Ottawa.

Department of Foreign Affairs and International Trade (DFAIT). 1999. *Canada and the Future of the World Trade Organization: Government Response to the Report of the Standing Committee on Foreign Affairs and International Trade*. Ottawa.

———. 2002. *Documents on Canadian External Relations*, vol. 23, ed. Greg Donaghy. Ottawa.

Dymond, W.A., and Michael M. Hart. 2002. 'Abundant Paradox: The Trade and Culture Debate', *Canadian Foreign Policy* 9, 2 (Winter): 15–33.

Economist. 1996. 'The Power of Suggestion', 18 May, review of books and multimedia section, 4.

Europe, Council of. 2000. 'Declaration on Cultural Diversity', adopted by the Committee of Ministers, 7 Dec. Available at: <cm.coe.int/ta/decl/2000/2000 dec2.htm>.

European Commission. 2002. 'The General Agreement on Trade in Services (GATS) and the New Round'. Available at: <europa.eu.int/comm/avpolicy/extern/gats _en.htm>.

Francophonie, Organisation internationale de la. 2001. 'Déclaration de Cotonou', 15 June. Available at: <www.francophonie.org/oif/publications/evenements/declaration_Cotonou.doc>.

Gagné, Gilbert. 2002. 'The Canada-US Border and Culture: How to Ensure Canadian Cultural Sovereignty', *Canadian Foreign Policy* 9, 2 (Winter): 159–70.

Garten, Jeffrey E. 1998. 'Cultural Imperialism Is No Joke', *Business Week*, 30 Nov.

Goff, Patricia. 2000. 'Invisible Borders: Economic Liberalization and National Identity', *International Studies Quarterly* 44, 4 (Dec.): 533–62.

House of Commons, Standing Committee on Foreign Affairs and International Trade. 1999. *Canada and the Future of the World Trade Organization: Advancing a Millennium Agenda in the Public Interest*. Ottawa.

International Network for Cultural Diversity (INCD). 2002. Newsletter 23, Sept. Available at: <www.incd.net/docs/Newletter23E.htm>.

International Network on Cultural Policy (INCP). 2000. 'List of International Agreements which Make Reference to Culture'. Available at: <206.191.7.19/ w-group/wg-cdg/list_e.pdf>.

————. 2002a. 'Draft Text of an International Instrument/Convention on Cultural Diversity'. Available at: <206.191.7.19/meetings/2002/instrument_e.shtml>.

————. 2002b. 'Options and Issues for the Implementation of an Instrument: Depositary, Mechanism and Strategy'. Available at: <206.191.7.19/meetings/ 2002/options_e.pdf>.

————. 2002c. 'Cape Town Statement'. Available at: <206.191.7.19/meetings/2002/ statement_e.shtml>.

————. 2002d. 'Strategic Options for a New International Instrument on Cultural Diversity'. Available at: <206.191.7.19/meetings/2002/strategic_e.shtml>.

Lindgren, April. 1997. 'Trade Negotiator Fears Sovereignty at Risk', *Ottawa Citizen*, 28 June, A1.

Liss, Jeffrey. 1999. 'The Impact of Technological Change on Canada's Affirmative Policy Model in the Cultural Industry and New Media Sectors', *Canada-United States Law Journal* 25: 379–88.

Magder, Ted. 1998. 'Franchising the Candy Store: Split-Run Magazines and a New International Regime for Trade in Culture', *Canadian-American Public Policy* no. 34 (Apr.): 1–66.

————. 1999. 'Going Global', *Canadian Forum* (Aug.): 11–16.

Mahant, Edelgard E., and Graeme S. Mount. 2001. 'The U.S. Cultural Impact upon Canada', *American Review of Canadian Studies* 31, 3 (Autumn): 449–65.

Mandate Review Committee—CBC, NFB, Telefilm Canada. 1996. *Making Our Voices Heard: Canadian Broadcasting and Film for the 21st Century*. Ottawa: Department of Canadian Heritage.

Maule, Christopher. 2002a. 'Trade and Culture: Rhetoric and Reality', *Policy Options* (Mar.): 39–44.

————. 2002b. 'Overview of Trade and Culture', *Canadian Foreign Policy* 9, 2 (Winter): 1–14.

Mendelsohn, Matthew, Robert Wolfe, and Andrew Parkin. 2002. 'Globalization, Trade Policy, and the Permissive Consensus in Canada', *Canadian Public Policy* 28, 3 (Sept.): 351–71.

Monchuk, Judy. 2001. 'Ottawa Wants International Body to Safeguard Culture in Trade Negotiations', Canadian Press, 11 June.

Morton, Peter. 1995. 'U.S. Draws up Canadian Culture "Hit List"', *Financial Post*, 4 Feb., 3.

————. 1996. 'Kantor's Attack on Canada Is Warning to World', *Financial Post*, 12 Mar., 7.

Naqvi, Yasir A. 1999–2000. 'Bill C-55 and International Trade Law: A Mismatch', *Ottawa Law Review* 31, 2: 323–53.

Palmateer Pennee, Donna. 1999. 'Culture as Security: Canadian Foreign Policy and International Relations from the Cold War to the Market Wars', *International Journal of Canadian Studies* 20 (Fall): 191–213.

Pearlstein, Steven. 1999. 'U.S., Canada Resolve Dispute: Deal Allows American Inroads in Neighbor's Magazine Market', *Washington Post*, 27 May, E3.

Pettigrew, Pierre. 2002a. 'Prime Time in Ottawa', speech to the Canadian Film and Television Production Association Conference, 7 Feb. Available at: <www.cftpa.ca/publications/ speeches_Pettigrew-feb72002.html>.

———. 2002b. 'The Next Step Forward for Trade and Culture', speech to the International Institute of Communications, 28 Nov. Available at: <webapps.dfait-maeci.gc.ca/minpub/Publication.asp?FileSpec=/Min_Pub_Docs/105745.htm&b Print=True&Language=E>.

Rabinovitch, Victor. 1998. 'The Social and Economic Rationales for Domestic Cultural Policies', in Dennis Browne, ed., *The Culture/Trade Quandary: Canada's Policy Options*. Ottawa: Centre for Trade Policy and Law, 25–47.

Raboy, Marc, et al. 1994. 'Cultural Development and the Open Economy: A Democratic Issue and a Challenge to Public Policy', *Canadian Journal of Communication* 19, 3–4 (Summer-Autumn): 291–315.

Ritchie, Gordon. 1997. *Wrestling with the Elephant: The Inside Story of the Canada–U.S. Trade Wars*. Toronto: Macfarlane Walter and Ross.

Royal Commission on National Development in the Arts, Letters and Sciences. 1951. *Report*. Ottawa.

Sallot, Jeff. 2002. 'Ottawa Urged to Open Markets', *Globe and Mail*, 4 Sept., B1.

Sands, Christopher. 2001. 'A Chance to End the Culture Trade Conflict between Canada and the United States', *American Review of Canadian Studies* 31, 3 (Autumn): 483–99.

Schoffield, Heather. 1999. 'Ottawa Seeks Global Deal to End Cultural Trade Wars', *Globe and Mail*, 20 Oct.

Schwanen, Daniel. 2001. 'A Room of Our Own: Cultural Policies and Trade Agreements', *Choices* 7, 4 (Apr.): 2–28.

Spicer, Nick. 1997. 'France Joins Copps' Fight Against U.S. "Culture Vulture"', *Calgary Herald*, 1 Feb., A15.

Taber, Jane. 1999. 'Talking Tough about Trade', *Ottawa Citizen*, 9 Jan., B3.

Tamburri, Rosanna. 1998. 'Canada Considers New Stand Against American Culture', *Wall Street Journal*, eastern edition, 4 Feb., A18.

Task Force on the Canadian Magazine Industry. 1994. *A Question of Balance: Report of the Task Force on the Canadian Magazine Industry*. Ottawa.

United Nations Development Program (UNDP). 1999. *Human Development Report 1999*. New York: Oxford University Press.

United Nations Educational, Scientific, and Cultural Organization (UNESCO). 2001. 'Universal Declaration on Cultural Diversity', adopted by the 31st Session of the General Conference, 2 Nov. Available at: <unesdoc.unesco.org/images/0012/001271/127160m.pdf>.

———. 2002. 'Culture, Trade and Globalisation: Questions and Answers'. Available at: <www.unesco.org/culture/industries/trade/html_eng/question.shmtl>.

United States Trade Representative, Office of the (USTR). 1997. 'WTO Appellate Body Expands U.S. Victory in Challenge to Canada's Restrictions on U.S. Magazine Exports', press release 97-62, 30 June. Available at: <www.ustr.gov/releases/1997/07/97-62.pdf>.

———. 1998. 'United States to Take Trade Action if Canada Enacts Magazine Legislation', press release 98–96, 30 Oct. Available at: <www.ustr.gov/releases/1998/11/98-96.pdf>.

————. 2002. '2002 Trade Policy Agenda and 2001 Annual Report of the President of the United States on the Trade Agreements Program'. Available at: <www.ustr.gov/reports/2002.html>.

World Commission on Culture and Development. 1995. *Our Creative Diversity*. Paris: UNESCO.

World Trade Organization (WTO). 1998. 'Audiovisual Services: Background Note by the Secretariat', document S/C/W/40, 15 June.

————. 2001. 'Communication from Canada: Canadian Initial GATS Sectoral/Modal/ Horizontal Negotiating Proposals', document S/CSS/W/46, 14 Mar.

Yong-shik, Choe. 2002. 'Free Trade Regimes Kill Cultural Diversity, says Canadian Activist', *Korea Herald*, 15 May. Available at: <www.koreaherald.co.kr/SITE/ data/html_dir/2002/05/15/200205150022.asp>.

7

Canada–US Defence Relations Post-11 September

DAVID BERCUSON

If William Lyon Mackenzie King were to magically reappear in the nation's capital today, he would no doubt be shocked at the extent to which the armed forces of Canada and the United States operate together and the extent to which Canada's defence has been so thoroughly integrated into the larger context of US defence concerns. King would be staggered by the range and number of treaty-level agreements and memorandums of understanding that tie the Canadian Forces to the US military structure. He would disapprove of the Canadian navy's now standard practice of integrating a Canadian warship into every US carrier battle group that goes to the Arabian Gulf to enforce UN sanctions against Iraq. He would be mortified by Canada's 29 August 2002 announcement of a pending agreement with the US to allow US troops onto Canadian soil in response to a terrorist attack. He would undoubtedly reject the notion that in matters of security and defence, the already close working relationship between Canada and the US ought to be tightened even further, or that a Canadian government ought to think seriously of a significant expansion of its defence budget in order to soothe rising US concerns about Canadian defence 'freeloading'.

In general, it still remains that the Canada–US defence relationship is one of the closest of any two sovereign countries on the face of the earth. As of January 2002, there were close to 90 bilateral treaty-level agreements governing the Canada–US defence relationship, some dating as far back as the early nineteenth century. Since the terrorist attacks of 11 September 2001, further close arrangements have been entered into, including the establishment of the Canada–US Bi-National Planning Group. The Group will prepare 'contingency plans to ensure a cooperative and well coordinated response to national requests for military assistance' on land and at sea, essentially to supplement NORAD (DND, 2002). Outside of the purview of strictly defence matters, the two nations have moved very close together on sharing cross-border intelligence, providing for border security, smoothing the flow of cross-border traffic, and generally in starting to shore up the continental perimeters to ward off attack.

Offshore, active Canadian military co-operation with the US, as well as with Canada's other NATO allies, predated the events of 11 September, with the Canadian air force contributing to the bombing of Yugoslavia during the Kosovo crisis of 1999 and a Canadian ground contingent being sent to Kosovo for two rotations in 1999 and 2000 to help KFOR pacify that nominally Yugoslav province. Most notably, Canada sent a large naval contingent to aid the US-led campaign against the Taliban and Al-Qaeda in Afghanistan in the fall of 2001, followed by a Canadian ground contingent sent to participate in a shooting war in the early spring of 2002. Close operational co-operation continues between the Canadian and US navies and air forces while Canadian defence contractors supply a myriad of military equipment to the US armed forces.

At one level, then, the Canada–US defence relationship continues much as it has evolved since the first post-World War II affirmation in February 1947 (Permanent Joint Board on Defence Resolution No. 36) that the close wartime continental defence relationship, initiated at Ogdensburg, New York, in August 1940, would continue into peacetime. And yet the post-11 September period saw an immediate upswing in US pressure—in public by the US Ambassador to Canada and in private by a wide range of government officials, political leaders, and influential private citizens—on Canada to beef up the Canadian military for both continental defence and offshore operations. Dwight Mason's essay in this volume accurately reflects the growing frustration that the US feels over Canada's shoddy treatment of its own armed forces because of the hard reality that the US's longest border, and perhaps its most vulnerable, is with Canada.

It is still too early to know whether all the forecasts that the terrorist attacks would 'change the world' were correct. As with all such sweeping generalizations, no one will really know until many years have passed. But one thing is certain: those attacks revealed just how vulnerable the US is to acts of planned mass mayhem. Thus the defence of the continental United States is now, once again, at the top of the US priority list, ahead of virtually every other American foreign policy concern. This has not been true since the end of the Cold War and not even since the era of the massive buildup of ICBMs in the USSR and the US, which began in earnest in the early 1960s. In many respects, then, Canada today is in virtually the same position it was during the 10 years immediately after World War II; due to geography alone, Canada is once again vital for the defence of the United States itself, whether Canadians are aware of that reality, whether they like it, or even whether they are prepared to pay for it. In that sense, 11 September returned Canada to a past that should not be forgotten.

Canadians remained wary neighbours of the US for more than six decades after the establishment of Canada in 1867. It is a continuing source of amusement to Canadian military historians that the first interwar defence plan put together by Canada's tiny interwar military had at its heart a Canadian cavalry attack into the US Midwest. It was not until 1938, when Hitler was well on the road to launching World War II, that the first very tentative but tangible steps towards Canada–US defence co-operation began after Franklin D. Roosevelt told a Queen's University audience in 1938 that the US would not stand idly by if Canada were threatened by a hostile power. King responded in kind a few days after (Thompson and Randall, 1994: 147). Two years later, as France lay in defeat, Canada initiated the first military-to-military talks ever between the two countries—but in secret, of course. Canadian officers soon began to pay secret visits to Washington, always going in mufti, to begin exploring concrete steps that the two countries might take in view of the growing threats overseas (Eayrs, 1965: 203).

Thus the fundamental pattern of the Canada–US defence relationship was set from the very beginning of that relationship: the US initiates, Canada responds (because it usually must), but generally reluctantly and often with great hesitation. The dynamic—as true today as in 1938—is rooted in the reality that the US has harboured global interests and ambitions since the late nineteenth century and Canada has not. Thus, with the exception of the 20 years between 1919 and 1939, the US has generally understood that global interests must be protected by global power, manifest in its many forms but especially military power, and that at a minimum, America's real security borders must be established far from its shores and its land boundaries with Canada and Mexico.

Almost none of that is true for Canada. When Canada's mandarins first awoke in the 1930s to the importance of reaching out for international markets—particularly but not exclusively in the United States—their strategy rested primarily on the power of reason and the pull of economic self-interest to tie Canada to the US and eventually the rest of the trading world (Granatstein, 1981: 66). Canada had economic interests in the Caribbean, for example, but no military capacity to force the peoples of that region to do its bidding. Besides, the US was perfectly capable of policing that area and shouldering the full costs of maintaining marines and naval units at the ready there.

The pattern of Canada–US defence relationships almost always has involved Canada responding to American initiatives; the pattern of Canadian-American trade relationships is almost exactly the opposite. From the first days of Confederation, Canada initiated contacts aimed at easing the cross-border trade flow, with the US responding. On three occasions—in 1910, 1947, and 1985—Canada initiated free trade discussions with the US, only to back away on the first two occasions and almost on the third.

The explanation for this peculiar train of events is simple. In matters of defence Canadians have long believed that the US needs strong Canadian defences far more than Canada does, while no one has to convince Canadians that in matters of trade, Canada badly needs US markets. In other words, when Canadians look south, they see jobs; when Americans look north, they see defence. This Canadian view of things is quite wrong, but most Canadians still seem to believe, as Senator Raoul Dandurand proclaimed at the League of Nations in 1924, that Canada lives in 'a fireproof house far from inflammable materials' and is thus unaffected by the onset of world crises and has no need to maintain a credible military between wars (Granatstein and Hillmer, 1994: 76).

The historical evolution of the Canada–US defence partnership in the post-World War II era was established early. In 1946 the Military Co-operation Committee (MCC) attempted to convince both governments that the air-atomic threat from the USSR was so grave and so imminent that both countries ought to move quickly to establish vast networks of radar stations and fighter fields to counter the threat (Jockel, 1987: 6–29). In fact, the MCC's view reflected the worst-case scenario held by some high-ranking generals in the US Air Force far more than it did official thinking in either US military or diplomatic circles. The Canadian government was not at first aware of that and feared that the MCC report was but the opening stage of a new campaign to pressure Canada to fortify its north. William Lyon Mackenzie King's misgivings were fed by news leaks emanating from Washington relating that Canada was being pressed to establish some sort of aerial 'Maginot Line' in the Far North. Some historians took Canadian reticence as a sign that Canada's view of the Soviet threat in that period was more moderate than could be found in Washington (Page and Munton, 1997). In fact, as closer examination of Department of External Affairs and Department of National Defence documents have since revealed, Canadian policy-makers on the whole were of the same mindset as those in the US. The difference in outlook between the two countries was that the Canadian defence budget was so much smaller that Canada's policy-makers were forced to subordinate their mistrusts of the USSR to the spending priorities of the Department of Finance. That department, under Douglas Abbott, took its cue directly from the Prime Minister, who was determined to shrink the military budget and shift financial priorities to paying down Canada's massive war debt and initiating the welfare state measures the government had promised in the June 1945 federal election. Not for the first time, Canada's defence planning was cut to fit the Finance Department's cloth (Bercuson, 1993a).

Although the US also made massive cuts to its defence budget after 1945, those cuts still left enough money for the US military to be more expansive in its planning than was the case in Canada. Besides, the US was forging ahead with the expansion of its nuclear attack capabilities and the design and building of new intercontinental bombers such as the B-47 and the development of air-to-air refuelling, which, it was believed, would provide the ultimate protection for the US and would be its ultimate guarantor against attack from the USSR (Conant, 1962: 16).

In almost every case in the late 1940s, Canadian ties to the US defence establishment developed out of US requests to Canada to map the Canadian North by air, or establish LORAN and weather stations, or allow cold-weather testing, or give access to US naval vessels and military personnel to practise joint land-sea exercises in the Arctic Archipelago. The US wanted the transcontinental radar station chains, the Strategic Air Command (SAC) lease of Goose Bay, the possible use of an emergency landing strip at Resolute, permission for its fighters to cross into Canadian airspace in hot pursuit of unknown radar contacts, the ability to overfly Canada with bombers armed with nuclear weapons, and the right to use Goose Bay to launch atomic attacks by air against the USSR without Canadian permission. Being the larger power, with a greater military and a far more sweeping list of potential threats, it was natural that the US would be the perpetual supplicant, Canada the perpetual respondent. And it was natural also that US defence requirements would so often distort Canadian budget priorities.

In the first 15 years or so of the Cold War, Canadian policy vis-à-vis defence relations with the Americans evolved from initial great reluctance, to a realistic appraisal of what measures would have to be taken to accommodate US requirements, to a renewed reluctance to be perceived as a mere cockboat following in the wake of the US man-of-war. From roughly 1945 through late 1949, the Canadian government's main strategy for dealing with US requests for defence cooperation was deceit of the Canadian people and delay in agreeing to the requirements of the Americans. When Canada agreed to the construction of LORAN and weather stations in the Far North, for example, the public never learned the military nature of the building program and US aircraft and ships detailed to carry construction supplies to the North were instructed to avoid Canadian population centres (Bercuson, 1993b: 158). To some degree the government's effort to mislead Canadians over the US presence in the Far North was rooted in the fear that the Anglophile Tory Official Opposition in Parliament would raise embarrassing questions over why Canada was tying itself ever more closely to the US in defence matters. The other main factor was King's reluctance to be seen as too activist in the Cold War and too close to the US line on the USSR. King officially retired from office in late 1948 and his successor, Louis St Laurent, was far less reticent to throw Canada's lot in with the US.

In these early years of the Cold War, Canada evolved a policy that amounted to defending its own sovereignty against possible US incursions by ensuring that it be seen by Washington to be doing as much as time and Canada's financial resources would allow in regard to defending the continent (Bercuson, 1990). The greatest fear among Canadian policy-makers was that failure to act at all, or to act sufficiently to give the US comfort, would prompt the US to shove Canadian sovereignty concerns aside and act in its own self-defence. There was an almost irrational fear, for example, that the US might challenge Canadian claims to sovereignty over the Arctic Archipelago, especially since Canada had no tangible presence on many of the Arctic islands and claimed sovereignty on the 'sector principle', which the US did not recognize (Smith, 1966: 214). Even if the US was not interested in formally challenging Canadian sovereignty over any Canadian soil, the danger persisted that heavy US presence in any concentrated area of Canada would have the practical result of the US assuming de facto control over parts of Canada, even if de jure control was not sought. That had appeared to happen in large areas of British Columbia and the Yukon in the lands contiguous to the Alaska Highway and the North West Staging Route during the war and could not be allowed to happen again

Thus a set of principles was worked out in Ottawa that was subsequently applied to almost all Canada–US defence projects on Canadian soil, with the notable exception of the Goose Bay SAC base, which was governed by a special lease negotiated by both countries. Included in that set of principles were provision for at least a symbolic Canadian presence on all joint bases and projects, ultimate Canadian ownership of any facility built, and applicability of Canadian law to US personnel (Bercuson, 1993b: 158).

Canada's reluctance to spend money on defence projects that appeared to be short-sighted and more beneficial to the US than to Canada melted away in the 12 to 14 months between the explosion by the USSR of its first nuclear weapon in late 1949 and the initial spectacular successes of the Chinese 'volunteers' in Korea beginning in November 1950. By the first months of 1951 Canada was as ready as the other Western powers (all affiliated to NATO) to spend massively on defence. An atmosphere of panic pervaded Washington, London, Paris, Bonn, and even Ottawa as the UN forces in Korea were pushed back from near the Korean border with China to south of the thirty-eighth parallel. Deep fear gripped these capitals that a

Communist victory over the UN forces in Korea would prompt the Communists to launch World War III with either an atomic attack on North America or an attack into West Germany, or both.

Canada's defence budget ballooned in early 1951 and kept climbing for the next half-decade; suddenly, Canada's hesitation over matters of continental defence faded away. From the early winter of 1951, Canada–US military co-operation grew apace as the Cold War deepened. Agreements were concluded that solved a host of minor issues arising out of the American presence at the leased bases in Newfoundland, a renewable 20-year lease was signed for a SAC base at Goose Bay, and provision was made for backup SAC facilities elsewhere. Canada undertook to build the Mid-Canada Line (or McGill Fence) and gave the US permission to build the DEW line. Canadian air defence resources expanded rapidly, with major increases in fighter forces deployed, bases maintained, and radar and ground control stations operated. A series of agreements deepened interoperability in air defence and led to the signing of NORAD in 1957 (Jockel, 1987: 91–117). At the same time a North American defence production agreement was concluded in October 1956, while co-operation in research on chemical, biological, and nuclear weapons increased. By the time John Diefenbaker received his massive 208-seat majority in the 1958 election, Canada had become a willing partner not only in Canada–US continental defence matters but also in NATO, where the previous St Laurent government had been a leader in the nuclearization of the alliance.

The Canadian defence effort, and Canada's commitment to an enthusiastic defence partnership with the United States, began to slip during Diefenbaker's five years in office. There were four main factors underlying this renewed lack of Canadian enthusiasm for defence in general and defence of North America in particular.

The first was the rapid slowing down of the Canadian economy in the first years of Diefenbaker's administration as the nation slid into its first serious post-war recession. Rising unemployment alongside Canada's first post-war devaluation of the Canadian dollar ushered in a period of severe federal restraint marked, for example, by the cancellation of the Avro CF-105, which was emerging as one of the most expensive defence undertakings in Canadian history.

The second factor was Diefenbaker's own mindset and his view that the Liberals had allowed Canada to slip much too far down the road of Americanization. Dief the Chief was determined to swim against the inexorable tide of continental economic history by thrusting Canada back into US markets and ensuring that Canada re-emphasize its ties with Britain and the British Commonwealth of nations (Robinson, 1989: 10). Diefenbaker gave his approval, almost automatically, to the NORAD agreement not long after he was first elected with a minority government in 1957, but this lack of any resistance was almost certainly due to the wiles of the Chairman of the Chiefs of Staff Committee, General Charles Folukes, who presented it to the Prime Minister as a done deal and one that only capped a series of agreements that were already in place—which was partly true. As Diefenbaker grew more comfortable in his unexpected interregnum, he questioned Canada–US defence relations more closely until eventually he balked completely over the matter of nuclear warheads for the newly acquired BOMARC-SAGE ground-to-air anti-aircraft defence systems. Diefenbaker also refused to fulfill commitments made to NATO about acquiring tactical nuclear warheads for the Honest John short-range missiles that the Canadian army was operating in Europe or for the CF-104 Starfighters that had been acquired to replace the aging RCAF Sabres.

Diefenbaker was not only suspicious of the 'Americanization' of the Canadian defence effort, he was also suspicious of the new President of the United States, John F. Kennedy. The poor personal relations between Diefenbaker and Kennedy are well known and need not be detailed here, but there can be little doubt that the two men were as intense in their dislike of each other as Lyndon Johnson and Lester Pearson or George W. Bush and Jean Chrétien. In part that dislike was based on sheer age and personality differences. But Kennedy was also determined to conduct an active, vigorous, and, where necessary, armed US foreign policy where his predecessor, Dwight D. Eisenhower, had seemed to rely more on diplomacy. Whenever there is great activity in defence and foreign affairs in Washington, Canadian governments find themselves challenged to help lead, to follow, or to get out of the way—a source of perpetual discomfort for most Canadian governments, which are by their nature hesitant and cautious, either for reasons of conviction or because of sheer politics. Thus when Kennedy announced the presence of Soviet intermediate-range ballistic missiles in Cuba in October 1962 and brought US military forces to the second highest state of readiness in anticipation of an invasion of Cuba and a war with the USSR, Diefenbaker refused to go along. As a consequence, the Canadian military itself took the unprecedented step of following the US lead in the absence of a lawful order from the Prime Minister, a clear violation of the principle of civilian control of the military (Granatstein, 1986: 114–16).

The final factor that led the Canadian government to distance itself from the Americans in matters of continental defence was the growing realization that the threat of the manned bomber was passing as the USSR and the US deployed increasing numbers of ICBMs and the age of the SLBM (submarine-launched ballistic missile) dawned. Since there was no effective defence against either of these two weapons systems, there was less need for Canada to continue devoting resources to anti-aircraft defence systems. US reliance on detection for purposes of defence shifted to detection for purposes of warning, with the first steps being towards the establishment of the BMEWS (Ballistic Missile Early Warning System) in 1959. By 1964 much of the continental radar warning system put in place after 1950 was destined to be closed and dismantled. Canada would thenceforth have a much smaller part to play in continental defence than it had had during the manned bomber era; in the age of MAD (mutually assured destruction) the US would defend itself by deterrence, a role in which Canada could play only a peripheral and unimportant part.

In 1963 John Diefenbaker lost power in the first election since 1911 that had an important defence issue to be decided. His refusal to agree to acquire the nuclear warheads that were vital for the effective operation of the BOMARC missiles (and the rocket warheads and tactical nukes designed for the Starfighters) gave Lester B. Pearson a winning election issue. Previously, while Leader of the Opposition, Pearson had opposed Canada's nuclearization. But that had been mere politics; he had been a willing proponent of NATO acquiring tactical nukes when he was still Secretary of State for External Affairs. In a calculated move to distance themselves from the Tories, the Liberals switched sides and won the 1963 election by campaigning that Canada had made commitments to the US and NATO and must now fulfill those commitments.

Once the Liberals were elected the nukes were acquired, but the government made it clear that it would abandon Canada's nuclear role as soon as possible. Pearson's main occupation in his five years as a minority Prime Minister was the completion of the welfare state and the laying of foundations for national bilingualism. The war in Vietnam reached fever pitch as Canadians welcomed American draft dodgers and demonstrated in increasing numbers against the 'war on

Vietnam'. Pearson's attempt to give Lyndon Johnson advice about that war stoked Johnson's anger and the Canada–US defence relationship cooled considerably, at least at official levels (Martin, 1982: 223–30). Pearson's successor, Pierre Elliott Trudeau, publicly distanced himself from closer defence ties with the US. He courted the Third World, was a leader in the start of the so-called North-South dialogue, and even tried to cultivate Canada–USSR ties in a vain attempt to make multilaterism actually work for Canada. He also cut Canada's military presence in NATO. And although he eventually gave his blessing to the acquisition of new Leopard tanks and the CF-18 fighter jets, he left the navy and much of the rest of the military in a dilapidated state. He trod a fine line when he gave the US permission to test cruise missiles in the Canadian Arctic while launching his round-the-world peace mission in the last year of his prime ministership (Granatstein and Bothwell, 1990: 377–83).

If Trudeau's pirouette around traditional Canada–US defence ties and long-standing Canadian defence commitments to NATO left the Americans unimpressed, Brian Mulroney tried to restore Canadian credibility in Washington by pulling Canada closer to the US in trade and on major foreign policy questions. Mulroney was determined to restore the credibility that Canada had once had in NATO and with the Americans, participating in the Gulf War of 1990–1 and slightly increasing the defence budget. His government set the Halifax-class frigate construction program in motion, began to plan for the acquisition of marine helicopters to replace the already-aging Sea Kings, and at one point even proposed that Canada acquire nuclear submarines and a Polar 8 icebreaker to guard Canadian sovereignty in the Arctic. The subs died when Canada's growing budget deficit and debt crisis dictated new cuts in defence expenditures. There can be no doubt, however, that Canada–US defence relations reached a new high point during his administration (Davis, 1989: 215–38).

Canada–US relations began to slide once again under Jean Chrétien and, more particularly, his longest-serving Minister of Foreign Affairs, Lloyd Axworthy. Axworthy was determined to show the world that Canada was not simply a pale reflection of the United States and used the greater freedom that the end of the Cold War seemed to allow Canada to encourage ties with Communist Cuba, to use the UN, multilateralism, and 'soft power' to achieve Canadian goals and to pursue goals—such as the anti-landmines treaty—that the US found diplomatically embarrassing. For the most part the Clinton administration more than tolerated Axworthy's ingenuous spin on Canadian foreign relations, possibly because it projected the image that it was itself more likely to act within a multilateral framework than its Republican predecessors were. But when George W. Bush was elected in 2000, the tone of the American administration quickly changed.

The new President made it very clear that the US would rebuild its military, that it would unilaterally withdraw from the Kyoto Accord, and that it did not trust international inspection regimes covering chemical and biological weapons. Ottawa was immediately challenged to either get on side with the new administration or keep its distance and await developments. The choice was complicated by the knowledge that President Bush had a long history of involvement with Mexico and was close to the new Mexican President, reformer Vicente Fox. One way to forestall a US-shift towards Mexico, several experts suggested, was to rebuild the Canadian military and strengthen the Canada–US defence relationship, as British Prime Minister Tony Blair was strengthening UK–US defence ties. The Chrétien government, as was its wont, chose caution, and even appeared to make a practice of denouncing alleged US unilateralism, becoming once again the 'stern daughter of the voice of God', as Dean Acheson had once described Canadian foreign policy (Granatstein and Hillmer, 1991: 183).

Almost immediately after the terror attacks of 11 September, Canada was once again in the Washington spotlight as a country that was suddenly very important for continental defence and the security of the United States. The closing of cross-border trade and the grounding of all air traffic in North America after the attacks grabbed the attention of the Canadian government almost immediately. The direct impact on the economy was devastating in its own right, but the ripples were felt right across Canada. One burgeoning young airline closed its doors permanently; the rest required bailouts. In companies large and small, retail, wholesale, and manufacturing, plants shut down—or nearly did—for lack of parts or lack of access to US markets. Border security leaped to the top of the Canadian government agenda.

From the very beginning of the war on terror, the Canadian government was an active and willing partner with the US in tightening border controls and increasing border security. Tough new internal security measures were adopted and billions in new resources were directed to perimeter and national security in the December 2001 budget. With $1.7 billion in daily cross-border trade at issue, it mattered much to Canada that the US was once again very concerned about its northern border.

That firmness was missing, however, when it came to beefing up the only Canadian agency capable of patrolling the littoral waters and the air over Canada, or of making any significant contribution not only to the war on terrorism at home but to the attack on terrorism abroad. Canada's Operation Apollo, heavy on naval forces, extremely light on air assets, and with a battle group insertion only in late February 2002 and incapable of a tour longer than six months, was the best Ottawa could do with the nation's badly depleted military. No matter what pressure was placed on the government by various domestic agencies, private and public, including the Senate Security and Defence Committee, the federal Auditor General, and the House of Commons Standing Committee on National Defence and Veterans' Affairs, the Prime Minister dug in his heels and refused to consider any significant increases in the national defence budget. It was then that the US Ambassador to Canada, Paul Celluci, began to openly disparage Canada's defence readiness and urged that Canada's military be bolstered (Gatehouse, 2002). Celluci's entreaties merely widened the rift that Trudeau, Chrétien, and Axworthy had already worked hard to create. One poll taken in mid-December 2002 showed that an astonishing 38 per cent of Canadians thought George Bush was more of a threat to world peace than Saddam Hussein.[1]

It is ironic that a nation so dependent on international trade, and so securely tied to the US economy, should have emerged early in the twenty-first century as so cool to the US, so isolationist in its foreign policy outlook, and so self-deluded as to believe that it matters much in world councils any longer. Tepid government leadership in foreign affairs, the gutting of the military, and the felt need of some Liberal ministers to cater to the illusions of the otherwise tattered Canadian left have produced a growing impasse with the United States. As in the early days of the Cold War, the US is looking to Canada for help; unlike those days, Ottawa is spurning Canada's only true neighbour and friend. If this policy trend is not reversed, the long-term implications for Canada will be devastating.

NOTE

1.   See <http://www.ekos.com>. Fifty-six per cent thought Saddam Hussein was more of a threat than Bush; 6 per cent could not make up their minds.

REFERENCES

Bercuson, David. 1990. 'Continental Defence and Arctic Sovereignty, 1945–1950: Solving the Canadian Dilemma', in K. Neilson and Ronald G. Haycock, eds, *The Cold War and Defense*. New York: Praeger.

———. 1993a. 'A People so Ruthless as the Soviets: Canadian Images of the Cold War and the Soviet Union, 1946–1950', in David Davies, ed., *Canada and the Soviet Experiment: Essays on Canadian Encounters with Russia and the Soviet Union, 1900–1991*. Toronto and Waterloo: Centre for Russian and East European Studies, University of Toronto/Centre on Foreign Policy and Federalism, University of Waterloo, 89–103.

———. 1993b. *True Patriot: The Life of Brooke Claxton, 1898–1960*. Toronto: University of Toronto Press.

Conant, Melvin. 1962. *The Long Polar Watch: Canada and the Defense of North America*. New York: Harper.

Davis, Mathwin S. 1989. 'Nuclear Submarines for Canada: A Technical Critique', in David G. Haglund and Joel Sokolsky, eds, *The U.S.–Canada Security Relationship*. Boulder, Colo.: Westview Press.

Department of National Defence (DND). 2002. 'Enhanced Canada–US Security Cooperation', Backgrounder, 9 Dec. Available at: <http://www.dnd.ca/site/newsroom/view_news_e.asp?id=509>.

Eayrs, James. 1965. *In Defence of Canada: Appeasement and Rearmament*. Toronto: University of Toronto Press.

Gatehouse, Jonathon. 2002. 'Why the Canadian Military Isn't Ready for a War', *Maclean's*, 30 Sept.

Granatstein, J.L. 1981. *A Man of Influence: Norman A. Robertson and Canadian Statecraft, 1929–1968*. Ottawa: Deneau.

———. 1986. *Canada: 1957–1967, The Years of Uncertainty and Innovation*. Toronto: McClelland & Stewart.

——— and Robert Bothwell. 1990. *Pirouette: Pierre Trudeau and Canadian Foreign Policy*. Toronto: University of Toronto Press.

——— and Norman Hillmer. 1991. *For Better or For Worse: Canada and the United States to the 1990s*. Toronto: Copp Clark Pittman.

Hillmer, Norman, and J.L. Granatstein. 1994. *Empire to Umpire: Canada and the World to the 1990s*. Toronto: Copp Clark Longman.

Jockel, Joseph T. 1987. *No Boundaries Upstairs: Canada, the United States and the Origins of North American Air Defence, 1945–1958*. Vancouver: University of British Columbia Press.

Martin, Lawrence. 1982. *The Presidents and the Prime Ministers*. Toronto: Doubleday.

Page, Don, and Don Munton. 1977. 'Canadian Images of the Cold War, 1946–1947', *International Journal* 32, 3 (Summer): 577–604.

Robinson, H.B. 1989. *Diefenbaker's World: A Populist in Foreign Affairs*. Toronto: University of Toronto Press.

Smith, Gordon W. 1966. 'Sovereignty in the North: The Canadian Aspect of an International Problem', in R. St J. Macdonald, ed., *The Arctic Frontier*. Toronto: University of Toronto Press.

Thompson, John Herd, and Stephen J. Randall. 1994. *Canada and the United States: Ambivalent Allies*. Montreal and Kingston: McGill-Queen's University Press.

8

US–Canada Defence Relations: A View from Washington

DWIGHT N. MASON

The US and Canada have enjoyed a strong and successful defence relationship for many years. Its focus is the defence of North America, but it also includes co-operation abroad. We were allies in the two world wars, in Korea, in the Gulf War, and in numerous United Nations (UN) and North Atlantic Treaty Organization (NATO) operations. We are members of many alliances, including NATO, North American Aerospace Defence Command (NORAD), the Organization of American States (OAS), and the Inter-American Defence Board to list a few. The strength of our defence relationship is based on this history, which reflects shared values and experience. These factors have created strong mutual confidence and trust.

We both know that when the chips are down we will be there for each other. For example, after the terrorist attacks of 11 September 2001, Canadians welcomed thousands of Americans as unexpected guests when the US closed its airspace. They showed support and affection for Americans in the immense gathering in front of Parliament on 14 September 2001, not to mention in thousands or tens of thousands of telephone calls and e-mails from Canadians to their friends in the US expressing sympathy and concern. Canadian law enforcement, intelligence, and border management co-operation were immediate after 11 September. It is doubtful that the US could have increased border security as effectively without this assistance. Canadian military help was also immediate. NORAD acted to secure North American airspace while at least one hijacked airplane was still in the air, and this was done under the direction of a senior Canadian officer, who was the Commander of NORAD's Combat Operations. Subsequently, Canada sent forces to fight beside those of the US in Afghanistan.

While US and Canadian law enforcement, intelligence, and border management co-operation continues to expand and to strengthen post-11 September, the story is different in the case of the Canadian military. The government of Canada has neglected its forces for many years. This situation did not materially change after 11 September. The Canadian Forces are fading away, unable to meet their fundamental mission requirements to defend Canada, work with the US in defending North America, and support efforts to promote a peaceful world abroad. As the forces fade, so will Canada's defence relationship with the US. So will its influence abroad.

Canada's neglect of its military affects US interests adversely to the extent that those forces are important to the defence of North America and more generally to the health of international defence alliances. The events of 11 September revealed that the Canadian Forces could be important to the defence of North America. The terrorist attacks also changed the way North America must now be defended. Those changes are likely to demand a greater Canadian defence effort and closer military co-operation with the US in the future.

Yet there seems to be little prospect that the Canadian Forces will be able to meet these new challenges. The forces received a modest increase in the government's 2003 budget. Even so, efforts to reverse course and restore the military to the point where it could again make a significant contribution to the defence of North America and to the UN and other alliances in promoting world order and stability will take a number of years and considerable money. From an American perspective, the policies that have brought Canada to this point look self-defeating and short-sighted.

THE BASIS OF THE CURRENT UNITED STATES-CANADIAN DEFENCE RELATIONSHIP

Today's US–Canada military relationship owes much to President Franklin D. Roosevelt. In the years before World War II, the President singled out Canada as a 'good neighbour' and encouraged informal staff talks between the two countries' armed services. In 1938, with the prospect of a war in Europe in mind, President Roosevelt used the occasion of a visit to Queen's University in Kingston to state (without consulting the Canadian Prime Minister in advance) that 'the people of the United States would not stand idly by if domination of Canadian soil is threatened by any other empire.' Prime Minister King replied a few days later, saying, 'we, too, have our obligations as a good friendly neighbour, and one of them is that, at our own instance, our country is made as immune from attack or possible invasion as we can reasonably be expected to make it, and should the occasion ever arise, enemy forces should not be able to pursue their way either by land, sea, or air to the United States across Canadian territory' (Eayrs, 1959: 177–83).

This exchange of statements became the basis of the existing defence relationship between the two countries (Granatstein, 2002: 3). The key point of this understanding is its recognition that North America is and must be managed as a single military theatre. It is important for Canadians to keep Prime Minister King's assurances in mind today. North America is still a single defence theatre, and the US can still be threatened from Canada. Terrorism is a prime example of such a threat.

STRUCTURE OF THE DEFENCE RELATIONSHIP

As World War II began, the Roosevelt-King understanding took on structure and depth. A process of co-operation often expressed through agreements and institutional arrangements developed rapidly.

The Permanent Joint Board on Defence
The first major step in this process was the establishment of the Permanent Joint Board on Defence (PJBD) by President Roosevelt and Prime Minister King in August 1940 at Ogdensburg, New York. The purpose of the Board was, as they put it, 'to consider in the broad sense the defence of the north half of the Western Hemisphere'

(Maloney, 1997: 5). It was intended to be a permanent arrangement, and it set the pattern for future US–Canadian defence co-operation.

The PJBD consists of US and Canadian 'sections'. Chairs appointed by the President and the Prime Minister respectively lead each section. Membership on the Board includes representatives of the several armed services, the Joint Staff, and the Department of State and their Canadian equivalents. The Board makes formal and informal recommendations to the two governments from time to time. Perhaps the most important functions of the PJBD are its ability to facilitate creativity in thinking about North American defence, to sort out problems before they become issues, and to establish strong, informal personal linkages between key officials of the two countries that have greatly strengthened and expanded co-operation.

Expansion of defence co-operation began almost at once. One of the first things the Board recommended was that a joint plan for the common defence of North America be prepared. This work continues today and is reflected in the Basic Security Document and the Combined Defence Plan. This planning is supported by a joint intelligence estimate that is regularly updated.

The Military Co-operation Committee

After the war, continental defence planning took on new dimensions and complexity in light of the evolving Soviet threat. This challenge was met by a further expansion of co-operation and institutional arrangements in the establishment of the Military Co-operation Committee (MCC) in 1946. It was patterned after the PJBD, and its core membership is the assistant PJBD members. It operates in the same manner as the PJBD except that the two chairs report to the Chairman of the Joint Chiefs of Staff and to the Chief of the Defence Staff, respectively. Although the MCC does not report to the PJBD, the two organizations work together closely. The PJBD often will refer matters to the MCC for study and suggestions, and the MCC regularly reviews issues before they come to the PJBD. Over time, the MCC has established several subgroups to manage or examine specific matters, including mapping and charting, weather, intelligence, interoperability, rules of engagement, oceanography, and information systems and operations (Maloney, 1997: 14–20). The responsibilities of these groups illustrate the growth and depth of bilateral defence relations.

One of the most notable aspects of these arrangements for bilateral military co-operation was the system of work that emerged: the

PJBD and the MCC work on the basis of consensus, respect, and equality. Planning for the defence of North America is done jointly. What was sought and achieved was a genuine partnership despite the disparities in power and world responsibilities. This style became and remains the norm for managing the bilateral military relationship. One by-product of this partnership has been a number of professional and personal relationships that have lasted long after the individuals left the PJBD or the MCC. A second by-product of participation in the PJBD and MCC has been unusual Canadian access to senior officials in the Department of Defense and the Joint Staff. This access can translate into influence.

One result of this collaboration was a vast increase in military-related agreements and organized contact between the two governments. The Department of National Defence estimates that by 2002 there were about 145 bilateral *forums* in which defence matters are discussed and that over 20,000 visits are made annually to the US by Canadian government and industry representatives on defence activities (DND, 2002a: 1). No one knows for certain how many agreements and arrangements there are, but the Department of National Defence puts it at about 330 including treaties, exchanges of notes, Memoranda of Agreement, and so on (ibid.).

The subject matter of these agreements illustrates the extent of the relationship. They provide for nearly every imaginable matter: refuelling, officer exchanges, communications, base agreements, logistics, information technology, rules of engagement, air defence and NORAD, maritime operations, meteorology, the various radar warning systems the countries installed in Canada, joint testing facilities, cooperative research and development, and search and rescue.

Defence Production Sharing Arrangements

A particularly significant focus of agreement was economic co-operation for defence, the idea being that not only was North America a single theatre but also that its defence required a common industrial base. This policy was expressed in a 1949 agreement establishing a Joint Industrial Mobilization Committee, another agreement in 1950 relating to economic co-operation for defence, the Defence Production Sharing Arrangements Agreement of 1959, and a 1987 agreement to form the North American Technology Industrial Base Organization. These agreements have allowed Canadian firms to compete on an equal basis with US counterparts in US defence markets in developing goods for the use of the US military. They have also allowed Canadian firms access to advanced US technologies and have contributed to the creation of high-technology industry and jobs in Canada (DND, 1994: 24). Trade flows related to defence were about $2 billion Canadian in 2002 (DND, 2002b: 3).

More recently, problems resulting from trade conducted under these arrangements stemmed from some unauthorized diversions from Canada of sensitive items to problematic countries. Discovery of these diversions led to suspension of Canada's special status under the US International Traffic in Arms (ITARS) regulations in 1999. The two countries were able to resolve most of the issues involved through negotiations expressed in an agreement in June 2001, in which the two countries committed themselves to take steps to prevent future diversions. Canada agreed to and did strengthen its legal regime governing exports for that purpose (Department of State, 2001).

NORAD

The continued evolution of the Soviet threat led in 1958 to the establishment of the North American Air (now Aerospace) Command or NORAD. These threats were increasingly lethal, included weapons of mass destruction (WMD), and their delivery systems were increasingly swift, a situation markedly different from that which prevailed during World War II and that dictated not just a co-operative air defence but also now an integrated one.

The system put in place—NORAD—was a truly binational, integrated air defence and later also space warning system that at once permitted very quick responses but also preserved each country's command and control systems. Both countries staff NORAD. The Commander (by custom a US officer) or in his absence the Deputy Commander (by custom a Canadian) reports to the President and the Prime Minister through their respective ministries of defence. A senior Canadian officer is sometimes in charge at the command centre, and Canadians hold senior positions throughout the command. It was a Canadian officer who directed NORAD's response to the events of 11 September 2001 and who put both Canadian and American fighters into the air that day (Macdonald, 2002: 4–5). NORAD has no forces permanently assigned to it, but the plans developed to implement the agreement permit the rapid assignment of forces by each country for specific missions. While NORAD may have operational control of elements of the US and Canadian air forces from time to time, command itself remains with the country providing the forces. Thus a decision to attack a target in Canadian airspace requires Canadian government authorization before American or Canadian aircraft carry out the order.

A key point about NORAD is that Canada and the United States were able to come to an agreement that contemplates defence of North American airspace on a genuinely binational and shared basis. Each country had sufficient confidence in the other to permit a situation where a military officer of one country might be in operational control of the assigned forces of the other at a critical juncture, as indeed happened on 11 September. Similarly, the general officer in charge of the NORAD command centre would be the person who advised the President and the Prime Minister though the two defence ministries of a threat or attack from air or space and NORAD's assessment of that threat or attack, key factors in the decision on whether and how to respond.

This degree of confidence is extraordinary and probably unique. It is a signal accomplishment. It is the fruition of years of working together ever more closely. It has not only resulted in a strong system for North American air defence but has also greatly expanded Canada's ability to patrol and control its airspace and sea frontier at minimal incremental cost.

Interoperability

Running parallel to and reinforcing the growth of co-operation and institutional arrangements has been a strong push for interoperability. Interoperability is a simple concept. It is the ability to work together in a practical sense, whether by shared radio frequencies, the use of common or compatible equipment and ammunition, or the co-ordination of information systems and operations.

What is new about interoperability is that the pace and impact of military modernization in the US have demanded an increasing level of sophistication in allied interoperability to permit practical co-operation with US forces while also creating the possibility, indeed, the probability, of increased allied dependence on US systems for battlefield awareness and effectiveness. Allied military effectiveness depends to a large extent on interoperability with the US. This is particularly true in the case of the defence of North America, and NORAD can be seen as an example of interoperability. Thus the

Canadian Forces have made interoperability with the US a high priority. As the Chief of the Canadian Defence Staff noted in his *Annual Report* for 2002, 'Maintaining interoperability is the key to the future relevance of the CF' (Henault, 2002: iii, 14, 26).

The Canadian navy is an excellent example of the power of interoperability. When its new frigates were built, they were designed to permit full interoperability with the US Navy. This was necessary for combined anti-submarine operations, one of the frigates' prime missions. But few probably foresaw where this would lead. Now these ships are fully capable of sailing and do sail as an integral part of US fleets if appropriate and agreed. This degree of interoperability has greatly magnified the frigates' ability to work with the US to protect the coast of North America. It has also enabled Canada to make a real contribution to US and allied naval operations abroad.

This ability is threatened by the inability of the Canadian Forces to recruit, train, and retain crews for its ships. The coming end of the useful life of the few fleet supply ships also threatens it. There appears to be no funding to replace those ships. Their absence will turn the Canadian navy into a coastal fleet and make it dependent on the US for support in blue-water operations.

Interoperability is also important for the Canadian Forces because of their lack of resources (Henault, 2002: 26; Middlemiss, 2002: 9–10). Interoperability offers an economical and efficient way to maintain military capability because others have often done much of the necessary research and development (although, in the case of Canada, some of this development may have been done in Canada through the Joint Defence Production Sharing Arrangements). Nevertheless, interoperability is not cheap, requiring constant investments in upgrading and training. Interoperability can be seen as a form of technology transfer.

In short, the United States and Canada over the last 60 some years developed a highly structured and rich bilateral defence relationship that has gradually been moving towards greater integration of defence effort. This trend was most pronounced in air defence, was incremental, and was a response to the evolution of threats to the security of North America. As the threats became more lethal and the time available to counter them shrank, effective co-operation demanded faster response times and more detailed planning, which in turn required more intense co-operation to the point of integration of effort, as in NORAD.

By 2001, this level of co-operation was beginning to be threatened by the lack of priority of funding that the government of Canada attaches to its defence program. It was also threatened by a shift in US focus. Until the advent of surveillance satellites, the US depended on ground-based radar systems for warning, assessment, and tracking of objects in the atmosphere and space. Many of these radars were in Canada. Indeed, the US and Canada built entire radar systems, such as the Pine Tree line, the Distant Early Warning line and the North Warning System. Shifting to space-based systems ended this dependency on Canadian territory. Similarly, as long as the primary threat was bombers, access to Canadian air facilities and airspace was critical so that fighters could be moved forward and operate in the Far North. Once the threat moved from bombers to missiles, this was no longer true, and the US focus shifted to missile defence, a policy that Canada did not support. In short, Canadian territory and defence cooperation mattered less to the US in light of changed US capabilities and the new threat perception. This situation tended to reduce the intensity of the bilateral military relationship as the US focus moved elsewhere.

Thus, in 2001, the US and Canada were working together closely in the defence of North America, but the policies and practices of both countries were diverging and held the prospect of diminishing the operational importance of their long-standing alliance to defend North America. This is where things stood before the terrorist attacks of 11 September 2001.

EFFECTS OF 11 SEPTEMBER: A NEW THREAT

After 11 September the situation changed. The threat to North America looked different and more complex. Canadian geography mattered again to the defence of the US. So did Canadian co-operation.

This perception of a new menace to North America began before 11 September. It derived in large part from the Year 2000 threat to computer systems. That threat (and the enormous effort to counter it) led to the realization that the US and Canada shared North America in a newly understood way: shared infrastructure ranging from oil and gas lines, electric power grids, rail and air transportation networks, financial services, and telecommunications networks. This realization generated in turn the idea of 'critical infrastructure' and an appreciation of its vulnerability, a new variant on the 'single theatre' view of North American defence.

One needed to look no further than the 1998 ice storm in eastern Canada to observe the effects of a major power failure, an example of both the interconnectedness of North American critical infrastructure and its vulnerability. The Canadian Forces were used to respond to that disaster (with some support from the US) and that experience informed Canada's preparations for Y2K—the military was put in charge of contingency planning for that event. Both countries had also begun to think about and to prepare for cyber attacks on North American critical infrastructure, and the Y2K experience reinforced that thinking by underscoring the vulnerabilities of networked systems as well as their immense reach and scope.

The 11 September 2001 terrorist attacks in the United States, while not so much directed at critical US infrastructure as against the World Trade Center and the Pentagon as symbolic targets, nevertheless affected that infrastructure because they weakened confidence in the air travel system and increased the costs of operating that system permanently. Indeed, the new, permanent costs have extended to the entire management of the US–Canadian border. The apparently unrelated anthrax mailings had similar effects on the US postal system.

More generally, the nature of US–Canada trade makes it vulnerable to disruption beyond the effects of shared infrastructure. This is true because a large part of that trade is in intermediate goods transported on a just-in-time basis. Border delays can become extremely costly very quickly. General Motors estimates that each minute of delay at the border costs it $1 million Canadian (Sands, 2002: 3). Or, to put it another way, the border itself should now be seen as shared, critical infrastructure.

Most importantly, however, these attacks pointed out the vulnerabilities of North America's critical infrastructure to small, terrorist attacks. The attacks also led the US and Canada to view the vulnerabilities of the North American infrastructure in a new way—as subject to attacks originating within the US or Canada with little or no warning—and demanded new thinking and new planning on how that infrastructure should now be defended.

Finally, by bringing home the notion of North American vulnerability to terrorist attack, these events caused both countries to consider the possible range of weapons available to terrorists and the potential impact of such attacks, particularly those involving weapons of mass destruction. Even if the target was in the United States, there was a good possibility that such an attack would affect Canada. One need only think of a WMD attack on Detroit, Chicago, or Seattle to realize that such an event might well affect more Canadians than Americans. In the words of the Council for Canadian Security in the 21st Century's *The Peoples' Defence Review*, 'Attacks on the infrastructure systems in the United States, especially from weapons of mass destruction, will also be, in effect, attacks on Canada. The effects will be devastating to our economy' (CCS21, 2002). This threat is not fully appreciated in Canada, as Marcus Gee noted in the *Globe and Mail* on 15 November 2002: 'And yet, listening to most government leaders, you can't avoid the sense they think this is someone else's fight . . . No Canadian leader has made it clear to the public why this is our fight too' (Gee, 2002). Indeed, some ministers have been dismissive (Van Rassel, 2002: 1). But Canadians cannot escape the fact of shared infrastructure with or of proximity to the United States.

The second lesson of the 11 September attacks was that this vulnerability once again made Canadian geography important to US security interests, and it made US geography important to Canadian defence as well. North America is a single theatre when it comes to defence against terrorism. This reality makes US–Canadian co-operation important: neither country can fully secure itself against terrorist attacks in North America independently.

A third lesson of 11 September is the speed of events. The creation of NORAD was in response to the very limited time available to react to attacks from the air and then, in addition, from space. Now, terrorists can strike with even less warning because there is no trajectory to track. Although it may take terrorists months or years to plan an attack, if that plan is not detected in advance with some precision, the actual event comes without any warning in a practical sense. In fact, it is possible that an attack could occur whose effects would only be detected later—the use of a biological weapon, for example. Since such an attack affecting both countries could take place in either country, both countries need a highly developed system of immediate, co-operative, and co-ordinated response such as an expanded NORAD.

ROLE OF THE MILITARY IN DEFENDING AGAINST TERRORISM IN NORTH AMERICA

The role of the military in protecting North America from terrorism is secondary but important. US and Canadian planning and attention have properly been focused on law enforcement, intelligence, and first response. But there is an important military aspect. The simplest example of the military role in protecting North America from terrorism is both countries' use of NORAD on 11 September as the attacks were in progress and afterwards. We used NORAD to secure North American airspace immediately. The new aspect of the 11 September attack was that it originated within North American airspace. Until then, the US and Canada had planned for attacks originating from beyond the continental perimeter (even if very close to it in the case of cruise missiles, for example). The fact that attacks could come from within North America not only vastly shortened warning and response times, but also made the availability and use of both countries' civilian air navigation and control radar systems essential to NORAD's ability to secure and defend internal North American airspace. Fortunately, both countries had already made provision for the availability of that data in the context of countering narcotics smuggling by air. But the key element here is that this information is not available to NORAD via satellite systems. Each country is dependent on the other for it.

The military has a broader role in the defence against terrorism, however. It is that of assistance to civil governments. This is the principal reason why US Northern Command (NORTHCOM) was created.

US NORTHERN COMMAND AND EXPANDED PLANNING FOR NORTH AMERICAN DEFENCE

The Commander of NORTHCOM has a presidential mandate to direct, plan, and conduct defence and civil military support operations within the United States. He assumes the continental defence planning responsibilities formerly exercised by Joint Forces Command. It is obvious that there must be a close relationship between NORTHCOM and NORAD in view of NORAD's continental aerospace defence mission. This is why the President appointed the US officer who is Commander of NORAD to be Commander of NORTHCOM. Before that, the Commander of US Space Command had also been the Commander of NORAD, but the President also combined Space Command with US Strategic Command.

Before 11 September the two countries' planning for air defence had been done at NORAD, and representatives of both countries at Joint Forces Command in Norfolk, Virginia, had done the planning for land and sea. This bifurcated process was long and a bit desultory. It could be argued that the land and sea planning suffered from a lack of priority and resources. With the US decision to create NORTHCOM and to combine those responsibilities with those of the Commander of NORAD, a new opportunity arose to strengthen and improve existing planning, and ultimately, capabilities for North American defence: they could be combined at NORAD.

As noted earlier, both countries' experience with NORAD has been very successful. NORAD could easily be seen and was seen as a model for expanded US–Canadian military co-operation in the defence of North America. Thus, when the idea of NORTHCOM began to emerge, members of the US section of the PJBD suggested informally in October 2001 that NORAD be expanded to include land and sea forces and that North American defence planning be centralized at NORAD. An additional reason for the idea that NORAD itself should be expanded was that the lack of warning time associated with the terrorist threat suggested the need for the kind of integration of effort prevailing at NORAD for air defence.

The two countries began discussions on how to strengthen North American defence shortly thereafter. On 5 December 2002, they agreed to combine and strengthen existing planning and related activities for North American defence and to do this at NORAD under the direction of the Deputy Commander of NORAD, a Canadian general officer, who would operate under the authority of the Commander of NORAD (US Embassy, 2002; DND, 2002d; DND, 2002e). Canada did not agree to a formal expansion of NORAD itself, and the US did not insist, anticipating that the logic of the strengthened planning arrangements would probably lead to the expansion of NORAD in the end. In any event, from the US perspective, it was the improved joint planning that mattered most—NORAD would be strengthened by the centralization of this planning. The key point here is that while it may be possible for the US to plan and prepare for natural and terrorist disasters in North America without Canadian help, that planning would be far more efficient and effective with Canadian assistance because those disasters potentially affect both countries and could require co-operation or joint action of some kind.

There is plenty of precedent for such co-operation in the case of natural disasters. For example, the US provided heavy airlift support to the Canadian Forces immediately after the 1998 ice storm. Dealing with disasters can make great demands on military resources. Canada deployed about 14,000 Canadian troops to Winnipeg during the last serious flood there. The US doubts that Canada now has sufficient military capacity to respond adequately to at least some potential major disasters, natural or otherwise. Whether this is true and to what extent will be revealed in the new continental defence planning process because that work not only will seek to identify possible problems but also will try to develop plans to cope with them, including identification of US and Canadian resources (or the lack of them) thought to be needed for specific contingencies.

In sum, by the end of 2002 the US and Canada were creating novel institutional arrangements to support a new level of integration of effort in the area of planning for North American defence. These plans probably will lead to new requirements for US and Canadian forces. Geography had again become important, and Canadian information and military resources were important to the defence of North America.

It was far from certain, however, that the needed Canadian resources would be available or that the government of Canada appreciated the possibility of such requirements. From an American perspective, it was also not clear that the Canadian government shared the US perception of the threat presented by terrorism. For example, Canada now lacks the heavy airlift capacity a major Canadian disaster may require and apparently has no plans to acquire it. It is not prudent to plan on last-minute rentals of aircraft in such situations because they may not be available, or the lessor might well be unwilling to allow the equipment to be used in a WMD disaster area for reasons of insurance or contamination. Similarly, the US military might not have the necessary equipment available immediately.

CANADIAN DEFENCE CAPABILITY AFFECTS
THE UNITED STATES

Canada's management of its national security and of its military forces affects the interests of the United States. This is true in the first instance because of proximity. What happens in Canada can affect America. This was true during World War II. It was less true after the US began to rely heavily on satellites for warning and assessment. Geography began to regain importance because of drug interdiction efforts. This importance increased as both countries began to understand the vulnerabilities presented by their shared critical infrastructure. But it took 11 September to refocus the US on the importance of Canadian geography to US security. Defence no longer began at the continental perimeter. Canadian law enforcement, intelligence, and military capabilities to manage that threat within Canada and to work with the US to counter it became very important.

Canadian co-operation on improving border security was immediate. In addition, Canada took important steps to strengthen its legal regime to manage issues related to terrorism. These actions were noted and well received in the United States. Similar attention has not been paid to strengthening Canadian military capabilities to deal with terrorism in North America. This, too, has been noted in the United States.

DECLINE OF CANADIAN DEFENCE CAPABILITIES

In recent years, the Canadian Forces have been a low priority for the government of Canada. The defence budget has been too small to sustain basic capabilities, and no serious thought has been given to increased military spending (Sands, 2002: 1). This neglect of Canadian military capability has had several effects. First, the situation in the Canadian Forces is disastrous. Second, the government of Canada's neglect of its military is undermining the US–Canada defence relationship. The armed forces lack the ability to offer the degree of co-operation with the US in North America that the current terrorist threat demands.

Third, Canada's ability to act militarily abroad without US logistical support is extremely limited, if it exists at all. This reduces Canada's ability to contribute to international military activities nearly to the point of symbolism, thereby weakening international institutions and multilateral activities. This undercuts Canadian foreign policy. Indeed, the linkage between stated Canadian foreign and defence policy seems to be very weak. The Department of Foreign Affairs and International Trade apparently has little interest or experience in dealing with military issues and policy other than arms control, and the relationship between that ministry and National Defence is not good (King, 2002).

The Situation of the Forces
The disastrous financial situation the Canadian Forces face is beyond dispute. It has recently been laid out in exhaustive detail in numerous studies, including reports by the Senate Standing Committee on

National Security and Defence, the House of Commons Standing Committee on National Defence and Veterans Affairs, the Centre for Military and Strategic Studies at the University of Calgary, the Council for Canadian Security in the 21st Century, the Conference of Defence Associations, the Center for the Study of the Presidency in Washington, and the Center for Strategic and International Studies in Washington. The Chief of the Defence Staff himself put the matter clearly in his *Annual Report* for 2001–2 when he stated, 'the *status quo* is not sustainable' (Henault, 2002: ii). The conclusions of these studies are that the Canadian Forces cannot meet the missions assigned in the *1994 Defence White Paper*. Those missions are, in summarized form: combat-capable forces able to protect Canada, to co-operate with the US in the defence of North America, and to contribute to international security.

Key findings of one or more of these studies include the following. Between 1993 and 1998 the Canadian defence budget fell by 23 per cent and the Department of National Defence's purchasing power by 30 per cent (SCONDVA, 2002: ch. 2, 2). Canadian defence spending amounts to 1.1 per cent of GDP (DND, 2002b: 10). The number of uniformed personnel has dropped from 87,000 in 1989–90 to somewhere between 50,000 and 55,000 today (ibid., 18, 16; Ferguson et al., 2001: 19; SSCNSD , 2002: 85). The requirements of the 1994 White Paper on defence cannot be met and the government policies stated in that paper cannot be sustained (SCONDVA, 2002: ch. 2, 2-3; Bland, 2002). There has been a significant deterioration in the Forces' equipment, and the capital account (the picture of the Forces' future) requires an immediate infusion of $4 billion (SCONDVA, 2002). The Forces face serious recruiting, retention, and training problems (SCONSAD, 2002: 82–3; Hénault, 2002: ii). Canada cannot now field, move, supply, or sustain even a small force abroad (Kenny, 2002). Without assistance, it is doubtful that the Forces have the capability to meet serious natural disaster and WMD challenges in Canada (Monchuk, 2002), including keeping order in large population centres during emergencies. This situation will be very difficult and expensive to recover from. Some of the deficits in trained personnel not only affect readiness now but also will take years to correct.

There seems little prospect for serious improvement while the present government is in office. The Prime Minister initially dismissed the notion of more funds for defence ('everybody would like us to spend more money') while finding $101 million in the defence budget for executive jets for his and the cabinet's use (Palmer, 2002). The 1 October 2002 Throne Speech contained nothing other than the promise of further study in the indefinite future. Although the Minister of Defence called for more defence funds on 25 October 2002 in his first major speech as minister, the government's response to the recommendations of the Standing Committee on National Defence and Veterans Affairs submitted on the same day by the same minister repeated the theme of the Throne Speech: study the problem (McCallum, 2002; DND, 2002c). Subsequently, the Minister of Finance acknowledged the problem, and the 2003 budget gave an 800 million dollar annual increase to the military. The Prime Minister said, however, 'It is not our highest priority, however, defence' (Fife and Trickey, 2002). The 2003 increase is probably not enough to maintain existing readiness levels.

Effects on the US–Canada Defence Relationship
From an American perspective, the government of Canada's neglect of its military threatens to diminish the historic US–Canadian defence for several reasons.

First, the less Canadian military there is and the less capability it has, the less military co-operation with the US (and other allies) there can be. This comes at a time when such co-operation looks more important to the US than it used to. The newly invigorated joint planning process to be established at NORAD will, for the first time in many years, bring high-level US attention to the planning and application of both countries' resources to the defence requirements identified in that process. Thus Canada may expect serious, high-level US attention to problems identified and pressure to correct them.

Second is the matter of North American missile defence. Here, although Canadian co-operation is not essential to the security of the United States (no radars or interceptors are needed on its territory), Canada may end up for the first time and by its own choice in the position of electing not to participate with the US in an important aspect of North American and possibly Canadian defence. The Canadian government's unwillingness to decide on participation despite very extensive briefings over a considerable period of time has left an impression with a number of American observers that Canada is not taking American concerns about this aspect of defence seriously and is instead focused on ideological issues associated with it—worrying about crossing bridges years in advance of when it might be necessary. In January 2003 it appeared that Canada was reviewing its position on missile defence, perhaps because the US has decided to deploy an initial system.

Time is running out for Canada on missile defence. The US program is moving forward steadily. The decision to deploy a first-stage system has been announced. It appears that command will be given to NORTHCOM. There can come a time when Canada will have waited too long, when new structures that do not include Canada have been put in place and have solidified. If that time arrives, there will be effects on Canadian interests. NORAD will not have a role in missile defence. This will reduce the importance of NORAD to the US and thus Canadian influence on how North America is defended. Canada would find itself cut off from access to much of the US military space program, including new technology and intelligence. The loss of access to this technology is likely to affect Canadian industry and Canadian jobs. Such a loss is also likely to diminish some important capabilities of the Canadian Forces.

Finally, there is a school of thought in Canada that holds that Canada need not and perhaps should not invest seriously in its own defence because the US must and will defend Canada for its own reasons in the last analysis. This latter point may be true, but if these notions should prevail in Canada, clearly the US would manage North American defence on its own terms and without much consultation with Canada. Most US observers would not welcome such an outcome and doubt that such a policy will prevail.

Canada's Ability To Act Abroad

The state of the Canadian Forces greatly limits Canada's ability to act abroad as a member of international alliances or coalitions. This reduces Canada's foreign policy effectiveness and influence on world affairs. It is no longer among the most important peacekeeping countries. It is barely at the table in NATO. It is unable to deploy even small forces abroad without the logistical assistance of an ally, and even then it cannot sustain them for very long. Senator Colin Kenny, chairman of the Senate's Standing Committee on National Security and Defence, described the situation bluntly: 'Well, given the deterioration of the Canadian military over the past decade, Canada has pretty well walked away from its international military obligations' (Kenny, 2002). For a country that has long stressed the importance of international institutions and multilateralism, this is a self-defeating policy.

THE FUTURE

Canadian defence policy is at a critical juncture. If the current situation continues, Canadian marginalization in North America and internationally will follow inexorably. In North America, it also guarantees more difficult relations with the US because Canada will be seen as pulling back from participation in the defence of the continent at a time when the US sees itself as seriously threatened at home and when Canadian participation in continental defence is valuable. This can only lead to a more unilateral US defence posture. Canadians should remember the Roosevelt-King understanding and realize that current Canadian defence policy is weakening it and the relationship based upon it.

Such a policy also threatens the US–Canada special relationship. The unique element of that relationship is defence. The rest—trade, proximity, and family and friends on both sides of the border—are also true for Mexico. US ties to Mexico are rapidly increasing and bilateral Mexican–American trade may one day exceed that with Canada (Cohen, 2002). If the special relationship fades away, the US will more and more see Canada in a narrower context, primarily through the lens of trade, border, and similar issues.

On the other side, over the last year there has been a strong, critical reaction in Canada to existing defence policy and its implications for the future of Canada. This has been noticed in Washington. Many in Washington hope and believe that Canada will be able to strike a new balance among its national priorities, one that preserves and strengthens the Canadian-American partnership in the managing of North America and its defence.

NOTES

1. Van Rassel (2002) quotes Finance Minister Manley: 'I think if we became aware of real threats, or a specific threat . . . . I don't believe that I have any greater threat than the broader threat we all know we live under in a free society.'

REFERENCES

Bland, Doug. 2002. 'Funding Canada's Defence Policy', Council for Canadian Security in the 21st Century. Calgary. Available at: <http://www.ccs21.org/ccspapers/researchpapers.htm>.

Cohen, Andrew. 2002. 'Canadian-American Relations: Does Canada Matter in Washington? Does It Matter If Canada Doesn't Matter', in Norman Hillmer and

Maureen Appel Molot, eds, *Canada Among Nations 2002: A Fading Power*. Toronto: Oxford University Press, 34–48.

Council for Canadian Security in the 21st Century (CCS21). 2002. *The Peoples' Defence Review*. Calgary: University of Calgary.

Department of National Defence (DND). 1994. *1994 Defence White Paper*.

————, Directorate of Western Hemisphere Policy. 2002a. 'Canada–United States Defence Relations'.

————, Finance and Corporate Services. 2002b. *Making Sense out of Dollars 2001–2002*. Apr. Available at: <http://www.dnd.ca/admfincs/financial_docs/msood/intro_e.asp>.

————. 2002c. 'Government to Respond to the Report of the Standing Committee on National Defence and Veterans Affairs', 25 Oct.

————. 2002d. Exchange of Notes (US Note), 5 Dec.

————. 2002e. 'Enhanced Canada–United States Security Co-operation', news room, 9 Dec.

Department of State. 2002. 'Defence Export Controls', press release, 19 June.

Eayrs, James. 1959. *In Defence of Canada*, vol. 2. Toronto: University of Toronto Press.

Fergusson, Jim, Frank Harvey, and Rob Huebert, 2001. *To Secure a Nation: The Case for a New Defence White Paper*. Calgary: Centre for Military and Strategic Studies, University of Calgary.

Fife, Robert, and Mike Trickey, 2002. 'PM Vows to Raise Military Spending', *Ottawa Citizen*, 22 Nov.

Gee, Marcus. 2002. 'When it comes to Osama, Canada doesn't get it', *Globe and Mail*, 15 Nov., A21.

Granatstein, J.L. 2002. 'A Friendly Agreement in Advance: Canada–US Defence Relations Past, Present and Future', *Commentary: The Border Papers*. Toronto: C.D. Howe Institute.

Hénault, R.R. 2002. *At a Crossroads: Annual Report of the Chief of the Defence Staff, 2001–2002*. Ottawa: Department of National Defence.

Kenny, Colin. 2002. 'Imagine If We Had Real Armed Forces', *Globe and Mail*, 13 Nov., A29.

King, David L. 2002. 'We Need a Romanow Commission for Defence and Foreign Policy', *Policy Options* (Apr.): 7–14.

McCallum, John. 2002. 'Speaking Notes, Toronto Board of Trade', Department of National Defence, 25 Oct.

McCarthy, Shawn, and Simon Tuck, 2003. 'Overstretched Military Likely to Get $2.4-Billion', *Globe and Mail*, 8 Feb. (on-line edition).

Macdonald, George, Lt. General, Vice Chief of the Defence Staff. 2002. 'Canada–US Defence Relations, Asymmetric Threats and the US Unified Command Plan', Statement to the Senate Standing Committee on National Security and Defence, 6 May.

Maloney, Sean M. 1997. 'Our Defended Borders: A Short History of the Permanent Joint Board on Defence and the Military Co-operation Committee, 1940 to the Present', *The 200th Meeting of the Canada–United States Permanent Joint Board on Defence*. Ottawa: Canadian Section, PJBD.

Middlemiss, Danford, and Denis Stairs. 2002. 'The Canadian Forces and the Doctrine of Interoperability: The Issues', *Policy Matters* 3, 7 (June): 1–40.

Monchuk, Judy. 2002. 'Military Report Says Canada's Emergency System Can't Cope With Large Disaster', *Ottawa Citizen*, 14 Nov.

Palmer, Randall. 2002. 'Canada PM doubtful on defence spending hikes', *Ottawa Citizen*, 30 May.

Sands, Chris. 2002. 'Canada and the War on Terrorism', *CSIS Canada Focus* 2, 3 (Oct.).

Senate Standing Committee on National Security and Defence (SCONSAD). 2002. *Canadian Security and Preparedness*. Ottawa: Senate.

Standing Committee on National Defence and Veterans Affairs (SCONDVA). 2002. *Facing Our Responsibilities; The State of Readiness of the Canadian Forces, Fourth Report*. Ottawa: House of Commons, 30 May.

US Embassy. 2002. 'US and Canada Sign Bi-National Agreement on Military Planning', press release, 9 Dec.

Van Rassel, Jason. 2002. 'Forces can't fulfill duties, Manley says', *Ottawa Citizen*, 17 Nov.

9

Canada–United States Intelligence Relations and 'Information Sovereignty'

There has been a remarkably pervasive ignorance about the nature and role of intelligence in Canada. This has been not only among the general public and the media, but even in the corridors of government where intelligence plays or should play an important role in understanding the world and making informed judgements. It seems strange that what might be the oldest professional field in government has been poorly understood even in Canada's public sector.

While this ignorance could be condoned during the Cold War when Canada had very little real say in the East-West conflict, it is no longer tenable in the face of the new security environment ushered in by the September 2001 terrorist attacks on New York and Washington. This environment has been described as constituting a 'Revolution in Terrorist Affairs' parallel to and reflective of the same causative factors that have contributed to the so-called 'Revolution in Military Affairs' (Abiew, 2002: 3).

The terrorist or security revolution, if there has been one, stems from a changed threat environment that has been described as 'doubly asymmetric in that it potentially involves both unconventional parties (terrorists) and unconventional means (weapons of mass destruction)' (ibid., 14). It is a threat environment in which intelligence necessarily becomes of central importance because the crucial objective has to be prevention, not merely defensive response.

Such a revolution necessarily requires significant adjustments to Canada's traditional approaches to domestic and international security, including its approaches to intelligence in all its forms. As part of this transformation, it would also be logical to expect changes in traditional approaches to intelligence co-operation with other countries and with multilateral institutions like the United Nations.

Within the galaxy of Canada's international intelligence relationships, it is already clear that no bilateral intelligence links will be more highly affected than the six-decade-old Canada–US intelligence relationship. But it is possible that the implications may be paradoxical. Whereas it was logical for the two countries to have highly integrated intelligence co-operation during the Cold War, when they faced a common external threat, the new security circumstances may require Canada to develop a greater degree of intelligence autonomy from the United States in order to deal with 'borderless' threats that can come from within either country and the neighbouring country may be seen as a threat or cause of a threat to the other (ibid., 29).

This factor, coupled with the changing international role of the United States, is producing an unprecedented intelligence challenge for Canada. It is one in which reliable information and expert understanding about the United States, both domestically and on the international stage, and in a depth never required before, have become a fundamental prerequisite for protecting Canada's future security and enhancing its ability to play a constructive role as a friendly neighbour and independent contributor to global peace and security.

In line with this reasoning, this chapter concludes that we have reached a point where Canada's intelligence policy has to distinguish more clearly between its international and its continental relationships and, as part of that, must deliberately strengthen its 'information sovereignty'.[1]

Arriving at sound intelligence policy and strategy on questions of this magnitude will require a much greater public awareness of intelligence issues than in the past. But this will not come easily to a country that remains one of the only countries with an international role not to have held a post-Cold War public review of foreign intelligence policy. A full review and public debate about the role of intelligence in Canada's future security, defence, and international relations, beginning with its place in co-operating and coping with the 'Colossus', is now urgent in the face of the new international and domestic security environment.

INFORMATION SOVEREIGNTY AND INTELLIGENCE

Canada has extensive, long-standing, and valuable international intelligence relationships, both bilateral and multilateral. They cover the traditionally distinct but increasingly convergent subfields of foreign, military, security, criminal, and enforcement intelligence. Of these, none has been of greater importance than the range of intelligence relationships with the United States. And no subfield of the intelligence relationship with the Americans is closer, amounting to near-integration, than the field of bilateral co-operation on foreign intelligence.

In the post-11 September world, that relationship has taken on increased importance and complexity because of the special importance of intelligence in a global war against state-sponsored and extremist terrorism. Adapting that relationship from its Cold War contours to meet the needs and expectations of an embattled, impatient, and insecure neighbour has become a major contemporary challenge for Canada, with implications across the whole spectrum of Canada's foreign relations.

Similarly, American pressure on Canada to take part in a 'perimeter defence' or otherwise to tighten continental security, using the leverage of continued smooth cross-border access to the US economy, has opened the door to even deeper co-operation than in the past in sharing information and databases. It is also forcing consideration of proposals for increased harmonization and near-integration in many areas of security, regulatory affairs, and economic administration that heretofore were entirely a matter of domestic concern. The bilateral intelligence relationship, with over a half-century of near-integration, offers useful lessons and insights for these possible new arenas of increased integration with the United States.

At the same time, changing circumstances pose an important paradox: whereas integration in foreign intelligence amounting to dependence made practical sense in the Cold War, when Canada was far less integrated with the United States in other respects, that degree of intimate intelligence relationship may need to be attenuated in the international environment Canada now faces. Seeking a greater degree of 'information sovereignty' may be an essential objective for Canada as a precondition for increased practical integration in other arenas of the bilateral relationship. Without the necessary degree of information sovereignty, ever-increasing economic, security, and administrative integration is more likely to pose all the risks of dependency and accelerate eventual complete absorption.

Information sovereignty as used here means a country's governors, legislators, and people having the autonomous capacity to acquire and have access to the information and expert knowledge needed to make sound and independent decisions in all areas of its interests. Information sovereignty at the international level is compatible with a close continuing bilateral intelligence relationship with the United States, but it is not compatible with an abject degree of dependence on that relationship. It is a matter of degree, not a question of principle. Past experience has shown that a high degree of integration does not require complete abdication of our ability independently to know and understand the world. However, it may have inhibited our ability to know and understand the United States adequately.

In an age where 'information warfare' and 'total information dominance' have strategic and tactical currency, 'made in Canada' information for decision-making and judgement, the quintessence of the intelligence function, is more necessary for Canada than ever before, and it is essential for the sound management of the increasingly integrated Canada–US relationship. Living with 'the Colossus' starts with knowing it much better, and in much greater depth.

THE 'CULTURE' OF INTELLIGENCE IN CANADA

If, in the vernacular of Sherlock Holmes, there has been an important 'dog not barking' in the study of Canada's international relations, it is probably what might be called the intelligence dog. Because the dog is not heard or heard about, it is mainly invisible in the media, in international relations research, and in Canada's schools of international studies. It is not surprising, consequently, in Canada's case at least, that until recently it has played no role whatsoever in public discussion of foreign, defence, and security policy.

Indeed, other than peripherally in the internal security context of the Macdonald Royal Commission in the 1970s (Canada, 1980), the government of Canada has never yet initiated a public debate about foreign intelligence in any context. Several parliamentary committees have, on the other hand, made serious efforts to address this blind spot, including, several years ago, the Subcommittee on National Security of the Standing Committee on Justice and Human Rights. More recently, the House of Commons Standing Committee on Foreign Affairs and International Trade has carried out hearings and made relevant and important recommendations.[2] The Standing Senate Committee on National Security and Defence has also taken an active interest in intelligence issues under the leadership of Senator Colin Kenny.[3] While these efforts have yet to ignite broader parliamentary or public interest and do not appear to have had the support of the government, the efforts of the parliamentarians is a sound basis for unleashing the needed public debate about Canada's future intelligence policy and co-operative relationship with the United States.

From a security point of view, all blind spots are dangerous. Canada's long-standing intelligence blind spot is important to understand because it may offer insight into our foreign relations 'culture', i.e., our ways of thinking (or not thinking) about the art and science of the conduct of international affairs. It is possible that Canadian preferences and habits of international altruism have inhibited adequate understanding of and therefore institutional reflection on our national intelligence needs because of their somewhat shady and unpalatable aura. If so, this is a weakness that needs to be addressed in the new security environment.

Overcoming our historical national inhibition against intelligence will begin by clear-sighted recognition that, in both offensive and defensive senses, intelligence has long had direct and sometimes pivotal effects on international relations. Consider, for example, Stalin's failure to heed accurate intelligence about German military plans leading to Operation Barbarossa in 1941 or, in June 1944, Hitler's initial acceptance of intelligence deception about 'the real D-Day' landings being targeted at the Pas de Calais. Closer to home, Canadians were jolted, reluctantly, into a temporary consciousness of intelligence issues with the defection of Igor Gouzenko in 1947, a turning point of the Cold War but not one of Canada's finest security hours. The foreign policy decision-makers, clearly unfamiliar or uncomfortable with the world of intelligence, and reflecting a cultural value system that continues to hound effective intelligence policy, looked eagerly for ways to avoid the potential embarrassment with Russia of allowing Gouzenko's defection.

In all three cases and innumerable others, intelligence shaped and will continue to shape international outcomes, for better and worse. It is an issue of governance that Canada can no longer afford to keep mute in a closet.

Beyond the unmistakable significance of intelligence in international relations, it is also important to address this Canadian blind spot because intelligence and intelligence relationships (a.k.a. networks) are increasingly relevant in a world experiencing an 'Information Revolution'. Information and knowledge are drivers of innovation and competitive advantage. Coupled with the fact that information networks spanning the world are essential to defend countries against globalized networks of international crime, drugs, disease, and terror, this means that intelligence and intelligence relationships are now more important than ever before for Canada.

SECRECY AND INTELLIGENCE

A full analysis of the reasons behind the Canadian intelligence blind spot also requires acknowledgement of the fact that study and informed debate about intelligence matters are made difficult by the need for high levels of secrecy. The justification for secrecy in intelligence is based on the need, in the first place, of protecting the sensitive information Canada possesses. It is less well understood that there is also a need for secrecy to protect against allowing adversaries to know what Canada does not know, or 'knows wrong'.

The most important explanation, however, is not the protection of information or the lack thereof, but rather the need to protect the 'sources and methods' from which or by which the information was provided. This is the cornerstone or stock-in-trade of effective foreign and domestic intelligence services of any description and it is the basis for maintaining effective international intelligence relationships. It follows that where a country is in a highly dependent information relationship with another country, protecting the sources and methods underlying intelligence received from that other country is even more important than protecting the receiving country's own secret information. Any inability or perception of inability to protect secrets will quickly guarantee loss of friendly sources.

Canada's high (some would say gross) dependence on American sources for information requires that secrecy and security of intelligence be strictly maintained by the Canadian intelligence services even beyond standards otherwise necessary for Canadian-sourced information. Canada's record in protecting information entrusted to it appears to be remarkably good, especially in contrast with the notorious 'leakiness' of American intelligence (often as a result of congressional lapses). But maintaining a spotless record for secrecy comes at a high price because it has a chilling effect on scholarship and public understanding of the intelligence function. Indeed, the 'need to know' principle, which severely (and rightly) restricts access to intelligence within government, also has the effect of chilling necessary information flows within government. The only way around this secrecy dilemma is to distinguish better between intelligence materials that are truly sensitive and need protection and intelligence materials that are not. Just because something is intelligence does not mean it has to be considered automatically secret.

It is sometimes suggested that governments and intelligence services use the secrecy argument to protect themselves from scrutiny and criticism and do so far beyond its real legitimacy. That is probably occasionally true, but in my experience in intelligence analysis it is not generally true. Indeed, for many in the intelligence services, the need for secrecy poses significant and frustrating impediments to optimal effectiveness. For example, natural links among analytical experts should include direct links with counterparts in that other major depository of scarce Canadian expertise about other countries, Canada's universities. Efforts have been made by the intelligence services in recent years to expand links with the universities, including by providing financial support to the Canadian Association for Security and Intelligence Studies, which plays an important role in bringing practitioners and academics together. However, the undeniable need for a high degree of intelligence secrecy will always pose impediments if not barriers to such otherwise highly desirable links.[4]

Consequently, in the interests of secrecy, sensitive intelligence records are not revealed to the public for decades after the events, if ever, leaving scholars, the information media, and even policy advisers with inadequate information to evaluate the nature and value of international intelligence and intelligence relationships. Is it any wonder, therefore, that there is so little public knowledge or debate about intelligence in Canada?

While perhaps understandable, this state of public awareness is no longer acceptable if Canada's security and other interests are to be protected in a dangerous world. Thus, it is suggested that there is clearly a need to overcome these obstacles and increase public awareness and interest in the field of intelligence. A prime area where this is desirable is with regard to the Canada–US intelligence relationship.

In the interests of increasing public awareness and debate about intelligence in Canada, the following sections will discuss briefly the meaning of 'intelligence' and 'intelligence relationships'. The focus will then turn on the Canada–US intelligence relationship, drawing lessons from the past and suggesting directions for the future in a rapidly integrating continental environment and, some fear, a rapidly disintegrating security environment.

UNDERSTANDING INTELLIGENCE AND INTELLIGENCE
RELATIONSHIPS

Intelligence, in its broadest definition, is the reliable knowledge required to make good decisions. The product called 'intelligence' is generated by a four-step process sometimes called 'the intelligence cycle'—tasking, collection, analysis, and dissemination. There are as many types of intelligence product as there are distinct sectors needing reliable information to make good decisions. So, to mention the main ones, there are foreign intelligence, security intelligence, military intelligence, criminal intelligence, immigration intelligence, transport intelligence, and so on.

In Canada's federal government, these functions are organized around 11 key departments or agencies:

1. The Privy Council Office (PCO), which has two units (cabinet secretariat and policy co-ordination plus analysis and assessment) that report to the Co-ordinator for Security and Intelligence, who is the senior adviser to the Prime Minister on security and intelligence issues and who provides co-ordination for the work of the intelligence community as a whole. He or she also has policy responsibility for the Communications Security Establishment (CSE). The PM traditionally carries overall responsibility for security and intelligence and has authority over appointments as well as the organization and priorities of government.

2. The Department of the Solicitor General, which has cabinet-level and supervisory responsibility for CSIS and the RCMP.
3. The Department of Foreign Affairs and International Trade (DFAIT).
4. The Department of National Defence (DND), which has administrative responsibility for CSE and also houses the Office for Critical Infrastructure Protection and Emergency Preparedness (OCIPEP).
5. The Department of Justice.
6. The Canadian Security Intelligence Service (CSIS).
7. The CSE, which provides Signals Intelligence and protects electronic information.
8. The Royal Canadian Mounted Police.
9. The Department of Transport.
10. The Department of Citizenship and Immigration.
11. The Canada Customs and Revenue Agency.

In the United States federal government, until the recent establishment of the Department of Homeland Security, 13 departments and agencies carried intelligence responsibilities. Major departments and agencies now include:

1. The Central Intelligence Agency (CIA), which has responsibility for foreign intelligence collection and analysis and is headed by the Director of Central Intelligence, who also has nominal responsibility for overall intelligence co-ordination in the US government but whose real clout varies from one administration to another;
2. The Department of Defence (DOD), whose Secretary has eventual responsibility for several intelligence agencies and by far the largest budget for intelligence purposes because some of the agencies are high-tech and high-cost (e.g., satellites for imagery surveillance);
3. The National Security Agency (NSA), which is responsible for communications intelligence and protection.
4. The State Department (equivalent to the diplomatic side of DFAIT).
5. The Department of Commerce (equivalent to the trade side of DFAIT).

6. The Federal Bureau of Investigation (FBI), which parallels the RCMP's federal policing responsibilities but has additional responsibility for counter-espionage and counterterrorism within the United States (parallel to the role of CSIS in Canada).

7. The new Department of Homeland Security established by President Bush as a response to the 11 September attacks, which entails the amalgamation and integration of over 170,000 employees and several agencies, including FEMA (emergency measures), Secret Service, Coast Guard, Immigration and Naturalization Service, Customs Service, Border Patrol, Transportation Safety Agency, the National Information Protection Centre, certain energy departments and laboratories, the Animal and Plant Inspection Service, and the Federal Protective Service (Abiew, 2002: 12).

The central purpose of the intelligence function in government is to acquire information needed for good governance and to validate, distill, and analyze it to produce *reliable knowledge.* The world is awash in data and information, as well as disinformation, and the job of modern intelligence services is to turn all the information 'noise' into coherent patterns and reasonably reliable insight and understanding (i.e., knowledge) about the international milieu and the specific settings in which a country has interests. This is a not very mysterious function and certainly has little to do with James Bond images. But it has become more important than ever in today's world.

It is significant to note that this broad definition encompasses a good deal of the raison d'être of diplomacy, which also generates information and insight for decision-makers. Indeed, in this respect, the role of diplomacy does overlap with the role of intelligence in government and this explains to a large extent the traditional discomfort among Canada's foreign policy practitioners with the intelligence functions as they emerged during and after World War II.

Nowhere is this discomfort more noticeable than when an intelligence analytical function is housed, as it was in Canada's DFAIT until 1993 and still is in the US State Department, within the foreign ministry's walls. Inevitably, despite significantly differing roles and purposes, this can create intra-organizational competition between foreign policy advisers and intelligence analysts. At its best, this competition is seen as constructive by decision-makers because it reduces their dependence on single analytical perspectives. At its worst, it leaves a minister with diametrically opposed analyses and confusion.

Two professional groups carry out seemingly overlapping but in reality distinct functions because their respective functions depend on information, but from different points of view: foreign policy analysts have the role of devising, promoting, and implementing foreign policy, while intelligence analysts are in the business exclusively of generating objective information and knowledge without any policy bias. Policy responsibility can skew interpretations of the facts because of the natural human tendency to see what you want to see. Because of this, a fundamental ground rule of intelligence in the Anglo-American model on which Canadian intelligence has been based is that intelligence analysis and assessment must stand at arm's length from policy-making if it is to be of any value. It seeks to be objective, while policy must be subjective.

If intelligence is concerned at its most basic level with producing (and protecting) reliable information for sound decision-making, why is it that it has such a marked 'James Bond' image in the popular imagination? This is because the function of intelligence is divided between two basic subfunctions—operations and analysis. Operations entail the collection of information, especially information an adversary does not want you to have—i.e., secret information. This sometimes requires covert activities. This is where the Bond image has some semblance with reality since some foreign intelligence services extend the skills and mindset necessary to acquire secret information to the conduct of 'covert operations', which have little or nothing to do with gathering information. At that point, the word 'intelligence' becomes a catch-all term for any type of secret and sometimes illegal activity carried out under the authority of the state—hence, the racy and sometimes unsavoury reputation of the function.

While intelligence can be defined by the subcategories or fields of subject matter covered, as reflected in the lists above (e.g., defence, security, etc.), there can be confusion because intelligence is also often categorized by the *means or processes* by which it is generated. There are a number of types of intelligence collection. These are often referred to by their acronyms—e.g., HUMINT (Human Intelligence) is information collected through and from individuals or agents; SIGINT (Signals Intelligence) is information collected from interception of communications; IMINT (Imagery Intelligence) is information from aerial/satellite photography and sensing; and OSSINT (Open Source Intelligence) is information that comes from open or 'grey', not secret, sources.

The traditional companion to intelligence collection is analysis. This also is a broad term with several layers of distinct meaning, from the relatively mechanical roles of collating and distilling concrete data and information and classifying and managing it so that it can be readily accessed, to the expertise required to validate its veracity, translate it, and interpret its implications, and eventually to the more speculative and imaginative analytical roles of assessing its portent and estimating warnings and forecasts about potential future developments.

The other two dimensions of the intelligence cycle, tasking and dissemination, have tended to receive too little attention even within the intelligence profession. Tasking involves the definition of the needs and interests of users while dissemination is the deceptively simple but actually very complex function of distributing intelligence production to users. Both these functions have become vastly more important and challenging in the electronic age in which not only the volume but the speed of information flows have eclipsed anything imaginable in the days of typewriters and telexes and in which, using the memorable insight of Marshal MacLuhan, 'the medium is the message'.

Because of these differentiations and nuances, the seemingly neat bifurcation of intelligence into collection and analysis is not so neat in practice. Indeed, there are few universally accepted definitions, and two of Canada's chief international partners do not even share common definitions of the word 'intelligence'. The British, whose intelligence ideas strongly influenced Canada's, see intelligence as principally about the collection and protection of secret information. The Americans, on the other hand, consider that they suffered Pearl Harbor not for want of information but for failure of analysis. They interpret intelligence very strictly as 'analyzed information'. Until data and 'raw' information have been analyzed by properly qualified Americans, they are not considered to merit the term of 'finished' intelligence.

Even within a single government, the term 'intelligence' will have differing meanings between one organization and another because of the differing uses to which intelligence is put, with resulting important practical and legal differences between, for example, foreign, security, and criminal intelligence.

These distinctions are not mere semantics. They have implications for international intelligence relationships because definitions drive organizations and expectations in every country. In the case of Canada's dealings with the United States, the overwhelming magnitude of US intelligence institutions and capacity means that Canada generally adapts to American definitions and their organizational implications when dealing with that bilateral relationship, with the three major exceptions that, in contrast to the United States, Canada has a capacity and experience of reasonably effective co-ordination of its overall intelligence effort, almost no legislative oversight, and very limited media scrutiny.

Because the US intelligence structure has chronically been characterized by a high degree of institutional balkanization, the bilateral intelligence relationship has tended to be carried out predominantly at the service-to-service and subfunction-to-subfunction levels. Therefore, a thorough understanding of the intelligence relationship between the two countries requires looking at each element of the larger picture. For the past 50 years and more, the overall intelligence relationship between the two countries has tended to be the sum of a number of vertical relationships among relatively discrete parts.

But the past can only be a limited guide for the future. With the new focus on terrorism ('Revolution in Terrorist Affairs'), the gradual implementation of 'perimeter security'[5] policies, the creation of the colossal Department of Homeland Security, and the parallel creation of a Northern Command in the US military, Canada faces an unprecedented change in how it will have to go about bilateral intelligence relations with the United States in the years ahead.

WHITHER THE CANADA–US INTELLIGENCE RELATIONSHIP?

Canada's intelligence relationship with the United States has not always been as peaceful and constructive as it was during the Cold War. Along old Ontario Highway 2 bordering the United States on the St Lawrence River, a historical plaque honours the service of Justus Sherwood, a United Empire Loyalist who carried out courageous intelligence activities against the revolting thirteen colonies during the War of Independence. Historians have also recorded that Toronto was a hive of intelligence agents during the American Civil War, with Confederate agents even mounting from Canada an assassination attempt (using, as we would say nowadays, a biological toxin) against the entire cabinet of Abraham Lincoln.

However, for the past half-century, starting hesitantly with World War II and intensifying with the Cold War, Canada's foreign intelligence relationship with the US has become one of unprecedented closeness, amounting, in some areas, to full, not just virtual, integration. One feature of this close relationship has been frequent exchanges of personnel and in-house liaison representation between respective services. Over the years this has resulted in close working relationships, extensive information-sharing, and open analytical exchanges.

From a quantitative point of view, this is far from a relationship of equals. American expenditures on intelligence organizations in the federal government are reportedly in excess of $30 billion. This is probably in the order of 100 times the equivalent expenditure by the Canadian government. (Intelligence expenditures are not made public in either country.)

Qualitatively, the picture is less uneven because Canada brings a number of advantages to the relationship, including its smaller, more flexible, and better co-ordinated structure. Moreover, the most valuable information and knowledge about the world for government decision-makers come not from volumes of data but from seasoned judgement and insight—i.e., estimation and assessment—about the meaning and implications of the data. That type of intelligence comes from rare and talented analysts with expertise nurtured and encouraged within the professional intelligence community over the years. Where Canada has people of this quality in its intelligence services, their value and contribution are seen as extremely important by American counterparts. In addition, Canada's geographical location and its multicultural and linguistic strengths also offer significant value to the United States.

Like the United States, Canada has intelligence relationships with many other countries, but, collectively, what they provide to Canada does not come remotely close to the volume of data and information received from the US relationship. Because of the magnitude of the American intelligence effort and the technological sophistication of its reach, US-provided intelligence data and information is overwhelmingly dominant in the flows used by Canadian intelligence analysts for understanding the world. This is a privileged position for

Canada that many other countries envy. Indeed, no country receives the degree of intelligence co-operation from the United States that Canada enjoys, with the possible exception of the UK.

However, inevitably, this creates a situation of and the associated behaviours of near-dependency in the Canadian intelligence community and government. When the government needs to understand specific international developments, what it receives from the intelligence community is heavily dominated by US-source information. This, unless guarded against, can negatively affect its credibility among Canadian policy readers.

This near-dependency on US-provided intelligence is paralleled by the dominance of US-source reporting in Canadian news organizations, few of which have foreign correspondents. While secret information can be of significant advantage in certain circumstances and can provide an 'information edge' to its users, Canadian intelligence analysts rely as much or more on 'open sources' of information to develop their analysis. Consequently, Canadian news media, which tend to be dominated by US-source news and perspectives, compound the risk of an 'Americanized' Canadian intelligence world view. This risk can easily be exaggerated because Canada and the United States share a host of common interests, values, and perspectives that would justify common world views on the majority of issues affecting the rest of the world. Where the risk is more serious is when Canadian views about Canada's bilateral relationship with the United States are *unwittingly* based on or shaped by American information and perspectives.

On the whole, during the Cold War when intelligence services in both countries concentrated primarily on the Soviet threat, such a high degree of information dependency was not a problem for Canada since Canadian and American interests converged. Moreover, tapping into the US information bank had the added advantage of allowing Canada to see the basis for American policy thinking and strategy. That factor continues to be an advantage to the Canadian government since understanding where the US is 'coming from' is of real value in shaping Canadian foreign policy. However, having access to and allowing oneself to become dependent on information in the control of another country are two different matters. As Canada becomes more highly integrated with the US in other sectors and implements policies to remain on good terms with the American vision of perimeter defence, and where the United States becomes increasingly unilateral in its foreign policy thinking and dealings, an independent flow of information and reliable knowledge becomes vital for Canada.

LESSONS FROM PAST NEAR-INTEGRATION IN INTELLIGENCE CO-OPERATION

To be sure, there are worthwhile lessons relevant to today's broad range of Canada–US bilateral relationship issues that can be learned from the experience of over 50 years of near-integration with the United States in the field of foreign intelligence.

The first and possibly most important lesson is that even very high levels of integration have not removed the capacity for independent judgement and action by Canada. Although American information has been vital to understanding the world, independent analytical capacity in Canada filtered that information and successfully achieved distinct Canadian perspectives about it. It is possible to maintain and even enhance distinctive Canadian interests despite closely embracing 'the Colossus'.

This conclusion mirrors a similar observation by George Hoberg, who, after reviewing research just prior to 11 September, concluded that 'the consequences of continental integration have not been as formidable as widely believed. Canada still retains significant room to manoeuvre, even in areas of policy most affected by growing economic integration' (Hoberg, 2002). This conclusion could probably still be upheld in the wake of intensified bilateral integration since 11 September, provided that the negotiated terms of such arrangements as the Smart Border agreement have left room for a reasonable degree of 'subsidiarity' (i.e., autonomous decision-making) to be exercised by Canada.

A second lesson from past high levels of bilateral co-operation and integration on foreign intelligence matters has been that the Americans, seeing advantage to their interests in maintaining a close foreign intelligence relationship with Canada, generally seem to have taken a long and balanced view. They have not allowed short-term tensions or disagreements, such as over Cuba or during the Vietnam War, to interfere with the maintenance of the relationship. Canada's dependence on intelligence information flows from Washington was not overtly used as a lever to extract concessions or to express policy displeasure. In other words, in a situation of high dependency and near-integration, the Americans were reasonable and often generous partners even when the larger bilateral relationship was under duress. (This is not to say that the Americans have always taken a benign view of criticism from allies. They ended bilateral intelligence co-operation with New Zealand in the 1980s because of displeasure over American nuclear warships being prohibited from entering New Zealand waters.)

A third lesson is that near-integration works in both directions despite the preponderant weight of the US. Working closely with the Americans and developing close working relations and personal trust created an environment in which Canadian information contributions and judgements could influence American thinking along avenues supportive of Canadian perspectives and interests just as much as vice versa. This is not to pretend that a 'Canadianized' American world view can or should be an objective in bilateral intelligence co-operation, but to make the point that, in the spirit of exchange, it is just as possible for one view to influence the other as vice versa.

Near-integration, in other words, is not necessarily threatening to Canadian interests and, on the contrary, may be advantageous to their advancement. Indeed, it could be one of the best ways for Canada to influence and shape American policies to be harmonious with Canadian policies and values.

A fourth lesson, on the negative side of the scale, is that near-integration in intelligence relations with a big and rich neighbour can create a temptation to dependency, leading a country to reduce its investments in autonomous capacity and to 'freeload' on the neighbour. Dependency, where it exists in the intelligence relationship, undermines institutional capacity and organizational morale. If the United States had not been prepared to share its intelligence resources so generously over the past six decades, Canada would have had to invest more in its own intelligence capacity than it has. The need to guard against the temptation to dependency is an important lesson from the near-integration experience in the bilateral intelligence relationship.

An extension of these points, and a fifth lesson, is that the objective in a near-integration situation should be to achieve interdependence between the partners. A one-sided or qualitatively disproportionate flow of benefits in the relationship is undesirable. Constant efforts need to be made where there is a quantitatively unbalanced sharing, as there inevitably will be most of the time with 'the Colossus', to ensure that as much reciprocity and value is provided by Canada as possible. Canada should offer quality in return for the American quantity.

THE FUTURE CANADA–US INTELLIGENCE RELATIONSHIP?

These largely positive lessons from the past bilateral foreign intelligence relationship between Canada and the United States would seem to suggest that near-integration has much to commend it as a bilateral relations strategy. Its downsides, notably the risk of overdependence, can be guarded against, and its advantages, notably the opportunities for synergies and efficiencies, can be used strategically to achieve Canadian objectives better than without near-integration. However, those are lessons from a Cold War context and the question to be addressed now is whether the 'Revolution in Terrorist Affairs' has so changed the situation that these lessons no longer apply. Does the bilateral intelligence relationship with the United States need to be changed to some other more autonomous approach, or does the policy of the past six decades continue to meet Canada's intelligence needs in today's changing international and continental environments?

This distinction between the international and continental contexts is an increasingly necessary and important conceptual distinction in addressing questions of relations with the United States. Perhaps it needs to be made more explicit in Canadian thinking about foreign relations. Perhaps we have to recognize more overtly that we now have a 'perimeter foreign policy' with a need for special concepts and organizational adjustments for dealing with the emerging continental realities and challenges. This trend, of course, has already been implicit in Canada's organization for and handling of the US relationship, with DFAIT and its minister having become essentially the 'ministry of offshore (i.e., international) foreign affairs' and the Privy Council Office and the Prime Minister or his delegate having become the de facto 'ministry of continental affairs'.

This kind of bifurcated reality is not new to the bilateral intelligence relationship. Continentalism has been implicit in Canada's defence, security, and foreign intelligence strategies for many years. The word 'foreign' as used in the term 'foreign intelligence' has not included and does not extend to coverage of our next-door neighbour because of a quite rigid adherence, presumably on both sides of the border, to the principle of 'friend on friend'—i.e., the trust-building principle whereby intelligence allies agree formally or informally not to spy on each other. While countries like Israel and France routinely break this principle vis-à-vis the United States and Canada, Canada has honoured it throughout the Cold War in its intelligence relationship with the US, even to the exaggerated degree of not carrying out systematic analysis of US developments in the Canadian intelligence services. The Americans have not taken the principle to that extreme a degree and have an impressive analytical understanding of Canadian developments based on open source and diplomatic information, not espionage. The question of whether or not this implicit distinction, whereby we avoid using intelligence services to achieve an in-depth understanding of 'the Colossus', still remains valid in today's world is an excellent example of the kind of issue that needs public review in the new security environment. Such a review would ask the question: do we now need a new continental or perimeter intelligence strategy of our own?

This is a truly pressing question for public policy in today's world. The shape of the international environment we are in now was clearly emerging and discernible through the 1990s, but it took the attacks on the Twin Towers and the Pentagon to usher in a completely new paradigm in Canada–US relations. That paradigm is based on an iron linkage between security and economic interests that began on 12 September 2001 with the closing of the Canada–US border by the American government. This will be a permanent shift and, as we have seen above, it forces us to adapt to US wishes and anxieties in a number of areas, whether we like it or not. It is a good question whether this process should continue to be done quietly and without obvious complaint (i.e., quiet diplomacy) to avoid arousing nationalist Canadian passions, or whether it should be done with the transparency and open debate merited by questions fundamentally affecting the future of our country.

Security has many dimensions covering virtually every governmental activity. An embattled and insecure United States can be expected to intensify pressures on Canada to bring its laws and administration closer to US thinking and preferences in a number of areas, including customs, immigration, transport, and policing. In the face of Canadian objections, the US administration gracefully soft-pedalled its initial post-11 September use of the term 'perimeter defence', but that term remains the motivating vision driving an aggressive American continental and international security policy, with which Canada has no choice but to co-operate.

The objective of American policy is to establish its security perimeter as far from the United States borders as it can. That has unavoidably serious consequences for Canada's future policies. It follows that, at least in the intelligence field but probably most others too, these consequences need to be the subject of the most extensive and well-informed public debate possible lest we discover that 'while we have slept' the quiet diplomats have thrown the Canadian baby out with the continental security bathwater.

Adaptation will be an ongoing process for several years as the Americans pursue their security needs with little tolerance for neighbourly differences of opinion. Perhaps the most challenging adjustments facing Canada in this respect, next to implementing and extending the Smart Border strategy of December 2001, will be, as mentioned earlier, coping with the new US Department of Homeland Security, a behemoth amalgamation of several departments and agencies with a staff nearly equalling the entire Canadian federal public service. Not least among the challenges of this new environment for both the Americans and Canadians will be integrating the provincial and even municipal levels of government into the emerging security 'perimeter'.

Adaptation not only will be about changed laws and new procedures but also will involve a major increase in intelligence co-operation with the United States in non-traditional sectors. Each of the areas of pressure for greater harmonization and integration entails a distinct element of information sharing—i.e., intelligence co-operation. There is also pressure to allow American extraterritorial law enforcement on Canadian soil and there are already many cases of American enforcement personnel working and collecting information in Canada. Much more of this can be expected as the US seeks to establish its defensive perimeter as far from the actual US border as possible.

Although bound to inspire unease among Canadians, the pragmatic and forthcoming approach adopted by the Canadian government in responding to these pressures seems justified by the preceding summary of the lessons from near-integration with the United States in the field of foreign intelligence during and after the Cold War. As noted above, harmonization and near-integration do not need to mean the loss of autonomous capacity or subservience, provided steps are taken to prevent sliding into abject dependency. They can even offer opportunities for enhanced attainment of Canadian objectives in a number of fields where increased co-operation with the Americans can create synergies and efficiencies. Nonetheless, this relatively optimistic assessment is only that—an optimistic assessment—and not one that should motivate policy behind closed doors without the Canadian public having a full opportunity to debate and understand the stakes and long-term implications.

In light of public views on the issues, which might perhaps be articulated by a Royal Commission or parliamentary process, a lot will then depend on Canada's strategic and policy-shaping skills to create an architecture for more integrated relations with the Americans while ensuring that they continue to be compatible with national needs and preferences. *A crucial precondition for the ability to exercise such skill successfully is having available the necessary depth of reliable information and knowledge about all relevant US realities.* That, in turn, requires having adequate, autonomous intelligence capacity for continental purposes.

Canada does not appear to have the necessary tradition, organization, or capacity to meet such ambitious information needs at this time. As noted earlier, a fundamental principle of the Cold War Canada–US intelligence relationship was that, in the interest of mutual trust, neither country carried out intelligence activities against the other. This 'friend on friend' principle of intelligence relationships made sense in the Cold War and still makes sense for co-operation in matters of mutual international interest (i.e., other than continental intelligence needs). However, the argument here is that the combination of over-adherence to this principle by Canada and allowing ourselves to become overdependent on American intelligence support has perhaps left Canada with the wrong foreign intelligence concepts, strategy, and capacity for meeting the country's needs in a more highly integrated continent experiencing a so-called 'Revolution in Security Affairs'.

It follows that Canada needs to review its approach to intelligence (i.e., as in information gathering and knowledge generation) vis-à-vis the United States with a view to developing a continental intelligence policy and strategy that meets today's needs better than the Cold War model. This does not have to mean throwing out the Cold War model, which remains relevant and mutually beneficial at the extra-continental level. What it means is that the changing continental reality requires us to design a two-pronged foreign intelligence policy distinguishing between our international and continental intelligence needs. To work on an increasingly integrated basis with 'the Colossus' on security and other matters requires greatly expanded capacity to understand American political and economic developments and policies in depth and across the complete range of public policy issues. If traditions of near-integration of foreign intelligence with the US inhibit our capacity to generate the necessary autonomous understanding of American realities, this would constitute an unacceptable lack of 'information sovereignty'.

It is the contention here that the traditional foreign intelligence relationship can be smoothly adapted to Canada's greatly increased information needs as it enters and manages a host of new arenas of near-integration with the Americans. The necessary information sovereignty can be maintained within the suggested two-pronged intelligence strategy for the future.

CONCLUSION

The special Canada–US intelligence relationship during the Cold War, and in particular the foreign intelligence relationship, has been an important but poorly understood dimension of the overall bilateral relationship between the two countries. It was the basis for a near-integration of effort against a common enemy long before the tragedy of 11 September prompted consideration of similar levels of integration across a much broader spectrum of arenas of co-operation. It offers useful lessons to those responsible for shaping harmonization or near-integration in these new arenas. Near-integration does not prohibit achieving Canadian goals with Canadian values, provided it is carried out appropriately.

Carrying it out appropriately means that Canada should start with efforts to generate much greater public awareness about the information, intelligence, and other challenges of the new security relationship with the United States. This awareness can be the primary objective of a much-needed public review and debate about future Canadian intelligence policy. Once decided, implementation of our future security-related directions will require strategic capacity, skilled people, and redesigned structures and processes to shape the opportunities in the continental integration process.

This, in turn, will require access to a rich and deep well of reliable knowledge and understanding about every relevant facet of the

United States. This is the kind of understanding that intelligence services are designed to provide and that Canada's services should be empowered to provide, in continuing co-operation with but not dependency on the Americans. The future role of Canada's intelligence services should be to assure that Canada has the information sovereignty it needs for the twenty-first century.

NOTES

1. Bertin (2003) reports the keynote speech of Thomas d'Aquino on behalf of the Canadian Council of Chief Executives in which he calls for a continental union agreement with the United States and only much later with Mexico 'because of security concerns'.
2. See House of Commons (2002: 97–8), where the text reads 'Professor Stuart Farson of Simon Fraser University told the Committee that the intelligence community would still benefit from both an independent review and increased parliamentary oversight .... the Committee agrees.' The Committee goes on in Recommendation 10 to call for the establishment of a Standing Committee on Security and Intelligence.
3. See Standing Senate Committee on National Security and Defence, chair's Web site. Available at: <http://kennyco@sen.parl.gc.ca>.
4. The Access to Information Act is designed to provide access to information and legal protection to citizens against abuse of secrecy requirements by government agencies. It contains important clauses permitting the government to exempt sensitive security and foreign relations information from release under the Act. University researchers often feel thwarted by the Act's 'weakness' in the security area. Practitioners, on the other hand, see the Act and its sometimes overzealous application by the Office of the Information Commissioner as potential threats to national security.
5. See 'Terrorism, Proliferation, and the Myth of American Independence' (Abiew, 2002: 37–44). The issues of multilateralism versus unilateralism are discussed and the author forecasts that Canada will have to live with inevitable US unilateralism in security matters for the future. In my opinion, the author is correct in principle but the language of state-to-state relations implied by the term 'unilateralism' does not accurately describe what is happening when a 'perimeter defence' is more or less imposed on Canada, 'whether we like it or not', through the exercise of economic and administrative leverage. This is already happening by other names (as with the 'Smart Border Agreement' of December 2001). Against such action and overpowering negotiation Canada probably has no choice but to acquiesce while negotiating the most favourable terms possible and insisting on the niceties of sovereign appearances. Indeed, this appears to sum up Foreign Minister John Manley's and the Canadian government's strategy since 11 September 2001 under considerable pressure from the Canadian business community (see note 1 above).

REFERENCES

Abiew, Francis Kofi. 2002. *Canadian Defence and the Canada–US Strategic Partnership*, Conference Report. Ottawa: Centre for Security and Defence Studies, Norman Paterson School of International Affairs, Carleton University.

Bertin, Oliver. 2003. 'CEOs Urging Stronger Ties to U.S.', *Globe and Mail*, 15 Jan., B3.

Canada. 1980. *Commission of Inquiry Concerning Certain Activities of the Royal Canadian Mounted Police*. Toronto: Micromedia.

Hoberg, George. 2002. 'Canada and North American Integration', *Canadian Public Policy* (Aug.): S35.

House of Commons, Standing Committee on Foreign Affairs and International Trade. 2002. *Partners in North America: Advancing Canada's Relations with the United States and Mexico*.

10

'A Special Case': Canada, Operation Apollo, and Multilateralism

GRANT DAWSON

Jean Chrétien's Liberal government gave a robust military response to the 11 September 2001 terrorist attacks on the United States that killed more than 3,000 people. In October, under Operation Apollo, Canada contributed ships, special forces, and transport and surveillance aircraft to support the US-led war against Osama bin Laden, his Al-Qaeda terrorist network, and the Taliban regime that was harbouring him in Afghanistan. Ottawa expanded Apollo by deploying the 750-person Princess Patricia's Canadian Light Infantry Battle Group to Kandahar to fight under US control in February 2002. During the crisis, Ottawa's priority was to match its desire for a significant role, ideally with the US, with the skill-sets, equipment, and personnel the Canadian Forces (CF) had available. Chrétien sought a noteworthy task, but he also hoped to reflect Canadians' comfort with peace operations and discomfort with war, and ensure that the country's engagement was consistent with its multilateral interests.

In the domestic debate concerning the country's role, some commentators argued that the government should reflect Canada's traditional strengths in fostering peace and multilateralism. Political scientist Janice Gross Stein argued that since 11 September, 'Canada has not been speaking with its traditional voice.' Putting 'our highly trained and skilled ground forces in harm's way to protect civilians in war', she said, was 'where we can make a difference' (Stein, 2001: A19). Former Foreign Affairs Minister Lloyd Axworthy (1996–2000) believed that multilateralism was the best way for Canada to play a distinctive role. As minister, he had focused on protecting the human security of individuals in civil conflict, non-military peace-building, and improving the timeliness of United Nations deployments (Dawson, 2001: 299, 308–9). He said Ottawa should select a 'Canadian strategy' that would 'design and promote effective international agreements and programmes to tighten the screws on the terrorists' (Axworthy, 2001a: A19). Axworthy and Stein reflected the preference of some Canadians for honest-broker diplomacy and norm-building, and their unease with the use of force and close military collaboration with the US.

Columnist Jeffrey Simpson and historian J.L. Granatstein, in contrast, believed that fighting terrorism was in Canada's interests. Simpson criticized the moralists who appealed for peace in the belief that an attack on Afghanistan would be equivalent to 11 September because it would cause civilian casualties. On this occasion, he noted, the 'brigades of the morally superior' were outnumbered by those who wanted Canada to 'go beyond the old dodge of offering all assistance short of help' (Simpson, 2001a: A15). Granatstein pointed to the national interests that would be served by a significant military role. He stressed that if Ottawa did not contribute to common security concerns, then Washington would provide the desired protection itself on its terms. If Canada failed to carry its own weight militarily, its usefulness to its more powerful partner would diminish. Those who warned against a robust engagement in the war against terrorism, Granatstein argued, needed to ask themselves '[w]hat will the Americans say to this? . . . Will anyone in Washington listen when Ottawa complains if we bring only rifle-carrying social workers to the table?' (Granatstein, 2001: A18).

Canada, however, did not offer troops immediately after the attacks because Chrétien wanted to encourage the US to proceed with a controlled and measured military response. In contrast with the United Kingdom and Australia, which both promptly put troops at Washington's disposal, Ottawa held back and avoided high-profile moves like visiting 'ground zero', the site of the destroyed World Trade Center in New York. It turned instead to quiet diplomacy. Chrétien did not want US President George W. Bush to doubt the country's commitment to combatting terrorism, but he hoped Washington could be persuaded to use restraint. The Prime Minister worried that the US would 'take sensational, short-term actions that could have negative effects over the long term for the whole population of the globe' (McCarthy, 2001a: A7). Chrétien displayed Canada's independence by not automatically providing forces, and symbolically he stressed the need to not lash out. He also criticized UK Labour Party Prime Minister Tony Blair, whom he called 'Tory Blair' during a fall 2001 Liberal caucus talk, for being so eager to fight (Fife, 2002: A6).

Chrétien's diplomatic pause, although criticized by some analysts, reflected the domestic mood. One scholar commented that 'it was not the lack of a sense of right and wrong that was so offensive in the behaviour of the Chrétien government, but its timidity. . . . No wonder so many Canadians were ashamed' (Cooper, 2002: A14). Yet the Prime Minister had read public opinion accurately. When the implications of participation in an anti-terrorist war were explained, Canadians pulled back, wanting neither military nor civilian casualties. An Ipsos-Reid poll taken in mid-September found that 73 per cent favoured a role in the US-led campaign. But, if this were to provoke a terrorist attack leading to civilian casualties in Canada, then only 43 per cent were supportive (McCarthy, 2001b: A1). In addition, an October Canadian Alliance poll showed that 66 per cent supported the idea of having the CF fight terrorists, but if this led to the deaths of hundreds of Canadian soldiers, then only 48 per cent approved (Laghi, 2001: A11).

Chrétien understood better than New Democratic Party leader Alexa McDonough the passions at play domestically. According to writer Lawrence Martin, the 'raw emotion' in Canada after the attacks was for some Canadians a 'big argument for getting closer' to the US (Martin, 2002: A15). McDonough, who believed that she spoke for the majority of Canadians, did not see it this way. She had 'grave reservations about a coalition of countries being the judge, jury and executioner' (Toughill, 2001: A18). However, McDonough's dissent cost her political support, even among party faithful. For example,

Bill Innis, an NDP supporter since 1969, said '[s]he lost my vote when I heard her on the news. I lost all respect for her . . . we would want the US and the UK to help us, but she doesn't want to help them' (ibid.). McDonough had been subjected to considerable pressure to change her views. 'It's been painful and frightening', McDonough said. 'There is immense pressure to just conform, to capitulate, [and] to suspend democracy' (ibid.). Chrétien moved carefully between cautious disagreement and support for the US. His response was 'the classic Liberal . . . approach, alternating between home-grown impulse and continentalist reality' (Martin, 2002: A15).

The Prime Minister's ambiguous approach proved difficult to maintain. If Ottawa tilted too much towards the US, this 'would have provided grist for the anti-American crowd and kindled the government's fear of a reflexive reaction in Canada against being too pro-American' (Simpson: 2001b: A13). At the same time, Bush's omission of Canada from his 20 September congressional address demonstrated that excessive caution could lead to controversy. The President failed to mention Canada or its accommodation of redirected US airline passengers on 11 September, but did acknowledge the assistance or sacrifices of the UK, Egypt, El Salvador, and other countries. According to David Frum, who helped draft the speech, the 'omission stung and shamed Canadians with the power of a savage and unexpected slap' (Frum, 2003: 149–50). Although the omission had not been an intentional slight, it had been abetted in part because Ottawa had not offered troops immediately after the attack. Canada was cut, Frum said, 'because it is easy to forget friends whose governments give you no cause to remember them' (ibid., 150).

In fact, Ottawa wanted to stand with the US, and it believed that this was in line with what most Canadians desired. Chrétien told the House of Commons on 17 September that Canadians 'know where our duty lies'. The country must 'stand with Americans. As neighbours. As friends. As family' (Chrétien, 2001a). Government officials believed that these statements captured the mood of the nation. They were aware that the public was paying attention to the way Ottawa responded to the situation and did not want Canada to remain passive. Jim Wright, a senior official in the Department of Foreign Affairs and International Trade (DFAIT), said he 'was not surprised that this was so. Those of us in government expected that this venture would and should enjoy the support of the Canadian people' (J. Wright, 2002). The desire to assist was clear-cut and catalytic, and this made the fall of 2001 stand out for DFAIT decision-makers. Jill Sinclair, for example, remarked that 'I think it is important [to] see Afghanistan as being different. Afghanistan was special' (Sinclair, 2002).[1]

The government grasped the enormous significance of what had happened, and it believed Canada had an obligation to participate in the US response. The Prime Minister argued that this was not merely an attack on the US, but a war against democratic civilization. 'So let us be clear', he said, '[t]hese cold-blooded killers struck a blow at the values and beliefs of free and civilized people everywhere. The world has been attacked' (Chrétien, 2001a). Ottawa believed that it had an interest in doing its part to eradicate terrorism because Canada was at risk, and supporting international peace and security efforts was central to its foreign policy. Canadian decision-makers assumed that since Canada was one of the world's few rich countries, it had a responsibility to do what it could to further international stability. Canada had an interest in fostering harmony, prosperity, and order because this made the global system easier to live in. As Minister of Foreign Affairs John Manley (October 2000–January 2002) noted, '[w]e're involved in Afghanistan because that's one of the things responsible countries need to do right now' (McCarthy, 2002a: A4).

Ottawa did not want or expect to exchange its contribution for progress on some other bilateral issue, but it did hope, as previous governments had, that Canada's military commitment would earn the country credit in Washington. It 'would be naive to believe', said Manley, that 'military support during [the US] action in Afghanistan . . . would result in a US policy change' regarding softwood lumber (McCarthy, 2002b: A6). However, it was clear to Ottawa that collaborating with the US was essential to the national interest because this increased the chances that the latter would listen to Canadian concerns. For example, Secretary of State for External Affairs Lester Pearson observed during the Korean War that '[t]here must always be in our minds the possibility that if we do not demonstrate our fundamental solidarity we should inevitably find it more difficult to get a favourable treatment in procurement and other problems.' In addition, when Ottawa deployed military personnel to Europe to bolster the North American Treaty Organization (NATO) in February 1951, it had been motivated in part by a desire to have its voice heard in Washington (Bothwell, 1992: 48; English and Hillmer, 1989: 37). The government's ground contribution in Afghanistan would achieve a similar result. Canada got 'all sorts of preferential treatment', noted one senior official, because of this role. 'We may not win every argument', the official added, but Washington was prepared to hear Canada 'because they know how difficult it is for leaders to put the lives of their citizens on the line' (Sallot, 2002: A5).

Initially, however, there were no specific tasks for the CF to perform outside of purely domestic roles like civil assistance. Within a week of the attacks, the National Defence Headquarters' Joint Staff had prepared a list of force package options and had passed them to the government. It took the US several weeks to determine its response and what it needed from allies, and as a result it did not immediately request forces from Canada (Côté, 2002). The CF, under Operation Support, did help national authorities cope with the arrival of 23,921 passengers from 142 flights that had been diverted from US destinations to six Canadian airports on 11 September (Department of National Defence, 2002: 4).[2] It also immediately assigned aircraft to a North American Aerospace Defence Command mission, named Noble Eagle, to protect the continental airspace. On 20 September, Minister of National Defence Arthur Eggleton authorized the more than 100 CF members on exchanges to participate in host unit actions in response to the attacks on the US (Eggleton, 2001).

When the US requested military contributions for its coalition on 4 October, Ottawa quickly agreed because it wanted to help and the coalition suited the country's multilateral instincts. Chrétien immediately instructed Eggleton to provide what was needed so that Canada could show that it stood 'shoulder to shoulder' with the US and that it refused to live in fear on 'terms dictated from the shadows' (Chrétien, 2001b). Ottawa's commitment also reflected the country's long-standing preference to work with the US in the company of other nations. As Pearson noted in his memoirs, 'for Canada, there was always security in numbers. We did not want to be alone with our close friend and neighbour' (Pearson, 1973: 32–3). Chrétien avoided this dilemma by accepting a role in the US-led multinational coalition. Canada, he said on 7 October, was 'part of an unprecedented coalition of nations . . . . I have made it clear from the very beginning that Canada would be part of this coalition every step of the way' (Chrétien, 2001b).

As a result, Eggleton announced on 8 October that a 2,000-person force of ships, planes, and Joint Task Force 2 commandos would be contributed to the anti-terrorist coalition. The aircraft provided inter-theatre transport, humanitarian airlift, and maritime surveillance, while the ships helped the coalition control the waters nearest Afghanistan. Chief of the Defence Staff General Raymond Hénault said the ships had been chosen because the CF and US fleets had trained together extensively and could operate as one (Sallot, 2001a: A7). The CF contributed a Naval Task Group (four ships) to a larger US Naval Task Force in the Arabian Sea.[3] The frigate HMCS *Toronto* joined NATO's Standing Naval Force Atlantic in the eastern Mediterranean. The HMCS *Vancouver* was the only ship from any navy fully integrated into a US Carrier Battle Group. This frigate replaced a US flag unit in the USS John C. Stennis Carrier Battle Group, and it was not the only CF ship capable of being so integrated (Garnett, 2002).

This interoperability enabled the CF to offer the US more support than some Canadian defence commentators predicted. Analysts such as David Charters stressed 'how limited the capabilities of the Forces are right now'. Scott Taylor, editor of the magazine *Esprit de Corps*, added that '[u]nless we shut down and pull out of Bosnia, we are fully committed right now in terms of soldiers' (Foss and Sallot, 2001: A7). The CF's seamless co-operation with US forces enabled it to surpass these expectations. Military leaders believed that twenty-first-century crises demanded flexible and rapidly mobile armed forces that could plug into coalitions where required, and that the complaints about the CF's size related to an outdated understanding of force structure that equated the magnitude of a contribution with its effectiveness (Garnett, 2002). For the government, interoperability was central because whenever the country went to war or participated in an intervention, it did so with a coalition. In addition, interoperability was necessary for budgetary reasons. Ottawa's conundrum was that Canadians wanted the country involved in world affairs, but did not support large armed forces. Afghanistan reflected decision-makers' conclusion that 'to play a significant role on the world stage, Canada has to get into bed with the United States' (Stairs and Middlemiss, 2002: 33).

Ottawa did not see military integration as an aberration, but its political decision to join the US coalition was made on a case-by-case basis. Close interaction with the US, whose standards and procedures had been at the heart of most ad hoc non-UN coalitions in the 1990s, was critical to the military's strategy. In his report for 2001–2, Hénault noted that '[m]aintaining interoperability remains key to the future relevance of the CF', and that this had enabled it to make 'major strides in laying a solid foundation to chart an affordable, strategic course for the years ahead' (Department of National Defence, 2002: 26). DFAIT officials saw integration as a normal reflection of the close Canada–US relationship (J. Wright, 2002). What was special was Ottawa's intense desire to help, to co-operate as effectively as possible with the US, and to be on the front line beside it. The 11 September attacks provided a uniquely powerful justification for this feeling. In the case of a possible war with Iraq in 2002–3, the government was much more reluctant to support the US (Sinclair, 2002; Ibbitson, 2003: A15).

For Afghanistan, Canada had to align itself with the US because NATO and the UN were not central to the anti-terrorism campaign. Washington had found the alliance's consensus-based decision-making process to be cumbersome during the 1999 Kosovo aerial intervention (Sallot, 2001b: A6). As a result, the US decided to organize its own multinational coalition. Ambassador David Wright, Canada's Permanent Representative to NATO, noted that the government favoured a more predictable, rules-based approach to crisis management. The UN was preferred, but NATO was also a reliable tool. Coalitions were less desirable because 'what unites a coalition in the short term may not survive after the initial crisis is past and may lead to instability' (D. Wright, 2002a). Yet, despite Ottawa's preference, it was what the US thought that mattered. Wright said that at 'present the ad hoc coalition approach, based on a specific mission, is the model on which Washington is focused' (D. Wright, 2002a).

Ottawa was nevertheless mindful of the significance of the first-ever invocation in principle on 12 September (confirmed on 2 October) of Article 5 of NATO's founding Washington Treaty. This collective defence provision stipulates that an attack on one member state will be considered an attack against all. Although Canada did not propose its use, it participated actively in the decision (J. Wright, 2002). Ottawa welcomed the activation of Article 5 because it showed that Canada was not alone in wanting to help the US. According to Michael Ignatieff, 'the invocation of Article 5 articulated this sense of a common transatlantic identity under attack' (Ignatieff, 2002: 8). In light of this, at the request of the US, alliance members agreed to eight measures to implement Article 5, such as improving intelligence sharing and co-operation both bilaterally and with NATO bodies (Bennett, 2001: 6). They also mounted Operation Active Endeavour, in which the NATO Standing Naval Forces Mediterranean and Atlantic were deployed to the eastern Mediterranean to monitor shipping. In addition, on 8 October, alliance members agreed to

Operation Eagle Assist, in which five NATO-crewed and owned Airborne Warning and Control System (AWACS) aircraft flew missions from the US for the first time.

The UN also had a role to play, but it was not central because the Afghanistan operation was quite different from its previous interventions. The Security Council supported the US by affirming, in Resolutions 1368 and 1373 (12 and 28 September), Article 51 of the UN Charter. The Council was recognizing 'the inherent right of individual or collective self-defence' (UN, 2001a, 2001b). This acknowledged that Afghanistan was a special case, in which the US had the legal right to pursue and punish bin Laden and his supporters and did not require UN sanction. The world body could support US efforts if it wished, but Washington did not require a resolution to act (Heinbecker, 2002). UN approval for a humanitarian intervention had been sought on several occasions in the 1990s, but this time the situation was completely different. As a result, the guidance provided by *The Responsibility to Protect* (2001), the report of the Canadian-sponsored International Commission on Intervention and State Sovereignty, was not applicable. It had been written to help states and the UN deal with humanitarian protection claims in other countries. It was not relevant to the Afghanistan case, where the central problem was a failed state that was harbouring terrorists guilty of an attack on US and other nationals. The Commission co-chairs said that the 'two situations in our judgement are fundamentally different' (Evans and Sahnoun, 2001: viii).

The UN was still important to Canada's anti-terrorist response because it established a global anti-terrorist legal architecture that the US welcomed. One of the UN's main tasks was to encourage states to ratify and implement the 12 anti-terrorist conventions that had been deposited with the world body. In addition, Security Council Resolution 1373 was historic because it required states to act to prevent terrorists from moving, acquiring weapons, finding safe haven, and raising capital in their territory. US Secretary of State Colin Powell said the UN 'took a critical step forward' by imposing these urgent and binding obligations on all nations (UN, 2001c: 16). The resolution created a 'global structure for countering terrorism' that was not time-limited (UN, 2002a: 3, 6). The resolution established a Counter Terrorism Committee to which states were required to report on their progress towards full implementation of its provisions. By June 2002, the Committee had received reports from 161 nations and four international governmental organizations (out of 189 states), and had seen ratifications of the existing anti-terrorist conventions rise 15 per cent from the previous year (ibid., 2002a: 3, 5).

In addition to this global legal and financial role, bodies like the UN were important to Ottawa because they multilateralized and legitimized the coalition effort in Afghanistan. According to former Prime Minister Brian Mulroney, Canada has always stood for a vision of an interdependent world, and '[w]e express our vision, we uphold our values, through our belief in multilateralism and multilateral institutions' (Mulroney, 2001). In this case, Washington had decided to use the UN as one of the means to fight terrorism, and the UN had shown that the coalition was backed by the collective will of the world community. Secretary of State (Asia Pacific) Rey Pagtakhan made it clear that Ottawa attached great value to this multilateral sanction. 'I do not have to repeat the rationale for the military action in Afghanistan', he said. 'Under the auspices of Article 51 . . . Canada has proudly contributed to the US-led military intervention' (Pagtakhan, 2001). In addition, Minister of Foreign Affairs Bill Graham commented in April 2002 that Canada joined the coalition because it had UN sanction (Graham, 2002).

However, the country's deployment options were narrowed by the UN's unwillingness to send peacekeeping forces into Afghanistan. This followed the recommendation of Lakhdar Brahimi, who had been reappointed Special Representative of the Secretary General in Afghanistan on 3 October 2001 (a position he last held in 1999), and had peacekeeping expertise because of his work in Liberia, Haiti, and Afghanistan and as the chair of the Panel on UN Peace Operations (2000). During Brahimi's first official Security Council briefing on 12 October, he noted that the UN 'should not rush to establish a peace-keeping operation in Afghanistan' (Lynch, 2001: A26). He repeated this on 13 November:

> UN peacekeepers have proven most successful when deployed to implement an existing political settlement among willing parties—not to serve as a substitute for one. Any security force established in the absence of a credible cease-fire agreement or political settlement, whether constituted by Afghans, international personnel, or both, could quickly find itself in the role of combatant. This is not a role for 'Blue Helmets'. (Brahimi, 2001)

The UN's approach was clearly reflected in Brahimi's terms of reference. His focus was on diplomatic peacemaking, humanitarian assistance, and peacebuilding (UN, 2001d: 2). Neither his UN Special Mission for Afghanistan nor the UN Assistance Mission for Afghanistan that took its place in accordance with Resolution 1401 (28 March 2002) (UN, 2002b) had a military role.

Although Canada could not deploy to Afghanistan with the UN or NATO, roles that were more broadly multinational continued to have appeal, as the media's discussion of peacekeeping in the Balkans demonstrated. On 4 October, Washington asked NATO members to be ready to 'backfill' selected assets needed for operations against terrorism (Bennett, 2001: 6). However, in Canada, it was reported that Ottawa was considering a request from US Ambassador to Canada Paul Cellucci to contribute extra peacekeepers to the NATO Stabilization Force (SFOR) in Bosnia-Herzegovina to free up 'crack US fighting units'. Key DFAIT officials, however, have stressed that this was never considered (Sallot, 2001b, 2001c; Sinclair, 2002; J. Wright, 2002). Peacekeeping was mentioned because it was seen as a natural Canadian role. Canadians viewed 'their country as a peace-keeping nation', noted analyst Martin Shadwick. 'It's a mindset that's made its way deeply into the Canadian psyche and it's difficult to dislodge' (Laghi, 2001b: A4).

The government also considered an ad hoc stabilization mission that would have been consistent with its multilateral peacekeeping impulse and desire for a significant role. In mid-November the US asked Ottawa to deploy the Princess Patricias to protect relief shipments and defuse tensions in the parts of Afghanistan secured by the Northern Alliance, anti-terrorism's Afghan ally. Chrétien said Canada wanted to 'bring peace and happiness as much as possible', but was, as Eggleton noted, prepared to take on 'a little bit more risk' than traditional peacekeeping (Thompson, 2001: A1; Campbell, 2001: A1). It was inevitable that the country would want to help in this way. Peacekeeping suited Canadians' anxious desire to serve as the world's conscience, and it had acquired a momentum as the automatic, instinctive Canadian response to crisis that no politician could ignore (Hillmer, 2002: 1). The government was keen to contribute, and as a result it placed the Princess Patricias on very short notice (forty-eight hours) for deployment. However, Ottawa stood down these forces on 20 October, once it became clear that the mission was neither wanted by the Northern Alliance nor needed since food was getting through.

Ottawa could have chosen another stabilization mission, the UN-sanctioned and UK-led International Security Assistance Force (ISAF), but the government was unable to find a suitable role for Canada. The 4,500-strong operation had been called for by Annex I of the Bonn Agreement (5 December 2001), which dealt with the reconstruction of government institutions in Afghanistan. With Resolution 1386 (20 December), the UN Security Council gave the UK-led force Chapter VII enforcement powers and mandated it to provide security in and around Kabul, Afghanistan's capital (UN, 2001e). This was noteworthy because the government had been discussing a possible ground role with the British and US since November. For Ottawa, it was not a question of deciding between combat and a stability task, or of close co-operation with the US versus a more multinational role. The main problem was finding the most effective way to get involved. In accepting the US offer, Eggleton said that 'we had to decide one or the other. We believe that this was the most effective way to use our troops' (Eggleton, 2002).

The US coalition was more attractive because the UK request did not suit the resources that Ottawa was prepared to commit. It became clear in early January that London's immediate need was limited to 200 engineers, who were in short supply in the CF. The British proposed that the rest of the 750-person battle group[4] wait to replace withdrawing UK forces in three months' time. This would not have been the clearest demonstration of Canada's commitment to fighting terrorism. 'We're not interested in giving a couple of hundred of guys here or there', said Jeremy Kinsman, Canada's High Commissioner to the UK. Canada had been waiting for an assignment that was 'identifiable' and 'self-sustaining' and did not want to supply forces that would be subsumed into a larger unit (Freeman, 2002: A1). Eggleton said it was 'absolutely wrong' to suggest, as some critics had, that Canada was not wanted by ISAF. The problem was 'the basis on which they wanted us' (Eggleton, 2002).

Ottawa was relieved when the US requested a significant force on 4 January 2002. The Princess Patricias were asked to deploy as part of the US Army's Task Force Rakkasan, which was built around the 187th Brigade Combat Team from the 101st Airborne Division. This made Canada the fourth largest coalition contributor, with almost 3,000 personnel in theatre under Apollo. The government was pleased with the new tasking because it wanted to show Canadians and the world that the country was a valued US partner. Eggleton stressed that the 'Americans recognized' CF skills, had 'specifically requested' its Coyote armoured reconnaissance vehicle, and were 'anxious that we get there' (Eggleton, 2002). Sending a token force would not have enabled the country to receive a task that was visible and identifiably Canadian. Retired Major-General Lewis MacKenzie noted that Ottawa was 'trying to send a message to the Americans that we are with them' and that it was right to have 'held out for a decent role' (Alberts, 2002: A6).

When it accepted this task, the government found that it had to struggle against the myth that Canadians were an unmilitary people. It may be that peacekeeping is the national métier, noted DFAIT's Jill Sinclair, but the government is not squeamish about using force when appropriate (Sinclair, 2002). Eggleton pointed out that Canada had been willing to use force in the past, such as in the Persian Gulf War (1991), Somalia (1992), the former Yugoslavia (1995), and Kosovo and East Timor (1999). He said Canada was 'good at peacekeeping, but if we have to be involved in combat we can do that too. We've demonstrated that time and time again in history. Canadians know how to fight when they have to fight' (Naumetz, 2002: A1). The Princess Patricias' February-July 2002 efforts demonstrated this. It fought Al-Qaeda and Taliban remnants, maintained security around Kandahar and its airport, explored sensitive areas, and provided humanitarian assistance and demining services. The battle group engaged in four coalition missions: Operations Anaconda, Harpoon, Torii, and Cherokee Sky. In addition, six CF snipers registered Canada's first confirmed combat killings since the Korean War during Anaconda (Leblanc, 2002: A1).

While this deep collaboration concerned some Canadians, the government's decision to withdraw its infantry from Afghanistan but not from the Balkans illustrated that its commitment to multilateralism remained strong. With the deployment to Kandahar, it began to seem that harmonization had again gone too far and that the country had moved too close to the US. Thomas Axworthy, for example, argued that the decision to fight with the US was another sign of Canada's integration into the US by increment. From border security to the move from peacekeeping, each step where Canada's approach was harmonized with the US 'nudges us ever so slightly more firmly into the American orbit' (Axworthy, 2002: A17). Lloyd Axworthy said that now the 'only test is how high we jump' (McCarthy, 2002c: A8).

Ottawa, however, demonstrated that it had other priorities, such as its multilateral obligation to SFOR. Canada stayed in Bosnia, David Wright has noted, because it had no choice. The government always maintained that it had gone in with its allies and would depart with them as well. Wright added that he never even discussed with Ottawa the possibility of withdrawing from the Balkans to support a second Afghanistan rotation (D. Wright, 2002b). The continuation of the role was also a sign and symbol of Canada's separate policy and approach to peace and security. The decision to withdraw from Afghanistan highlighted the fact that the period immediately after 11 September was a special time of sympathy and vulnerability for Canada, and that once these feelings faded the old preferences and priorities resurfaced.

Ottawa demonstrated this by deciding on 12 February 2003 to contribute troops to ISAF (now led by Germany and the Netherlands), rather than declare support for a US-led war against Iraq. Chrétien said that Canada 'firmly supports the objectives' of the US in 'forcing Saddam Hussein to abide' by UN Resolution 1441 (8 November 2002), which demanded that Iraq comply with a UN inspections regime designed to ensure the full and verified dismantling of its weapons of mass destruction (UN, 2002c; Chrétien, 2003). However, Canadians did not want to wage war alongside the US without UN approval. Even with UN sanction, only 60 per cent of Canadians favoured a combat role with the US in Iraq, and 18 per cent disapproved whether Washington received UN authorization or not (Sallot, 2003: A9). The ISAF enabled Ottawa to avoid having to choose between supporting the US and UN-centred multilateralism. This was because Minister of National Defence John McCallum (May 2002-present) and US Secretary of State Donald Rumsfeld had agreed that a Canadian contribution to ISAF would further the US interest in Afghanistan's stability. In addition, the task was attractive, McCallum noted, because it was 'in the peacekeeping tradition of Canadians' (Leblanc, 2003: A1).

The size of the ISAF role made it unlikely that Canada would provide significant infantry support in the event of war with Iraq. McCallum announced that the CF would deploy to Kabul, for two six-month rotations of up to 3,000 troops, starting in the late summer of 2003. The CF contingent would consist of a battle group and some of the infrastructure for a brigade headquarters. With the ISAF role, however, the CF would be fully committed to coalition operations in Afghanistan and Bosnia. Journalist Daniel Leblanc wrote that, in light of McCallum's announcement, a ground commitment in Iraq was 'virtually impossible'. McCallum seemed to concur, noting that it 'is true that the more one sends to one place, the less one may have available for other places' (Leblanc, 2003: A1).

The government wanted to contribute military forces to assist the US response for several reasons. It believed Canada needed to demonstrate its concern, that it had a responsibility to share the risks borne by its allies in the name of peace, and that Canadians wanted to be involved. When Ottawa engaged in October and February, it did not see the CF's integration into US formations or the prospect of using force as problems. Its main concern was to help in the most effective way possible, however possible. The government thought that integration was not an aberration but a demonstration of the trust and familiarity existing between the two militaries. It was also clear that close military co-operation was unavoidable because Canadians wanted the CF engaged globally but were unwilling to pay for a large military. The government also repeatedly asserted that combat was not a break from Canadian traditions, and that it had always fought when it had to.

The Chrétien government joined the US-led coalition mindful that it had UN and NATO sanction. Participation in the US force was consistent with Canada's multilateral foreign policy because the Security Council had affirmed Article 51 of the UN Charter and NATO had activated Article 5 of its founding treaty. Both organizations, however, were peripheral to the military effort in Afghanistan. The UN was secondary because the attacks in Afghanistan were entirely different from the interventions previously considered by the Council, and the world body knew that deploying blue helmets into Afghanistan's hostile and fluid environment was out of the question. Washington formed a US coalition rather than use NATO because it believed that the alliance's decision-making process was cumbersome. Although Ottawa would have preferred the coalition to be under NATO or the UN, it had to accept this decision.

The government considered roles in the British-led ISAF and the US coalition. It desired to work as closely as possible with its US friends, but it negotiated with both parties at the same time to locate a task. The ISAF did not have an edge because it was a less aggressive peace operation. The British did not reject Canada; rather, Ottawa decided that the US request for a battle group best suited the kind of contribution it wanted to make, while the British wanted the bulk of the Canadians to wait and only a few hundred engineers to deploy immediately. The country was interested in helping in an immediate and significant way, and the CF's interoperable units enabled it to integrate into US land and sea formations.

While Ottawa wanted to support the US after 11 September, there was another side to this response that reflected Canada's traditional needs and impulses. Ottawa hesitated before offering military support because it hoped to encourage the US to use restraint, and Canadians expressed unease about engaging in combat. The government showed that Canada was independent by not automatically offering troops to the US after 11 September. It hoped to convince Washington not to use its power excessively because this could have negative long-term consequences for the world. Chrétien's cautious but supportive approach reflected the national mood. While many Canadians called for prompt and unquestioning support of the US, many others feared casualties and were unenthusiastic about joining the global war against terrorism. But excessive caution was also risky because it could result in Canada being overlooked by Washington.

Ottawa contributed to the US anti-terrorist effort with the view that this would earn Canada credit in Washington and because the coalition reflected the country's multilateral instincts. The government had no intention of using its military contribution to secure more favourable treatment on a specific bilateral issue. But Ottawa hoped, as had previous governments, that its demonstration of solidarity would enable Canada to be heard in Washington, and would help make the management of bilateral ties easier. Decision-makers sought to contribute to the anti-terrorist effort because they believed that Canada had a responsibility to do what it could to further international peace. In addition, the coalition's multinational nature reflected Canada's long-standing desire to avoid being alone with the US on the world stage.

The country's comfort with the mediatory and usually non-violent characteristics of peacekeeping was another reflection of Canada's preference for multilateralism. Canada's peacekeeping instincts led the media to highlight stabilization activities in the Balkans in October, and led the government to consider a humanitarian relief and security operation in Afghanistan in November. The withdrawal from Afghanistan and not Bosnia in July 2002 also indicated its co-operative instincts. Canada stayed in SFOR because it had agreed that it would not unilaterally depart from the NATO force. However, Canada's continued presence in Bosnia also showed Canadians and the world that it had other priorities besides the US anti-terrorist campaign, and that multilateralism continued to push policy strongly. As the events of 11 September and their immediate aftermath receded, this priority was reasserted.

Ottawa's support of the US coalition was special because it was driven by Canada's strong desire to help defeat terrorism. It was clear why military action was appropriate and why the marginalization of the UN and NATO was justified.

NOTES

1. Wright was Assistant Deputy Minister (Global and Security Policy) at DFAIT. Sinclair, who reported to him, was Director General of the International Security Bureau.
2. In total, Canada received 226 aircraft and 33,000 diverted passengers. See Manley (2001).
3. The Canadian Naval Task Group initially comprised the following vessels: the frigates HMCS *Halifax* and *Charlottetown*, the destroyer HMCS *Iroquois*, and the auxiliary oiler/replenishment ship HMCS *Preserver*.
4. The battle group consisted of two Princess Patricia's Light Infantry companies: a Lord Strathcona's Horse (Royal Canadians) squadron with Coyote light-armoured reconnaissance vehicles and a logistics group from 1 Service Battalion.

REFERENCES

Alberts, Sheldon. 2002. 'Canadians Know How to Fight', *National Post*, 8 Jan., A1, A6.

Axworthy, Lloyd. 2001. 'Canada to the Rescue', *Globe and Mail*, 28 Sept., A19.

Axworthy, Thomas. 2002. 'Integration by Increment', *Globe and Mail*, 17 Jan., A17.

Bennett, Christopher. 2001. 'Aiding America', *NATO Review* 49, 4 (Winter 2001): 6–7.

Bothwell, Robert. 1992. *Canada and the United States: The Politics of Partnership*. Toronto: University of Toronto Press.

Brahimi, Lakhdar. 2001. 'Lakhdar Brahimi's Briefing to the Security Council', UN verbatim transcript. New York, 13 Nov. Available at: <http://www.globalpolicy.org/wtc/un/unindex.htm>. Accessed 27 July 2002.

Campbell, Murray. 2001. 'New Afghanistan Takes Shape but Canada's Role in Doubt', *Globe and Mail*, 21 Nov., A1.

Chrétien, Jean. 2001a. 'Address on the Occasion of a Special House of Commons Debate in Response to the Terrorist Attacks in the United States on Sept. 11, 2001', Ottawa, 17 Sept. Available at: <http://canada.gc.ca/united-states/press-us_e.html>. Accessed 11 Jan. 2003.

———. 2001b. 'An Address to the Nation Concerning the International Campaign Against Terrorism', Ottawa, 7 Oct. Available at: <http://canada.gc.ca/united-states/press-us_e.html>. Accessed 18 Jan. 2002.

———. 2003. 'An Address by Prime Minister Jean Chrétien to the Chicago Council on Foreign Relations'. Available at: <http://pm.gc.ca>. Accessed 13 Feb. 2003.

Cooper, Barry. 2002. 'Looking Back on Our Timid Response to 9/11', *National Post*, 9 Sept., A14.

Côté, Gaston. 2002. 'Interview with Canadian Forces Colonel Gaston Côté, Director of the Directorate of Peacekeeping Policy', 16 Oct.

Dawson, Grant. 2001. 'In Support of Peace: Canada, the Brahimi Report and Human Security', in Fen Osler Hampson, Norman Hillmer, and Maureen Appel Molot, eds, *Canada Among Nations 2001: The Axworthy Legacy*. Toronto: Oxford University Press.

Department of National Defence. 2002. *At a Crossroads: Annual Report of the Chief of the Defence Staff, 2001–2002*. Ottawa: Department of National Defence.

English, John, and Norman Hillmer. 1989. 'Canada's American Alliance', in Hillmer, ed., *Partners Nevertheless: Canadian-American Relations in the Twentieth Century*. Toronto: Copp Clark Pitman.

Eggleton, Arthur. 2001. 'Minister of National Defence Press Conference: Canadian Military Contributions', Ottawa, 8 Oct. Available at: <http://www.forces.gc.ca/site/operations/apollo/news_e.htm>. Accessed 21 Jan. 2002.

———. 2002. 'Minister of National Defence Arthur Eggleton and Chief of the Defence Staff Raymond Henault Give Press Conference on the Deployment of Canadian Forces to Afghanistan', Ottawa, 7 Jan. Available at: <http://www.forces.gc.ca/site/operations/apollo/news_e.htm>. Accessed 21 Jan. 2002.

Evans, Gareth, and Mohamed Sahnoun. 2001. *The Responsibility to Protect*. Report of the International Commission on Intervention and State Sovereignty. Ottawa: International Development Research Centre.

Fife, Robert. 2002. 'Ottawa denies rift with Britain', *National Post*, 11 Jan., A6.

Foss, Krista, and Jeff Sallot. 2001. 'What Will Canada Contribute?', *Globe and Mail*, 20 Sept., A7.

Freeman, Alan. 2002. 'Canada Shuns Minor Peace Role', *Globe and Mail*, 4 Jan., A1, A7.

Frum, David. 2003. *The Right Man: The Surprise Presidency of George W. Bush*. New York: Random House.

Garnett, Gary. 2002. 'Interview with Vice Admiral (ret'd) Gary Garnett, former Canadian Forces Vice Chief of the Defence Staff', Ottawa, 13 Jan.

Graham, Bill. 2002. 'An Address to the Canadian Institute of International Affairs on "Affirming Canadian Sovereignty in an Interdependent World"', Toronto, 4 Apr.

Granatstein, J.L. 2001. 'Old Ideas Never Die', letter to the editor, *Globe and Mail*, 20 Nov., A18.

Heinbecker, Paul. 2002. 'Interview with Ambassador Paul Heinbecker, Permanent Representative of Canada to the UN', 16 Aug.

Hillmer, Norman. 2002. 'The Inevitability of Canadian Peacekeeping', unpublished manuscript.

Ibbitson, John. 2003. 'Do We Stand with Our Friends?', *Globe and Mail*, 11 Jan., A15.

Ignatieff, Michael. 2002. 'The Divided West', *Financial Times* (London), 31 Aug., 8.

Laghi, Brian. 2001a. 'Support for Forces Funding Limited, Alliance Poll Finds', *Globe and Mail*, 2 Oct., A11.

———. 2001b. 'No Clear Mission for Troops', *Globe and Mail*, 21 Nov., A4.

Leblanc, Daniel. 2002. '"Deadly" Canadian Snipers Cut Down Enemy Fighters', *Globe and Mail*, 14 Mar., A1, A4.

———. 2003. 'Canada Takes Afghan Mission', *Globe and Mail*, 13 Feb., A1, A13.

Lynch, Colum. 2001. 'Envoy Urges UN Not to Send Peacekeepers', *Washington Post*, 17 Oct., A26.

Manley, John. 2001. 'Address to the US Foreign Policy Association', New York, 5 Nov. Available at: <http://webapps.dfait-maeci.gc.ca/minpub/default.asp>. Accessed 5 Jan. 2003.

Martin, Lawrence. 2002. 'A Canuck in the Closet', *Globe and Mail*, 7 Feb., A15.

McCarthy, Shawn. 2001a. 'PM Plans Trip to US to Discuss United Force', *Globe and Mail*, 19 Sept., A7.

———. 2001b. 'Canadians Reject War if Civilians Put at Risk', *Globe and Mail*, 22 Sept., A1, A4.

———. 2002a. 'Manley Defends Deployment', *Globe and Mail*, 9 Jan., A4.

———. 2002b. 'Grow Up, Manley Tells Canada', *Globe and Mail*, 4 Sept., A1.

———. 2002c. 'Pulled Ever Further into US Orbit', *Globe and Mail*, 8 Jan., A6.

Mulroney, Brian. 2001. 'Speech to the United Nations Association of Canada', Toronto, 31 Oct., *National Post On-line Extra*. Available at: <http://nationalpost.com/mulroney>. Accessed 31 Oct. 2001.

Naumetz, Tim. 2002. 'Canadians Are "Ready for Combat"', *Globe and Mail*, 8 Jan., A1, A4.

Pagtakhan, Rey. 2001. 'An Address to the South Asia Partnership on the "Afghanistan of Tomorrow: Realistic Prospects for a Lasting Peace"', Ottawa, 22 Nov. Available at: <http://webapps.dfait-maeci.gc.ca/minpub/default.asp>. Accessed 5 Jan. 2003.

Pearson, Lester. 1973. *Mike: The Memoirs of the Right Honourable Lester B. Pearson*, vol. 2, eds John A. Munro and Alex I. Inglis. Toronto: University of Toronto Press.

Sallot, Jeff. 2001a. 'Canadians Head Off to War', *Globe and Mail*, 9 Oct., A1, A7.

———. 2001b. 'NATO Seeks Canadian Troops for the Balkans', *Globe and Mail*, 8 Oct., A6.

———. 2001c. 'Will Canada Send Soldiers to Free US Peacekeepers?', *Globe and Mail*, 4 Oct., A4.

———. 2002. 'Bittersweet Homecoming Awaits Troops', *Globe and Mail*, 15 July, A1, A5.

———. 2003 'Canadians Oppose US Stand, Poll Says', *Globe and Mail*, 8 Feb., A9.

Simpson, Jeffrey. 2001a. 'Canada's Help: Who Are We Kidding?', *Globe and Mail*, 19 Sept., A15.

———. 2001b. 'And Nary a Mention of Canada', *Globe and Mail*, 22 Sept., A13.

Sinclair, Jill. 2002. 'Interview with Jill Sinclair, Director General of the International Security Bureau', 29 Nov.

Stairs, Denis, and Danford W. Middlemiss. 2002. 'The Canadian Forces and the Doctrine of Interoperability: The Issues', *Policy Matters* (Institute for Research on Public Policy) 3, 7 (June).

Stein, Janice Gross. 2001. 'Bravo for Soldiers of Peace', *Globe and Mail*, 16 Nov., A19.

Thompson, Allan. 2001. 'Canadian Troops on Hold', *Toronto Star*, 20 Nov., A1, A6.

Toughill, Kelly. 2001. 'McDonough's Anti-War Stance Under Fire', *Toronto Star*, 13 Oct., A18.

United Nations Security Council. 2001a. Resolution 1368, 12 Sept.

———. 2001b. Resolution 1373, 28 Sept.

———. 2001c. 'Statement of US Secretary of State Colin Powell to the Security Council', Security Council provisional verbatim record, S/PV.4413, 12 Nov.

————. 2001d. 'Special Representative for Afghanistan—Terms of Reference', Annex to 'Letters from the Secretary-General to the President of the General Assembly and the President of the Security Council', A/56/432–S/2001/934, 3 Oct.

————. 2001e. Resolution 1386, 20 Dec.

————. 2002a. 'Threats to international peace and security caused by terrorist acts', Security Council provisional verbatim record, S/PV.4561, 27 June.

————. 2002b. Resolution 1401, 28 Mar.

————. 2002c. Resolution 1441, 8 Nov.

Wright, David. 2002a. 'Address at McGill University on "Ad Hoc Coalitions and the NATO Alliance"', Montreal, 8 Oct.

————. 2002b. 'Interview with Ambassador David Wright, Permanent Representative of Canada to the North Atlantic Treaty Organization', 11 Nov.

Wright, Jim. 2002. 'Interview with Jim Wright, Assistant Deputy Minister (Global and Security Policy)', 23 Dec.

11

Dispelling the Myth of Multilateral Security after 11 September and the Implications for Canada

FRANK P. HARVEY

The emerging consensus in the literature on the terrorist attacks of 11 September 2001 suggests that the attacks destroyed, once and for all, the myth of American independence. According to this view, US officials can no longer remain complacent in the belief that they are somehow isolated from global conflict or that they have the power independently to protect the US from external (and internal) attacks. As the world continues to transform, state-centric models of international politics will become increasingly obsolete. These outdated frameworks no longer provide a useful analytical tool for predicting international behaviour, and have become almost useless as a guide for foreign and security policy (Cilluffo et al., 2001; Cilluffo and Berkowitz, 1998: 1–72).

The American myth of independence is not the only casualty of September 11. Traditional realist paradigms fail us today also because our adversaries

are no longer motivated by 'interest' in any relevant sense, and this makes
the appeal to interest in the fashion of realpolitik and rational-choice theory seem merely foolish. (Barber, 2002)

The death of independence, in turn, will have a profound impact
on US foreign and security policy. American unilateralism will
inevitably be replaced by a strong preference for multilateralism,
because only multilateral strategies and institutions can provide the
coalitions and international co-operation required to address the
security threats created by the mutually reinforcing pressures of globalization, proliferation, and terrorism. Predictions and recommendations regarding the inevitable and rational move towards greater
dependence on multilateralism represent the conventional wisdom
on the subject.

But these predictions do not appear to match the US response to
the acts of terrorism. Instead, the evidence confirms that the more
insecure the US becomes as a result of the globalization of terrorism and the proliferation of weapons of mass destruction (WMD)
technology, the more effort, money, time, and energy the US will
invest in re-establishing independent, autonomous, self-directed, sovereign, and unilateral control over American security and economic
affairs.[1] In other words, despite the reality of *inter*dependence,
increasing levels of US vulnerability and sensitivity, and the myth of
American independence, US officials will continue to implement policies that prioritize re-establishing American independence. Officials
in Washington, while requesting support from other states to assist
in their war on terrorism, are committed to becoming less dependent
(or reliant) on contributions from other states and international organizations for the safety of American citizens, less dependent on the
United Nations, less dependent on European allies, and less dependent on Russia for multilateral arms control.

Washington is unlikely (and apparently unwilling) to heed the
concerns expressed by proponents of multilateralism. Nor is the current American government likely to accept the obsolescence of geo-
graphic boundaries or suddenly acknowledge the death of its own
independence. When it comes to protecting Americans after 11
September there is little evidence to indicate that American officials
are becoming more dependent on the UN, NATO, or, for that matter,
any other state, alliance, multilateral coalition, organization, institution, or regime.

Critics are correct to warn that unilateral, state-centric approaches to security may not succeed, but the futility of unilateralism is not entirely relevant. What is relevant is that major powers will struggle to re-establish independent control over their own security despite the enormous challenges associated with mounting effective unilateralist strategies. How does one explain this powerful fixation with US independence in a globalizing world? Doesn't this imply a preference for strategies that are not particularly rational, that are unlikely to enhance security, and that may actually make things worse?

On the contrary, what appears on the surface to be an irrational response to the contemporary realities of globalization is in fact a perfectly rational strategy derived from an objective assessment of the costs, benefits, and risks of available alternatives. Unilateral approaches to security are rarely evaluated (and selected) in isolation —they are always compared to the successes, failures, and overall potential of multilateral alternatives. With respect to that comparison, it is becoming increasingly apparent that multilateral approaches to security have not succeeded and that unilateral strategies offer a better return for one's security investment, with fewer risks.

The debate between supporters of ballistic missile defence (BMD unilateralism) and their critics who favour reliance on the nuclear non-proliferation, arms control, and disarmament regime (NACD multilateralism) encapsulates the divide in the security community. It also helps to explain the post-11 September preference in Washington for unilateral solutions to WMD proliferation. The impasse within the UN over Iraq and how to enforce United Nations Security Council Resolution 1441 provides another illustration of the potential problems American officials face when relying exclusively on multilateral consensus.

UNILATERAL-MULTILATERAL CONTINUUM

Several points should be noted regarding the 'choice' between multilateral and unilateral approaches to security. First, the choice is rarely driven by preferences alone; the decision is often a product of systemic pressures that push leaders in one or another direction— uncontrollable imperatives, not preferences, often explain behaviour. 'People and countries might shape systems, but systems shape countries and people. It is impossible to divorce the exercise of power from the context in which it is set. . . . A singularly unipolar political

structure will produce, absolutely inevitably, a unilateralist outcome. . . . The sole viable alternative to unilateralism is not multilateralism, but isolationism' (Hanes, 2002).[2]

Second, there are no pure unilateralists or multilateralists. One's
preferences are likely to vary from issue to issue, region to region,
and threat to threat. Moreover, the application of these strategies is
likely to vary for specific states in different contexts. For example,
unilateral strategies were entirely acceptable to France when dealing
with ethnic conflict in its former African colonies; and to Russian officials when combatting ethnic violence in Chechnya; and to China
when confronted with challenges to its unilateral control over Tibet
and Taiwan. Yet these same three states were quick to emphasize the
importance of multilateralism in the context of US policies in Iraq
circa 2003. There is nothing particularly surprising about the selective application of these strategies. Historically, American foreign policy has exhibited elements of both, although Washington tends to
receive far more criticism for its unilateral initiatives than praise for
its contributions to multilateralism. This bias often creates an exaggerated impression that Washington is decidedly unilateral even if the
record is far more balanced.

A slightly different approach to measuring US unilateralism focuses
on the extent to which, prior to 11 September 2001, US officials were
decidedly disengaged internationally. As Andrew Cohen (2002: 44)
points out, 'until Sept. 11, less foreign news was presented in America
in recent years, as measured in minutes on television news and space
in newspapers and magazines, than was the case in the past. By one
measure, *Time* magazine ran fewer cover stories on foreign subjects
in the 1990s than it did in the 1960s. In Congress, it has been said
that almost a third of the representatives do not have passports.' Still
another approach to assigning unilateral/multilateral labels to major
foreign policy initiatives focuses on 'outcomes'. Unilateral initiatives
can conceivably produce multilateral benefits—for example, the
international community (including France) will gain some measure
of multilateral security if the US succeeds in its efforts to disarm Iraq,
despite the fact that many of these states (including France) were initially opposed to US intervention in Iraq.

Third, there are two distinct dimensions to the various disputes
among proponents of multilateralism and unilateralism. Both illustrate the difficulties with classifying any major foreign policy initiative in these terms: (1) debates about whether the US, its allies, and

their opponents are (or are not) acting unilaterally or multilaterally, and (2) debates about whether unilateral or multilateral approaches are more or less effective at enhancing global, regional, or domestic security. The first set of debates raises several difficult questions about how one actually measures unilateralism or multilateralism, the second raises both normative and empirical questions about the probability of success and failure. All of these debates are taking place simultaneously without any effort to apply a more systematic framework of analysis.

With respect to the first debate, it is important to begin by noting that there are no purely unilateral or multilateral strategies or policies—virtually every major foreign policy initiative falls somewhere on a continuum ranging from purely unilateral, to bilateral, to multiple bilateral, to coalitional, to à la carte multilateralism, to purely multilateral. Most states practise some combination of these strategies for different policies across different issues with different partners for a variety of reasons. It is simplistic in the extreme to assign a single title of 'unilateral' to encapsulate, for example, US pre- or post-11 September foreign policy. Unfortunately, we tend to be very selective (and decidedly unsystematic) when applying these terms, often because our impressions are formed by our views about the foreign policy initiative in question. Proponents of US intervention in Iraq, for example, are likely to interpret US behaviour in multilateral terms (e.g., unanimous support for Security Council Resolution 1441), while critics are likely to characterize US foreign policy in unilateral terms.

A more systematic approach to the problem would acknowledge that one could measure in several ways the presence and/or absence of multilateral support for any foreign policy initiative by compiling evidence on, for example: (1) multilateral diplomacy and/or dialogue through international organizations and institutions; (2) explicit offers of political, economic, and/or military support for the foreign policy initiative in question; (3) implicit (non-public) offers of multilateral political, economic, and/or military support; (4) tactical (e.g., logistics) and/or operational (over-flight access) and/or strategic military support, etc. Moreover, evidence of assistance across each of these dimensions of multilateralism must be measured on a continuum ranging from no support to extensive support. This approach obviously poses significant challenges for anyone interested in providing a truly systematic (and accurate) assessment of the extent and nature of multilateralism in the system.

Among the questions that emerge from this approach are the following. How much more or less weight should we assign to explicit, public support versus implicit (behind-the-scenes) support? How does one distinguish the value of political versus military support for American foreign policy in Iraq? How does one measure the value in multilateral terms of the letter signed by eight European leaders (or the subsequent letter signed by another 10 world leaders a few days later) supporting US intervention in Iraq? Where on the unilateral-multilateral continuum does one place the quiet military and operational support offered to the US by several allies in Europe and the Middle East. For example, although Germany and France were opposed to US intervention in Iraq, they will nevertheless be required to provide tactical, logistical, and operational support to the US campaign through NATO—e.g., the provision of AWACS and Patriot missiles to Turkey. Comments by the German Ambassador to Canada, Christina Pauls, illustrate some of these measurement challenges—she claimed that Germany will not participate in any military operation against Iraq, but when asked about German airmen flying in AWACS and the logistical support Germany would have to provide US troops deployed from German bases in coalition operations against Iraq, her response was, yes but 'you will not see "German" ground forces or naval forces or air force participating in armed conflict against Iraq' (Wells, 2003). How exactly should one measure Germany's indirect military support when calculating the extent and nature of US unilateralism/multilateralism? Skeptics will no doubt point out that this approach leaves out of the calculation many critics of US foreign policy who prefer to remain quiet, but there is no reason why those who prefer to remain quiet are any more or less likely to support US policy. Several allies in the Middle East are unlikely to be vocal about their support for US policy in Iraq (or openly critical of Saddam Hussein) for obvious domestic political reasons.

The period following the unanimous passage of Resolution 1441 serves well to illustrate other measurement problems. Consider, for example, the extensive political support on the US side of the zero-sum equation—Spain, Italy, Turkey, Denmark, Netherlands, Lithuania, Kuwait, Qatar, Saudi Arabia, Australia, Poland, Czech Republic, Hungary, Bahrain, Oman, Uzbekistan, Bulgaria, Pakistan. Consider, too, the combined population of Britain, Spain, Italy, Denmark, Portugal, the Czech Republic, Hungary, and Poland (at 232 million) versus France and Germany (at 143 million). Clearly, the French coalition appears to be closer to the unilateral end of the continuum, at least within Europe. Consider also the fact that only three out of 19 members of the NATO alliance (France, Germany, and Belgium) are critical of US policy and, at least initially, vetoed contingency plans to mobilize NATO troops in support of Turkey. The fact that NATO cannot act unless support is unanimous is not a policy conducive to multilateralism; it is a policy in support of unanimity and, in essence, gives more power to fewer states with a unilateral agenda. Ironically, the most recent experience with NATO multilateralism will likely have the effect of pushing the US towards a strategy of multiple-bilateralism whereby the US will obtain specific commitments from allies one at a time, rather than depend on (and wait for) consensus to unfold through NATO or the UN.

A second but related dimension of the debate between proponents of multilateralism and unilateralism focuses on the capacity of these respective strategies to enhance global, regional, or domestic security. It is important to note that there is nothing inherent in unilateralism or multilateralism that makes either approach any more or less likely to succeed. Some threats will be addressed more effectively through unilateral strategies, while others will require a multilateral response. Consequently, valid assessments (or predictions) of success and failure must be based on the specific threats in question, the policy initiatives put in place to address those threats, and an objective assessment of success and failure. With respect to the proliferation of weapons of mass destruction, for example, an objective assessment of the costs, benefits, and risks of available alternatives suggests that unilateral ballistic missile defence is a valuable addition to any credible strategy to address the security threats from WMD proliferation and terrorism. Despite the claims by staunch defenders of multilateralism, there is very little evidence that the nuclear arms control, non-proliferation, and disarmament regime is capable of addressing these threats. Again, evidence of rampant multilateralism is not evidence of successful multilateralism.

THE DEMISE OF CANADA'S 'WEAK-STATE' STRATEGY

In a post-11 September environment the imperative to be confident and proactive when crafting Canadian foreign and security policy has never been greater, and the dangers of a blind commitment to the default 'weak-state' strategy of 'distinction first, security second' have never been more apparent. As Christopher Sands (2002: 71–2) points out:

> A weak state strategy for Canada would consider the threat of international terrorism largely a US concern, and seek to placate US pressures within minimum efforts while husbanding Canadian sovereignty and avoiding commitments to undertake new responsibilities with regard to the defence of North America. . . . If [Ottawa] continues to adopt a weak country strategy it will fade in its ability to represent and defend Canadian interests in the United States, while fading in its attractiveness as a partner for Washington in the management of cross-border issues.

Perhaps this is Canada's destiny—as US power continues to expand and as the status and influence of a growing number of very active 'middle powers' continues to develop, Canada will, by definition, become increasingly marginalized. In this context perhaps we should expect Canadian officials to work that much harder at maintaining the false impression that Canada actually has some choice left, that we are relevant, that we still have control over our priorities and our own destiny. Perhaps the 'weak-state' strategy is all we really have left.

The most recent example of Canada's 'weak-state' foreign and security policy was clearly illustrated by Foreign Affairs Minister Bill Graham's insistence that the social and military wings of Hezbollah be considered distinct. This position was maintained and defended despite extensive evidence to the contrary compiled by US and Canadian intelligence sources (see Bell, 2002). Notwithstanding this evidence and the overwhelming consensus in the terrorism literature that recruitment and funding are rapidly spreading in liberal democracies, Ottawa continued to explain and defend the distinction between Hezbollah's social and military wings with repeated references to Canadian 'values'. There are at least four reasons why this policy undermined the security of Canadian citizens. First, the message received by American officials was that Ottawa was less committed than the US to fighting terrorism. Second, Graham's insistence that the distinction was not only fair but worthy of defending conveyed to prospective terrorists that their funding networks could function more efficiently in Canada—what other message could they possibly derive from Canada's policy? Third, from Washington's perspective Ottawa was perceived as willing to accept the costs and risks of being wrong about Hezbollah (perhaps because those costs were more likely to be paid out in American lives) rather than the costs and risks of appearing to support a very straightforward and rational US security policy—a rationality Ottawa was finally forced to accept after comments by a prominent Hezbollah leader calling for renewed suicide attacks against Israel. Fourth, perhaps most disconcerting for US officials was the fact that the Liberal government was not compelled to push for a distinct position on Hezbollah as a way of avoiding the domestic political costs of supporting an unpopular US policy—without a credible opposition, there were (are) no political costs for the Liberal government to worry about. In other words, it has never been easier for the Liberal Party to do the right thing for Canadian security, yet, for some reason, DFAIT officials decided the wrong policy made more sense, despite the evidence compiled by a far superior US intelligence-gathering network.

There is another interpretation of Canada's position on Hezbollah that is perhaps even more distressing—it was a policy driven by unilateral self-interest designed to avoid the wrath of terrorist groups by demonstrating that Canadians are not Americans (a post-11 September variation on the appeasement theme). The 'weak-state' explanation, while perhaps more accurate, is certainly disconcerting. The 'appeasement' explanation, while less accurate, is particularly dangerous even if it applies only to a small minority of opinion in Canada. The most important question, of course, is which of these two interpretations is considered by officials in Washington to be more accurate, and what are the implications for Canada?

UNILATERALISM AS A PREREQUISITE FOR MULTILATERALISM

Canadian and European proponents of multilateralism often refuse to admit that multilateralism typically requires a major push, primarily because most states have different, and often mutually exclusive, self-interests. Each aspiring multilateralist state brings to the diplomatic game a set of very specific interests and objectives. These unilateral interests determine states' positions regarding which multilateral coalitions to join, which ones should be ignored, and which ones should be challenged by forming a competing coalition. These efforts seldom, if ever, have anything whatsoever to do with noble efforts to create a universal standard of values and norms embedded in international regimes and multilateral institutions. That image of multilateralism is a dangerous myth. Instead, multilateral strategies are typically selected by states for entirely 'unilateral' reasons—e.g., to acquire some combination of power, status, influence, domestic political survival, economic and financial gain, etc. For example, the enormous (unilateral) economic investment by France and Russia in oil extraction and production facilities in Iraq define their interests— 'values' associated with global justice and multilateral security have nothing to do with their position in Iraq.

Given these competing self-interests, coercive diplomatic threats of unilateral action have become an almost essential prerequisite for pushing the multilateral juggernaut into action. It took US threats of unilateralism to move the bargaining space towards the multilateral consensus that produced a stronger and more robust inspections regime through Resolution 1441. Without those threats, and associated fears on the part of Europeans and Russians that they were on the verge of being bypassed (and that their interests in a post-Saddam Iraq were in jeopardy), the UN would not have come close to achieving a unanimous resolution. Proponents of multilateralism are not likely to acknowledge the need for coercion, but the evidence to the contrary is overwhelming.

In essence, the US has become an indispensable nation for UN credibility and successful multilateralism. Few analysts would disagree with the observation that the essential prerequisite for a return of UN weapons inspectors (UNMOVIC) to Iraq was the deployment by the US and the UK of close to 100,000 troops to Kuwait, Qatar, and Turkey. The prerequisite for the unanimous passage of Resolution 1441 was the US Senate vote on 11 October 2002 of 77–23 authorizing President Bush 'to use all means that he determines to be appropriate, including force, in order to enforce the United Nations Security Council Resolutions (regarding Iraq), defend the national security interests of the United States against the threat posed by Iraq, and restore international peace and security in the region'. The House, by 296–133, approved an identical resolution. The passage of this resolution was driven by a very strong conviction held by members of the US Congress that the only way to get France, Russia, China, and other members of the UN Security Council to sign onto Resolution 1441 was to convey to these states that the US was resolute in its determination to respond (alone if necessary) to what the Bush administration perceives as a growing threat to security. That resolve convinced other European powers that Resolution 1441 was essential. And the only reason the Iraqi regime allowed UN inspectors back into Iraq (with a significantly more robust mandate than the previous inspection regime, UNSCOM) was the successful application by the US administration of coercive diplomacy throughout this period. Hard power prevailed. Take away the coercive diplomacy of the US and the UK and none of this 'multilateral' activity would have unfolded. There was no 'soft power', multilateral alternative that would have come close to achieving what coercive and credible threats of US unilateralism achieved in Iraq—in fact, the evidence suggests that UN multilateralism from 1998 to 2002 produced four years of opportunity for Iraq to proliferate. There is no rational reason to expect that Iraqi officials did not take advantage of that opportunity.

DISHONEST MULTILATERALISM AND CANADA'S FUTURE AMONG NATIONS

Given Canada's declining status as a middle power and the relatively insignificant influence this carries on the international stage, an almost religious commitment to multilateralism has emerged as the only game in town for Canada. There is nothing wrong with this— Canada has done a good (although not error-free) job as the world's favourite multilateralist (at least in the eyes of DFAIT officials). But Ottawa should not assume that the priorities Canada is forced to accept by virtue of our declining position in the world are the only priorities that should be imposed on the rest of the world.

> Never has the world meant more to Canada; never has Canada meant less to the world. . . . If indeed Canadians want a somewhat distinctive foreign policy vis-à-vis Washington, then they have to pay for it. Having failed to make that investment, they fill the vacuum with moral superiority that acts as a false substitute for having real assets, tangible commitments and the ability to make real choices. (Simpson, 2003)

Regardless of how commendable one's goals are of establishing a truly multilateral global order, the refusal to acknowledge the deficiencies of multilateralism is morally suspect. This is particularly true given the lack of any compelling evidence that multilateral approaches have contributed to enhancing global security. In fact, a little less multilateral apathy in Rwanda in 1994 and a little more unilateral (independent) initiative would have saved hundreds of thousands of lives; a little less dependence on multilateralism in Bosnia *circa* 1990–5 and a little more support (throughout this period) for a US initiative to lift the arms embargo against the Muslims and to strike Serb targets would have saved potentially tens of thousands of lives; US unilateral pressure to push for a military solution in Kosovo *without* a UN Security Council resolution (given the inevitable veto by China and Russia) proved to be the right strategy at the right time against the right person (Milosevic) for the right reasons.

Assuming Canadian security is in fact a priority, honest multilateralism would at least acknowledge the many deficiencies that plague the approach and would accept, at least occasionally, the potential utility of alternatives. The unintended consequence of maintaining an unwavering commitment to multilateralism is that all other approaches are dismissed, not because they provide less security for Canadians but because they tend to marginalize Canada, Canadian approaches, and Canadian officials. Moreover, Canada's 'distinctive' emphasis on 'soft power' does not provide Canada with anything distinctive—every state on the planet has some level of soft power. The assertion that Canadian officials somehow corner the market on the intellectual tools required to apply this kind of diplomacy effectively is a tad insulting to every other state on the planet that lacks hard power. In reality, as Proudman, in Chapter 17 of this volume, correctly points out, 'soft power is useless—it is not power at all (and) can result in a kind of ideologically induced blindness to the existence of real and intractable conflict.' He goes on to point out that, 'in very human ways, international actors emphasize those types of power that they have the ability to exercise, and simultaneously deny those problems with which they are ill-equipped, materially or ideologically, to deal.' Proudman's observation explains the backwardness of Canadian foreign and defence policies—they tend to be derived not from a balanced assessment of our values, interests, and strengths, but from a balanced assessment of our weaknesses. If Canada cannot sustain a meaningful contribution to, say, a war to disarm Iraq, then it is better to emphasize the benefits of letting diplomacy work through multilateral institutions. At least that approach is more likely to postpone the inevitable demonstration that Canada cannot afford to contribute to multilateral security. The result is a kind of dishonest multilateralism that is vigorously supported by Canadian officials not because the approach maximizes Canadian security but because it maximizes the false impression that Canada has a meaningful contribution to make to global security by pushing for multilateral solutions.

An honest commitment to Canadian security would acknowledge that all options available for dealing with terrorism and proliferation, including unilateral options, should be considered and evaluated in terms of their capacity to solve these problems. And in the context of evaluating alternatives, Canadian officials should be willing to engage the mounting evidence that exclusive reliance on multilateralism has failed. An honest approach requires answers to the following questions. If US unilateralism is not the answer, then what is? How exactly will 'multilateralism' work to address the specific problem in question, and what precisely are the costs and security risks to Canadians if that approach fails? Canadian officials have an obligation to provide answers to these questions, but they rarely do. The default recommendation is that multilateralism will solve the problem if given enough time, an assertion that is often put forward by DFAIT officials as a self-evident 'truth' with no explanation required. This dishonesty plays out in much of what passes as Canadian foreign policy today. Four recent illustrations are outlined below.

1. In the weeks prior to the unanimous passage of Resolution 1441 (designed to create a more robust inspections regime in Iraq), DFAIT officials were constantly repeating Canada's five main concerns about a US unilateral intervention in Iraq: (1) many other 'rogue' states are just as bad as Iraq and we can't attack them all; (2) there is no clear proof of a link between Iraq and the terrorist attacks of September 2001; (3) there is no clear proof of WMD proliferation by Iraq; (4) there is no clear proof of WMD deployment by Iraq; and (5) there is no clear proof of an intention to use WMD. Put differently, unless the US produces a picture of Saddam Hussein with his finger a few inches from a big red button, the US has no right to attack Iraq. But it became apparent that the same Canadian officials did not require the same evidentiary prerequisites to establish a just and moral cause for intervention in Iraq if the intervention was sanctioned by a UN Security Council resolution. In that case, none of the five conditions applied, as if a multilateral operation sponsored by a UN Security Council resolution (such as 1441) automatically established the moral clarity required to attack another country. It was clear that Canada's position had (has) nothing to do with a balanced and

honest assessment of the threats and the best available strategy to address them. Instead, Canadian priorities are derived from a preference for process. But 'just war' theory says nothing about a preference for multilateralism because there is nothing about the process itself that increases the probability of success, ensures proportionality, or protects innocent civilians—the cornerstones of 'just war' theory.

2. Defence Minister John McCallum's reaction to President Bush's advice to Canada (and other NATO allies) at the 2002 NATO meeting in Prague provides another example of dishonest multilateralism. In response to the US President's plea to NATO ministers to increase defence expenditures, McCallum responded by pointing out that this was 'a Canadian matter' and that 'a number of Canadians were a little bit ticked off.' Consider the irony here: we have the world's favourite multilateralist (at least in the eyes of many Canadians) rejecting a suggestion from the world's least favourite unilateralist that Canada (and other NATO members) spend more on defence, in large part, to become more effective contributors to multilateral security, peacekeeping, and peace support operations. On the surface, Bush's advice was entirely appropriate considering that most Canadians preferred to see a more sustained deployment of Canadian troops in Afghanistan (beyond the 800 troops that returned after six months). That reasonable suggestion was dismissed by McCallum because, as he correctly points out, Canada reserves the right to make unilateral (sovereign) decisions about how to make Canadians more secure. In other words, no state or collection of states has the right to define Canada's security priorities and defence imperatives. Yet Canadian officials, namely Prime Minister Jean Chrétien and Foreign Affairs Minister Bill Graham, reserve the right to demand from US officials that they avoid unilateral approaches to protecting American citizens from terrorism and WMD proliferation in favour of a multilateral consensus on how the US should deal with these emerging threats. This selective application of multilateralism by Canada is dishonest, especially given the dismal record of multilateral solutions to these threats.

3. The dishonesty with which Canadian officials practise multilateralism can also be seen in pronouncements by Prime Minister Chrétien that the international community must work towards resolving global poverty, because of obvious linkages to terrorism. These statements are dishonest for two reasons. First, there is no empirical

evidence to support the linkage between poverty and terrorism. In fact, in one study on the subject, Krueger and Maleckova (2002: 29) conclude the exact opposite is true. According to the authors:

> The evidence we have assembled and reviewed suggests there is little direct connection between poverty, education and participation in terrorism and politically motivated violence. Indeed, the available evidence indicates that, compared with the relevant population, participation in Hezbollah's militant wing in the late 1980s and early 1990s were at least as likely to come from economically advantaged families and have a relatively high level of education as they were to come from impoverished families without education opportunities.

These findings corroborated similar results in the work of Charles Russell and Bowman Miller (1983, cited ibid.): 'the vast majority of those individuals involved in terrorist activities as cadres or leaders is quite well educated. In fact, approximately two-thirds of those identified terrorists are persons with some university training, university graduates or postgraduate students.' Since education is clearly related to social status and class, the implications regarding the link between poverty and terrorism is obvious. As Krueger and Maleckova (2002: 31) suggest, 'educated, middle or upper class individuals are better suited to carry out acts of international terrorism than are impoverished illiterates because the terrorists must fit into a foreign environment to be successful'.

The second problem with Chrétien's recommendations is that he promised in 1994 to raise the level of Canadian aid and development assistance to 0.7 per cent of GNP, yet Canada's level of aid fell during his reign as Prime Minister to 0.25 per cent of GNP. In other words, Canada's efforts under Chrétien to combat poverty fell from eighth among OECD nations to 17 out of 22. Recent figures place Canada's ranking at 19 out of 22 in regard to spending as a portion of GNP, and 11 out of 22 for overall spending among OECD members (Simpson, 2003). All of this occurred at a time when Canada successfully raised its own standard of living (and associated quality-of-life indicators) to be ranked by the UN as the best country in the world to live, a statistic the Prime Minister repeatedly and enthusiastically repeated. Thus, Canada's quality of life increased at a time when Canada's contribution to the quality of life of the planet's less fortunate declined. If we follow the logical implications of these two trends, Canada is arguably more responsible than other OECD states (including the US) for the poverty that, according to Chrétien, induces the terrorism inflicted on American citizens. As Hillmer and Molot (2002: 24) point out:

> Chrétien has put considerable effort into what will be the last [G-8] summit [Kananaskis] in Canada under his leadership. . . . Helping (Africa) pull itself up by the bootstraps is a laudable enough goal, if one can get past the understandable skepticism that Africa is merely the flavour of the month and that good money will be thrown after bad. . . . Good works are usually the sign of a leader winding down.

The final and perhaps saddest irony of Chrétien's Kananaskis plan for Africa is that Africa, the poorest continent on the planet, does not produce terrorists. Comparatively wealthy countries in the Middle East, such as Saudi Arabia, do. I doubt very much that the Canadian International Development Agency has any plans to shift a significant portion of its development assistance to the Middle East, for very good reasons—the terrorists that flew planes into the World Trade Center and the Pentagon hate liberal democracies for what they are, not for what they have.

4. Finally, a more extreme form of dishonest multilateralism emerges from the position on Iraq expressed by both the outgoing (and incoming) NDP leaders in Canada. The official policy line is that to avoid being sucked into the vortex of American unilateralism, Canada should refuse to support an American-led war in Iraq. But war in Iraq should be rejected even if sponsored by a unanimous UN Security Council resolution. In other words, Canada under an NDP government would reserve the right to act unilaterally in opposition to any multilaterally sanctioned intervention to disarm Iraq.

CONCLUSION

Andrew Cohen (2002: 37) observed that 'Canada has always struggled for attention in Washington, but it will now have to work harder to remain on the radar screen. The danger is that as Canada fades as a power in the world—in the reach of its military, the impact of its foreign aid, the influence of its diplomacy, the absence of foreign intelligence gathering—it risks becoming a fading presence in Washington, too.' But Canada will continue to fade not only because of what Canadian officials are doing wrong, but because of what other emerging powers are doing right. To deal with this decline Ottawa has to reshape its perceptions of itself and apply its strengths in a post-11 September environment more strategically.

Canada has only one key asset that other emerging states do not—our relationship with the United States. Yet we are not using this resource as effectively (and as ruthlessly) as we should. 'Saying yes to the US—in Kuwait or Kosovo or Afghanistan [or Iraq]—is no shame if that is where we see ourselves rather than where we would like the United States to see us. But those choices should be made from strength' (ibid., 47). While the 'distinction first, security second' strategy may not have been very costly to Canada before 11 September and its aftermath,, Ottawa can no longer afford to miss valuable opportunities to support US policies at the right time—bad timing and missed opportunities to gain important concessions from the Americans on a variety of economic and political issues make no sense, especially if we inevitably support US policies anyway and for the right reasons (e.g., Iraq 1991; Bosnia 1995; Kosovo 1999; Afghanistan 2001/2; Iraq 2003; etc.).

Canadians must engage Americans on the right debates, with the right arguments derived from the right evidence. As Robert Fulford (2001) observed:

> we Canadians love to lecture Americans on their shortcomings in world affairs, not because the Americans listen but because it makes us feel we are part of great events and bring to them a superior wisdom. While we habitually denounce all generalities made about culture, we are able to identify with ease what we consider the sins of the United States. . . . The idea of dealing even-handedly with both sides holds a particular appeal for Canadians. It, too, provides a feeling of cool superiority. Unfortunately, it may also leave us incapable of the one act that has always been essential to survival, distinguishing friends from enemies.

If Ottawa remains committed to a default strategy of privileging distinction over security, officials in Washington will continue to ignore the mounting costs to Canada produced by America's ongoing unilateral responses to emerging threats of terrorism and proliferation. Canada's support for US policies at the right time will go a long way towards persuading American officials (not to mention the US public) that Canada matters as a friend and ally. Unfortunately, Ottawa appears to have lost the ability to manage the US relationship in a way that enhances Canadian interests, values, status, and influence in the world. Unless Canadian officials reconsider the utility of what is obviously a failing strategy, Canada and Canadian interests will continue to fade.

NOTES

1. Lael Brainard, in Cilluffo et al. (2001), writes: 'The aftermath of September 11 confronts America with countervailing pressures. When a sense of safety previously taken for granted is profoundly undermined, there is a natural tendency to pull up the drawbridges and pull back from the world. And when jobs and economic security are put at risk, there is a tendency to look towards protectionist solutions.

2. As Hames correctly points out, 'Genuine multilateralism requires a multipolar order. That can only be achieved when authority is distributed evenly across a number of players (a transient event in human history so far) or if the largest power chooses, for some reason, to shrink itself to meet the occasion. That was the essence of American foreign policy in the decade between the Gulf War and September 11.'

REFERENCES

Barber, Benjamin. 2002. 'Beyond *Jihad* Vs. McWorld', *The Nation*, 21 Jan. 2002. Available at: <http://www.thenation.com/doc.mhtml?i=20020121&s=barber>.

Bell, Stewart. 2002. 'Blood Money: International Terrorist Fundraising in Canada', in Norman Hillmer and Maureen Appel Molot, eds, *Canada Among Nations 2002: A Fading Power*. Toronto: Oxford University Press, 172–90.

Cilluffo, Frank, and Bruce Berkowitz, eds. 1998. *Cybercrime, Cyberterrorism, and Cyberwarfare: Averting an Electronic Waterloo*. Washington: Center for Strategic and International Studies.

———, Joseph J. Collins, Arnaud de Borchgrave, Daniel Gouré, and Michael Horowitz. 2001. *Defending America in the 21st Century: New Challenges, New Organizations, and New Policies* (Executive Summary). Washington: Center for Strategic and International Studies.

Cohen, Andrew. 2002. 'Canadian-American Relations: Does Canada Matter in Washington? Does It Matter If Canada Doesn't Matter?', in Hillmer and Molot, eds, *Canada Among Nations 2002*, 34–48).

Fulford, Robert. 2001. 'From delusions to destruction: How Sept. 11 has called into question the attitudes by which our society lives', *National Post*, 6 Oct. Available at: <www.nationalpost.com>.

Hames, Tim. 2002. 'Arrogance, ignorance and the real new world order', *The Times* (London), 15 Feb. Available at: <www.thetimes.co.uk>.

Krueger, Alan, and Jitka Maleckova. 2002. 'Education, Poverty, Political Violence and Terrorism: Is There a Causal Connection', unpublished manuscript.

Molot, Maureen Appel, and Norman Hillmer. 2002. 'The Diplomacy of Decline', in Hillmer and Molot, eds, *Canada Among Nations 2002*, 1–33.

Sands, Christopher. 2002. 'Fading Power or Rising Power: 11 September and Lessons from the Section 110 Experience', in Hillmer and Molot, eds, *Canada Among Nations 2002*, 63–73.

Simpson, Jeffrey. 2003. 'If only moral superiority counted as foreign aid', *Globe and Mail*, 21 Jan., A17.

Wells, Paul. 2003. 'Germany, France: The sum of all fears', *National Post*, 30 Jan., A13.

12

Canadian Leadership and the Kananaskis G-8 Summit: Towards a Less Self-Centred Foreign Policy

ROBERT FOWLER

At the Kananaskis Summit of G-8 leaders, Prime Minister Jean Chrétien nudged the pendulum of Canadian foreign and economic policy back towards a posture more sensitive to the needs and aspirations of the ever-larger number of poorer people in developing countries. Nowhere was the widening gap more significant than in Africa, by far the most marginalized and least developed part of the world. The Prime Minister ensured that African concerns would have their full place at Kananaskis, inviting the creators of the New Partnership for Africa's Development (NEPAD) to join the debate at the Summit. By reversing the long-declining trend in Canadian development assistance with a commitment at Monterrey (subsequently expanded on in the Speech from the Throne in September 2002) to double Canada's official development assistance (ODA) performance by 2010 through annual increases of 8 per cent and by assigning, at Kananaskis, half of that increase to Africa, Chrétien was resetting Canada's international image, which had become a little hard-edged.

This change of focus was very much on the Prime Minister's mind when he set in motion, at Genoa, the notion of appointing personal representatives for Africa who would be charged with the creation of a G-8 Africa Action Plan. On the road to Kananaskis, Chrétien often returned to the themes of Africa's unique and pressing need, of the unacceptably widening gulf between rich and poor nations, and of the importance of finding more effective means to come to the assistance of those in Africa who were doing the right things to help themselves.

Jean Chrétien, indeed, had begun to prepare his management of Kananaskis well before the Genoa Summit of July 2001. At Genoa he was the elder statesman among the participants, having been longer in office and having attended more summits than any of his peers. Prime Minister Chrétien knew what he needed out of the Genoa meeting in order to set the stage for the Summit he would chair in Canada in the summer of 2002, and he had a very good idea of what he did and did not want that encounter to achieve. He also had some clear ideas of what he hoped the meeting in 2002 would accomplish.

BECOMING SHERPA

On 30 July, a week after Genoa, Prime Minister Chrétien appointed me to become his Personal Representative for the next year's G-7/ G-8 meeting in Kananaskis and made me his Sherpa, responsible for both the substance and the organization of the meeting. He also, insisting on one-stop shopping, appointed me to the newly established position of his Personal Representative for Africa (APR), a position I will retain until the next G-8 meeting in Evian. To acquit these responsibilities effectively, and after only eight months as Ambassador in Rome, while promising my wife, my staff, the Italians, and myself that I would return as soon as possible, I moved to Ottawa to set up the Summit Office in the Old City Hall on Sussex Drive.

In Rome, as the new Ambassador to Italy, I had watched my Italian hosts gear up for their Summit in Genoa. I have attended 10 summits—principally as the Foreign Policy Adviser to Prime Ministers Trudeau and Mulroney—and have had something to do with preparing a few more. I had never been given the responsibility of preparing one of these meetings, but was well aware of what this entailed and not a little relieved that such responsibilities had eluded me. 'Sherpa' is a title that, early in summit history, was given to the personal representatives who were charged by G-7 Leaders with the preparation of the annual meetings, and evokes the responsibilities of those tireless Nepalese guides who helped Edmund Hillary in 1953, and subsequently so many others, to conquer Everest. The Sherpas' task is to act and take decisions in the name of heads of government, and in their interests, in all matters relating to the organization and substantive preparation of these meetings. Sherpas do not act on any kind of ad referendum basis but, rather, settle issues as they arise based on an understanding of their principals' views and objectives. It is diplomacy at the sharp end.

My first day as Sherpa and APR was 10 September 2001. On the morning of my second day, as I fiddled with the television set I found there (simply to see if it worked), our world changed with the terrorist attacks on New York and Washington. So, too, did my job. Although the package of Summit assignments was already sufficiently daunting, I was reassured by three thoughts. First of all, while the Prime Minister is an exacting boss, working directly for him is like no other job in Ottawa. It makes getting things done an awful lot easier, and I knew well that I would need all the help I could get if what he wanted to achieve at Kananaskis were to be accomplished in 10 months. Second, I already knew I would have the ultimate interdepartmental 'Dream Team' to work with, but the reality of the exceptional and dedicated people who had come together to make Kananaskis a success exceeded even these expectations. Third, I would have the satisfaction of knowing that as I approached the end of my career I would have another—this time unique—opportunity to assist Africa, a continent and a people that have held my fascination and deep affection for all of my adult and professional life.

PRIME MINISTERIAL LEADERSHIP

The Prime Minister insisted that fundamental changes be brought to the way the 2002 Summit in Canada would be organized and conducted. He knew the form of the meeting would have a significant impact on the outcomes he was anxious to achieve, but he also wanted to change the way summits were conducted, simply because changes were so evidently required to preserve the effectiveness and credibility of the Summit instrument. In naval parlance, every institution needs to have its bottom scraped from time to time, and the barnacles had grown thick on the Summit hull after 27 years. Specifically, Canada's Prime Minister wanted to engineer a different kind of Summit, rather than simply a Summit done differently.

In contrast to those stratospheric numbers at Okinawa or Genoa (where one delegation had nearly 1,000 rooms), we offered each delegation 25 rooms at Kananaskis and agreed that each could put up to an additional 11 people in those rooms. A small number of 'day-trippers' from each delegation were allowed to commute to the site. There was a little cheating around the edges, but to everyone's surprise it worked very well. With regard to security, the advantages of an isolated site were manifest in light of the Quebec City (Summit of the Americas) and Genoa experiences, where the very proximity of the meeting in a constrained urban context seemed to incite violence. Whatever the history, circumstances changed utterly following the horrors of 11 September. After the attacks on the Twin Towers and the Pentagon no compromise regarding access to the site was possible, even were it deemed desirable.

Prime Minister Chrétien was adamant that we find a way to allow reasonable access to the media for Summit participants while protecting, without compromise, the safety of Summit leaders and the integrity of the Summit proceedings. The answer, we believed, lay in the installation of state-of-the-art optical fibre video conferencing facilities between Kananaskis and the media centre in Calgary, which would enable any leader or spokesperson to have instant access to their national media contingent or, if they preferred, to talk to and be seen throughout the entire media centre in Calgary, and at any time of their choosing. Indeed, a few could use these facilities simultaneously. In the event, the system lived up to its billing and worked flawlessly throughout the meeting. Whatever was lost in the limitation of face-to-face encounters with the media was, in the view of this observer, more than offset by the security comfort afforded by an essentially closed site and by the increased relaxation and spontaneity that was the result of the media not being in constant and close proximity to Summit participants.

If we had accomplished nothing else, Kananaskis would have been remembered for its efficiency and informality. Much of that is due to the selection of a site which allowed the near elimination of protocol, formality and, above all, the need to organize and protect complex and time consuming motorcades.

SUMMIT PLANNING AND PRIORITIES

In the days and weeks immediately prior to the Kananaskis meeting, a story developed remarkably long legs that what was presumed to be President Bush's anti-terrorist agenda (terrorism was on everybody's agenda!) was poised to supplant Prime Minister Chrétien's African priority. From my perspective as the chair of both the Sherpa preparations, where terrorism was being discussed, and the meetings of personal representatives for Africa charged with creating the Africa Action Plan, this was an utterly false and fabricated dichotomy. Certainly, strong views were expressed on all sides as to the size, scope, and cost of both of these major initiatives and specific aspects of each were debated hotly. After all, each of these complex undertakings engaged unheard of resources and involved fundamental issues of political philosophy and principle. There was never, however, any doubt expressed, at least in my hearing, as to whether either might be unnecessary or inappropriate for consideration at the Summit table generally or in the context of the Kananaskis agenda.

From Genoa, in July 2001, it was crystal clear that Prime Minister Chrétien would insist that the Canadian Summit he would host in 2002 would feature an all-encompassing effort to end Africa's exclusion from the rest of the world and reverse the downward-spiralling trend in the quality of life of the vast majority of Africans. From the moment Al-Qaeda terrorists flew planes into the World Trade Center and the Pentagon, it was equally clear that the next G-8 Summit would have to engage the matter of international terrorism, and particularly the possibility that such individuals would gain access to weapons and materials that would have an utterly cataclysmic impact on our collective way of life. Thus, beyond the fact that all such initiatives compete for places within national budgets, there was no suggestion that Kananaskis should deal with only one of these vitally important and pressing issues, or that one would diminish the other.

Stories in the Canadian media, repeated in Parliament, questioned whether President Bush was even going to attend the Summit. It was confidently asserted that the US President could not be separated from hundreds of advisers and battalions of Secret Service agents. It seemed to be assumed, in Canada, that the Americans believed that

Canada could not adequately protect their President. This was nonsense from the outset. We were, of course, at pains to do it right and provide security arrangements—in the post-11 September environment—that satisfied all Summit leaders, and we knew that that would take some doing—and a lot of spending.

The collaboration among the RCMP, the Canadian Forces, and the Calgary police was simply outstanding. From the first advance visits from G-8 leaders' offices (the Washington contingent was among the first), it was evident that they were entirely satisfied with our extensive security arrangements. Nevertheless, the more we dismissed this shibboleth, the more it seemed to take root. It was, though, a quintessentially Canadian preoccupation: we simply could not, it was widely assumed, be good enough to bring this off. It would be nice to think that Kananaskis might dispel some of our tendency to self-doubt.

In this regard, it is worth recalling that there was not a single cracked pane of glass in Calgary attributable to the Summit. No tactical troops were used or even appeared. No gas or pepper spray was deployed and the only arrests were of a couple of guys spray-painting rail cars prior to the meeting.

When asked about a specific issue in the Venice communiqué, Prime Minister Trudeau told a journalist at the concluding press conference in the summer of 1980 that he had not read the communiqué emerging from that meeting and, further, that he had absolutely no intention of doing so. I heard Chrétien say something very similar on three public occasions in Genoa. Perhaps the best line to emerge from Genoa on the relevance of summit communiqués was from the American Under-Secretary of State for Political Affairs, Mark Grossman, who wryly noted that it would be wonderful if more people read communiqués than wrote them.

I believed that summit communiqués had become an exercise in anti-communication. They were turgid, dense, and essentially not readable, and virtually nobody did. Certainly I had never met a journalist who had admitted doing so. The pretense that these lengthy, over-negotiated examples of bureaucratic excess actually emerged from the discussion among leaders had expired a long time ago and was utterly void of credibility. Indeed, over a number of years, communiqué battles at Sherpa meetings, and even brought to the Summit table, had served to weaken significantly the utility of the entire Summit vehicle. Such battles rarely settled outstanding complex issues and, instead, served only to paper over profound differences, which did not benefit from being disguised.

At our first meeting in Ottawa following my appointment, I reminded the Prime Minister of the comments he had made about the communiqué to the media at Genoa, and wondered if he wished me to try to eliminate it from the Kananaskis context. Bearing in mind that all Summit decisions are by consensus, neither of us knew whether such an entrenched tradition could be easily dispensed with, but he urged me to give it a try.

In view of the evident dissatisfaction with normal communications methods and channels, we established an extraordinary outreach program. It extended over the 10-month period in which we prepared the Kananaskis meeting and reached into most major population centres across Canada and abroad to most G-8 capitals and beyond to Africa and the international organizations. The effort to reach out to Canadians to discuss the Summit agenda and priorities and to get their feedback was, at least for me, a thoroughly enjoyable and useful experience. We also put in place layer upon layer of outreach activities to talk to Canadians.

At my first Sherpa meeting in December 2001, still under the Italian presidency, from the Genoa meeting, I put forward, on behalf of the Prime Minister, a firm agenda proposal for the Kananaskis meeting. It was a little early for us to be making hard and specific agenda proposals, but we believed that if we were to counter effectively the anti-globalization protest movement we would have to demonstrate a genuine commitment to transparency, along with very clear and steadfast messaging about why those ought to be the Summit priorities.

On the basis of this logic, I wanted to get an agenda agreed among Sherpas as quickly as possible and then explain it forcefully and consistently at every possible public occasion. Thus we sought approval for a three-item agenda, which was both relevant to the lives and priorities of Canadians and sufficiently encompassing to resist the inevitable pressures to accommodate new themes in the intervening months before the Summit at the end of June. We proposed three broad challenges as the 'Kananaskis Agenda': (1) strengthening world economic growth; (2) building a new partnership for African development; and (3) combatting terrorism.

As it happened our agenda proposal was agreed by the end of December and never changed. Thus, as we had hoped, our

Kananaskis agenda became a remarkably stable and effective communications tool. Then, to the consternation of some of my new Sherpa colleagues, we proposed the elimination of the summit communiqué. While there were still a few doubts, by the end of that first meeting in early December there was general agreement that we would all recommend to our principals a 'Chairman's Statement', which would be very short (no more than three pages) and replace the discredited communiqué. The preparation and content of the Chairman's Statement would become the responsibility of the host, who, of course, would give the other leaders a look at it prior to its being issued at the conclusion of the meeting. It would not, though, be pre-negotiated, for the practical reason that it could not be written until the meeting was almost over. The chair would take full responsibility for reconciling any last-minute differences among Summit participants.

THE AFRICA ACTION PLAN

At Genoa, G-8 leaders accepted the proposal by African leaders to establish a new and forward-looking relationship based on the principles and the realism of what came to be called NEPAD, aimed at making African nations full and equal partners in the global economic and trading system and, above all, at attracting significant levels of foreign investment to that continent. Canada's Prime Minister had a great deal to do with that decision. In a late-night meeting at the conclusion of the first day of the 2001 Summit, Jean Chrétien insisted that G-8 leaders respond to the African initiative firmly and forcefully, and proposed—for the first time in the 28 years of Summit history—that a new group of personal representatives be established to address a single issue, in this case, to draw up an 'Africa Action Plan' (AAP) in response to the NEPAD proposal. This group, which was to be separate from the regular Sherpas or personal representatives, was charged with presenting such a plan to the next G-8 meeting.

This proposal, championed by Chrétien, was agreed upon relatively expeditiously and announced the next day. Further, because G-8 leaders accepted that the task of producing such a complex and comprehensive plan, in full consultation with our African partners, international institutions, and other major aid donors, would necessarily take more than a few months and would require continuity of leadership, they immediately charged Canada, as the next host, with chairing this group, rather than awaiting the end of the year when the responsibility for summit preparations usually passes from one chair to the next.

The personal representatives for Africa met six times, usually for two and a half days, on the road to Kananaskis. The first meeting was in London in October, and subsequently we gathered in Addis Ababa (December), Cape Town (February), Dakar (April), Maputo (May), and Kananaskis (June), during which time our Africa Action Plan progressively took shape. At all but the final meeting, we included the personal representatives of the members of the NEPAD Steering Group, led by Professor Wiseman Nkuhlu, South African President Thabo Mbeki's outstanding economic adviser and head of the NEPAD Secretariat. Representatives of the 15 members of NEPAD's Heads of State Implementation Committee also participated in parts of our deliberations. Over the course of these meetings with our African colleagues we established a remarkably frank and effective dialogue, which has served both sets of partners very well. We also met on occasion with representatives of African civil society, and at the Maputo meeting we included representatives of the nine donors beyond the G-8 that each provide more than US $100 million in annual development assistance to Africa.

In addition, each of us held extensive domestic consultations. In this regard, I met with 105 organizations and 121 individuals and groups across Canada having interests in Africa. It soon became evident that the centrality of the African initiative was widely, even fervently, supported, as was to a lesser degree the need to co-ordinate action at the highest level to fight terrorism.

I also held four in-depth discussions with the African diplomatic corps in Ottawa. Wearing both my APR and regular Sherpa hats, I was invited to join my Japanese, French, British, German, and Italian colleagues for meetings with interested groups and civil society representatives in their countries and accompanied the Prime Minister to meetings of the World Economic Forum (in New York) and the Commonwealth Heads of Government in Australia, as well as on his pre-Kananaskis travels to Summit capitals where the G-8 African initiative was discussed extensively.

Our outreach effort engaged the Prime Minister in numerous meetings at home and abroad with influential individuals and ordinary citizens who had views about the conduct of the Kananaskis encounter. He visited six key countries in Africa in April and met with groups of West African leaders in Nigeria and with Southern African leaders in Johannesburg. He spoke to the Economic Commission for Africa and the Organization for African Unity in Ethiopia and made speeches all over the world in support of the African centrepiece of the Kananaskis agenda. In addition, the Parliamentary Standing Committee on Foreign Affairs and International Trade undertook hearings across the country on the Kananaskis agenda, and the Foreign Minister, Bill Graham, and the Governor General played roles in this outreach effort from Calgary while the Summit was taking place in the Rockies.

The creation of the Africa Action Plan, with more than 100 specific commitments, was thus as comprehensive, inclusive, and exhaustive as we could make it. The AAP does not purport to respond to every element of the NEPAD; rather, it offers an impressive degree of consensus within the G-8 on where and how G-8 governments ought, collectively, to respond to NEPAD's promise. This response highlights areas where we believe G-8 countries have particular value to contribute at this time, in the context of what both G-8 and African partners have agreed to be an ongoing dialogue in the context of a decades-long new partnership.

G-8 partners have undertaken to make every effort to avoid duplicating the efforts of other countries or of institutions and organizations already working effectively in many of the areas highlighted in the NEPAD. Further, our G-8 Africa Action Plan is a road map that each of us will follow as we develop our partnership with Africa. It is not a formula for collective endeavour, although we Canadians very much anticipate that on occasion two or three or more of us might combine our efforts, perhaps with other donors and/or institutions, to make our contributions more effective.

Canada would have wished to see more co-ordination among G-8 players in the on-ground delivery of our collective AAP commitments, more and better attempts at co-operation on the ground, and greater efforts to avoid overlap and duplication in an effort to acquit our undertaking to achieve greater effectiveness. This said, for a group of countries severely allergic to institutionalizing themselves in any way (the G-8 has no secretariat and employs not a single employee), we did not do too badly. The results are and will be substantial, substantive, and eminently measurable, particularly with regard to increased performance in development assistance. Perhaps the best and most important example of 'one plan, many executions' is with regard to the all-important concept of 'enhanced partnership'—the keynote innovation in the AAP, which aims to develop privileged relationships among those African countries demonstrably committed to the implementation of NEPAD in all its aspects.

G-8 partners agreed that our response to NEPAD could not be business as usual. We agreed, furthermore, that our individual and collective efforts to assist with Africa's development over the past 40 years have not been crowned with great success; that 'Africa' is in fact a vast collection of very different states, governments, political cultures and systems, and resource and agricultural histories, as different and diverse as on any other continent. Our G-8 collective response to each African nation had to be different, quite possibly also different as among G-8 members. We were, however, unanimous that we had to start rewarding success rather than persistently reinforcing failure.

THE NEW PARTNERSHIP WITH AFRICA

With regard to hard decisions and announcements, the Kananaskis meeting, the first to include non-G-8 participants directly in its deliberations, was productive. Specifically, the Summit leaders agreed on the Africa Action Plan. It also provided a long-term framework for a productive partnership between G-8 countries and the 53 nations of Africa.[1]

The first element of this partnership commits G-8 countries to respond to the basic human needs of 800 million Africans without reference to the types of government with which they are blessed or afflicted. The guiding principles behind this engagement are our collective adherence to the 'Millennium Development Goals' agreed upon at the United Nations in the fall of 2002. The second, and more innovative, aspect of this new partnership with Africa, as articulated at Kananaskis, is founded on the realization that the past 40 years of development assistance in Africa have produced, at best, very mixed results. To achieve NEPAD's goal of attracting desperately needed investment to Africa, G-8 countries will henceforth focus the bulk of their new development programming on those countries that act on the principles contained in NEPAD and will seek to inspire confidence in potential investors by putting in place the kinds of policies to attract and retain foreign direct investment.

Thus, the Kananaskis Africa Action Plan foresees that 50 per cent of the significant new development resources committed at the Monterrey meeting on Financing for Development in March of last

year (which the Development Assistance Committee of the OECD estimates to be some US $16 billion) would go to Africa, being directed
to a small group of 'Enhanced Partners' to be selected by each G-8
nation. G-7 leaders at Kananaskis issued a statement following their
meeting (without Russia) on the first morning, which committed them
to ensuring that this highly indebted poor countries (HIPC) initiative,
launched following discussions at the Cologne Summit in 1999,
would indeed deliver on the debt reduction promised to HIPC-eligi-
ble countries, 34 of 42 of which are in Africa, and pledged that 'we
will find our share of the shortfall in the HIPC initiative, recognizing
that this shortfall will be up to US $1 billion'.

CANADA FUND FOR AFRICA

Academics and our African visitors to Kananaskis were both compli-
mentary and realistic in what the Summit achieved; particularly with
regard to the Africa Action Plan, writing in the *Calgary Herald* on the
day following the Summit (June 28), Professor John Kirton of the
University of Toronto's G-8 Information Centre said in an article
entitled 'A Summit of Historic Significance: A Gold Medal for the
Kananaskis G-8':

> . . . At Kananaskis in 2002, the G-8 has finally delivered. It has thus ended
> the cold war and its destructive global legacy, and brought the G-7's
> central democratic values to critical areas of the developing world. The
> Kananaskis G-8 Summit has thus proven to be a strikingly successful sum-
> mit, indeed one of the most successful ever held since the Summit started
> work 28 years ago.

The UN Secretary-General, Kofi Annan, put it very succinctly when
he spoke to the press at the conclusion of the Summit:

> . . . If Africans really stick to the commitments they have made in NEPAD to
> themselves, and to each other, and if the G-8 really carry out the Action Plan
> they are announcing today, this Summit might come to be seen as a turn-
> ing point in the history of Africa, and indeed of the world. That is a chal-
> lenge for all of us to live up to. . . .

To highlight Canada's deep commitment to the evolving Africa
Action Plan, the government had set aside $500 million in a special

Fund for Africa in the December 2001 budget. This fund was used to finance the comprehensive package of major initiatives that Prime Minister Chrétien announced during his final press conference immediately following the conclusion of the G-8 meeting in the afternoon of 27 June. While not a 'Kananaskis deliverable' (because these were strictly Canadian announcements), the Prime Minister believed it was important that, as host and chair of the process that led to the creation of the AAP, he 'walk the talk' in terms of putting the brave words of the AAP into immediate, significant, and far-reaching action. This package of initiatives was, by any Canadian measure, a truly impressive package of projects and policy prescriptions that demonstrated a commitment to making the AAP a living reality. While largely overlooked by the media in Kananaskis and Calgary, it was very much noticed on the ground in Africa and contributed significantly to the credibility of the Kananaskis undertaking to engage in a new and substantive partnership with the peoples and those governments in Africa truly committed to the NEPAD vision.

The 27 June package reinforced the economic-growth elements of the NEPAD, with the opening of Canada's markets to almost all products from the least-developed countries as of 1 January 2003; with the provision of trade-related capacity-building to help African partners benefit from increased market access; with $100 million in federal funding to be matched by the private sector in an African Investment Fund; and with initiatives to help bridge the digital divide. A substantial portion of the package sought to reinforce African capacity in governance and peace, including innovative arrangements intended to ensure that the capacity-building provided to parliaments and public services corresponds directly with what is sought by African partners. Support was also provided for civil society engagement on NEPAD in Africa.

The most substantial portion of the package directly addressed the educational and health needs of the people of Africa, including substantial new funding for the eradication of polio and for African research towards an AIDS vaccine. Prime Minister Chrétien announced that Canada would double its investment in basic education in Africa by 2005 as part of the Canadian initiatives to support the G-8 Africa Action Plan. Canada will invest $100 million annually by 2005 to help achieve the goal of universal primary education in Africa. These resources are additional to Canada's commitment to double its assistance. On 27 June the Prime Minister also spoke to a new manner of working with African partners—for example, by indicating Canada's steadfast engagement to follow through on its commitment to untie its official development assistance and to deliver aid more effectively on the basis of country-driven strategies and priorities.[2]

FIGHTING THE SPREAD OF MASS WEAPONS

Building on the intense and productive activity of G-8 ministers and security officials, who had been creating a new anti-terrorist architecture over the weeks and months following 11 September, Summit leaders took the decision, which only they can take, to mobilize national efforts and put the necessary resources behind such an enormous undertaking. Clearly, one of the most notable achievements of the G-8 Summit in Kananaskis was the launch of the Global Partnership Against the Spread of Weapons and Materials of Mass Destruction, under which G-8 leaders agreed to raise up to US $20 billion over the next 10 years to address a number of non-proliferation, disarmament, counterterrorism, and nuclear safety issues, initially in the Russian Federation. The leaders also issued a statement in which they agreed on a series of measures to promote greater security of land, sea, and air transport in the post-11 September 2001 environment.

The horrors perpetrated on 11 September demonstrated that a relatively small group could inflict disproportionately high damage, typifying a trend in terrorism towards mass casualties. Canadian officials reasoned that terrorists would increasingly seek to acquire weapons of mass destruction (WMD) to intensify their campaigns appallingly and, as a consequence, proposed a set of principles to prevent such an outcome. These principles involved, in the first instance, strengthening the laws, rules, and norms underpinning the international non-proliferation regime, supplemented by a series of concrete measures including: securing WMD materials and facilities that house them; strengthening border controls, export controls, and law enforcement efforts to deter, detect, and interdict in cases of illicit trafficking in WMD items; and, finally, reducing overall quantities of WMD materials in existence. Also included in the principles was a call to assist countries lacking the necessary resources to implement these measures.

The US supported wholeheartedly these principles and specified that assistance should be directed where the proliferation risks are most acute, namely in Russia and former Soviet Union countries.

Furthermore, the US indicated that it would contribute US $10 billion over the next 10 years if that amount were collectively matched by other countries, especially those in the G-8. While G-8 members were receptive to the proposal, they noted that a series of implementation problems hampered progress on existing projects in Russia, and, if a very significant expansion of activities in this area were to be credible, these impediments would need to be addressed.

As a result, Canada drafted a series of guidelines as the framework for new or expanded co-operation projects covering, among other things, access, monitoring and transparency, tax exemptions, liability, procurement practices, intellectual property protections, and privileges and immunities. Prime Minister Chrétien sent a special envoy to Russia to present the guidelines. Following a series of intense negotiations, including by the leaders themselves at Kananaskis, the guidelines were agreed on and the initiative was launched. In the statement, leaders identified among their priority concerns the destruction of chemical weapons, the dismantlement of decommissioned nuclear submarines, the disposition of fissile materials, and the employment of former weapon scientists. Leaders also issued an invitation to other countries prepared to adopt the principles and guidelines to enter into discussions with the G-8 on participating in and contributing to this initiative. This was done in recognition of the fact that countering the WMD terrorist threat is in every country's interests. The recently adopted United Nations General Assembly Resolution 57/68, which recognized the global importance of the partnership and called on all countries to commit to its principles, reflected this view.

Since Kananaskis, all G-8 members have taken steps to implement the global partnership and the group is close to the $20 billion target. Additional partners are expected to join the initiative and countries are now in the process of developing and implementing specific project proposals with Russian authorities, in keeping with the four priorities identified by leaders at the Summit. Canada, for its part, has pledged up to $1 billion over the next 10 years to address the WMD terrorist threat. Working in conjunction with all those participating in the global partnership, Canada will continue efforts to ensure that the potentially catastrophic human, economic, and social consequences of a WMD attack can be prevented.

While the launch of the global partnership, under Canadian leadership, represents one of the most significant international security initiatives of the post-Cold War era, its expeditious and effective implementation will be the true measure of its success. Thus, achievements will not be assessed on the basis of ethereal or laudatory prescriptions but rather on how many chemical weapons have been destroyed, how much weapon-grade plutonium has been disposed of, and how many nuclear submarines have been dismantled. In sum, the vast quantities of weapons and materials of mass destruction that now exist have created for the world a dangerous legacy. The global partnership is an attempt to manage collectively that legacy so present and future generations may live in safety.

The Kananaskis decision to establish the global partnership demonstrated the value of having the Russian President inside the G-8 tent and contributed significantly to the legitimacy of the decision to offer Russia the opportunity to host the Summit in 2006, ending the ambiguity of Russia's membership credentials.

REFLECTIONS

Over the course of the four Sherpa meetings I attended and the six encounters among the personal representatives for Africa, there were issues that Canada would have wished to have seen treated more fully or comprehensively, but the G-8 is a consensus body and the consensus achieved by Prime Minister Chrétien at Kananaskis last June exceeded by far what any G-8 observers (including this one) and international meeting anthropologists had anticipated.

By responding directly to NEPAD's underlying objective of attracting much greater private investment to Africa and of recoupling Africa to the global trading system, the Africa Action Plan stands to generate far more than US $6 billion in additional annual financial resources for Africa. NEPAD indicates that Africa requires some US $64 billion in new financial resources from all sources, both inside (including national budgets) and outside Africa. The AAP will significantly help to bolster Africa's ability to generate those resources.

African need and priorities were highlighted by the fact that the G-8 had engaged as forcefully and as publicly as it had in support of NEPAD, with the high-profile naming of personal representatives of G-8 leaders charged with finding solutions and the resulting energizing of the administrations in all G-8 capitals and within the European Commission to assist in that search. Leaders were evidently committed and the resources were found. Africa became once again a legitimate area of endeavour. Concern for Africa had become respectable. Afro-pessimism was no longer in vogue. The perception of Africa's need changed from that of a desperate situation to become a challenge to the rest of the world.

In fairness, some steadfast and generous nations, principally the Nordic countries and the Dutch, had never lost faith, though perhaps they had begun to waver. That group of countries, which delights in calling itself 'the G.7', had largely sustained their very high levels of ODA contributions, generally well over double the G-8 average, while the G-8 countries were allowing theirs to slip. The participation of such stalwart development performers and experts in our joint endeavour will remain essential, but as the statistics show only too clearly, it is the huge volume of G-8 actual and promised contributions that must necessarily make the difference to Africa's future. Thus, huge new commitments were made at Monterrey: an additional US $12 billion for ODA, including an annual additional $5 billion from the US alone; at Kananaskis, more than US $6 billion was promised to Africa. The AAP in large part made Monterrey possible, as well as being its principal beneficiary.

Both of the Kananaskis initiatives—on Africa and on terrorism—are the real stuff of summitry. Neither could have been taken in any other decision-making forum. No other has the competence, reach, authority, or capacity to commit $120 billion (Cdn) over the next decade to such newly emerging imperatives. Kananaskis demonstrated the flexibility and agility of the G-8 instrument, both in its ability to absorb fundamental change in the manner and in the context in which such meetings are conducted, and in its adaptability to new and challenging circumstances.

The G-8, more than any other world body and certainly far more than the UN Security Council, is a truly capable crisis management vehicle. Kananaskis proved that, responding to the challenge of Africa and to the imperative of denying a new, more effective, and more ruthless brand of terrorist access to cataclysmically dangerous weapons. In fact, however, the G-8 heads of government at Kananaskis had another major crisis to manage, that of the rising tide of doubt on the part of their constituents that they and their governments were up to managing the challenge of the anti-global, essentially anti-government, movement that, in the spring and summer of 2001, seemed to be taking over the streets. Their forthright and large-scale prescriptions for Africa and for the containment of weapons of mass destruction and their firm commitment to manage any threat to public order in the aftermath of 11 September showed the world and each other that they were entirely capable of rising to such significant challenges.

The Kananaskis Summit, with high expectations and aspirations, worked the way it did because the timing was right, the players were the correct ones, and Canadians are adept at this kind of diplomacy— at reconciling differences and finding a high common denominator among decision-makers who want to reach agreement. Indeed, there are those who believe that setting the bar so high was unrealistic and thus that these impressive outcomes are unlikely to be realized. I disagree, but acknowledge that such profoundly complex and expensive commitments will require constant vigilance to see that they are achieved.

Social and economic indicators in Africa will not soon be comparable to those in the rest of the world. It will take time, patience, and enormous effort to set Africans—even in those few African nations that have got most things right—on a different and productive track, one on which measurable improvements in their individual circumstances will be evident and therefore will reinforce what is known in economic circles as a virtuous cycle. If the Africa Action Plan, with its particular emphasis on rewarding success through enhanced partnerships, is successful in changing the trend line for a few in Africa, their positive experience will serve as a beacon of 'best practices' to other nations whose governments still do not understand or accept what must be done to help themselves.

The biggest impediment to the successful application of the Africa Action Plan is our own tendency to expect and require instant and comprehensive satisfaction from any high-profile endeavour, no matter how complex. As our pace of life heats ever upward and information overload becomes ever more acute, we tend to narrow our focus on instant 'up or down', 'black or white', 'winner or loser' judgements. We do not seem to have time for or to be willing to make the effort to produce more subtle analyses. Yet real-world issues affecting the lives of hundreds of millions of people in a vast continent of 53 disparate nations do not lend themselves to such simplistic thinking.

In the same vein, our own expectations of what can be achieved in Africa and how quickly, even in the most promising sub-regions, need to be tempered with healthy doses of reality. We will, I expect and hope, continue to rail against the human and material ravages of the senseless wars and revolutions that occur with distressing regularity across the African continent, all too often in the parts we thought secure. We will also tend to put from our minds, as we do this, the tens of millions killed and the nations destroyed in wars in our part of the world over the last century. Perhaps, too, we will finally rise to the challenge of AIDS (President Bush's 2003 State of the Union commitment of US $15 billion over the next five years is a very promising start) before it completely drains future generations of Africans of what hope and dignity and decency they might otherwise have expected from their short and hard lives.

Africa, over the 30–40-year course of our planned new partnership, will necessarily take a few steps forward and then a few steps back. Through the Action Plan, we will endeavour to ensure that there is net forward progress, but there will be setbacks, even among our chosen 'enhanced partners'. We must weather these delays and disappointments while maintaining a realistic appreciation of the reasonableness of our expectations, though without reducing our standards and performance criteria.

Our African partners must also preserve a sense of realism with regard to the speed and consistency of the application of our AAP commitments. G-8 leaders have pledged a great deal of their taxpayers' money and have indicated unequivocally the circumstances under which it will and will not be used. They have also pledged to use their huge contributions and considerable influence within international organizations and financial institutions to promote national, regional, and sectoral infrastructure development throughout Africa.

Nevertheless, these resources and undertakings, at least initially, may not have an immediate or evident impact on the lives of many Africans and, in many cases, will be introduced slowly. Putting certain of these enhanced partnerships into place will also take each of us varying amounts of time and, to an extent our African partners might from time to time choose to forget, will depend on their meeting their own NEPAD undertakings, including the introduction of a credible and effective African peer review mechanism. Thus, patience, goodwill, and understanding on all sides must not be in short supply over the coming decades if this brave Kananaskis initiative is to succeed.

NOTES

1. To view the entire NEPAD document, please refer to: <http://www.avmedia.at/nepad/indexgb.html>.
2. Details of these 27 June announcements by the Prime Minister can be found under 'Canada helps build a New Partnership with Africa', available at: <http://www.g8.gc.ca/statements/20020627-en.asp>.

APPENDIX: G-8 AFRICA ACTION PLAN HIGHLIGHTS

What is the New Partnership for Africa's Development

- The New Partnership for Africa's Development is first and foremost a pledge by African leaders to the people of Africa to consolidate democracy and sound economic management, and to promote peace, security, and people-oriented development.
- African leaders have personally directed its creation and implementation, focusing on investment-driven economic growth and economic governance as the engine for poverty reduction, and on the importance of regional and sub-regional partnerships within Africa.

Why we are supporting this initiative

- Half of Africa's population lives on less than US $1 per day, and alone among the continents, Africa is becoming poorer and poverty is on the rise. Alone among the continents, the average lifespan in Africa is becoming shorter and is now 16 years less than in the next-lowest region and has dropped three years in the last 10. The rate of illiteracy for persons over 15 is 41 per cent, and Africa is the only region where school enrolment is declining at all levels, and particularly among women and girls. While Africa accounts for 13 per cent of the world's population, Africa's exports account for less than 1.6 per cent of global trade, and that figure is falling. Africa currently attracts less than 1 per cent of global investment and is the only major region to see per capita investment and savings decline since 1970; indeed, as much as 40 per cent of Africa's own savings are not invested within the continent. Total net official development assistance (ODA) to Africa has fallen from previous levels of US $17 billion to US $12 billion today.

- African leaders have emphasized good governance and human rights as necessary preconditions for Africa's recovery. They have formally undertaken to hold each other accountable for their individual and collective efforts to achieve NEPAD's economic, political, and social objectives.

The new 'Enhanced Partnership' we are offering

- We commit ourselves each to establishing enhanced partnerships with African countries that are committed to and implementing the NEPAD. We will match Africa's commitment by our own efforts to find peace in Africa, to boost expertise and capacity, to encourage trade and direct growth-oriented investment, and to provide more effective official development assistance.
- This will lead us to focus our efforts on countries that demonstrate a political and financial commitment to good governance and the rule of law, investing in their people and pursuing policies that spur economic growth and alleviate poverty. Our partners will be selected on the basis of their commitment and the results they show.
- G-8 governments are committed to mobilize and energize global action, marshal resources and expertise, and provide impetus in support of NEPAD's objectives. Our Action Plan focuses on a limited number of priority areas where, collectively and individually, we can immediately add value. These areas are: 1) peace and security; 2) political and economic governance; 3) trade, investment, economic growth, and sustainable development; 4) debt relief; 5) education and information and communications technology (ICT); 6) health and HIV/AIDS; 7) agricultural productivity; and 8) water resource management.

What we will do

- The G-8 Africa Action Plan provides significant new initiatives in support of the New Partnership for Africa's Development. Highlights of the Action Plan include commitments to:

Resource mobilization
- Allocate to Africa at least 50 per cent of G-8 share of the US $12 billion per year in increased ODA that we pledged at

Monterrey, which will mean at least US $6 billion per year in new resources that will go to Africa;

- Increase the use of grants rather than loans for the poorest debt-vulnerable countries; and provide up to an additional US $1 billion to meet the projected shortfall in the highly indebted poor countries (HIPC) initiative;
- Work towards the objective of duty-free and quota-free market access for all products originating from the least-developed countries (LDCs), including African LDCs;
- Work towards enhancing market access—consistent with WTO requirements—for trade with African free trade areas or customs unions.

Peace and security
- Immediately strengthen efforts to maintain and consolidate the peace in Angola and Sierra Leone;
- Ensure that by 2010 African regional and sub-regional organizations are able to engage effectively to prevent and resolve violent conflict on the continent;
- Develop a framework for regulating and making more transparent the activities of international arms brokers and traffickers, and help to eliminate the flow of illicit weapons to Africa;
- Ensure better accountability and greater transparency with respect to those involved in the import or export of Africa's natural resources from areas of conflict.

Governance
- Expand capacity-building programs related to political governance in Africa, including support for African efforts to ensure that electoral processes are credible and transparent, that elections are conducted in a manner that is free and fair in accordance with NEPAD's commitment to uphold and respect 'global standards of democracy';
- Intensify international efforts to facilitate the freezing of illicitly acquired financial assets and the return of the proceeds of crimes;
- Assist African countries in their efforts to combat money laundering and terrorist financing in African countries.

Human resources

- Significantly increase the support provided by our bilateral aid agencies to basic education for African countries with a strong policy and financial commitment to education;
- Provide scholarships and other educational support for African girls and women;
- Work with the pharmaceutical industry to make life-saving drugs more affordable in Africa, and with African countries and other stakeholders to ensure effective distribution—especially with respect to HIV/AIDS and other communicable diseases;
- Provide the resources needed to eliminate polio by 2005; and
- Continue funding and support for the Global Fund to Fight AIDS, Tuberculosis and Malaria; and help Africa enhance its capacity to participate in and benefit from the Fund.

Source: From Kananaskis Summit, 2002.

13

NEPAD and the Renaissance of Africa

STEVEN LANGDON

External perspectives on Africa have been bleak for many years. Even in the early years of independence in the continent, many analysts found catastrophes on which to concentrate—from the breakdown of the first Congo government, to civil war in Nigeria, to the Uganda coup that brought Idi Amin to power. The litany of internal turmoil, state collapse, famine, and disease can be traced through the rest of the twentieth century—from mass starvation in Ethiopia, to internal wars in Angola and Mozambique, to genocide in Rwanda, to despairing refugee flows from Liberia, Sierra Leone, southern Sudan, Somalia, and elsewhere. Systemic and structural pressures in sub-Saharan Africa kept the crises coming and produced the socioeconomic dilemmas.

But Africa has also, in its own way, in certain regions and at certain times, been a place of vivid hopes and significant miracles. Small-scale farmers won the chance to grow cash crops for the first time in much of East Africa, with huge success; there have been massive percentage increases of women getting schooling in many countries; the mainly peaceful transition to majority rule in South Africa defied all expectation; and community-based civil society movements helped establish democratic transitions in Ghana, Benin, Nigeria, Zambia, Malawi.

By the new millennium, though, the overall balance sheet seemed grim. Africa had become marginalized in the global economy, and many Africans were experiencing exclusion and insecurity. The development models pursued by the newly independent states had virtually all failed, and the growth record of Africa lagged far behind that of most Asian developing countries (which had been at similar starting points around 1960). Deep poverty conditions had increased in many nations. Disease remained prevalent, including the serious new spread of HIV/AIDS. Internal and external conflict crippled a dozen regions, even though some peacemaking was proving successful in parts of West Africa.

That is the context to which the New Partnership for Africa's Development (NEPAD) responded. The goal, said South African President Mbeki, is to achieve an 'African Renaissance' that will 'give hope to the emaciated African child that the 21st century is indeed Africa's century' (NEPAD document, sec. 207).

This chapter analyzes this important initiative in terms of Canada's international policies in 2002. A first section reviews three key factors shaping the African context—the spread of poverty, widespread governance problems, and the impact of HIV/AIDS. The next section discusses the NEPAD framework and Canada's response to it within the G-8. The final section explores the significance of this Canadian role in a world of changing US policy actions and the potential of NEPAD to achieve successful development results for Africa.

THE POLITICAL ECONOMY CHALLENGES OF AFRICA

Three broad problem sets confront Africa in the new millennium— the extent and roots of mass poverty, the dilemmas of ineffective and weak governance, and the potential social destructiveness of HIV/AIDS. To understand why the NEPAD initiative has emerged and the form it has taken, it is necessary to examine each of these problem sets.

Mass poverty and debt relief. Using a simple but robust definition of poverty (a personal income level less than the US purchasing power of US $1 per day), we find that many of the poorer countries of the world have exhibited extensive poverty in the last 30 years. But in most of Asia and Latin America two basic trends have been evident. First, poverty has broadly declined over time, so that the percentage of those considered poor has fallen significantly. Second, most countries have been able to access private foreign capital flows directly to accelerate growth and thereby to allow them to push those poverty levels even lower.

From China, to Indonesia, to India these dynamics have been evident, as they have been in Brazil, Mexico, Chile, and elsewhere in Latin America. There have been a few exceptions in each of these continents, such as Cambodia and Nepal in Asia, and Bolivia and several Central American countries in Latin America.

The African norm, however, has been entirely different. Even resource-rich countries like Nigeria have seen poverty rise dramatically—from 45 per cent of people in 1985 to 66 per cent in 1999. Increases have been identified in many countries, including Kenya, Cameroon, Côte d'Ivoire, Tanzania, Zambia, and Burkina Faso.[1] Just as important, African countries have generally not gained access to private capital inflows, so they have had to rely heavily on loans from the IMF and the World Bank—and the burden of these loans in turn has required debt relief that meant external agreements had to be implemented (and respected) on how development policies were to be implemented.

A whole new emphasis from the international financial institutions has led to drafting Poverty Reduction Strategy Papers (PRSPs) in most African countries; these demonstrate how countries will use debt relief and new finance to counter poverty in order to achieve loan (and interest) forgiveness and are approved on that basis by the boards of the IMF and the World Bank. As of September 2002, of the 63 countries involved in this PRSP process internationally, 36 of them (57 per cent) were from Africa. South Africa represented the main African exception to PRSP involvement.

This African focus on poverty reduction efforts means, first, that there is a keen preoccupation with actions that can be taken to reduce poverty (and thus this has also become the main thrust of NEPAD). Second, the PRSP approach has also underlined the external capital-flows dependency of African countries and therefore encouraged NEPAD as an indigenously based mechanism to seek to take back direction for development decision-making in Africa. Finally, at the same time, the realities that PRSP relations represent mean that

NEPAD has been formulated in terms of a partnership with key OECD countries from which financial resources will have to come.

Governance concerns. Underlying rising poverty has been a widespread failure in governance in post-independence African states, sometimes leading to state collapse, sometimes explaining policy mistakes. Throughout the continent, the characteristics of this failure differed somewhat, but certain common realities were evident:

- Most new states lacked powerful indigenous economic forces driving forward capital investment and growth, and so the state itself became the dominant economic actor—and the (usually narrow, often ethnically based political) groups in control generally came to use this state economic leverage to direct benefits to themselves rather than broadly sharing economic opportunities and gains.
- The regulations, controls, and state-owned assets misused to do this in turn distorted economic performance badly, usually hurting domestic agriculture and reducing exports—with consequent foreign exchange shortages and severe economic constraints.
- Foreign borrowing accelerated to cover the foreign exchange crisis; but the limits to such foreign borrowing soon pushed high domestic borrowing (to cover budget gaps) and led to very high inflation, commonly crippling public service salaries. This further weakened state performance and spurred petty corruption among police, customs officials, and other poorly paid public servants.
- These factors, as they led to greater poverty, less security, and diminished public integrity, often brought in their wake military takeovers or internal civil strife, which soon resulted in even poorer governance and yet further corruption among a new group of rulers. This led to even more difficulties in achieving good economic performance.
- More insecure, short-term political regimes often turned to even more blatant self-enrichment to build up personal fortunes for when they were ousted, increasing economic distortions and reducing funding for delivery of social services.

By the nineties, this governance failure was widespread in many countries and was generating growing state decay. New forces for change had to emerge across Africa, and these took various forms.

In some cases, such as Uganda, Ethiopia, and Eritrea, lengthy armed struggles resulted in the overthrow of corrupt, authoritarian regimes by movements shaped by a democratic 'bush' ethos of co-operation and equality. In other cases, like Ghana, Benin, and Malawi, emerging civil society groups provided leadership in moving to new democratic constitutions that restored the rule of law. Some one-party regimes evolved into pluralism under exemplary leadership, as in Senegal and Tanzania. Some military regimes collapsed under their own incompetence, as in Nigeria. And the dramatic liberation of a democratic South Africa provided a major new impetus towards rebirth.

Led by new leaders reflecting these changes (Mbeki of South Africa, Wade of Senegal, and Obasanjo of Nigeria), NEPAD is both an outgrowth of these new democratic governance trends and a reaction against the state failures and patterns of corruption, arbitrary coercion, and economic weakness that had spread too widely in Africa. As the NEPAD analysis puts it:

> There are already signs of progress and hope. Democratic regimes that are committed to the protection of human rights, people-centred development and market-oriented economies are on the increase. African peoples have begun to demonstrate their refusal to accept poor economic and political leadership. These developments are, however, uneven and inadequate and need to be further expedited. (Ibid., sec. 7)

Thus NEPAD stresses 'corruption and bad governance' as crucial impediments to be tackled, and identifies as central to its plans a 'democracy and governance initiative' to respect 'global standards of democracy', including political pluralism, free elections, transparency and accountability, integrity, respect for human rights, and the rule of law. There will be a peer review system to monitor and further country-by-country progress towards such 'good governance'.

The impact of HIV/AIDS. NEPAD, then, represents a self-directed African effort to overcome poverty, based on clear recognition that improved governance is crucial. But does any of this economic and political endeavour matter, given the devastating expansion of HIV/AIDS that some analysts say is now overwhelming Africa?

UN statistics show that the estimated number of Africans with HIV/AIDS has gone from 10.5 million in 1997 to 29.4 million in 2002; Africa now contributes 77 per cent of all deaths from the disease

(2.4 million people). As Stephen Lewis put it at the Barcelona AIDS Conference in 2002, 'by the year 2020, the number of deaths from AIDS in Africa will approximate the number of deaths, military and civilian combined, in both world wars of the 20th century.'[2]

Some $25 billion will be required from the richer countries to overcome the crisis, say the HIV/AIDS activists. And it is time to stress this reality above all else, they say, time for 'the world to come to its senses'.

Yet there is an uncomfortably apocalyptic narrowness to this fervour.

Last year, students I help supervise in poor rural parts of northern Ghana reviewed all the records for people coming to health clinics in a district near the main commercial city of Tamale (where truckers heading north and south might have been expected to be a key source of HIV/AIDS infection). In the thousands of cases dealt with by the clinics, there was not a single instance of HIV/AIDS; over 80 per cent of illness was diagnosed as malaria.[3] Many other parts of Africa also have low incidence levels of HIV/AIDS, including Senegal (0.5 per cent of adults in 2001), Nigeria (5.8 per cent in 2001), and Madagascar (0.3 per cent).

There is no question that HIV/AIDS is a huge health assault in a minority of African countries in southern and eastern Africa, such as Kenya, Botswana, Zimbabwe, and South Africa. But the picture even in those countries is not unremittingly grim. In Uganda, for instance, vigorous countermeasures cut the prevalence rate from 16 per cent in the 1990s to 5 per cent in 2001. And in Zambia prevalence was reduced by four percentage points among both urban and rural younger women between 1996 and 1999. Recent evidence also shows a decline from 21 per cent in 1998 to 15.4 per cent in 2001 in prevalence among pregnant teenage women attending antenatal clinics in South Africa (UNAIDS, 2002: 17–18).

The fact is, too, that many of the alarmingly high numbers for parts of southern Africa are projections of the future rather than detailed snapshots of an existing reality that has already come to pass. Take the high prevalence statistics from Botswana, for instance (38.8 per cent according to the recent UN report). These data are based for men on testing males who go to health clinics with sexually transmitted diseases (already a high-risk category). For women, the basis is quite small numbers of tests done in selected prenatal clinics—and there is wide variation in the results from different clinics. Thus, one HIV estimate for Botswana in 2001 is 260,000 persons (using assumptions based on lower incidence responses from some samples), while the possible estimate using some higher-incidence samples is 390,000—a variance of 50 per cent.

It is common for HIV/AIDS activists to express this level as a percentage of adults 15–49 years of age. But taking, instead, the whole population of Botswana, some 1.7 million, that lower estimate would be 15 per cent of the total—or 23 per cent with the higher projection.

In either case, this level represents a serious strain on health services (especially since Botswana is committed to providing anti-retroviral treatment, and will pay 80 per cent of drug costs). But the challenge is far less paralyzing than suggested by levels described as 38.8 per cent.

The point is not to minimize the importance of HIV/AIDS in some parts of Africa. But the huge amount of money some say is needed and the projections of mass mortality tragedy for the future have the effect of making out Africa to be, once more, a collapsing basket case that needs massive charity just to survive. That is an unfair and inaccurate picture.

Thus, NEPAD highlights HIV/AIDS as one of the key communicable diseases to fight (along with malaria) and commits to seeking international financial support to help, but does not portray Africa as paralyzed and overwhelmed by this challenge. The HIV/AIDS reality is placed in context as one of a number of policy priorities.

NEPAD AND CANADA

The previous section suggests what spurred NEPAD. It can be seen as a process, developed step by step in the context of Africa-wide politics—the Millennium Africa Plan Renaissance Programme (MAP)[4] was developed by the Organization for African Unity (OAU) with South Africa playing a leading role; the OMEGA[5] plan was initiated by Abdoulaye Wade of Senegal. Both of these initiatives were then integrated so as to avoid internal conflicts within the continent. NEPAD was the result, and should be seen as fundamentally an initiative of African leaders. It is not a detailed plan but a vision of infrastructure improvements, economic integration, social reforms, and governance strengthening that will counter poverty, accelerate economic growth (to 7 per cent per year), and achieve democratic, accountable, and transparent government throughout the continent.

At the heart of the vision is the notion of 'peer review'—a concept that Canadian G-8 representatives saw as a serious commitment 'by some of Africa's most progressive leaders' to shift the development aid relationship to a policy of 'reward success and refuse to reinforce failure', based on improving political and financial governance. For countries that achieve such improvements, there would be higher and sustained aid commitments, at the expense of those countries failing to improve.[6]

NEPAD thus represents a combination of both hope and commitment on the African side, involving a tough-minded effort to achieve solid political and economic performance—which would be sustained by increased aid from key donors—with the risk that failure to perform effectively, as judged by peers, would incur significant aid-flow cuts. NEPAD is not a cry for help from an overwhelmed continent devastated by HIV/AIDS; it is a proposal for a serious bargain to end marginalization for at least some African countries.

What is striking is the Canadian leadership in responding to this initiative. In part, this might be seen as circumstantial. At the Genoa G-8 Summit in 2001, a delegation of African leaders presented an earlier version of NEPAD (the New African Initiative), and this was dealt with positively. It was agreed that personal representatives of the G-8 leaders would work with the African leaders to develop a concrete Action Plan for implementation, to be reviewed at the June 2002 Summit held in Canada. The Canadian representative, Robert Fowler, became chair of this working group.

The reality, however, is that three leaders became very serious about the process and the potential of NEPAD—Jean Chrétien, Tony Blair, and Jacques Chirac. Chrétien and Blair, in particular, visited Africa and spoke out strongly in favour of the initiative. And Chrétien, above all, engaged in detailed discussions with a range of the key African leaders to assure high priority for them and for NEPAD at Kananaskis. Fowler became deeply convinced of the seriousness of the African vision and saw to it that extensive work was done (in his role as 'Sherpa' for the Summit) to promote the NEPAD agenda. Indeed, Canada became so energetic in advocating NEPAD that various African civil society groups and parliamentarians became suspicious that this was really a Canadian set of proposals being circulated through key African leaders!

Despite the Canadian leadership, however, and the positive views of Blair and Chirac, the immediate results of the Summit were disappointing for NEPAD, mainly because of tepid US perspectives on the African approach. The G-8 meeting had explicitly been excluded as an occasion for funding pledges. But NEPAD leaders did hope for long-term commitments in principle to larger resource flows and improved trade arrangements. A number of countries promised increased financial flows, but without specifics and without an overall response from the G-8 that signalled significant acceleration of flows.

Nevertheless, the G-8 Action Plan for Africa enunciated at Kananaskis is a quite comprehensive and serious outline, emphasizing support for improved security measures against armed conflicts and the arms trade, moves to help democratic governance and anti-corruption, trade access and enhancement steps, greater debt relief, support to upgrade education (especially for girls), more action on health (with a focus on HIV/AIDS), steps to support agricultural productivity, and improvements to water supplies and management.

Canadian commitments were particularly specific and enthusiastic, including:

- $100 million risk capital fund for private investments in Africa;
- $50 million for water management and sanitation in Africa;
- $50 million per year for basic education in Africa;
- $50 million for two HIV/AIDS initiatives in the continent;
- $50 million for polio eradication;
- $40 million for African agricultural research;
- $28 million to strengthen public-sector competency;
- $25 million for e-initiatives and connectivity in Africa;
- $15 million for ECOWAS peace and security efforts;
- $15 million for African parliamentary and local governance support.

Trade access steps have also been taken by Canada, including assistance for African countries to work out their own trade strategies. As of January 2003, all tariffs and quotas were eliminated for 48 least-developed countries (34 of them in Africa) in all product areas except dairy products, poultry, and eggs.

CONCLUSIONS AND IMPLICATIONS

This review has shown that NEPAD represents an important response by African leaders to the increasing poverty and problematic governance that marked post-independence Africa. It presents both a tough-minded bargain that meeting financial and governance standards can achieve higher sustained aid to a number of well-performing countries, and a vision aiming to rekindle a sense of hopefulness. This discussion has outlined how Canada made promotion of NEPAD to its G-8 partners a major foreign policy priority in 2002 and committed significant resources to help implement the initiative.

Two questions are raised by this analysis. First, what does this case say about Canada's overall foreign policy framework, with its necessary preoccupation with the US relationship? Second, what are the longer-run implications of NEPAD for Africa itself?

There is no question that Canada provided significant leadership on the G-8 relationship with Africa and the response made to NEPAD. No other country has come close to the enthusiasm of Canada in responding to the African leadership. This needs to be stressed in the context of any analysis of living in close partnership with a US increasingly prone to unilateralism in international relations. There are still parts of the world where Canada can exercise quite differentiated leadership and have a significant impact apart from the relationship with the US.

The Prime Minister's own personal commitment on the African file is also important to underline. Those working closely on this issue with him report a deep sense of personal engagement and a strong sense of identification with issues of poverty in Africa. He has reportedly developed good personal relations with a number of the key African leaders, particularly President Mbeki of South Africa.

But the case also demonstrates the limited influence Canada can exercise in the present US context—the unenthused American response to NEPAD at the G-8 Summit shows that Canadian efforts could not raise Africa higher on the US agenda, as had been hoped. That inability to convince the US constrained the G-8 response to NEPAD to longer-term help, rather than initiating a major and immediate co-ordinated effort. The US decision to announce Mideast policy initiatives very close to the start of the Summit and the George Bush focus on security points during the Summit—while they seem to be explained by scheduling pressures facing the White House rather than any deliberate effort to undercut the Canadian concern with Africa—nevertheless underlined the differences in perspective between the Canadian and US governments.

What did this unproductive interaction with the US spur on the Canadian side? It is hard to avoid the conclusion that the Chrétien government's unease with US world views was significantly strengthened. Several weeks later, Prime Minister Chrétien made his now famous comments about the 11 September attacks on New York and Washington:

> ... it is a division in the world that is building up. And I knew that it was the inspiration of it. For me, I think that the rest of the world is a bit too selfish, and that there is a lot of resentment. I felt it when I dealt with the African file for the Summit of the G-8. You know, the poor, relatively, get poorer all the time. And the rich are getting richer all the time. . . . You know, you cannot exercise your powers to the point of humiliation for the others. And that is what the Western world, not only the Americans, the Western world has to realize, because, you know, they are human beings too, and there are long-term consequences if you don't look hard at the reality in 10 or 20 and 30 years from now. And I do think that the Western world is getting too rich in relation to the poor world. And necessarily, you know, we're looked upon as being arrogant, self-satisfying, greedy and with no limits. And the 11th of September is an occasion for me to realize it even more.[7]

This conveys the sense of concern and frustration of many about the apparent unwillingness of the US to analyze present world conflicts in a broader, balanced framework, where overcoming social injustice and fighting terrorism both matter. Yet such commentaries in turn spur unease on the US side about the 'reliability' of Canada—and further complicate difficult aspects of the US–Canadian relationship, from border crossing procedures to joint defence strategy.

What about the potential impact of NEPAD itself? Having worked so hard to advance NEPAD on the international agenda, Canada now has a special responsibility to follow through on the initiative with financial support and continuing engagement of Canadians. That includes ongoing assessment of NEPAD implementation (such as Prime Minister Chrétien's recent letter to President Mbeki, requesting clarification on peer review procedures as applied to governance).

NEPAD has now received wide endorsation from African leaders and governments throughout the continent. The African Union has replaced the Organization for African Unity, which was continually hobbled by internal conflicts among competing blocs of countries. The AU seems to be moving forward with a consensus around NEPAD and its call for complementary infrastructure investments, economic harmonization, and improved governance.

But, so far, serious problems remain in the leader-based character of NEPAD decision-making. One sign of this is the unwillingness of African leaders to put more public pressure on Robert Mugabe of Zimbabwe (a fellow leader, after all) to respect the 'global standards of democracy' to which NEPAD stands committed. It is true that there are constraints within southern Africa that help explain this, too, in particular, South Africa's fear that action against Zimbabwe would increase already costly refugee movements into South Africa. But public reticence on Zimbabwe does threaten NEPAD credibility with G-8 and other donor countries.

The top-down tendencies in NEPAD also worry many Africans. MPs with whom I work in Ghana have insisted strongly that this approach has to change, so the people the political leaders represent might have a say in NEPAD planning and proposals. African citizen groups have been making the same case for a different vision. 'It is important that the political and business leaders behind NEPAD realize the need for broader society's involvement in Africa's economic recovery', says Mary Wandia from the African Women's Development and Communication Network.

There is, increasingly, a community-based vision of Africa, based on local civil society groups, that is far more powerful than it has ever been in the past. And this perspective has not yet been integrated into NEPAD, even though the most effective capacity for meeting people's needs, especially for the poor, has been shifting to that community level. That is where poorer rural populations can have input into democratic local governments and see to it that the schools, the feeder roads, and the health clinics they need are implemented effectively.

In northern Ghana, for instance, citizen groups like JIDA in Salaga are the active agents delivering new water supplies and sanitation in partnership with poor rural villages. The Maata N Tudu women's development association in Bolgatanga is organizing micro loans to undertake economic initiatives, plus providing literacy training for villagers. The Neighbours in Need Foundation is working with the district assembly in Walewale on expanded access to safe water.

Increasingly, international institutions have come to realize that serious poverty reduction will come through working with community citizen groups and decentralized institutions. For truly democratic governments in Africa, too, where local voters choose legislators and endorse or reject presidents, responsiveness to community needs and citizen groups will determine future election results. Improved lives for African people and democratic freedoms will be linked closely together.

If the NEPAD vision is to succeed, it must come to terms with that bottom-up community-based vision. African presidents will have to be just as concerned about building relations with citizen groups in Salaga and Walewale as they are with lobbying George Bush and Jean Chrétien at G-8 meetings.

Is that possible for NEPAD? Can the new thrust succeed at the community level, even as African leaders carry forward world-level negotiations to achieve new relationships with the G-8? The challenge is a difficult one. Jean Chrétien could work on the world stage and host the G-8 Summit, yet discover his constituency had deserted him and enforced his own retirement. Drawing the links between their communities and their own international roles will be even more difficult for a group of diverse African leaders. It may be that NEPAD will stay mainly at the level of vision, and the real work of reducing poverty will also have to be carried forward, country by country, in differing ways, at the community level.[8] Local civil society groups and elected local politicians may also be crucial leaders in bringing about changes that matter to the varied communities of poorer Africans throughout the continent. It may be a time for 'grassroots heroes' in Africa, as well as for global spokesmen.

Canada has played a key role in helping shape a positive response to NEPAD. The conclusion from this review is that Canada should extend that role to encourage this deeper vision of Africa: one of community-based democracy.

NOTES

1. See World Bank Institute (2002). This reports the findings of detailed Poverty Reduction Strategy Papers and other documents that indicate the trends noted in the countries named during the 1990–2000 period.
2. See UNAIDS (2002: 17–18). Other comments and data below are drawn from presentations made, and background documentation, at the UNAIDS International Conference in Barcelona, 2002.
3. This documentation was gathered in the health clinics of Savelugu district, 20 km north of Tamale, by Ms Bromley Frey, Trent University development studies student, on a field placement in the Trent-in-Ghana Year-Abroad

Program (directed by Prof. J. Solway, International Development Studies, Trent University).

4. The Millennium Africa Renaissance Programme is a declaration of a firm commitment by African leaders to take ownership and responsibility for the sustainable economic development of the continent. The focus of the program is not increased aid, but increased investments in viable infrastructure and business opportunities with target aid and technical support to address capacity constraints and urgent human development priorities.

5. The OMEGA Plan sets goals and defines financial means for African countries to narrow the structural gaps of infrastructure. It was unveiled by Senegalese President Abdoulaye Wade at a meeting of the UN Commission on Africa in Algiers in May 2001. The text of the Plan is available at: <http://www.sapn.org.za/NEPAD/Omega.pdf>.

6. Perspectives of Canadian insiders on the initiative are outlined in revealing ways in Parliamentary Centre (2002). Robert Fowler, Senior Adviser to the Canadian government for the G-8 Summit, and David Angell, Deputy Director of the Canadian Secretariat for the Summit, were both present and spoke to participants.

7. This transcript is drawn from the Prime Minister's comments as found on the CBC's Web site. The commentary was released 11 Sept. 2002 but recorded in July 2002. Available at: <http://www.cbc.ca/news/features/chretien_interview.html>.

8. Steps in such a 'grassroots' poverty reduction strategy are suggested in Langdon (1999: 185–206).

REFERENCES

Langdon, Steven. 1999. *Global Poverty, Democracy and North-South Change.* Toronto: Garamond Press.

Parliamentary Centre. 2002. *Canada-Ethiopia Parliamentary Capacity Building Project: Workshop Sharing African Experience with Parliamentary Oversight and the New Partnership for Africa's Development (NEPAD).* Addis Ababa, Ethiopia, 9–11 Apr.

UNAIDS. 2002. *AIDS Epidemic Update, December 2002.* Geneva: UNAIDS/WHO.

World Bank Institute. 2002. *Handbook for Parliamentarians on Policies to Reduce Poverty.* Washington: World Bank.

14

Canada at the United Nations in the New Millennium

ELIZABETH RIDDELL-DIXON

We have entered a new century and a new millennium with a new US President, whose unilateral impulses appear stronger than his commitment to the United Nations. In contrast, Canada views the UN as a vital tool for promoting an equitable international community based on international law; hence the UN continues to be the most important multilateral institution for Canada. It is, therefore, not surprising that Canada's macro-level priority relating to the UN is to ensure that the organization functions effectively, with the US as a co-operative participant. Canada shows great leadership within the UN in launching initiatives, developing policies, and generating ideas. It has frequently been less effective in establishing priorities among these initiatives, policies, and ideas and in committing the resources necessary to implement them.

In the past 17 months, two developments have preoccupied the UN agenda: the desire to counter terrorism in the aftermath of 11 September and, more recently, the need to 'manage' the US in the wake of its unilateral threats to wage war against Iraq in retaliation for the latter's non-compliance with UN resolutions to disarm. The world did not change on 11 September 2001 when the terrorists attacked the US. It did, however, bring home to the people and governments in the US and Canada what is a daily reality for many around the world. The events of 11 September profoundly affected perceptions of vulnerability, especially among northern countries, with the result that counterterrorism measures became the Security Council's number-one preoccupation and continued to be so until President Bush issued his threat of unilateral action against Iraq. At that point, the chief focus became trying to persuade the US to abandon its unilateral stance and to work co-operatively through the Security Council.

Although Canada has worked from the sidelines to promote the development and implementation of counterterrorism provisions and to persuade the US to work through the Security Council, it has not been a principal player in either case. The task of addressing these two very high-profile issues has been the responsibility of the Security Council—a body of which Canada is not currently a member. The issues are, nonetheless, of great importance to Canada. Furthermore, the preoccupation with them has made it more difficult for Canada to pursue some of its own priorities, including promoting the International Criminal Court and the Canadian-sponsored 2001 report, *The Responsibility to Protect.*

The chapter will begin with a brief examination of the two dominant issues on the Security Council agenda before examining Canada's success in realizing its priorities in the areas of peace operations (including reforms to the Security Council), human security (especially the responsibility to protect and international impunity), human rights, and sustainable development. All come under the rubric of peace and security, broadly interpreted to include not only security for states but, more importantly, security for civilians—not just from the dangers of physical violence but also from the untold suffering that results from dire poverty, environmental degradation, and poor health. Some observations about Canadian leadership at the UN are also offered.

THE UNITED STATES AND IRAQ

In his speech to the General Assembly on 12 September 2002, US President George Bush issued his definitive threat to go to war against Iraq if the latter failed to comply with UN resolutions to disarm. The US decision to confront Iraq directly, instead of referring the matter to the Security Council—the international body authorized under international law to deal with international peace and security—threatened the credibility of the Security Council. Most members of the UN, including Canada, are skeptical of the American motives in making the threat. No evidence has been presented linking the Iraqi government to the terrorist attacks on the US. There are also questions to be asked about timing: why did President Bush decide to take action in September 2002? Iraq's non-compliance with UN resolutions is not new—it was all too apparent in the late summer and early autumn of 1990 when Iraq refused to withdraw from Kuwait—and the ongoing problem of Iraq's violations of UN resolutions is well-known. It has been suggested that the threat of war is motivated by electoral concerns: President Bush would rather campaign for re-election as a war President than as a recession President.

The first positive breakthrough came when the Bush administration backed down from proceeding with unilateral action and returned to the negotiating table, a move prompted by both international and domestic factors. International opinion clearly favoured a multilateral solution and the vast majority of UN members opposed a unilateral attack on Iraq. Within the US, public opinion polls showed that most citizens were opposed to going to war alone (CBS *News World*, 2002a, 2002b).

The negotiations among the permanent members of the Security Council took place at the highest political levels. In particular, France and the UK and, to a lesser extent, Russia deserve a great deal of credit for negotiating a solution acceptable to all permanent members of the Security Council. Credit is also due to the negotiating skill of Colin Powell, US Secretary of State. On 8 November 2002, the Security Council unanimously[1] approved Resolution 1441, which requires Iraq to disarm or face serious consequences. The resolution called for UN arms inspectors to be sent back into Iraq to determine if Iraq is complying with UN resolutions. The inspectors are authorized to make such determinations and they will report to the Security Council. What will happen after the inspectors submit their reports remains to be seen. The US claims that it can act against Iraq under Security Council Resolution 678, adopted on 29 November 1990 and authorizing member states to 'use all necessary means' to expel Iraq from Kuwait. The resolution provided the international sanctioning for Operation Desert Storm. Canada and most of the UN membership say

that a new Security Council resolution would be necessary to authorize a fresh attack—Iraq, after all, has had no presence in Kuwait since
the Gulf War.

Canada is concerned about how little thought has been given to
the aftermath of a war. The war, itself, would likely be short-lived.
Iraq was much more powerful in 1991 and even then the war was
over in a few months. Iraq lost most of its armed forces in 1991 and
it has been under sanctions for the past 12 years. In addition, its
finances, at least to some extent, have been controlled by the UN. As
a result, Iraq has been weakened and defeating it would not be the
most difficult task; the much tougher challenge would be trying to
rebuild the country after a war. Who would replace Saddam Hussein?
How could democracy be implemented? How could the differences
between Shiite and Sunni Muslims be reconciled? How would the
position of the Kurds be addressed? Would there be a Kurdish uprising that would trigger a civil war in Turkey?

The crisis over Iraq raises many vital issues: the credibility and
viability of the UN, the American commitment to work within the UN,
the threat of war, and the overwhelming prospects of peacebuilding
in the aftermath of a war. Canada, along with most members of the
UN, would prefer to ensure that the inspectors are able to fulfill their
mandates and that the UN takes measures necessary to ensure compliance. War against Iraq is not a preferred option, most particularly
because of the dire consequences that would follow. Yet in this
debate, Canada can only support from the sidelines because it is not
privy to the major negotiations taking place in the Security Council.
Likewise, and for the same reasons, Canada has not been a key
player in the counterterrorism campaign—the other major preoccupation of the Security Council.

COUNTERTERRORISM

The UN reacted quickly to the 11 September terrorist attacks and
undertook a range of activities to counter terrorism. Twelve coun-
terterrorism treaties have been developed under the auspices of the
UN—two within the last year. Prior to 11 September, only the UK and
Botswana had ratified all the treaties. Now 24 countries, including
Canada, have ratified all 12. On 28 September 2001, the Security
Council passed its landmark Resolution 1373, which forbids countries
from harbouring terrorists, from providing a safe haven for their

funds, or from permitting the raising of funds for terrorist activities within their borders. Furthermore, states are obliged to ensure that anyone planning, financing, or participating in terrorist activities is brought to justice. On the same day the Security Council also established a Counter-Terrorism Committee, as recommended in Resolution 1373. The Committee is the most important international body for determining the needs of countries in fulfilling their treaty obligations and their responsibilities under Resolution 1373. The Committee monitors compliance, holds countries accountable, and provides support and advice when changes are required. A major impediment to the implementation of the resolution is the lack of domestic infrastructure in many countries to allow them to fulfill their obligations, such as monitoring capital flows. Thus, Canada and the UN have been concerned with capacity-building.

Canada has been clear in asserting that terrorism is a problem requiring global solutions and, hence, that the UN is the pre-eminent organization to address the issue. For Canada, the response to terrorism must be global, both in the sense that all countries must participate in finding solutions and in the sense that efforts to combat terrorism must encompass a broad range of areas—not just border and airport security but also the conditions that foster terrorist sentiments. Canada's objectives are, therefore, to have the international community, working through the UN, committed to addressing both the direct threats of terrorism and the conditions propitious to its development.[2] In order to have a global response to terrorism it is necessary to develop common assessments of the threats, as well as common values and interest in addressing the problem in all its dimensions.

In addition to having ratified all 12 counterterrorism treaties, Canada is one of the countries most in compliance with Resolution 1373. Canada's Philippe Kirsch chaired the working group that drafted the most recent of the 12 counterterrorism treaties: the International Convention for the Suppression of the Financing of Terrorism and the International Convention for the Suppression of Terrorist Bombings. Two further treaties are contemplated: a treaty on nuclear terrorism and a comprehensive convention on terrorism. Canada has devoted considerable effort to making them a reality, but in both cases the negotiations are stalemated. Debates over the nuclear terrorism treaty tend to pit the nuclear powers, which are in favour of prosecuting others but want exemptions for their own troops, against members of the non-aligned movement, which fear the treaty would prejudice the debate on the legality of nuclear weapons and undermine the advisory opinion provided by the International Court of Justice in 1996 declaring nuclear disarmament to be required under international law. Negotiations of a comprehensive convention on terrorism have floundered over definitions of 'terrorist', which reflects the old controversy over who is a terrorist and who is a freedom fighter. It was possible to get agreement on the 12 existing conventions because they criminalize certain types of activities without defining a terrorist. Through the Human Security Program, Canada has assisted countries in developing the legislation necessary to fulfill their obligations under the 12 counterterrorism treaties.

In addition to supporting UN efforts to combat terrorism, Canada has been active in adopting counterterrorism measures unilaterally and in co-operation with the US. In October 2001, Canada passed two new bills. The Anti-Terrorism Act contains measures to 'identify, prosecute, convict and punish terrorists; provide new investigative tools to Canadian law enforcement and national security agencies; and ensure that Canadian values of respect and fairness are preserved through stronger laws against hate crimes and propaganda' (DFAIT, 2002a: 3). The Public Safety Act is designed to 'increase the government's capacity to prevent terrorist attacks, protect Canadians, and respond swiftly should a significant threat arise' (ibid.). An Ad Hoc Cabinet Committee on Public Security and Anti-Terrorism was established to strengthen Canada's capacity to combat terrorism and ensure public security. The Committee is chaired by Deputy Prime Minister John Manley. In December 2001 the Canadian government approved a budget of $7.7 billion to be spent over five years 'to enhance security for Canadians and make Canada's borders more secure, open and efficient' (DFAIT, 2002b: 3). The same month, Canada and the US signed the Smart Border Declaration and the Action Plan, which outline provisions for sharing information and co-ordinating activities to combat terrorism while keeping the border open to legitimate trade. There is no doubt that combatting terrorism has been a major priority for the Canadian government since 11 September, as evidenced by the direct involvement of the most senior levels of government and the extensive resources allocated to the campaign.

The threat of terrorism has not only preoccupied the Security Council for most of the past 17 months but has also had a profound effect on how the UN and its member states conduct business. The

UN no longer receives mail directly. Instead, the mail is rerouted to a clearing house in Florida to be checked for the anthrax virus before being delivered to the UN. Canada is by no means alone in facing this threat and, like others, has changed some of its standard business procedures. For example, far greater use is now made of e-mails and faxes to minimize the amount of mail received at the Canadian mission.

Although counterterrorism and the crisis resulting from Iraq's failure to prove that it has disarmed are receiving most of the media attention, the UN is far more than the current preoccupations of the Security Council. The media focus on debates at the UN headquarters in New York and generally ignore the work being done in other parts of the system, which is at least as important and which has become all the more salient in the post-Cold War era. One cannot talk about social peace and social justice without referring to the International Labour Organization. The World Health Organization is central to the fight against HIV/AIDS and other pandemic diseases. Discussions of social and political turmoil must involve the High Commissioner for Refugees and the High Commissioner for Human Rights. The International Telecommunication Union is central to addressing issues of high technology. The UN is a multi-institutional tool with the capacity to address problems in a functional way. A narrow focus on New York, to the exclusion of UN bodies based elsewhere, fails to present a comprehensive or accurate picture. Even in New York, the Security Council's current preoccupations are only part of the story. They have, for example, in no way dampened Secretary-General Kofi Annan's commitment to implementing the Millennium Development Goals. Canada's chief ongoing priorities at the UN are closely related to several areas outlined in these goals. In particular, they pertain to peace operations, human security, human rights, and sustainable development.

PEACE OPERATIONS

The 2000 *Report of the Panel on UN Peace Operations* (the Brahimi Report—named after the panel's chair, Lakhdar Brahimi) was welcomed by most analysts as a realistic, doable plan for improving peace operations in several interrelated areas of activity: conflict prevention (early warning and peacebuilding capacity), peacekeeping (realistic mandates, adequate resources to fulfill mandates, more secure funding, enhanced quality and quantity of training for all participants, and the rapid deployment of experts as well as troops), peacemaking, and the reform of UN bodies involved with peace operations, particularly the Department of Peacekeeping Operations and the Department of Political Affairs. The Brahimi Report reflected many Canadian objectives, including providing troop-contributing countries with a larger voice in the Security Council's decision-making process, enhancing the UN's rapid reaction capability (e.g., equipment, experts, logistical improvements), and strengthening the civil police component in peace operations.

Since the Security Council is the executive body responsible for international peace and security, its effectiveness is closely linked to the efficacy of peace operations. Two of Canada's three top priorities during its 1999–2000 term on the Security Council related to the latter's reform: making it more effective and credible, and making it more transparent and accountable (DFAIT, 2001: 3–4). Of particular concern to Canada was the regular failure to hold meaningful consultations with troop-contributing countries.

Democracy requires that elected national governments are responsible for decisions made about how and when their troops are deployed. The Security Council has traditionally operated in a very autocratic way and has frequently made decisions—including the decision to change the mandate of a mission—without consulting the troop-contributing countries. For example, the Security Council expanded the mandate of the Sierra Leone mission after troops were already in the field, requiring them to control the countryside. The troops of the contributing countries, India and Jordan, did not have the capability to control the countryside so each country recalled its troops. This completely undesirable situation strengthened the arguments being made by Canada and other troop-contributing countries for the Security Council to hold more regular and more co-operative meetings with them. On 13 June 2001, the Security Council unanimously adopted Resolution 1353, in which it undertook to keep troop-contributing countries fully informed of the mandates for missions and to hold meetings with them:

> in particular, when the Secretary-General has identified potential troop-contributing countries for a new or ongoing peacekeeping operation, when considering a change in, or renewal or completion of a peacekeeping mandate, or when there is a rapid deterioration in the situation on the ground,

including when it threatens the safety and security of United Nations peace-keepers. (UN Security Council, 2001: 6)

The meetings, which can be held either publicly or privately, may be called at the request of the contributing states. Significant progress has been made: the Security Council is now meeting more regularly and more co-operatively with the troop-contributing countries. There is, however, still room for improvement as the substance of the consultations is rarely well reflected in policy outcomes.[3]

Although Security Council decision-making is by no means transparent, the Council is holding more meetings to which the broader UN membership is invited. For example, it held open meetings on women and security in October 2002, on human security in December 2002, and on children and armed conflict in January 2003. The Security Council is also introducing greater transparency into its operations. Resolution 1441 was circulated in advance to the broader UN membership before being adopted by the Security Council. This move was a complete departure from traditional practice.

The Brahimi Report also recommended the development of rapid deployment capability—an objective long advocated by Canada. In 1996 seven states responded to a Danish initiative to established a brigade-size, rapid deployment force, known as the Stand-by High Readiness Brigade (SHIRBRIG).[4] It was established in close co-operation with the UN Secretariat and both bodies continue to work closely. The SHIRBRIG aims to deploy 4,000 to 5,000 troops quickly (i.e., in 14 to 30 days) after the Security Council has authorized a peace operation under Chapter Six of the Charter. The SHIRBRIG is designed to be a stop-gap measure to secure a conflict area in the period between the Security Council authorizing a peace operation and the arrival of the larger UN mission. Participation in the SHIRBRIG is entirely voluntary and member states decide whether to deploy on a case-by-case basis. The missions are sent for a maximum of six months.

The SHIRBRIG was not used during the first four years of its existence. To be fair, it took time to marshal a force of sufficient size and calibre, to undertake the necessary pre-deployment planning and training, to develop common operating procedures, and to ensure that members were contributing equipment that was mutually compatible. The slow start, however, was not good for credibility. The SHIRBRIG was first deployed in the autumn of 2000, after the Security

Council had decided to establish a mission for Ethiopia and Eritrea, under Chapter Six of the Charter. The deployment of Dutch, Canadian, and Danish personnel took some 90 days—well beyond the 30-day target specified in the Brahami Report. It took only three days for the Canadian cabinet to authorize the deployment of Canadian troops but it took significantly longer for the Dutch parliament to approve the deployment of its troops. Once the approvals were secured there were greater delays—the Canadian troops spent 25 days travelling by sea because Canada had no airlift capability. The SHIRBRIG's first six-month mission to Ethiopia and Eritrea was considered a success and it was redeployed in May 2001.

Canada would like to see the SHIRBRIG improved in two respects. First, its membership needs to be more geographically representative. At present there are no southern members. Two southern states have observer status: Senegal, which never attends the SHIRBRIG meetings, and Jordan, which comes regularly and reports back to the Group of 77. There is increasing support among the SHIRBRIG members to abolish the observer category and to force the current observers either to join or to stop attending the meetings. Canada and Sweden strongly opposed such a move on the grounds that it is important to have greater southern involvement. It is also much better to have Jordan reporting back to the Group of 77 so the latter knows what is happening from one of its own members rather than hearing reports from northern states, whose accounts might be regarded with suspicion. The Steering Committee—the SHIRBRIG's executive organ—has compiled a list of countries to approach about becoming members.[5]

Second, Canada would like to see the SHIRBRIG mandate expanded so that it can be used not only in peacekeeping operations carried out under Chapter Six of the UN Charter operations, but also enforcement missions under Chapter Seven, such as Sierra Leone and the Congo. There is, however, great opposition to expanding the SHIRBRIG mandate. The Netherlands has threatened to pull out of the SHIRBRIG if the latter's mandate is expanded to include Chapter Seven missions. At a meeting a year ago in Copenhagen, the Steering Committee agreed on a compromise: the SHIRBRIG would remain a Chapter Six instrument but its deployment to Chapter Seven missions could be considered on a case-by-case basis. Although Canada has not changed its position on expanding the mandate to include Chapter Seven missions, it realizes that it would be futile to push further on this issue at this time. Instead, it is concentrating on trying to enhance the versatility of the SHIRBRIG and to promote strategies to enhance the capacity of peacekeepers.

In February 2002, Canada organized a 'lessons learned' exercise in New York, which drew over 100 participants from all the major peace-keeping countries, the UN Secretariat, and the General Assembly's Special Committee on Peacekeeping Operations. Its report concluded that deployment to Ethiopia and Eritrea had been fairly rapid and effective, although securing national approval for troop deployments needed to be expedited and procedures for transferring authority from the SHIRBRIG to the incoming UN force needed to be improved. The report, nonetheless, provided a ringing endorsement of rapid deployment. In January 2003 Canada began a one-year term as president of the SHIRBRIG; hence it is now well positioned to seek progress on its key objectives, including enhancing the SHIRBRIG's capacity and expanding its membership.

The main weakness of the Brahimi Report was the failure to include an implementation plan. Consequently, there was the very legitimate fear that its recommendations would be shelved. The Special Committee on Peacekeeping Operations was, in fact, ready to shelve the report on the grounds that more study was necessary and the Secretariat had to be convinced of the need to table an implementation plan. As vice-chair of the Special Committee, Canada's Michel Duval effectively negotiated behind the scenes to lay the groundwork for the eventual adoption of the Brahimi recommendations for enhancing UN peacekeeping capacity.[6] The latter were controversial, especially since they required new resources, including the creation of over 200 additional staff positions. The Group of 77 quickly saw the predominantly northern desire to enhance the effectiveness of peace operations as an opportunity to bargain for additional resources for economic development and made its acceptance of the Brahimi recommendations conditional on receiving corresponding increases in the resources allocated to economic development. To court southern allies, Canada lobbied hard among major southern troop-contributors—states with vested interests in ensuring that peace operations received adequate resources. The Special Committee on Peacekeeping Operations moved from its initial insistence that the report needed more study—a position that would, at best, have seriously delayed implementation and, at worst, have resulted in the report being shelved—to working for its implementation. Canada got agreement that the recommendations would be adopted as a package and not negotiated individually. In March 2002, the Special Committee adopted most of the Brahimi Report's recommendations for enhancing UN peacekeeping capacity. Their acceptance was made possible by the combined backing of member states, the Secretariat, and the Secretary-General. To secure this level of support required effective diplomacy and hard work by Canada and its like-minded allies.

All but one of the new staff positions recommended to enhance peacekeeping capacity have been adopted. The Group of 77 remains resistant to creating the position of a gender adviser on peacekeeping.[7] Some of its members say the position is unnecessary because the UN already has a Special Adviser for Gender Issues and the Advancement of Women. Others reject the concept of gender and still others resist because the position is seen to reflect northern—rather than southern—priorities. Canada remains firmly committed to the creation of the position for practical as well as symbolic reasons. Its existence would highlight the importance of gender analysis to sound policy. Nonetheless, Canada chose not to push this issue when the other provisions were to be adopted for fear of reopening debate on all the Brahimi recommendations. Having the Brahimi recommendations for improving peacekeeping accepted is a significant victory. Canada and its like-minded allies are now working to ensure that these recommendations are reflected in the mandate of each new peace mission.

HUMAN SECURITY

Promoting human security was one of Canada's three principal goals when it served on the Security Council in 1999–2000. Canada defines human security as 'a people-centred approach to foreign policy which recognizes that lasting stability cannot be achieved until people are protected from violent threats to their rights, safety or lives' (DFAIT, 2002d: 1). Human security became a central pillar of Canadian foreign policy under Lloyd Axworthy and it has continued to be so. In June 2000, the Department of Foreign Affairs and International Trade established the Human Security Program, which funds projects around the world that 'strengthen the ability of the global community to respond to threats to Human Security and support peaceful governance' (DFAIT, 2002c: 1).

Canada brought the concept of human security to the Security Council in spite of the skepticism expressed by many countries about putting the protection of civilians on the agenda. Canada, along with its like-minded allies, continues to promote human security whenever it gets the opportunity, particularly in the General Assembly, the Human Rights Commission, and the Executive Committee of the Office of the High Commissioner for Refugees. Of the five pillars that comprised Canada's platform on human security when it sat on the Security Council, highest priority is now given to the protection of civilians and good governance, which includes addressing international impunity.[8]

Addressing International Impunity

No one accused of genocide or crimes against humanity should be exempt from prosecution. Three sets of international institutions are designed to deal with international impunity: the International Criminal Court, the International War Crimes Tribunals for the Former Yugoslavia and Rwanda, and the special courts being established to deal with war crimes in Sierra Leone and Cambodia.

The International Criminal Court (ICC) is the first permanent international court dedicated to trying cases of genocide, war crimes, and crimes against humanity. The ICC has two main objectives: to punish those who have committed genocide, war crimes, and crimes against humanity; and to deter further perpetrators of such crimes. The Court is intrinsically important to international law and justice. Its very existence reflects a shift from a laissez-faire attitude to impunity to an increased demand for accountability.

Although it became an independent institution on 1 July 2002, when the Rome Statute of the International Criminal Court entered into force, the Court was developed under the auspices of the UN. The ICC's Preparatory Commission was a UN body, chaired by Canada's Philippe Kirsch. Canada, along with the EU, played a pivotal role in creating the ICC. Canada established a group of like-minded states at the start of the Rome Conference, which it continues to chair. Membership in the group has grown from some 20 states to over 60 states, including members of the European Union, Australia, New Zealand, Norway, Argentina, South Africa, and Lesotho. Canada and other members of the group remain strongly committed to making the Court an effective tool of international justice and to getting as many states as possible to ratify the enabling statute. The pro-ratification campaign has met with considerable success and 87 states have ratified. Canada has organized numerous conferences and workshops to educate countries so they will have the legislation in place necessary to fulfill their obligations under the statute. At home, the Canadian government has adopted the legislation necessary to make the Canadian legal system compatible with the fulfillment of its commitments under the ICC. In his speech to the Assembly of States Parties in September 2002, Canadian Foreign Minister Bill Graham committed Canada to spending $1.5 million over the next year on projects promoting ratification and implementation of the ICC statute (DFAIT, 2002e: 4). Most of these funds will be drawn from the Human Security Program.

At its first session, held 3–9 September 2002, the Assembly of States Parties adopted instruments developed by the Preparatory Commission that are necessary to the functioning of the Court. Judges and prosecutors were elected in February 2003. Once elected, the judges chose from among their numbers Philippe Kirsch of Canada as the president of the ICC. Canada had nominated Kirsch as a candidate for the bench with the hope that he might also be elected as the ICC president.

The success in creating the ICC has been undermined by President Bush's formal rejection of it. The US actively opposes the ICC on the grounds that American soldiers and government officials could be subjected to politically motivated accusations and trials. In response, Canada and other like-minded states have pointed out that the ICC is designed to complement—not replace—national courts. An individual accused of war crimes, crimes against humanity, or genocide can only be brought before the ICC if the courts of his/her own country are unable or unwilling to try the case. As a result, the ICC would only have jurisdiction to prosecute US officials and members of its armed forces if US courts failed to try them.

Initially, the US sought complete exemptions for all US citizens— a position that ran contrary to Canada's belief that no one should be above the law. When most states were unwilling to accede to its demand for exemption, the US took the draconian measure on 30 June 2002 of vetoing the renewal of the mandate for the UN peace operations in Bosnia. Canada's Permanent Representative to the UN, Paul Heinbecker, wrote to the British chair of the Security Council, asking for an open meeting at which the Security Council could hear the views of the broader UN membership on this issue. When nothing came of the request, Heinbecker sent a second letter, which he circulated throughout the UN. These efforts generated enough pressure from the broader membership and from sympathetic members of the Security Council to prompt the Council to hold a meeting in July, at which delegates from some 50 countries criticized the US stance. The US has since backed away from seeking an automatic exemption. Instead, it seeks to limit its exposure by referring to Security Council Resolution 1422 (July 2002), which, in turn, refers to Article 16 of the ICC statute. Article 16 allows for the deferral of investigations pertaining to UN peacekeeping missions. It was intended to be used in complex peace negotiations where, in order to get key officials to attend the talks, it was necessary to guarantee that they would not be prosecuted during the peace process. The US has interpreted this provision as a blanket deferral—an interpretation that goes against the spirit and the letter of the law. Under Resolution 1422, the deferral has to be renewed each year; hence the issue will be revisited in July 2003. The outcome, as Heinbecker noted, was 'a two-thirds victory for the US and a one-third victory for Canada'.

The US seeks to negotiate bilateral agreements with all members of the UN. Although fewer than 15 mostly small states have entered into such agreements with the US, the American efforts in this regard may have a chilling effect on ratification. Some countries that appeared to be moving towards ratification are now backing away, although the overall number of ratifications keeps increasing. Canada is continuing to promote the ICC and to encourage ratification. Within the UN, support for the ICC appears to be growing, as it is often mentioned in UN resolutions and in Kofi Annan's speeches.

In contrast to the ICC, the International War Crimes Tribunals for Rwanda and the Former Yugoslavia are not permanent and their mandates are geographically limited. Both are functioning with little need for outside involvement. The Security Council is, however, still active in two regards. First, its support is essential because it alone has the authority to pressure governments to ensure that individuals accused of war crimes and crimes against humanity are prosecuted. Second, Security Council involvement is necessary to develop exit strategies. The tribunals are expensive[9] but establishing timetables for completing their work is problematic. A backlog of cases, for example, waits to be tried by the International War Crimes Tribunal for Rwanda. The situation with Yugoslavia is complicated because some of the key accused, including Radovan Karadzic and Ratko Mladic, have yet to be apprehended. In addition, there is an ongoing, low-intensity conflict in Macedonia that may produce additional cases for the tribunal.

Unlike the tribunals established for Yugoslavia and Rwanda, the special courts for Sierra Leone and Cambodia are not being created by the Security Council. The Security Council held informal negotiations to get processes moving and passed resolutions highlighting the importance of establishing them, but it did not pass a resolution setting up the court for Sierra Leone nor will it do so for a Cambodian court. Neither is yet functioning but the court for Sierra Leone is close to being operational. It was set up under a bilateral agreement between the UN Secretariat and the government of Sierra Leone, with support from funding countries. Canada has provided significant support. In addition to furnishing $2 million, it established a Management Committee—an informal mechanism to secure funding and to provide guidance on the court's functioning, budget, and the hiring of its officials. Fifteen states have now volunteered to serve on the Management Committee, which is chaired by Canada.

Establishing a court for Cambodia has been much more problematic. The Cambodian people want closure and the court would be an important part of that process. In contrast, the government has not been co-operative, largely because its leader was formerly in the Kumar Rouge and he does not appear keen to have the court proceed. In this case, it is necessary to find balance between what is achievable, given the past Kumar Rouge associations of many government officials, and what is compatible with the criteria of international justice. The process has been further complicated by the unhelpful positions of China and Vietnam, which appear to value their trade with Cambodia more than international law and justice. They seem unwilling to risk alienating Cambodia by supporting UN efforts to establish the court.

Australia took the lead in proposing a resolution to set up the court but Cambodia refused to co-sponsor it, thereby indicating an unwillingness to co-operate. Without Cambodia's co-sponsorship, the resolution could not succeed and had to be abandoned. Cambodia might be willing to co-sponsor a resolution if the mandate of the court is severely restricted, but this would seriously undermine the court's efficacy. Consequently, plans for the court are on hold, much to the chagrin of Canada, Australia, the Netherlands, and, to some extent, the US. A UN resolution was recently passed requesting the Secretary-General to restart the talks but the outcome of these efforts is uncertain at this point. If a special court were to be set up for Cambodia, it is expected that Canada would contribute money and officials, as it has done in Sierra Leone.

In addition to the current frustrations in dealing with Cambodia, Canada is concerned that UN credibility not be harmed by the functioning of the special courts. The UN's reputation would be damaged if the trials were seen to be shams, which is unlikely to happen in Sierra Leone but is a distinct possibility with Cambodia, especially since Cambodia wants each trial chamber to be dominated by Cambodian judges. The UN would also come under criticism if the courts ran out of money before completing their mandates. Blaming the UN for its members' lack of political will is a long-standing, although unfair, practice. The UN Secretariat did ask for three years of guaranteed funding for the special court for Sierra Leone but countries were unwilling to make this length of commitment.

Responsibility to Protect

In December 2001 the Canadian-sponsored Commission on Intervention and State Sovereignty submitted its report, *The Responsibility to Protect*, to Secretary-General Kofi Annan, who had it circulated as an official UN document. The report begins with two basic principles (ICISS, 2001: xi). First, the sovereign state bears primary responsibility for protecting its people. Second, in cases where a state is either unwilling or unable to protect its people from serious harm, the international responsibility to protect takes precedence over a deference to the principle of non-interference. Military intervention is seen as justified in cases where there is either large-scale loss of life or large-scale ethnic cleansing. The Security Council is designated as the appropriate body to authorize military intervention in such cases. The report refocuses attention away from debates over the degree to which sovereignty should remain sacrosanct to the duty to protect people when their state is unwilling or unable to do so.

Translating the recommendations of the report into action is recognized to be a longer-term project and Canada has yet to decide on the degree to which specific norms need to be adopted. Canada does, however, want the report to receive careful consideration and expects follow-up action by the Security Council, so that in future it is better prepared to act and the horrors of the Rwandan genocide are not repeated.

Canada is pursuing a two-track strategy to ensure that the report is not ignored: promoting it within UN circles, both in New York and Geneva; and building support for it in civil society. Although it is early in the process, there are some reasons for optimism. In May

2002 the Security Council held a retreat, during which a session was held on *The Responsibility to Protect*. Kofi Annan is a strong supporter of the report and he regularly incorporates its language into his speeches. Canada's Permanent Representative to the UN, Paul Heinbecker, has held consultations on a technical resolution to ensure that the report is given further consideration by the member states and that the Secretariat facilitates this consideration. From the consultations, it is evident that even such a modest resolution would face resistance from some southern countries, which argue that the issues raised in the report require further discussion. As a result, Canada has decided to organize events in New York to facilitate further discussions before officially tabling a resolution on *The Responsibility to Protect*.

In addition to promoting the report within UN circles, Canada recognizes that the longer-term implementation of the report will require cultivating the support of civil society. Canada is encouraging the establishment of NGO networks similar to those that existed for the landmines campaign. Canada's efforts in this regard have received some financial support from large US foundations, including the MacArthur Foundation. On 4–6 November 2002 the Canadian government held a conference for Parliamentarians for Global Action, at which some 100 parliamentarians discussed *The Responsibility to Protect* as well as the International Criminal Court. Other conferences and events to promote the report are scheduled to be held in all regions of the world.

The timing of the report affected its reception both positively and negatively. The report deals with prevention, intervention, and rebuilding—all of which are relevant to today's crises. Afghanistan exemplifies what can happen when a situation is ignored. Conditions deteriorated and religious extremists took control, thus creating a situation ripe for the development of Osama bin Laden's Al-Qaeda operations. Afghanistan also exemplifies the need to rebuild and to create the conditions for a lasting peace in the future. Having the report released as the campaign in Afghanistan was being waged heightened its relevance.

In some ways, however, timing has not been propitious. The current preoccupation with the Iraq situation is making it harder for Canada to promote *The Responsibility to Protect* because some states fail to distinguish between the situations addressed in the report, in which a state is unable or unwilling to protect its people, and the current situation, in which a functioning state is defying UN resolutions requiring it to disarm. The Iraqi government has committed grave human rights violations against its own citizens, but this is not the primary motivation for President Bush's threat of war. Canada is devoting time and energy to explaining the distinction between the Iraq crisis and the conditions being addressed in *The Responsibility to Protect*, when it would prefer to be expounding on the merits of the report's recommendations. The utility of the report depends on the implementation of its recommendations. The international community has yet to respond to the gross violations of human rights, including the loss of life, that are taking place today in Zimbabwe and the Ivory Coast, where the governments are clearly unwilling or unable to protect their peoples from serious harm. Intervention into such dangerous situations would be costly. Failure to act indicates that the report's recommendations are not being taken seriously.

HUMAN RIGHTS

Canada is a world leader in promoting the development of international human rights norms. It has proposed more resolutions than any other state at the Commission on Human Rights and has been very active in promoting the establishment and implementation of norms on a broad range of issues, including women's rights (especially the elimination of violence against women and reproductive rights), children's rights (especially education and protection in armed conflict), freedom of expression, impunity, indigenous peoples, and gender mainstreaming. The events of 11 September make human rights more important than ever, as the link between the deprivation of human rights and terrorism is recognized. Yet the past 17 months have been extremely difficult and challenging for those concerned with human rights. Highly contentious political debates over the Middle East preoccupied participants at the World Conference Against Racism and at the annual meetings of the UN Commission on Human Rights.

Preparations for the Conference Against Racism, which was held in Durban from 31 August to 7 September 2001, had been long and arduous. At the conference, the US and Israel walked out because their efforts to have anti-Israeli language deleted from the text were being thwarted. Canada was the first country to speak after the Declaration and Programme of Action were adopted, expressing agreement with most of their provisions but dissociating itself from the passages on the Middle East—a stance that left it fairly isolated. The discomfort of the Canadian delegation was exacerbated when its speech was booed by NGOs. The latter were unwilling to see criticisms of Israel's treatment of Palestinians derail support for the many important issues on which critical progress had been made, such as protecting migrants and refugees from discrimination and intolerance, declaring slavery a crime against humanity, and promoting gender equality (Human Rights Watch, 2001: 1). Thus Canada—a country that prides itself on promoting human rights and that enjoys relatively good relations with NGOs—was unable to endorse fully an important human rights document, much to the consternation of many southern countries and most NGO participants. The outcome at Durban is all the more lamentable because issues of racism, including racial profiling, are all the more important after 11 September.

Just as the Durban conference got diverted from its central purpose by geopolitical discussions on the Middle East, debates about the Middle East permeated all debates at the March 2002 session of the Commission on Human Rights. About half of the time available at the session was spent on the Middle East situation, which, as Marie Gervais-Vidricaire of the Global Affairs Bureau at DFAIT has noted, left little time for the numerous remaining items on the agenda.

In addition to the preoccupation with the Middle East, two other developments have caused Canada concern. The African states have become much more unified in collectively opposing discussion of their members' human rights records, especially if such discussion could be construed as criticism. As a result, it is extremely difficult to address grave human rights abuses taking place in countries such as Zimbabwe and Sudan. The chair of the Commission on Human Rights rotates among the regions and it is now Africa's turn to preside. The African states nominated Libya—a country with an abysmal human rights record[10]—and it was elected in January 2003. So the prospects for the March 2003 session of the Commission on Human Rights are not rosy. Conflict in the Middle East has been intensifying, not diminishing, thus much of the debate is likely once again to focus on the politics of that region and, to make matters worse, Libya will be in the chair.

A further challenge has been to prevent backsliding, especially in the area of women's reproductive rights. Canada was particularly disturbed by the tough stand taken by the US at the UN Special Session on Children in May 2002. At the Johannesburg World Summit on Sustainable Development, Canada once again had to struggle to prevent the Vatican and the US from rolling back progress achieved at previous conferences and summits.

In an otherwise rather gloomy picture, there were, nonetheless, a few important bright spots. Human rights comprise one of the six categories of objectives outlined in the Millennium Development Goals. In 2000, the UN Security Council unanimously passed a resolution on women, peace, and security that recognized 'the urgent need to mainstream a gender perspective into peacekeeping operations'.[11] The mandates of the International Criminal Court and the International War Crimes Tribunals for Rwanda and the Former Yugoslavia all explicitly require that sexual crimes against women be considered when deciding on the jurisdiction and when judging cases. The Optional Protocol to the Convention on the Rights of the Child on the Involvement of Children in Armed Conflict, which came into force in February 2002, was seen as a major breakthrough in the campaign to protect children affected by armed conflict. It seeks to limit their involvement and raises the minimum age for recruitment to 18. Canada continues to pressure for ratification and has contributed funds from the Human Security Program to promote this objective. Also in 2002, the Economic and Social Council established the Permanent Forum on Indigenous Issues to address indigenous concerns pertaining to economic and social development, education, health, human rights, culture, and the environment. Its 16 members include eight indigenous-nominated experts and eight government-nominated experts. Canada's indigenous groups welcomed the new body, and a Canadian, Wayne Lord, has been elected as one of the government-nominated experts.

Within UN circles there is growing disillusionment with holding further mega-conferences on human rights. The meetings themselves are costly and the follow-up is weak. A breadth of substantial norms now exists; hence, the focus needs to be on implementation, not on further norm development. Canada strongly endorses this focus.

SUSTAINABLE DEVELOPMENT

Sustainable development is defined as 'development that meets the needs of the present without compromising the ability of future generations to meet their own needs' (World Commission on Environment and Development, 1987: 43). Intrinsically important in its own right, sustainable development is also closely linked to the other issue areas discussed in this chapter. Economic rights comprise a set of human rights as exemplified by the Convention on Economic, Social and Cultural Rights, one of six principal treaties in the human rights regime. The link between terrorism and economic privation was made apparent in President Bush's National Security Strategy,[12] as well as in Prime Minister Chrétien's speech of 16 September 2002 to the General Assembly (PMO, 2002: 2). The relationship between peace and development is well established:

> It doesn't get more basic than this: without peace, there can be no lasting development. It is no coincidence that half of the 47 countries with the lowest human development index have experienced serious conflict in the past decade, and that 15 out of 20 of the least-developed countries have been involved in violent conflict. (Brown, 2000: 1)

The linkage between peace and development is also clearly depicted in the Brahimi Report, *The Responsibility to Protect*, and the Carnegie Commission's 1997 report, *Preventing Deadly Conflict*.

The World Summit on Sustainable Development (WSSD) was held in Johannesburg, South Africa, 26 August–4 September 2002. Its objectives were to provide further strategies and mechanisms for implementing the recommendations of the 1992 World Conference on the Environment and Development, to identify fresh challenges and the means of addressing them, and to stimulate greater global commitment to sustainable development. Although the WSSD was the largest-ever single gathering of heads of state and government, US President Bush refused to attend. Colin Powell represented the US and, while it would have been more encouraging to have had presidential participation, Bush's absence did not have any significant impact on the Summit's success.

Canada went into the Summit with five priorities: to promote better health and environmental safeguards and to recognize the interrelationship between them; to develop, and to ensure the implementation of, innovative strategies for promoting sustainable development and partnerships, especially those involving the private sector; to produce sustainable communities, particularly in cities where population growth is greatest and where infrastructures are frequently inadequate to match this growth; to promote stewardship and conservation, especially of the natural resource sectors but also of parks and the Arctic; and to improve international environmental governance.

The Summit established targets for increasing access to clean water and adequate sanitation; increasing access to energy for those currently without; improving health; enhancing agricultural productivity; and better safeguarding biodiversity and better managing the world's ecosystems. Some of these issues (e.g., health and agriculture) were already being addressed within the UN system but needed a higher profile, and the linkages between them needed to be made more explicit. Other issues, in particular water and energy, had received little attention. No UN bodies are devoted to safeguarding water or to ensuring that all peoples have access to sustainable sources of energy. In dealing with all five issues and addressing the linkages between them, the Summit made significant contributions. It also made important headway in developing and expanding mechanisms to ensure partnerships to promote sustainable development among northern and southern countries, the private sector, and NGOs. Prior to the Summit, over 220 such partnerships, with a total of US $235 million in resources, had been identified and an additional 60 were announced in the course of the Summit (WSSD, 2002: 1).

The success of the WSSD was due in large measure to being able to incorporate provisions negotiated in other forums into its Declaration on Sustainable Development and Plan of Implementation. The Millennium Development Goals had been developed by the UN Secretariat without being widely negotiated by member states. They set targets to be achieved by 2015, which include halving extreme poverty and hunger; ensuring that all girls and boys receive primary education; promoting gender equality and empowering women; reducing child mortality by two-thirds; decreasing maternal mortality by three-quarters; combatting HIV/AIDS and other pandemic diseases; promoting sustainable development (in particular, access to clean water and significantly improving the lives of slum dwellers); and developing partnerships for development, involving northern and southern states, the private sector, and NGOs. Although the goals had been championed by Secretary-General Kofi Annan, they had not been heartily endorsed, let alone implemented, by member states. At the WSSD, the Millennium Development Goals were refined, given higher profile and greater credibility, and endorsed by member states and the NGO community.

The balance struck between northern and southern interests at the March 2002 Monterrey Conference on Financing for Development was adopted at the WSSD. Southern countries agreed to create the conditions necessary for development within their respective countries, including commitments to democracy, good governance, and human rights. In turn, northern states promised to increase foreign aid, assist with debt relief, encourage southern trade, and promote investment in the South.

The chapter on Africa in the Johannesburg Plan of Implementation drew heavily on the New Partnership for Africa's Development, which is discussed in greater depth by Stephen Langdon in Chapter 13. At the G-8 Summit in June 2002, Canada, with support from the UK and France, was successful in making African development a major focus. The Summit adopted the G-8 Africa Action Plan, which served as a further impetus for the WSSD chapter on Africa.

The Doha ministerial meetings of the World Trade Organization are much more focused on development issues than any previous trade round has been. They are discussing such critical issues as agricultural subsidies, which frequently prevent southern sales to major northern markets, and southern access to patent medicines. While the details of such agreements remain to be worked out, the need to make progress on these development issues was recognized at the Doha meetings and subsequently at the WSSD.

At the WSSD, the importance of the Kyoto Protocol to the United Nations Framework Convention on Climate Change was affirmed and Prime Minister Chrétien committed Canada to ratifying it. The Summit also benefited from documents produced by the OECD and the UN's five regional economic commissions, as well as its own preparatory meetings.

The WSSD realized many Canadian objectives. Its documents contain strong language linking the environment and human health. The impact of the former on the latter had never been as clearly defined before. Canada led the campaign to get commitments to address the social, political, and environmental problems associated with mining, which comprises the principal export sector for many southern countries. Canada also led the efforts to get recognition of the need for further work on chemicals and the environment. After a tough struggle, Canada, with support from Norway, Australia, Switzerland, and the EU, managed to prevent fundamentalist Islamic states, led by

Egypt, as well as the US and Argentina, from rolling back progress made on reproductive rights at previous negotiations.

As president of the UN Environment Program since 2001, Canada's Minister of the Environment, David Anderson, is credited with getting the campaign to improve international environmental governance launched. At the WSSD, some countries within the Group of 77, including Venezuela, India, and Indonesia, were eager to roll back the provisions for good governance that had been adopted at Monterrey. Again, a reneging on previous agreements was prevented. Furthermore, provisions were included for improving the financing of the UN Environment Program and for improving its linkages with other UN bodies working on environmental issues.

Although most of Canada's priorities were reflected in the Summit documents, there were a few disappointments. The treatment of globalization is not as substantial as it might have been and Canada would have preferred stronger language on good governance. For example, it would have liked even more concrete recommendations to enable the UN Environment Program to co-ordinate its work more effectively with other UN bodies. Overall, the WSSD was a success, both in terms of UN and Canadian objectives.

LEADERSHIP

The issue of Canadian leadership arises in many chapters in this book. Leadership can be defined in many ways, ranging from entrepreneurial leadership (forming like-minded coalitions, engineering agreements, and facilitating the negotiation of compromise solutions), to intellectual leadership (offering fresh ideas, new perspectives, and creative ways of conceptualizing problems), to providing resources to translate the ideas into concrete, effective programs (Young, 1991: 281). Canada is well known for its entrepreneurial leadership. As noted in this chapter's discussion of peace operations, human security, human rights, and sustainable development, Canada has an excellent record of forming coalitions with like-minded states. It is not, however, always very willing to share the credit for new ideas and initiatives with its like-minded allies. Ministers' names often become associated with a new idea, which makes it harder for Canada to share the limelight. At times, it needs to be more sensitive to the frustration that other countries may feel when their contributions are not fully recognized publicly.

Canada has been, and it continues to be, one of the world's foremost intellectual leaders at the UN. Recent examples include the campaign to create the International Criminal Court and Canadian-sponsorship of the International Commission on Intervention and State Sovereignty. Canada has also been a leader in promoting gender equity and the rights of children. Overall, Canada's intellectual leadership is highly commendable. However, a cautionary note is in order. Canada proposes a great many ideas but at times quantity seems to prevail over quality and the need for more clearly defined priorities is evident. Canada's initial human security agenda was incredibly broad, comprising five pillars: the protection of civilians, peace support operations, conflict prevention, governance and accountability, and public safety. It would be hard to think of many issues that would not come under at least one of the pillars. They could include eliminating landmines, promoting economic development, organizing anti-malaria campaigns, ensuring adequate food distribution, countering terrorism, limiting the use of child soldiers, and even installing traffic lights to curtail accidents. Examples of excellent human security priorities for Canada include assisting a broad range of countries to develop the domestic legislation and the structures necessary to facilitate good governance, to combat international terrorism, and to comply with the statute of the ICC. For the international community to function well, it is essential that each member state have a well-functioning system of governance based on international law.

In many cases, Canada's intellectual leadership has not been matched at the implementation stage. Speeches by Canadian officials to the UN laud Canada's contributions to peacekeeping, yet concerns are increasingly being raised as to whether the rhetoric continues to be supported by action. Canada now ranks thirtieth in terms of contributing peacekeeping troops to UN operations, while many of the top 20 contributors are southern states. Canada refused to send troops to Sierra Leone, largely for fear of casualties and the political consequences that would follow. This fear has been heightened after four Canadians were killed by 'friendly fire' in Afghanistan. Canada's failure to deploy to some of the world's most serious crises, most of which are in Africa, raises questions about its commitment to non-European conflicts.

Canada can, and does, justifiably claim to offer intellectual leadership, which is based on its long and distinguished history of participation in UN peacekeeping missions. Its past record and its experience are internationally recognized. Canada also contributes experts and significant funding to peacebuilding. Does Canada need to continue to contribute peacekeeping troops to be seen as a peace-keeping country? Will a failure to send troops hurt Canada's reputation abroad and its credibility in peacekeeping decision-making at the UN? Are intellectual and entrepreneurial leadership and the contribution of non-military resources sufficient?

Patterns of strong intellectual leadership not being matched at the implementation stages are evident in other areas of endeavour. Canada asserts the need to implement the Millennium Development Goals, while the percentage of its gross national income devoted to international development assistance remains far below the international target of 0.7 per cent. Giving only 0.22 per cent of gross national income, Canada ranks nineteenth out of 22 OECD donor countries. At the Monterrey conference Prime Minister Chrétien promised to double Canadian overseas development assistance by the end of the decade. Time will tell if this commitment is realized. In Chapter 15, Inger Weibust points out that Canada has ratified the Kyoto Protocol but that it has the third highest per capita emissions of greenhouse gases of northern countries. As Denis Stairs has pointed out, there are indeed cases where Canada's rhetoric exceeds its performance (Stairs, 1999: 339).

CONCLUSION

Although we have entered a new millennium and the specifics of the issues preoccupying the UN are somewhat different from those taking precedence at the end of the twentieth century, developments at the UN, and Canada's foreign policies, are better characterized as part of an ongoing historic progress than as something brand new. US unilateralist impulses and Canada's desire to keep the US participating multilaterally are themes that have been present since the creation of the UN in 1945. Canada's chief preoccupation during the Korean War was maintaining the integrity of the UN. As such, it sought both to discourage the US from proceeding unilaterally and to keep the UN from becoming a tool of US foreign policy (Keating, 2002: 34). Today there is the struggle to have the US address Iraqi non-compliance through the Security Council. US unilateralism is very much in evidence in the US refusal to ratify the ICC statute, the

Kyoto Protocol, and the Convention on the Prohibition of the Use, Stockpiling, Production, and Transfer of Anti-Personnel Mines and on Their Destruction.

Yet, in spite of the gloom cast by the threat of terrorism, the threat of an impending war with Iraq, and the potential long-term consequences of such a war, the picture is not all bleak. In 2001 Kofi Annan and the UN won the Nobel Peace Prize in recognition of their contributions to world peace and the promotion of human rights and their efforts to combat new challenges, such as HIV/AIDS and international terrorism. Annan has worked to streamline the UN, to clarify and improve its priorities, and to better allocate resources to coincide with priorities. Significant progress has been made on many other fronts, especially in the development of norms and procedures to increase the efficacy of peace operations and to ensure that those who have committed crimes against humanity do not escape punishment. The responsibility to protect represents a major conceptual shift from a preoccupation with preserving state sovereignty to a focus on protecting people. The finances of the UN have improved largely because the US has paid a significant amount—although not all—of its arrears. In his 12 September speech to the UN, President Bush committed the US to participating in UNESCO after an absence of 19 years. US support for the UN has ebbed and flowed over the decades and there is every reason to expect the pattern to continue. Coping with the American Colossus involves persuading it to work as a co-operative participant within the system rather than having it gravitate to the extremes of either acting unilaterally or seeking to reduce the UN to being a tool of its foreign policy, both of which threaten the UN's credibility and viability.

NOTES

Much of the research for this chapter was drawn from interviews with federal public servants. In particular, I would like to thank Richard Ballhorn, Director General, Environment and Sustainable Development Affairs Bureau, DFAIT; Susan Brown, Chief, Peacebuilding Unit, CIDA; Terry Cormier, Director, International Crime Division, DFAIT; Marie Gervais-Vidricaire, Director General, Global Affairs Bureau, DFAIT; Paul Heinbecker, Ambassador and Permanent Representative of Canada to the United Nations; John Holmes, Director, UN Human Rights and Economic Law Division, DFAIT; Vanessa Kent, Peacekeeping Desk Officer, Regional Security and Peacekeeping Division, DFAIT; Patricia Lortie, Director General, International Organizations Bureau, DFAIT; Isabelle Massip, Director, UN

Commonwealth Affairs Division, DFAIT; Mark Moher, Canadian Ambassador to Ireland; and Peter Taylor, Deputy Director, United Nations Section. The author acknowledges assistance from the Office of Research Studies, University of Western Ontario.

1. Kofi Annan's effective diplomacy is credited with ensuring that even Syria supported the resolution.

2. 'Address by Prime Minister Jean Chrétien on the Occasion of the United Nations General Assembly High-Level Plenary Debate on the New Partnership for Africa's Development', New York, 16 Sept. 2002. Available at: <http://pm.gc.ca/default.asp?Language+E&Page' newsroom&Sub' newyorknepad20020916_e.>. Accessed 9 Jan. 2003. Also CBC News Online, 'Chrétien Interview on September 11', 16 Sept. 2002. Available at: <http://www.cbc.ca/printablestory.jsp>. Accessed 9 Jan. 2003.

3. See General Assembly, 'Special Committee of Peacekeeping Operations Ends Two-Day Debate on Need for Rapid Deployment of Peace Operations', press release, GA/PK/175, 12 Feb. 2002. Available at: <http://www.un.org/News/Press/docs/2002/GAPK175.doc.htm>. Accessed 28 Nov. 2002.

4. Those with full membership in the SHIRBRIG include Austria, Canada, Denmark, Italy, the Netherlands, Norway, Poland, Romania, and Sweden. Five other countries (Finland, Lithuania, Spain, Portugal, and Slovenia) also participate. For a more comprehensive analysis of the SHIRBRIG, see Peter Langille, *Bridging the Commitment-Capacity Gap: A Review of Existing Arrangements and Options for Enhancing UN Rapid Deployment* (Wayne, NJ: Centre for UN Reform Education, 2002), esp. 50–9.

5. The list of potential members includes Ghana, South Africa, Uruguay, Japan, Thailand, and Slovakia.

6. The most important proposals in the Brahimi Report pertain to conflict prevention. Yet these recommendations have been more rhetoric than reality.

7. Some southern countries, such as Fiji, speak out in favour of gender mainstreaming. For example, see the speeches by Amraiya Naidu to the Special Committee of Peacekeeping Operations, General Assembly, 'Special Committee of Peacekeeping Operations Ends Two-Day Debate on Need for Rapid Deployment of Peace Operations', 1, 8.

8. In 1998 Canada and Norway created the Human Security Network. The Network's current membership includes Austria, Canada, Chile, Greece, Ireland, Jordan, Mali, the Netherlands, Norway, Slovenia, Switzerland, and Thailand. South Africa participates as an observer. See George MacLean, 'Building on a Legacy or Bucking Tradition? Evaluating Canada's Human Security Initiative in an Era of Globalization?', *Canadian Foreign Policy* 9, 3 (2002): 65–83; and the human security Web site of the Department of Foreign Affairs and International Trade at: <http://www.human security.gc.ca>.

9. For example, the 2002–3 budget for the International War Crimes Tribunal for the Former Yugoslavia is US $223,169,800. UN, International War Crimes Tribunal for the Former Yugoslavia, 'ICTY Key Figures: General Information', 4 Dec. 2002, 6. Available at: <http://www.un.org/icty/glance/keyfig-e.htm>. Accessed 16 Jan. 2003.

10. The list of human rights abuses committed by the government of Libya includes extrajudicial and summary executions, the systematic use of torture, arbitrary arrests, and long-time detention without trial. Human Rights Watch, 'Libya Confirms Why it is Wrong for UN Rights Chair', press release, Aug. 2002, 1.

11. UN Security Council, S/2000/1044, 31 Oct. 2000, 2. Available at: <www.frauen. spoe.at/download/uno_resolution.pdf>. The resolution set important standards and principles. Unfortunately, it has not been effectively implemented.

12. According to the US National Security Strategy, 'poverty, weak institutions, and corruption can make weak states vulnerable to terrorist networks and drug cartels within their borders.' US, The National Security Strategy of the United States of America, Washington, Sept. 2002, 3. Available at: <http://www.whitehouse. gov.nsc/nss.pdf>. Accessed 12 Jan. 2003.

REFERENCES

Brown, Susan. 2000. *Why Conflict Prevention?* Ottawa: CIDA.

Canada. Parliament. 2000. *Crimes Against Humanity and War Crimes Act.* Ottawa, 29 June.

CBS News. 2002a. 'War with Iraq: Americans in No Hurry', New York. 7 Oct. Available at: <http://www.cbsnews.com/stories/2002/10/06/opinion/polls/main 524496.shtml>. Accessed 9 Jan. 2003.

———. 2002b. 'Americans Worry About Iraq', New York, 7 Nov. Available at: <http://www.cbsnews.com/stories/2002/11/02/opinion/polls/printable527933. shtml>. Accessed 9 Jan. 2003.

Department of Foreign Affairs and International Trade (DFAIT). 2001. 'Statement by Ambassador Paul Heinbecker, Ambassador and Permanent Representative of Canada to the United Nations on "Canada and the UN Security Council: Putting People First, An Overview"', Ottawa, Mar. Available at: <http://www.un.int/ canada/html/s-march2001/heinbecker.htm>. Accessed 30 Oct. 2002.

———. 2002a. 'Canada's Actions Against Terrorism Since September 11th— Backgrounder', Ottawa. Available at: <http://www.dfait-maeci.gc.ca/can-am/ menu-en.asp?act=v&mid=1&cat=10&did=1684>. Accessed 10 Jan. 2003.

———. 2002b. 'Canada–US Cross Border Crime and Security Cooperation', Ottawa. Available at: <http://www.canadianembassy.org/border/crime-en.asp>. Accessed 10 Jan. 2003.

———. 2002c. 'Human Security Program', Ottawa. Available at: <http://www.human security.gc.ca/psh-e.asp>. Accessed 4 Dec. 2002.

———. 2002d. 'Human Security Program: Human Security Program in Brief', Ottawa. Available at: <http://www.humansecurity.gc.ca/psh_brief-e.asp>. Accessed 4 Dec. 2002.

———. 2002e. 'Notes for an Address by the Honourable Bill Graham, Minister of Foreign Affairs to the Assembly of States Parties, International Criminal Court', New York, 9 Sept. Available at: <http://www.un.int/canada/s-09Sep2002 Graham.htm>. Accessed 30 Oct. 2002.

Gervais-Vidricaire, Marie. 2002. Director General, Global Affairs Bureau, DFAIT. Interview, Ottawa, 15 Nov.

Heinbecker, Paul. 2002. Ambassador and Permanent Representative of Canada to the United Nations. Interview, Waterloo, Ontario, 8 Nov.

Human Rights Watch. 2001. 'Anti-racism Summit Ends on Hopeful Note: Progress Amid Controversy', New York, 10 Sept. Available at: <www.hrw.org/prss/2001/09/wcar0910.htm>. Accessed 9 Dec. 2002.

International Commission on Intervention and State Sovereignty. 2001. *The Responsibility to Protect*. Ottawa: International Development Research Centre.

Keating, Tom. 2002. *Canada and World Order: The Multilateralist Tradition in Canadian Foreign Policy*, 2nd edn. Toronto: Oxford University Press.

Organization for Economic Co-operation and Development (OECD). 2003. 'Net ODA in 2001—as a Percentage of GNI', available at: <http://www.oecd.org/pdf/M00037000/M00037873.pdf>. Accessed 23 Jan. 2003.

Prime Minister's Office (PMO). 2002. 'Address by Prime Minister Jean Chrétien on the Occasion of the United Nations General Assembly High-Level Plenary Debate on the New Partnership for Africa's Development', New York, 16 Sept. Available at: <http://pm.gc.ca/default.asp?Language+E&Page=newsroom&Sub=newyork nepad20020916_e>. Accessed 9 Jan. 2003.

Stairs, Denis. 1999. 'Canada and the security problem: Implications as the millennium turns', *International Journal* 54, 3: 386–403.

United Nations Security Council. 2001. Resolution 1353. S/2001/573. 13 June. Available at: <http://www.un.org/News/Press/docs/2001/SC7070.doc.htm>. Accessed 11 Nov. 2002.

World Commission on Environment and Development. 1987. *Our Common Future*. Oxford: Oxford University Press. Available at: <http://www.gcrio.org/edu/pcsd/endnotes.html>. Accessed 19 Jan. 2003.

World Summit on Sustainable Development (WSSD). 2002. 'Johannesburg Summit 2002', Johannesburg, Sept. Available at: <http://www.johannesburgsummit.org/html/whats_new/feature_story39.html>. Accessed 18 Dec. 2002.

Young, Oran. 1991. 'Political Leadership and Regime Formation: On the Development of Institutions in International Society', *International Organization* 45, 3.

15

Implementing the Kyoto Protocol: Will Canada Make It?

INGER WEIBUST

On 17 December 2002, Canada became the one-hundredth country to ratify the Kyoto Protocol. The federal government pushed ahead with ratification over the protestations of several provincial governments, most notably Alberta, and major industry groups. By ratifying, Canada has lined up on the side of the angels, with the European Union, on the climate change issue. Meanwhile, the non-ratifiers, the Americans and Australians, will presumably burn in hell (or perhaps in uncontrollable forest fires). Although we have cast our lot with the Europeans, the challenges we face in implementing Kyoto place us in the American-Australian camp, not the European one.

Discussions over Kyoto ratification and proposals for implementation exposed two perceived constraints on Canadian foreign policy, particularly on Canada's ability to uphold its self-image as a good international citizen and global leader. The first constraint is our bilateral relationship with the United States and the extensive integration of our economy with the American economy. This has led to concerns that Canada will be disadvantaged, so long as the US remains outside Kyoto. The second constraint, which has received less attention, is the reality of executive federalism and constitutional restrictions, which limits our ability to fulfill international commitments. Although federal-provincial tensions have arisen in the context of other international issues, nowhere are they more acute than in the issue of climate change because the interests of Alberta and Quebec, in particular, are diametrically opposed on Kyoto.

It turns out that, in achieving our Kyoto commitments (or any stabilization of greenhouse gas emissions), Canada is far more constrained by domestic politics than by the provisions of Kyoto or what the US does. Unfortunately, the policy options that result in the lowest cost of compliance are those that disproportionately affect emissions-intensive sectors and therefore the regions where they are found. By the same token, commitments to ensure that no region or sector of the economy bears an unreasonable burden have the effect of substantially increasing total costs of compliance.

Canada's self-image as a good environmental citizen, if not actually a leader, runs counter to our track record on greenhouse gas emissions and climate change policies. Canada has chosen to rely heavily on voluntary actions to meet its Kyoto targets, despite the low success rate of such efforts compared with tools such as emissions trading. This choice was dictated largely by Canadian political considerations, particularly palatability to Canadian business interests, not outside constraints. Canada cannot simultaneously aspire to a mantle of international environmental leadership and insist that our policies remain in lockstep with those of the US.

THE STATUS OF KYOTO: WHO IS IN AND WHO IS OUT

Under the Kyoto Protocol, Canada is committed to a 6 per cent reduction of greenhouse gases below 1990 levels by 2008–12. This is a smaller percentage reduction than what the US agreed to (7 per cent, by the same deadline). Canada's commitment means a reduction of 240 megatonnes in annual emissions of greenhouse gases measured in CO_2 equivalents (unless the emissions grow at a different rate than economic growth projections assume). Only parties to Annex I of the Protocol are required to commit to emissions reductions. Annex I parties are the industrialized countries and those of the former Soviet bloc.

Article 25 of the Protocol specifies that for Kyoto to enter into force, 55 signatories accounting for 55 per cent of developed-country (Annex I) emissions in 1990 must ratify the Protocol. As of 19 January 2003 a total of 102 countries have ratified or acceded to the Protocol. Thus far, these account for only 43.9 per cent of emissions, although the EU member states and Japan have ratified the protocol. Because the United States counts for 25 per cent of global emissions, the failure of the US to ratify has dealt a serious, perhaps fatal, blow to the Kyoto process.

The Kyoto Protocol now requires only Russia's ratification to enter into force. Russia's 17.4 per cent of emissions are crucial in reaching the 55 per cent target, although Russia now appears to be hesitating in ratifying (Cattaneo et al., 2003: 1). Russia has more incentive to ratify than many other countries because Russia's current emissions, due to the collapse of the Soviet economy, are well below 1990 levels. This means that Russia is in a position to sell credits for the emissions it is entitled to emit but does not actually emit (these credits are sometimes referred to as 'hot air'). If Russia fails to ratify, the viability of the international market in pollution credits is reduced because Russia would have supplied a large proportion of those credits.

THE HOLDOUTS

Of the industrialized countries that signed Kyoto, to date only Australia, Switzerland, and the United States have yet to ratify. Most of these countries were in the JUSCANNZ coalition that emerged, largely in opposition to the European Union bloc, during successive rounds of negotiation within the United Nations Framework Convention on Climate Change, leading up to the Kyoto Protocol. The core members of the coalition were: Japan, the US, Canada, Australia, and New Zealand. Norway, Iceland, and Switzerland sometimes supported the coalition. JUSCANNZ was loosely allied with the countries of the Organization of Petroleum Exporting Countries (OPEC) until the Second Conference of Parties, in Geneva. Although these countries were less enthusiastic about Kyoto than the EU countries, Japan, Norway, and Canada have gone on to ratify the treaty.

Australia's current leadership has decided against ratification. This refusal is disconcerting because Australia is one of a handful of Annex I countries whose target allows for an increase in emissions, not a reduction.[1] However, Australia's per capita greenhouse gas emissions (but not CO_2 emissions) are among the highest in the world, even higher than those of the US, as shown in Figure 1 (Turton and Hamilton, 2002: 5). Although Australia's per capita emissions fell by 3 per cent between 1990 and 1999, per capita emissions in the European Union fell by 7 per cent in the same period (ibid.). Australia's total emissions continue to increase more rapidly than those of Canada and the US (Figure 2).

Despite the challenges that Kyoto ratification would pose for Australia, a poll of Australians released in July 2002 indicated that 71 per cent of those polled thought that ratification was in Australia's interest (Environment News Service, 2002). In place of multilateral co-operation, the governments of Australia and the US have opted for limited bilateral co-operation. The two countries have signed a bilateral Climate Action Partnership, focused on monitoring, information exchange, and research but not emissions reductions per se.

Figure 1

National Greenhouse Gas Emissions: Total and Per Capita

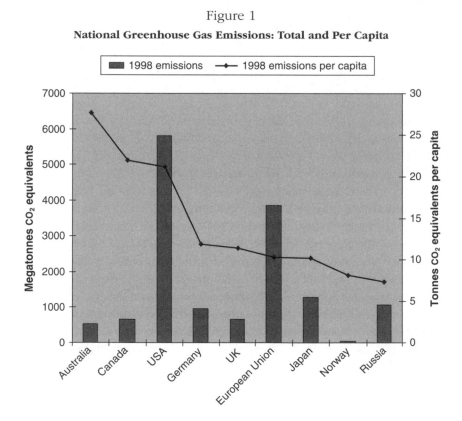

Figure 2

Change in Per Capita Greenhouse Gas Emissions, 1990–1999

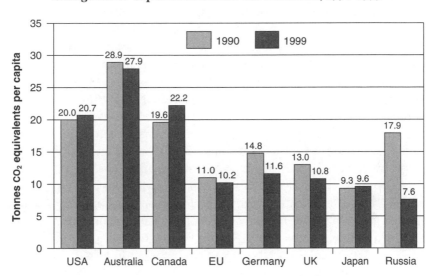

THE UNITED STATES: CLIMATE CHANGE POLICIES
WITHOUT KYOTO

The most conspicuous ratification holdout is the United States, which
signed the Kyoto Protocol on 12 November 1998. Under Kyoto, the
US should reduce emissions to 93 per cent of 1990 levels in the
2008–12 window. The United States accounts for approximately 25 per
cent of global emissions of greenhouse gases. US per capita emissions
have continued to increase, by 4 per cent between 1990 and 1999
(Figure 2) (ibid.). Because the US population continues to grow much
faster than that of many developed countries, total US emissions continue to grow. Because the US accounts for such a large proportion
of emissions, stabilizing global emissions without US participation will
be particularly difficult. Developing countries are not committed to
emissions reductions under Kyoto, which recognizes 'common but differentiated responsibilities' in addressing climate change.

To the extent that the current US administration acknowledges the
threat of climate change, it has a limited action plan to address it.
In February 2002, President Bush reaffirmed American commitment
to the goal of the treaty his father signed in 1992: the stabilization
of greenhouse gas emissions at levels that will prevent dangerous

climate change (Revkin, 2002a). However, the objective of the US policy is to reduce the greenhouse gas *intensity* of the US economy, that is, greenhouse gas emissions per unit of GDP, not total greenhouse gas emissions. The justification for this strategy is that action on climate change should not in any way constrain growth of the American economy. The target is to reduce greenhouse gas intensity by 18 per cent by 2012 (US Department of State, 2002: 5–6). There is no explicit target on emissions. These reductions are to be achieved through voluntary measures and technological advances. Because this policy does not entail any commitment to stabilization, much less reduction, of total US emissions, it has been harshly criticized by environmental groups.

Despite the administration's cautious, go-slow approach, action and calls for action on climate change are coming from many quarters. In January 2003, a bipartisan bill to reduce greenhouse gas emissions was introduced in the US Senate by Senators Joe Lieberman and John McCain, two respected senior senators. Although their plan would not bring the US into compliance with Kyoto, it would reduce US emissions to 1990 levels by 2016, using a cap and trade approach modelled on a successful trading component of the 1990 Clean Air Act (Lazaroff, 2003). If the bill were passed in its present form, it would represent a huge shift in US federal legislation on climate change and would have significant impacts on greenhouse gas emissions and the US economy as a whole.

State governments are taking action independent from the federal government. A recent report by the Pew Center on Global Climate Change surveyed action by nine state governments (Rabe, 2002). While state-level action is no substitute for national action, it could have significant impacts. Many individual states have greater greenhouse gas emissions than individual countries. For example, Texas has greater annual greenhouse gas emissions than France (Pegg, 2002). Texas requires that 2.2 per cent of the state's electricity portfolio come from renewable sources by 2009 (Pegg, 2002). This initiative has proven so successful that 16 states have now enacted legislation modelled on it. However, not all states seem to take climate change seriously. In 1999, 16 state governments passed legislation or resolutions critical of the Kyoto Protocol.

If these are the views of American governments, what about Americans? Polls indicate that Americans are aware of the climate change issue and are concerned about it. They are less skeptical about global warming than might be expected, given the Bush administration's focus on the uncertainty and the need for further research before acting. As of March 2001, 61 per cent of Americans polled stated that most scientists believe that global warming is occurring. Fifty-four per cent of those polled stated that the effects of global warming 'had already begun' and 61 per cent believed global warming is caused by human activity (Gallup, 2002: 90).

However, climate change is not at the top of the list of Americans' environmental concerns. When asked in March 2001 if they worried personally about the issue, 63 per cent indicated they worried 'a great deal' or 'a fair amount' about global warming (ibid., 89). Those who worried 'a great deal' about global warming were 33 per cent, slightly more than half of the 63 per cent total. However, in the same poll, global warming ranked twelfth out of 13 on a list of environmental issues, substantially lower than drinking water pollution but above acid rain. The Gallup Poll began asking the question about climate change concern in 1989. Since 1989, the percentage who worried 'a great deal' or 'fair amount' has ranged from a low of 50 per cent in October 1997 to a high of 72 per cent in April 2000. When asked in 2001 about the President's decision not to ratify Kyoto, 41 per cent approved and 48 per cent disapproved. Thus we see that while Americans regard climate change as a reality, they differ in their level of concern and what should be done about it.

Although the Bush administration shows no signs of reversing its position on Kyoto, it is coming under increasing pressure to take stronger action on climate change. In December 2002, White House officials stated at a meeting of climate change experts that President Bush was no longer 'locked into' a purely voluntary approach (Revkin, 2002b). In particular, the administration is taking aggressive steps to prove that the voluntary approach can yield reductions (Revkin, 2003). In February 2003, the White House and industry leaders will unveil industry pledges to make concrete, measurable reductions in greenhouse gases. The White House had rejected industry offers to commit to non-specific actions.

The position of American business on climate change has also shifted. The highest-profile industry group opposing action on climate change, the Global Climate Coalition, disbanded in 2002 (Global Climate Coalition). Its membership included many major corporations, and until 1997 it was housed within the National Association of Manufacturers. Leading corporations began to withdraw from the group in 1997, including American Electric Power, Dow, DuPont, Ford Motor Company, General Motors, Texaco, and Royal Dutch Shell (PR Watch). A number of major American corporations have decided that regulation of greenhouse gas emissions is inevitable and are taking early action (Revkin, 2003). In 2002, the Chicago Climate Exchange was launched. It aims to support voluntary greenhouse gas emissions trading between major corporations. Founding members include American Electric Power, DuPont, and Ford Motor Company (Chicago Climate Exchange, 2003).

CANADA: HOW ARE WE DOING?

Because of Canada's small population, it has been argued that its contribution to global greenhouse gas emissions is negligible and that therefore (1) Canada has little incentive to act and (2) Canada bears little responsibility for emissions reduction. The difficulty with the first argument is that *no country* has an incentive to act unilaterally. Climate change represents a classic collective action problem because climate is a public good. No country can capture the benefits of unilateral action on climate. What happens to the climate will depend on what most or all countries do. Any effective action on climate change is predicated on international co-operation.

With regard to the second claim, the significance of Canada's contribution to emissions depends on the metric one chooses to apply. Canada's emissions are about 2 per cent of global emissions. However, Canada's total emissions are approximately equal to those of the United Kingdom, a much more populous country with a much larger economy (Figure 1). To make the case that Canada's contribution to total emissions is trivial, one would have to make the same argument for the UK and any number of other countries.

In comparative terms, Canada's performance is particularly bad on two criteria: per capita emissions and growth in emissions. Canada's per capita emissions of all greenhouse gases and CO_2 are among the highest in the developed world. In developed-country CO_2 emissions per capita, we rank third behind the US and Australia (Figure 3) (Carbon Dioxide Information Analysis Center). A few OPEC countries have higher per capita emissions because oil production (quite apart from oil consumption) generates such substantial CO_2 emissions. In per capita greenhouse gas emissions, we rank behind Australia but are tied for second place with the US. Compared to

Figure 3

Per Capita CO_2 Emissions for 1998

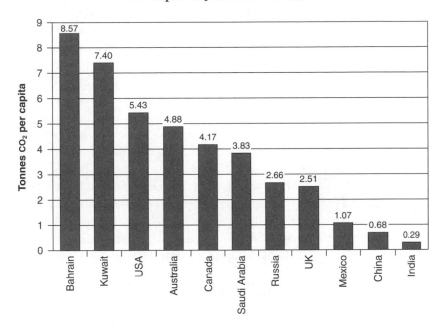

other countries, Canada, Australia, and the US have much higher per capita fossil fuel combustion (Turton and Hamilton, 2001: 4).

Canada's emissions profile compares unfavourably with most European countries. Canada's per capita emissions of greenhouse gases, on average, are approximately twice those of Japan and the European Union countries (Figure 1). This is due in part to the substantial gains in energy efficiency these countries achieved in the wake of the oil shocks of the 1970s. Climate cannot account for all of the difference between Canada and the Europeans. Sweden and Finland are cold, sparsely populated countries. Their per capita emissions are 22 per cent and 58 per cent of Canada's, respectively (ibid., 3). Even Norway, a sparsely populated northern country and major petroleum producer, has per capita emissions that are only 37 per cent of Canada's (ibid., 3).

One significant difference between Canada and the average European country is energy use and emissions from the transportation sector (Government of Canada, 2001: 10). Canada has relatively greater amounts of passenger travel and freight transport than

European OECD countries. An average Canadian car travels about 17,000 km per annum compared to about 14,000 km per annum for the average European car, not to mention that Canadian cars generally are larger and less energy efficient. The transportation of freight also results in higher energy use. Measured in tonne-kilometres per capita, Canada moves three times as much freight as Japan and major Western European countries.

The contrast is even more striking if we compare Canada's per capita CO_2 emissions to those of developing countries (Figure 3). CO_2 emissions are used here instead of greenhouse gas emissions because accurate measures of the latter are not available for all developing countries. Canada's per capita emissions are approximately four times higher than Mexico's, six times those of China, and 14 times those of India. Canada's total energy consumption is about the same as India's, a country with 1 billion people (US Department of Energy, 2002). The proportions would be even higher for countries less developed than these middle-income countries.

It is important to remember that because greenhouse gases persist in the atmosphere for many decades, current atmospheric levels are the product of past fossil fuel combustion by the industrialized countries. If climate change leads to longer and more frequent droughts and more serious storms and rises in sea level, developing countries will be suffering from the effects of a phenomenon that was not of their making. Thus, quite apart from the issue of being able to pay for mitigation, there are legitimate reasons for insisting that the developed countries bear a heavier burden in achieving reductions or, at least, must strive for a more equitable allocation of per capita greenhouse gas emissions (Paterson, 2001). One does not have to be a radical egalitarian to object to the existing per capita distribution of greenhouse gas emissions.

With regard to growth in per capita greenhouse gas emissions, Canada's have grown even faster than those of the US (Turton and Hamilton, 2002: 5). While US per capita emissions grew by 4 per cent between 1990 and 1999, Canada's increased 13 per cent during the same time period (Figure 2). The federal government's own statistics estimate the increase for this period at 15 per cent, but the government argues that the growth has slowed (Government of Canada, 2001: 1; Environment Canada, 2002). Based on projections for the future, by 2010 Canada will have to reduce its greenhouse gas emissions by 19 per cent to meet its Kyoto target. The federal report argues, however, that in the absence of the Canadian government's current climate change plan the reduction in 2010 would have to be 31 per cent.

With greenhouse gas emissions growing at such a rapid rate, Canada clearly faces a great challenge in reducing or stabilizing emissions. The challenge is made even greater by distributional issues. The costs and potential benefits of mitigation and costs of climate change itself are distributed very unevenly among the provinces. These distributional conflicts will only worsen if current projections in the growth of emissions are accurate. For example, Canada's progress report to the United Nations Framework Convention on Climate Change projects that between 1990 and 2010 the emissions of British Columbia, Alberta, and Saskatchewan will increase by 39 per cent (Government of Canada, 2001: 86). In the same period, Quebec's emissions are projected to increase by only 14 per cent and Ontario's by 16 per cent.

HOW TO CUT EMISSIONS? HOW TO ALLOCATE CUTS?

Allocating resources is always difficult, particularly if we are divvying up pain rather than gain. Historical experience with regulatory regimes shows that it is easier to create regulations that impose small costs on large numbers of people, than those that impose substantial costs on a small number of clearly defined groups. In situations where regulations clearly create winners and losers, it may be necessary to provide compensation to the losers in order for measures to be taken (Oye and Maxwell, 1994).

Policy options for reducing emissions are usually assessed on criteria such as efficiency, equity, efficacy, and political acceptability. Economists favour mechanisms that provide incentives to achieve reduction at the lowest possible unit cost, such as tradable permits or taxes. Such measures change consumer behaviour by changing the relative prices consumers face. These measures are intended to attach a cost to socially harmful actions that are currently costless. A permit scheme must cap total emissions, which makes permits scarce and hence valuable. (If an infinite supply of permits were issued, permits would be costless.) Because of the need for a cap, permits must be issued for a quantity below current emissions, or they can be set at current levels if emissions are projected to increase.

In a tradable permits scheme, those facing high unit costs of reduction purchase emissions permits from those who can make more money by selling their permits and cutting emissions instead of holding those permits. The distributional impacts of tradable permits schemes depend on the initial allocation of permits. Economists prefer an initial auction of permits. However, past experience shows that permits are almost always grandfathered, which discriminates against new entrants to the market. Grandfathering permits (allocation on the basis of current emissions) punishes those who have already taken measures to reduce emissions before the permits were allocated.

Equal, across-the-board cuts (e.g., everyone must cut 5 per cent) are sometimes suggested on the grounds of fairness and equity. The Kyoto Protocol is based on across-the-board cuts. On efficiency grounds, economists oppose them unless they are accompanied by trading. Reducing emissions through an across-the-board cut will always cost more per unit of emissions than a scheme that permits trading. It also means that greater cuts could be achieved at the same cost, had trading been permitted. Such measures have also been criticized on equity grounds because there is no guarantee that equal cuts are equal in impact. It is much easier for a person who consumes and wastes a lot of energy to cut consumption by 5 per cent than for someone who has been practising conservation to do the same. While the percentage may be equal, the pain of adjustment will not be. As with grandfathering of permits, across-the-board cuts can be seen as punishing those who have already taken steps to conserve.

To an economist, taxes on emissions and subsidies for emission reductions are two sides of the same coin. Either instrument can be seen as efficient because each changes relative prices and thus would be expected to have similar impacts on decisions about consumption and investment. They differ in their impact on income distribution, which raises questions about equity. Taxes are consistent with the 'polluter pays' principle—that those who pollute more should bear greater costs (Paterson, 2001: 122). In theory, the same price incentives could be created using subsidies to reward reductions, but those who pollute less will subsidize reductions by those polluting more. Those who already had low emissions may resent subsidizing later emission reductions by others.

WHAT WILL KYOTO COMPLIANCE COST CANADA? WHAT DOES US NON-PARTICIPATION DO TO THOSE COSTS?

The projected costs of Kyoto compliance depend heavily on the tools used to implement the policy. The good news is that, under particular conditions, certain policy tools can dramatically reduce the total cost of Kyoto implementation. The bad news is that Canada is making limited use of these tools, such as tradable permits and taxes. Several econometric projections of Kyoto impacts, using a variety of models, have estimated costs to Canada in the range of 0 to 3 per cent loss in GDP by 2010, relative to business-as-usual (BAU) scenarios (Wigle, 2001: 5). According to the federal government's modelling exercise, Kyoto compliance represents the difference between 29 per cent growth in GDP by 2012 and 31 per cent growth under business as usual (Government of Canada, 2002b: 15). According to the models, the glass is very much half full, not half empty.

The models are quite sensitive to changes in particular assumptions for each scenario. One general result is that policy tools such as emissions trading and taxes have significant negative impacts on energy-intensive sectors and, therefore, on provinces with large fossil fuel sectors (ibid., 16). The results differ dramatically based on whether or not emissions reductions are achieved only domestically. Allowing international emissions trading substantially reduces the total cost of compliance, in GDP terms (Wigle, 2002: 1). Based on his model of sectoral impacts in the Canadian economy, Wigle concluded that, with international emissions trading, the important negative sectoral impacts 'largely disappear' (ibid.).

On the other hand, Wigle's model of sectoral impacts found that, the greater the exemptions for particular sectors of the economy, the higher the total cost. In particular, if we assume exemptions for the most energy-intensive sectors, then abatement costs must be achieved in other, less energy-intensive sectors. Wigle concludes that, under this scenario, 'the welfare costs are staggering . . . Such restrictions would make Kyoto targets unachievable' (ibid., 23). Canada's actual implementation plan makes only limited use of emissions trading and does seek to shield the provinces from unequal costs of adjustment, an approach that will almost certainly increase the total cost of compliance.

Wigle has also modelled Canadian Kyoto compliance costs without US participation, and reaches a surprising conclusion (ibid., 1). Wigle cites an earlier study using a global computable general equlibrium model, which found that, without US participation, the cost of international emissions permits would fall substantially, because the US was expected to be the largest single market for such permits. Wigle's results for the Canadian economy were that Canada's cost of compliance *fell by half* when the US was not a participant in inter-national emissions trading, from 0.55 per cent of GNP to 0.25 per cent (ibid., 14). He concludes:

> This will probably not surprise trade-oriented people, but conflicts with the normal presumption that US non-compliance is likely to make on Canada. As expected, however, US non-compliance does make adjustment to Kyoto more severe, particularly for the energy-intensive sectors and fossil fuel sectors . . . Notwithstanding this observation, under any reasonable assumptions, both the cost of compliance and the adjustments associated with it are likely to be relatively modest *if* some type of emissions trading scheme is available.

In part, this result obtains because the price of permits is lower inter-nationally but also because energy-intensive goods from the US become relatively cheaper. Because the US is the major source of our imports, this lowers the cost to Canada.

Business groups and other Kyoto skeptics have argued that any Canadian action must be conditional upon the actions of our major trading partner. Otherwise, so they assume, the costs of compliance will be too high. In general, this position finds little support from the econometric models. First, there is nothing in the models to suggest that the costs of Kyoto compliance are so prohibitively high that Canada cannot afford to act on greenhouse gas reduction. Second, according to the models, those costs are not substantially increased in light of US non-participation. The models do not support the con-clusion that Canada has no choice but to adopt the US approach. Canada's chosen path to emissions reductions is far more constrained by the commitment that no province should bear 'an unreasonable burden of adjustment' than by decisions in the US.

THE PROVINCES AND KYOTO

On Kyoto, where you stand depends on where you sit, or rather, how much you emit. There is enormous variation between the provinces in their total and per capita emissions of greenhouse gases. By 1998, Alberta had overtaken Ontario as the province with the highest total annual emissions, with 200 megatonnes in emissions of CO_2 equiva-lents. In 1998, Alberta's per capita emissions were 5.5 times those of Quebec and more than three times the Canadian national average (Figure 4) (Government of Canada, 2001). In general, Saskatchewan's

Figure 4

Per Capita Annual Greenhouse Gas Emissions, 1998

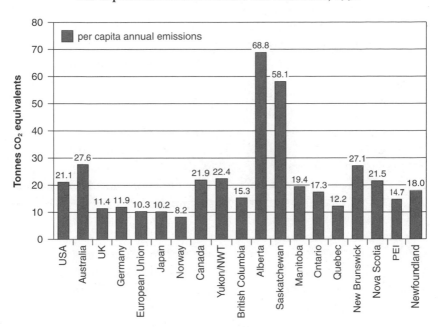

and Alberta's per capita emissions are much higher than those of any other Canadian province. However, even Quebec, which is the lowest per capita emitter in Canada, has higher per capita emissions than many European countries, such as Germany and the UK.

Although the provinces, Alberta in particular, argue that they have been kept in the dark on federal climate change policy, these claims are disingenuous. Failure to reach complete agreement is not the same as lack of consultation. The issue of global warming or climate change has been discussed in Canada since the late 1980s and extensive consultations have been held with the provinces, particularly through the Joint Energy and Environment Ministers' Meeting (JEEMM). It is over 10 years since the federal government presented its National Action Strategy on Global Warming to the Canadian Council of Ministers of the Environment in November 1990. In November 1993, the federal government began to develop the National Action Plan on Climate Change in consultation with provincial energy and environment ministers, which was announced in 1995. In November 1997, the JEEMM achieved agreement on two key points: the need for action on climate change and the desirability of reducing greenhouse gas emissions to 1990 levels by 2010 (Halucha, 1998: 299). Macdonald and Smith note that, after a flurry of provincial protests in 1997, around the time Canada signed Kyoto, '[Alberta premier Ralph] Klein and the oil and coal industries have seen no need to continue their public protest following the Kyoto meeting' (Macdonald and Smith, 1999–2000: 108).

In other federal-provincial battles, Alberta and Quebec have made common cause against the federal government, which won't happen over Kyoto. It will be very difficult to reconcile the demands of these two provinces in particular. As an important producer and exporter of hydroelectricity, Quebec sees Kyoto as an opportunity. Quebec has also made more progress in developing renewable energy sources such as wind (Mittelstaedt, 2002: A4). The Parti Québécois government has emphasized that an independent Quebec would have ratified Kyoto much sooner.

Kyoto has been suggested as a reason for Alberta to secede, for the opposite reason. In 1997, the Alberta Environment Minister warned that the use of the federal taxation power to alter energy consumption patterns would lead Alberta to contemplate secession (Macdonald and Smith, 1999–2000: 108). In November 2002, the Alberta government announced that it might seek a reference from the Alberta Court of Appeal on the question of whether the federal government has the right to sign an international treaty that infringes on provincial jurisdiction (Gillis and Toulin, 2002: A1).

Although substantial disparity of interests already exists among the provinces, it is set to grow in the future. Oil production from Atlantic Canada is increasing, from the Jeanne d'Arc Basin. Newfoundland already has the Hibernia and Terra Nova oil fields in production and the White Rose field is scheduled to start producing in 2004. Other potential developments are on hold because of the high cost of developing these reserves (US Department of Energy, 2002). British Columbia may revisit a ban on exploration in the Pacific Ocean. Oil and gas reserves in the area of the Queen Charlotte Islands are thought to be greater than those of the Jeanne d'Arc Basin.

The biggest challenge for the future concerns Alberta's oil sands. The Athabaska oil sands deposit is one of the two largest in the world (ibid.). There are smaller deposits elsewhere in Alberta and the Canadian Arctic. Canada has been described as a Saudi Arabia of oil sands because of the magnitude of these deposits. Current output from the oil sands is less than that from conventional oil fields because the production costs are much higher. Kyoto poses an added challenge: greenhouse gas emissions from oil sands production are substantially higher than those for conventional oil production (Government of Canada, 2001: 15). On an optimistic note, new technology has made it possible to reduce greenhouse gas emissions from oil sands extraction by 22 per cent in the last decade, and by 2010 oil sands producers hope to have reduced emissions per unit of output by 45 per cent from 1990 levels (ibid.).

Minister of Health Anne McLellan, one of only two Liberal MPs from Alberta, has stated that Kyoto cannot be allowed to hinder oil sands development (Chase et al., 2002: A4). Now that Canada has actually ratified Kyoto, we can assess the impact of ratification on oil sands development. In January 2003, True North decided to shelve its $3.5 billion oil sands project and cited Kyoto as a factor. However, some analysts argue that other factors, such as the cost of labour in Alberta, were far more decisive (Yedlin, 2003: B2). Other firms, such as Suncor, the largest oil sands player, are forging ahead. Suncor has announced that it regards the costs of Kyoto as negligible and plans to double oil sands production by 2010 (Reguly, 2003: B2). Shell Canada also continues to plan new oil sands investments (Brethour, 2002: B3) and aims to reduce net per barrel greenhouse gas emissions from oil sands to below those for conventional oil production. Most of these reductions would be achieved by purchasing offsets from other industries that have reduced emissions, not by implementing technology to reduce emissions from oil sands extraction. The oil sands production process would remain largely unchanged.

HOW TO ALLOCATE EMISSIONS REDUCTIONS IN CANADA

Given these dramatically different sectoral and provincial impacts, how should emissions reductions in Canada be allocated? According to the efficiency criterion, we should seek to cut those emissions that can be cut at the lowest possible cost. It seems reasonable to assume that cuts can be more easily achieved from those sources that account for a substantial proportion of total emissions, instead of making larger cuts from sources that contribute less to the overall problem. According to the equity criterion, it seems reasonable that measures should not penalize those who have already taken steps to reduce emissions. Judged by the efficacy criterion, measures must be likely to produce changes in behaviour. Measures that change relative prices are known to be effective in changing consumer behaviour.

Although market mechanisms can meet all of the above criteria, they fail on political acceptability. In the Canadian context, any of the above measures would face opposition from one or more provinces. A tradable permits scheme would force Alberta and other oil-producing provinces to either reduce emissions or purchase permits from other provinces to cover increasing emissions, no matter how the permits were initially allocated. Alberta has indicated its vehement opposition to the use of taxation.

Recent proposals on Kyoto implementation seem to call for greater subsidies. At their October 2002 meeting in Halifax, the JEEMM agreed on 12 principles that must be reflected in any national climate change plan. One of the principles is that:

> no region or jurisdiction shall be asked to bear an unreasonable share of the burden and no industry sector or region shall be treated unfairly . . . . The plan must incorporate appropriate federally funded mitigation of adverse impacts of climate change initiatives. (Government of Alberta, 2002)

The federal government's Climate Change Plan, announced 21 November 2002, 'recognizes the importance of no region bearing an unreasonable burden' (Government of Canada, 2002a). It seems likely that there will be considerable disagreement over what constitutes 'an unreasonable burden'.

A subsidy scheme of sufficient size to reduce total emissions would have serious consequences for balancing the federal budget. Political acceptability would also be a concern, particularly if the scheme involved ordinary taxpayers subsidizing major oil companies to make emissions reductions. The JEEMM principle spelled out above would seem to require federal compensation for any costs incurred by policies to limit emissions. Economists would call that applying the brake and accelerator simultaneously: for incentives to change behaviour, you cannot undo their impact by applying a subsidy of equal and opposite effect. It also seems unlikely that taxpayers in the rest of Canada would be willing to pay higher taxes to compensate oil-producing provinces, which are wealthier than other Canadian provinces.

It may not be possible to square this circle. Changing incentives requires changing relative prices, which means some sectors will be favoured over others. In particular, it is difficult to imagine how emissions reductions can be achieved without substantial changes in how oil is produced and, possibly, how much oil is produced. This, in turn, will mean impacts will be felt more in major oil-producing provinces than in others. More weatherstripping in Ontario and more cardigans in Quebec cannot compensate for the very large and rapidly growing contribution of oil production and fossil fuel consumption to total emissions.

VOLUNTARY ACTION

On the criterion of political acceptability, voluntary action is the preferred option for implementation. Voluntary actions, particularly by corporations, have been the cornerstone of Canada's policy and the basis of Australian and American plans as well. It is easy to account for the popularity of this approach. It fits well with the deregulation/anti-regulation ideology of more conservative governments and faces less opposition from business groups than regulations or policy instruments that change prices. However, the efficacy of such measures is very much open to question. Experience with other forms of voluntary environmental regulation has shown that such measures are most effective when they serve to supplement, not replace, conventional regulations and when government presents a credible threat of new, potentially more onerous regulation (Harrison, 1999). Clearly, these conditions do not apply to present climate change policy.

Canada's policy has relied on voluntary measures and seems destined to continue to do so. The National Action Plan on Climate Change, announced in 1995, was intended to meet Canada's goal of stabilization, as set out in the United Nations Framework Convention on Climate Change. The three prongs of this policy initiative were: (1) more research, (2) adaptation to climate, and (3) mitigation of climate change through emissions reductions (Government of Canada, 2001: 55). A key component of Canada's plan has been the Voluntary Challenge and Registry (VCR), a joint business-government initiative announced in 1995.

The Pembina Institute and the David Suzuki Foundation have assessed the performance of the VCR since its inception. They find that there have been some success stories—firms that have acted to reduce emissions. There are also 'unsuccess stories' such as Imperial Oil, whose production dropped between 1990 and 2000 but whose emissions increased anyway (Pembina Institute, 2002). The VCR is unlikely to bring about emissions stabilization, never mind cuts in emissions. Among participating firms, many have failed to report on their emissions (Bramley, 2002). Among those participants that have reported, most show increased emissions in the reporting period.

As the debate around ratification of the Kyoto Protocol heated up in the fall of 2002, there was little discussion of tools for achieving reductions. The debate was framed in terms of Kyoto versus a made-in-Canada solution. This is, in some respects, a red herring. If Canada intends to stabilize or reduce emissions within the next 30 years, difficult questions of how to allocate cuts will remain, whether Canada acts unilaterally, bilaterally with the US, or multilaterally.

ACTING UNILATERALLY OR MULTILATERALLY?

For all the claims about a unique plan for Canada's unique needs, Alberta's made-in-Canada alternative to Kyoto borrowed very heavily from the Bush administration's plan. It focused on cuts to be achieved in the distant future, employing technologies that do not yet exist. As with the American plan, the objective was to reduce the intensity of emissions rather than to reduce total emissions or per capita emissions (CBC News Online, 2002b).

Advocates of the made-in-Canada plan argued that the Kyoto framework is too constraining. However, there is a great deal of flexibility within Kyoto. Because one unit of greenhouse gas makes the same contribution to climate change no matter where it was emitted, there are compelling reasons to allow countries or firms to pay for emissions reductions elsewhere that can be achieved at lower cost. The JUSCANNZ group fought for these provisions during the negotiations leading up to the Kyoto Protocol in 1997. They were opposed by the European Union, which saw these measures as ways for the JUSCANNZ group to avoid making domestic cuts. On efficiency and efficacy grounds, there is little substance to these objections. However, it may be that the EU wishes to see some equalization for the improvements in domestic energy efficiency that EU members have achieved since the 1970s, improvements not matched in most JUSCANNZ countries, with Japan as the notable exception.

The three flexibility mechanisms available under Kyoto are: international emissions trading, joint implementation, and the Clean Development Mechanism. Under international emissions trading,

Annex I countries may purchase emissions credits from Annex I countries that are currently below their target. Some Canadian Kyoto critics have described this as 'sending our money abroad' (Myers, 2002). However, Canada would only purchase credits if we could achieve compliance more cheaply through purchasing credits than by reducing emissions domestically. Under joint implementation, companies can transfer credits for emissions reductions in any Annex I country to any other Annex 1 country, on a project-by-project basis, as long as the exchange is approved by both countries. The Clean Development Mechanism is the same concept as joint implementation but is applied to countries not in Annex I, which means developing countries. Unfortunately, Canada's implementation plan makes limited use of these mechanisms. Purchasing credits count for only 12 megatonnes of our 240-required megatonne reduction.

MADE IN CANADA, BUT NOT RECOGNIZED ANYWHERE ELSE: CLEAN ENERGY EXPORTS

One consequence of US non-participation in Kyoto is Canada's demand for credits for clean energy exports (primarily to the US) under the Kyoto Protocol. It is worth remembering that if the US ratified Kyoto, Canada would have no basis for its request because credit for reduced emissions would accrue to the US, the end consumer, not Canada, the producer. Canada has requested that 70 megatonnes of its total required reduction be allotted to credits for clean energy exports (Government of Canada, 2002b: 15).

Principle 10 of the 12 principles agreed to in October 2002 at the JEEMM in Halifax is that Canada must continue to demand such credits (Government of Alberta, 2002). At the Eighth Conference of Parties to the United Nations Framework Convention on Climate Change in New Delhi in November 2002, Environment Minister David Anderson repeated Canada's request that clean energy exports, such as selling natural gas to the United States, count towards Canada's emissions reduction. Thus far, these demands have fallen on deaf ears.

The European Union, in particular, is implacably opposed to credits for clean energy exports (CBC News Online, 2002a). The EU was not particularly pleased with the flexibility mechanisms that the JUS-CANNZ group asked for, and got, in the negotiations leading up to Kyoto. The EU also made concessions to Canada and the US on credits for carbon sinks (David Suzuki Foundation, 2002). These were seen as a necessary compromise to improve the odds of getting the US to sign Kyoto. Now that the US is clearly not going to participate, the EU has little incentive to accede to what they see as special pleading by the Canadians. The European Environment Commissioner has stated that agreeing to Canada's demand would mean reopening negotiations on Kyoto (CBC News Online, 2002a).

Agreeing to credits for clean energy exports to the US would undermine the Kyoto Protocol. Because there are, as yet, no penalties for non-compliance, one of the few mechanisms that the Protocol has for rewarding participation is to exclude non-ratifiers from participation in flexibility mechanisms such as the Clean Development Mechanism. Agreeing to give Canada credits for exports to a non-ratifier such as the US would set an unacceptable precedent. There is also no guarantee that such exports reduce emissions. In the absence of any cap on US energy consumption, Canada's exports do not necessarily displace consumption of dirtier sources of energy. Consumption of Canadian natural gas could occur in addition to, not in the place of, the consumption of dirtier fuels such as coal.

CONCLUSION

Although Canada has ratified the Kyoto Protocol, the significance of ratification is diminished in the absence of an implementation plan that might reasonably be expected to produce emissions reductions. It appears likely that Canada will follow in the footsteps of the world's other profligate greenhouse gas emitters, the United States and Australia, if not in word, then in deed. The United States and Australia, not wishing to impose any constraint on future growth in their economies, have opted for voluntary approaches, more research into technological fixes, and a wait-and-see attitude. There is little reason to believe that such approaches will result in the stabilization of emissions, much less the reduction of emissions.

The Canadian plan's heavy reliance on voluntary measures, as opposed to policy tools that have proven effective, makes it less likely that Canada's policy will achieve its objective. Limited use of emissions trading and the goal of ensuring that no province or sector bears an 'unreasonable burden' mean that the cost of compliance is higher than necessary. The choice of voluntary measures over economic instruments is driven far more by domestic political factors, particularly a goal of equalizing adjustment across provinces, than external constraints imposed by the Protocol itself or economic cost.

Canada's plan for achieving Kyoto is at odds with its image as a good global citizen and is not the plan of a global leader on the environment. The Bush administration has indicated that it will not be constrained by the demands of multilateralism, any more than it unilaterally chooses to be constrained. Canada still pays obeisance to the multilateralist creed while continuing to demand special treatment under Kyoto through its demands for clean energy export credits. Canada's self-image as a good global citizen may survive this challenge but its image and credibility in the eyes of other countries may be in tatters.

NOTE

1. Australia's target is 108 per cent of 1990 emissions, whereas most signatories of Annex I are committed to reductions of between 0 and 8 per cent.

REFERENCES

Bramley, Matthew. 2002. 'The Case for Kyoto: The Failure of Voluntary Corporate Action', Pembina Institute and David Suzuki Foundation. Available at: <http://www.pembina.org/publications_item.asp?id=140>.

Brethour, Patrick. 2002. 'Shell Canada to Spend Billions on Oil Sands', *Globe and Mail*, 29 Nov., B3.

Carbon Dioxide Information Analysis Center. 'Ranking of World's Countries by 1998 CO_2 Per Capita Emissions Rates'. Available at: <http://cdiac.esd.ornl.gov/trends/emis/top98.cap>.

Cattaneo, Claudia, Tony Seskus, and Steven Edwards. 2003. 'Russia Said Wavering on Kyoto Pact', *National Post*, 16 Jan., FP1, 7.

CBC News Online. 2002a. 'Canada's Kyoto "Energy Credits" Slammed by EU', 15 Apr. Available at: <http://www.cbc.ca/stories/2002/04/14/kyoto_020414>.

————. 2002b. 'Alberta Offers its Version of Kyoto', 18 Oct. Available at: <http://www.cbc.ca/stories/2002/10/17/kyoto_alberta021017>.

Chase, Steven, Patrick Brethour, and Jill Mahoney. 2002. 'Can't Risk Oil Sands for Kyoto, McLellan warns', *Globe and Mail*, 28 Nov., A4.

Chicago Climate Exchange. 2003. Available at: <http://www.chicagoclimatex.com/html/about.html>.

David Suzuki Foundation. 2002. 'Canada Challenged to Ratify Kyoto, End Clean Energy Credit Stall', news release, 15 Apr. Available at: <http://www.davidsuzuki.org/campaigns_and_programs/climate_change/news_releases/newsclimatechange04150201.asp>.

Environment Canada. 2002. *Canada's Greenhouse Gas Inventory*. Factsheet 1. Available at: <http://www.ec.gc.ca/pdb/ghg/factsheets/fact1_e.cfm#anchor1.2>.

Environment News Service. 2002. 'U.S., Australia Climate Plan Cuts No Emissions', 12 July. Available at: <http://ens-news.com/ens/jul2002/2002-07-12-02.asp>. Accessed 15 July.

Gallup, George, Jr. 2002. *The Gallup Poll: Public Opinion 2001*. Wilmington, Del.: Scholarly Resources.

Gillis, Charlie, and Alan Toulin. 2002. 'Provinces Stepping Up Kyoto Fight', *National Post*, 26 Nov., A1.

Global Climate Coalition. Home page. Available at: <http://www.globalclimate.org>.

Government of Alberta. 2002. 'Resolution Calls for a National Climate Change Plan Based on Provinces' 12 Principles', news release, 26 Nov. Available at: <www.gov.ab.ca/can/200211/13555.html>.

Government of Canada. 2001. *Canada's Third National Report on Climate Change*. Available at: <http://unfccc.int/resource/docs/natc/cannce3.pdf>.

———. 2002a. Climate Change Plan for Canada. Available at: <http://www.climate change.gc.ca/plan_for_canada/summary/index.html>.

———. 2002b. A Discussion Paper on Canada's Contribution to Addressing Climate Change. Available at: <http://www.climatechange.gc.ca/english/actions/what_ are/canadascontribution/Report051402/englishbook.pdf>.

Halucha, Paul. 1998. 'Climate Change Politics and the Pursuit of National Interests', in Fen Osler Hampson and Maureen Appel Molot, eds, *Canada Among Nations 1998: Leadership and Dialogue*. Toronto: Oxford University Press.

Harrison, Kathryn. 1999. 'Talking with the Donkey: Cooperative Approaches to Environmental Regulation', *Journal of Industrial Ecology* 2, 3: 51–72.

Lazaroff, Cat. 2003. 'U.S. Senate Bill Would Cap Greenhouse Gas Emissions', Environment News Service, 8 Jan.

Macdonald, Douglas, and Heather A. Smith. 1999–2000. 'Promises Made, Promises Broken: Questioning Canada's Commitments to Climate Change', *International Journal* 55, 1 (Winter): 107–24.

Mittelstaedt, Martin. 2002. 'Fossil Fuel Producers Main Foes of Treaty', *Globe and Mail*, 16 Feb., A4.

Myers, Jayson. 'Put your money where your Kyoto mouth is', *Globe and Mail*, 9 Aug., A13.

Oye, Kenneth, and James Maxwell. 1994. 'Self-Interest and Environmental Manage-ment', *Journal of Theoretical Politics* 6, 4 (1994).

Paterson, Matthew. 2001. 'Principles of Justice in the Context of Global Climate Change', in Urs Luterbacher and Detlef F. Sprinz, eds, *International Relations and Global Climate Change*. Cambridge, Mass.: MIT Press.

Pegg, J.R. 2002. 'U.S. States Combat Climate Change on Their Own', Environment News Service, 15 Nov.

Pembina Institute. 2002. 'Voluntary Action to Reduce Greenhouse Gas Emissions Flawed, Ineffective: New Study', 17 Oct. Available at: <www.pembina.org/news item.asp?newsid=61&section=media>.

PRWatch. 'Global Climate Coalition', *Impropaganda Review: A Rogues Gallery of Industry Front Groups and Anti-Environmental Think Tanks*. Available at: <http://www.prwatch.org/improp/gcc.html>.

Rabe, Barry. 2002. *Greenhouse & Statehouse: The Evolving State Government Role in Climate Change*. Prepared for the Pew Center on Global Climate Change. Available at: <http://www.pewclimate.org/projects/states_greenhouse.cfm>.

Reguly, Eric. 2003. 'Kyoto Will Work Best on Market Rules', *Globe and Mail*, 18 Jan., B2.

Revkin, Andrew C. 2002a. 'Can Global Warming Be Studied Too Much?', *New York Times*, 3 Dec.

———. 2002b. 'Temperatures Are Likely to Go from Warm to Warmer', *New York Times*, 31 Dec.

———. 2003. 'U.S. Is Pressuring Industries to Cut Greenhouse Gases', *New York Times*, 20 Jan.

Turton, Hal, and Clive Hamilton. 2001. 'Comprehensive emissions per capita for industrialised countries', Australia Institute. Available at: <www.tai.org.au/WhatsNew_Files/Whats New/Percapita.htm>.

——— and ———. 2002. 'Updating per capita emissions for industrialised countries', Australia Institute. Available at: <www.tai.org.au/WhatsNew_Files/WhatsNew/Percapita070802.pdf>.

United Nations. 2002. Available at: <http://www.un.org/law/ilc/texts/treaties.htm>.

United Nations Framework Convention on Climate Change. 2002. Available at: <http://unfccc.int/resource/kpstats.pdf>.

United States Department of Energy. 2002. 'Country Analysis Briefs: Canada'. Available at: <http://www.eia.doe.gov/emeu/cabs/canada.html>.

United States Department of State. 2002. *US Climate Action Report—2002. Third National Communication of the United States of America under the United Nations Framework Convention on Climate Change.* Available at: <http://unfccc.int/resource/docs/natc/usnc3.pdf>.

Wigle, Randall. 2001. 'Sectoral Impacts of Kyoto Compliance', Industry Canada Working Paper no. 34. Available at: <http://strategis.ic.gc.ca/pics/ra/wp34_e.pdf>.

———. 2002. 'The Kyoto Protocol Revisited', paper prepared for the Canadian Economics Association meeting, Calgary. Available at: <http://www.wlu.ca/~wwwsbe/faculty/rwigle/co2/cea-02.pdf>.

Yedlin, Deborah. 2003. 'True North's Claims Just Don't Add Up', *Globe and Mail*, 17 Jan., B2.

16

A Multilateral Affair: Canadian Foreign Policy in the Middle East

MIRA SUCHAROV

An analysis of Canadian policy towards the Middle East necessarily looks quite different than it did a decade ago. The September 1993 Oslo agreement between Israel and the PLO appeared to be ushering in a new era of peace in the region, and in the afterglow of the Gulf War Saddam Hussein seemed an impaired, if not altogether obsolete, threat to regional and Western security. But at the end of 2002 the Oslo framework had all but crumbled under the weight of a renewed Palestinian uprising (Intifada) and Israeli reprisals. The United States today is also attempting to construct a coalition for another war against Iraq, claiming that Saddam Hussein has been secretly stockpiling an arsenal of chemical, biological, and possibly nuclear weapons. This chapter will investigate two aspects of Canada's Middle East policy against the backdrop of Canada–US relations: Canada's diplomatic involvements in the Israeli-Palestinian conflict and peace process, policies that are focused on forging peace

between actors locked in a protracted conflict; and its evolving decision on whether to support a US-led war against Iraq, a policy stance
involving the definition of, and response to, a global threat.

I will argue that, on issues of both war and peace, Canadian
Middle East policy is shaped by an ethic of multilateralism that has
often been said to define Canadian foreign affairs in general. Yet
unlike others (Pratt, 2001) who view ethics and interests in the
Canadian context as opposing analytical frameworks, I contend that
Canada's commitment to multilateralism represents an approach constituted by national interests. These interests include a desire to forge
a foreign policy course distinct from that of the US, while not wanting to damage the Canada–US relationship. Specifically, on both of
these issues—the Israeli-Palestinian conflict and the threat posed by
Iraq—Canada's multilateralist bent enables it both to maintain an
image of itself as an international team player on the world stage,
something that accords with its focus on human security (Paris, 2001),
and to differentiate itself from American unilateralist tendencies,
when policy divergence may exist, without having to challenge US
power and interests directly. This latter benefit is especially important in light of Canada's close trade and security ties with the United
States, a relationship characterized by what has come to be called
'asymmetrical interdependence', certainly in the realm of trade and
largely in the realm of security as well (Cohen, 2002; Molot and
Hillmer, 2002). This interdependence has only intensified since 11
September at the same time that the Canada–US relationship has
been placed under increased scrutiny by Americans concerned about
burden-sharing on the issue of homeland security, and by Canadians
worried about maintaining autonomy (what Canadians oddly refer to
as maintaining 'sovereignty'—by most measures a legal category that
states possess by virtue of being a member of the international system, regardless of the types of foreign policies the state adopts).

The Canadian preference for multilateralism has been internalized
to such a degree that it indeed represents a particular ethical
approach to human affairs, but one that happens largely to derive
from a particular strategic context (Thomas, 2001). This understanding of multilateralism coexists partly in concert and partly in tension
with the most common scholarly understanding of multilateralism,
what John Ruggie (1993: 11) defines as 'an institutional form that
coordinates relations among three or more states on the basis of generalized principles of conduct . . . without regard to the particularistic

interests of the parties or the strategic exigencies that may exist in any specific occurrence'. While we could concur that Canada has adopted an entrenched multilateral interest that transcends *particular* strategic exigencies, its adoption and internalization have certainly been influenced by the material context within which Canada finds itself, as a fading power (Molot and Hillmer, 2002) attempting to forge a foreign policy course distinct from its much larger neighbour to the south.

From a pure capabilities standpoint the US could effectively go it alone in its various policy initiatives, yet it certainly prefers to have the material and moral support of its allies, in part for the purposes of distributing the burden but also largely for cloaking its actions with a measure of international legitimacy. When it does manage to achieve a certain degree of co-ordinated action, as it has in the war in Afghanistan, US officials believe, at least rhetorically, that they are acting 'multilaterally'. At a business engagement in China in October 2001, US Secretary of State Colin Powell quipped, 'Nobody's calling us unilateral anymore. That's kind of gone away for the time being; we're so multilateral it keeps me up twenty-four hours a day checking on everybody' (US Department of State, 2001). Thus, it is not enough, in the eyes of Canadian elites, for the country to participate in a multi-state endeavour led by the United States. Instead, in foreign policy, Canada has tended to adhere to its commitment to pursue formal institutional channels for action, namely through the United Nations—on both the Israeli-Palestinian issue and regarding any potential war on Iraq. This does not mean, however, that an outright Canadian attempt to oppose US unilateral initiatives will not have adverse effects on the Canada–US relationship or on Canadian security, as close Canadian defence co-operation with the US on any given issue inevitably helps to maintain a voice on future policy decisions (CSDS, 2002).

Nevertheless, in the Israeli-Palestinian context, this multilateralist approach has translated into an active role in regional and multi-party initiatives that take their inspiration from UN resolutions. Therefore, the breakdown of the Middle East multilateral working groups in 1996 has meant that Canada's negotiating role in the Middle East has been greatly curtailed. In keeping with its multilateral tradition, Canada has been careful to maintain its image within the region as an honest broker, in part to avoid alienating either the Jewish or Arab constituencies in Canada and in part out of the belief that its diplomatic and developmental efforts will be most effective if neither regional party feels Canada is biased against the other (DFAIT, 2002c). At the same time, Canada has parted course with the US on particular policy statements.

On the issue of Iraq, Canada has thus far overtly committed to a military action against Saddam Hussein only in the context of a UN resolution, something that has yet to materialize. At the same time, Canadian officials have also been careful not to distance themselves too much from the positions of the United States, such that in recent weeks some have been more ambiguous in their stance towards Iraq, in effect suggesting that Canada might take a more forthcoming role in backing a US-led war in the region. This policy ambiguity has so far enabled Canada to adhere outwardly to its multilateralist ethic while not unduly alienating the US. *Ambiguity*

CANADA AND THE ISRAELI-PALESTINIAN NEXUS

Both Canada and the United States have centred their Middle East foreign policies on supporting a peace agreement between Israel and the Palestinians, as well as between Israel and the rest of the Arab states. But Canada has been more outspoken in its support for the establishment of a Palestinian state, which sits at the crux of the conflict and is a policy the US, under President Bush, only recently has begun to advocate. Bush has also been more openly critical of Arafat. Bush's early October 2001 declaration of support for a Palestinian state may have indeed been accelerated by the attacks of 11 September, as when Bush refused to answer a reporter's question to that effect.[1] And almost one year later, as Palestinian suicide bombings escalated, Bush demanded that Arafat be replaced before the United States would back a Palestinian state (Bumiller and Sanger, 2002), while Chrétien expressed skepticism that it was possible to force regime change (Sanger, 2002). Despite these different rhetorical tacks, both Canada and the United States have attempted, in accordance with their widely varying capabilities and diplomatic influence in the region, to help shepherd the Israelis and Palestinians towards a peaceful settlement of the conflict. While the US is the most visible and influential external player in the region, Canada does not seem to structure its peace-process policies around US preferences, even refraining, at times, from including the US in its projects, knowing that an American presence could raise a 'red flag' for the regional actors (DFAIT, 2002c).

While the Oslo agreement has been the most visible framework for peace between Israel and the Palestinians throughout the last decade, Canada's most active diplomatic role evolved out of a multilateral and international context—the multilateral working groups that emerged from the 1991 Madrid talks. That conference, established as the Cold War was ending and in part as an opportunity for Moscow and Washington to display a degree of unprecedented diplomatic co-operation on the global stage, brought Israel together with its Arab neighbours to negotiate a framework for bilateral as well as regional peace. While the summit opened with much fanfare, the talks ultimately achieved little. Madrid's lack of success can be attributed in part to an Israeli government, led by Likud Prime Minister Yitzhak Shamir, that was inhospitable to peace between Israel and the Palestinians, as well as to the lack of direct PLO participation: Israel stipulated that the Palestinians could participate only within the context of a joint Jordanian-Palestinian delegation and without any PLO representation, which was effectively circumvented by the PLO controlling the Jordanian-Palestinian delegation's negotiating strategies from its Tunis headquarters.

In addition to the Arab-Israeli bilateral tracks, consisting of Israel negotiating separately with Egypt and the Palestinian-Jordanian delegation, five working groups emerged to address broader regional issues that would be essential to any comprehensive peace in the region. These meetings became known as the 'multilaterals'. For the working group on refugees (RWG), Canada was invited to serve as chair, or 'gavel-holder'. The other working groups included the environment (chaired by Japan), regional and economic development (chaired by the EU), water resources (chaired by the United States), and arms control and regional security, chaired jointly by the US and Russia. In line with Canada's sustained focus on human security, the RWG's mandate was to improve the living conditions of the 3.5 million registered Palestinian refugees, to explore possibilities for family reunification, and to work towards a better understanding of the refugee problem—one of the three 'final-status issues' that the subsequent Oslo agreement chose to defer until later stages of negotiation. (The other two questions were Jerusalem and the final borders and legal status of the emerging Palestinian entity, including the fate of the Israeli settlements in the West Bank and Gaza.)

While all of these regional concerns are crucial to conflict and co-operation in the Arab-Israeli sphere, the topic of refugees is particularly sensitive in its intimate relation to the roots of the Israeli-Palestinian conflict and hence to questions of moral and material responsibility. Canada's position as gavel-holder for the RWG also ensured that it would be able to contribute—even indirectly—to a final settlement between Israel and the Palestinians. Moreover, the multilateral format of the working group was well suited to the Canadian style of internationalism, which supports multilateral efforts for their ability, in the words of the official RWG statement of Canada's Department of Foreign Affairs and International Trade, to get 'governments and peoples of the region [to] see each other as partners across the spectrum of activities—whether it be trade, environmental co-operation, maritime safety', and to ensure that 'one side does not win at the expense of the other' (Axworthy, 1999). Canada is necessarily attuned to such strategies in light of its asymmetrically interdependent relationship with the United States.

Only two years after the launch of the Madrid talks, the September 1993 Oslo agreement emerged out of secret negotiations that had taken place during much of that year between senior Israeli and PLO officials. The change of government in Israel from Shamir's Likud regime to Yitzhak Rabin's Labour government signalled a shift on the part of Israelis, in part generated by the protracted six-year Intifada that had ignited the occupied territories. The news of Oslo, an agreement that laid out a multi-year framework for negotiations on the evolving status of the Palestinian territories and political independence for their 3 million Palestinian inhabitants, necessarily relegated the multilateral tracks to the background, and a bilateral peace treaty between Israel and Jordan soon emerged in 1994. (Israel had already signed a peace treaty with Egypt, in 1979, following the 1978 Camp David Accords.) Oslo signified a watershed in relations between Israel and the Palestinians, because Israel had, in 1986, outlawed contacts with the PLO and had long refused to recognize the Palestinian people as a distinct nation, a step that would be crucial for any meaningful discussion of autonomy arrangements and certainly for movement towards the establishment of a Palestinian state. Whether one was for or against the parameters of the agreement, most observers felt Oslo to be a momentous occasion: it was seen as either ushering in a framework to achieve full peace between Israelis and Palestinians, or else creating an unjust formula that would prejudice a final settlement to the conflict. Either way, it was viewed to be historically significant in creating a new context within which Israeli and

Palestinian politics would operate, capped by the likely establishment of a Palestinian state.

The optimism that Oslo engendered among the parties themselves, an enthusiasm that would be matched only by the receipt of the Nobel Peace Prize by Rabin, Arafat, and Israeli Foreign Minister Shimon Peres, no doubt enabled the multilaterals to continue operating formally for another three years, even though bilateral peace between Israel and Jordan had already been achieved two years earlier. Moreover, the Israelis and Palestinians were consumed with the halting progress of the Oslo framework, amid accusations by each side that the other was not adhering to its commitments. In 1996, the Arab states decided to withdraw formally from the multilaterals, frustrated by lack of progress over negotiating the redeployment of Israeli troops from the West Bank town of Hebron (Peters, 1999). Informal contacts through the working groups continued, however, until September 2000, when the second Palestinian uprising, dubbed the al-Aqsa Intifada (or Intifada II), broke out, in the wake of the failure of Israel (under Prime Minister Ehud Barak) to reach a final agreement with Arafat over the fate of the territories, refugees, and Jerusalem. Analysts of the multilateral track note that they failed because of lack of focus, rivalry between Israel and Egypt and between the US and the EU, concerns of the Arab states about Israel's nuclear capabilities, and Israel's overriding focus on achieving recognition (referred to as 'normalization' in Israeli diplomatic parlance) within the region (Peters, 1999; Kaye, 2001). Since 1996, then, the multilaterals have ceased to exist altogether, and they have been relegated mostly to a historical footnote for observers of the Arab-Israeli peace process.

Canada's official position is that it is attempting to keep the refugee working group network 'alive' (DFAIT, 2002a), an attempt that in practice has mostly been restricted to convening a series of informal meetings of interested third-party donors, as well as assisting the Palestinian-based Refugee Co-ordination Group to acquire funding for various projects investigating possible solutions to the refugee problem. Accordingly, the Canadian role in the peace process has necessarily faded, and Canada has taken a decidedly back seat to the United States in Israeli–Palestinian affairs. And when Canadian officials have attempted to put forth solutions to the refugee problem—as Foreign Minister John Manley did when he suggested in early 2001 that Canada might take in a number of Palestinian refugees in the context of an Israeli–Palestinian peace agreement—the regional response has been swift and hostile. Following that announcement, Palestinian protestors in the region burned him in effigy. Aside from sporadic policy pronouncements, Canada is still engaged in modest humanitarian efforts, but in light of its declared dedication to development issues and peacebuilding—issues crucial to the success of any Israeli–Palestinian peace agreement—it is curious that the demise of the multilaterals has caused Canada's work as regional facilitator to be stymied to such a degree.

This puzzling retreat arguably has to do with three processes. First, Canada's absolute and relative diplomatic influence in the region has declined from that of a middle power to a minor power at best, at the same time that other third parties, such as the European Union, have taken an increasingly active role in international affairs. Since Canadian foreign policy is partly shaped by its desire to forge a course different from that of the United States, Canada's relative lack of visibility in the Israeli-Palestinian sphere can be attributed in part to the rise of the EU and its accompanying attempt to craft a new, unified European foreign policy. Even if not articulated directly, Canada seems content to 'free-ride' on the efforts of the EU to serve as a friendly counterweight to American actions. Some observers, countering the conventional wisdom that China is the biggest threat to American primacy, have argued that Europe represents the newest and most significant challenge to American hegemony (Kupchan, 2002). Whether or not Canadian officials would agree with this precise assessment, it is obvious that other global contenders—among them the EU—share a similar outlook to that of Canada on many global issues, including the Middle East, and they can check the power of the United States in the region.

Indeed, a significant part of EU foreign policy has been directed towards the Middle East. And the EU certainly sees itself as being a major player in the region, as evidenced by its own Middle East policy statement claiming that 'the EU plays a pivotal role as a major global political and economic actor in the Israeli-Arab Peace Process' (EU, 2002). Along with the UN, Russia, and the United States, the EU is a member of the 'Quartet', an elite group charged with helping bring about a peaceful solution to the Israeli-Palestinian conflict. With the increased interest of the EU in the Middle East, Canada now enjoys less diplomatic clout in the region than it once did. And with the lack of a consensual negotiating framework through which to engage the parties, there is simply less of a role for a declining middle power to exert influence.

A second reason for Canada's lack of visible involvement in the peace process is the absence of formal institutional channels for Canadian participation. Canada prefers to work within multilateral frameworks. Currently, the most prominent of these engaging the Middle East conflict is the Quartet, from which Canada is obviously absent. And with the breakdown of the multilaterals, Canada has been left without any direct channel for influence. Many, including Arafat's Palestinian Authority, would have welcomed more Canadian involvement in the conflict; Arafat actually called on Canada some months ago to intervene. Similarly, one Sri Lankan human rights activist stated that 'none of us in the human rights community would think of appealing to the US for support for upholding a human rights case—maybe to Canada, to Norway or to Sweden—but not to the United States' (Friedman, 2002).

Finally, Prime Minister Chrétien is less intrinsically interested in the politics of the Middle East than other regions, and his current foreign policy agenda shows him being focused on development issues in Africa, an initiative he has defined as one of the priorities for Canada's overall policy agenda, ranked along with solving the Canada–US softwood lumber dispute and improving the state of health care in Canada (PM, 2002). At the 2002 G-8 Summit in Kananaskis, Chrétien identified Canada's relationship with Africa as one of three central issues, along with sustainable development and the war on terrorism, that defined Canada's agenda for the conference. This, even though the Intifada had by then raged for almost two years and the Israeli-Palestinian conflict was certainly a high priority of the United States, particularly in light of the region's relationship to the broader war on terrorism.

Now, with the outbreak of the al-Aqsa Intifada—the Palestinian uprising that began in September 2000 and has shown no immediate signs of abating—the most pressing problem remains less the multilateral working-group issues such as arms control and environmental co-operation, though these are still important, but getting Israel and the Palestinian Authority back to the table. The breakdown of the Oslo framework since the failure of Israelis and Palestinians to reach agreement at the Camp David summit in July 2000 thus simultaneously represents a challenge for any meaningful Canadian involvement, due to the lack of attention now devoted to the multilateral working groups, as well as an opportunity for Canada to take a more active role, since new solutions are needed to reroute the actors back towards a negotiating framework. Yet any direct Canadian diplomatic influence will likely not be automatic. Canada's notable absence from the Camp David framework, especially given that one of the main sticking points turned out to be the question of refugees, means that Canada has certainly not been a visible player, even when the issues it has invested in are front and centre in the peace/conflict spiral.

Given this, the most obvious, if indirect, way that Canada can contribute to creating a more hospitable atmosphere for helping the actors return to the table is through development assistance. Most observers agree that the Oslo agreement was hijacked by the lack of commitment from both sides to fulfill the spirit and the letter of the agreement (Makovsky, 2001). Successive Israeli governments have continued a sustained policy of building settlements in the contested West Bank, leaving a potential Palestinian state without contiguous territory, and Yassir Arafat's Palestinian Authority has not done enough to thwart the increasing spate of suicide bombings launched from the occupied territories into Israel. No doubt the sustained levels of poverty within the territories have fuelled Palestinian anger and increased support for extremist rejectionism spearheaded by the Islamic groups Hamas and Islamic Jihad, as well as the al-Aqsa Martyrs Brigade, a militant offshoot of Arafat's own Fatah party. It is impossible to know what drives these young men and women to blow themselves up in the service of killing Israelis, though most observers agree that better living conditions in the occupied territories would result in less incentive for these groups to recruit followers based on economic resentment alone.

On the other hand, the rise of suicide bombing as a form of resistance among Palestinians *succeeded* the Oslo agreement, rather than having preceded it. The question of how to address the phenomenon of Islamic terrorism in the Israeli–Palestinian sphere is, in large measure, mirrored by the nagging questions engendered by 11 September regarding whether poverty and general economic disenfranchisement are the ultimate causes of Islamic terrorism, or whether religious fanaticism itself gives rise to overtly anti-Western (or anti-Israel) sentiment. The way Hamas itself presents its objectives appears to provide more evidence for the latter explanation than the former. As the Hamas Web site states, the 'conflict' it is waging against

Israel 'aims to restore (from the occupiers) the entire Palestine with its Mandate borders and . . . . Hamas rejects the issue to be limited to the lands occupied in 1967' (Hamas, 2002). These pronouncements obviously imply a rejection of any form of peaceful agreement the Palestinian Authority may be able to reach with Israel. Whatever the self-declared aims of Hamas and Islamic Jihad, it is difficult to argue that the devastating socio-economic conditions in the occupied territories do not help these organizations, in some way, to gain adherents. This is especially so since Hamas operates largely as a charitable organization within the occupied territories, providing the sorts of civil society functions—including food rations, health clinics, and kindergartens—that the Palestinian leadership, through lack of resources or ability, cannot. The economic situation within Palestine is certainly grave. Gross national income in the West Bank and Gaza in 2001 was $1,350 (US) per person, compared to $21,340 (US) in Canada (CIDA, 2002). Paradoxically, perhaps, these conditions are in part fed by Israel having closed its borders—since the rise of terrorist attacks within pre-1967 Israel—to Palestinian day labourers. These jobs were once a significant source of income for the Palestinian economy, and Israel has now replaced these Palestinians with guest workers from Thailand and Romania.

The association of poverty with violent conflict is a relationship that is well understood by the Canadian government, as evidenced by its 2001 report to the UN, *The Responsibility to Protect*. That document states that '[i]gnoring these underlying factors [poverty, political repression, and uneven distribution of resources] amounts to addressing the symptoms rather than the causes of deadly conflict' (paragraph 3.19). To this end, Canada is a member of the Ad Hoc Liaison Committee, a body formed to co-ordinate international economic assistance to the Palestinian Authority. In recent years, Canada has taken on additional development projects related to the refugee issue, including the contribution of over $130 million to development efforts in the region and the organizing of efforts such as a project funded by Canada, Qatar, and others to provide scholarships to Palestinian refugee women in Lebanon and another to rebuild a refugee camp in Syria. The latter project would effectively demonstrate one in a series of options for addressing the refugee problem, given that a wholesale return of *all* refugees to Israel and/or Palestine is unlikely (DFAIT, 2002c). More recently, Canada is discussing transitional peacekeeping options with Israeli and Palestinian officials, and is currently planning a trip with Palestinian security officials to Bosnia and Macedonia to show them how a peacekeeping force might operate in the occupied territories (Amir, 2002; Adams, 2002). Peacekeeping in the Israeli-Palestinian sphere has been something that the parties have not yet agreed to, though the Palestinians have tended to be more hospitable to outside involvement of this kind than have the Israelis. Thus, while Canada retains a foothold in the region, with various projects aimed at bettering the situation economically for Palestinians or at getting the parties to contemplate a post-conflict security order, Canadian activities in the Middle East are modest at best.

What are the implications of all this for Canada–US relations? As discussed above, the fact that the EU has risen as a significant counterweight to American primacy means that Canada can take a less active role in the Middle East, knowing that another significant power is viewed as a different form of 'honest broker' from the US by the players in the region. However, Bush's declaration of support for a Palestinian state means that Canadian and American interests in the Middle East are now closely aligned. While Canada wants to contribute its fair share to alleviating poverty and encouraging development, its resources are limited. Domestically, issues surrounding health care loom large, as does the state of the country's military. Moreover, Canada can stand on the sidelines of the Middle East conflict in the knowledge that its southern neighbour will wield the diplomatic clout it lacks in the attempt to bring Israelis and Palestinians back to the table.

WAR ON IRAQ

The second major issue in the Middle East on which Canadian political interests are keenly focused is the impending war on Iraq. While Iraq represents a more traditional geopolitical issue related to regional and global security, the types of development problems intrinsic to the Israeli-Palestinian conflict also constitute an important part of the Iraqi situation. The increasingly apparent anti-Western sentiment that gains momentum from the ongoing Israeli-Palestinian conflict, the domestic repression that the Iraqi regime has meted out, and the debate as to whether international sanctions (Gordon, 2002) or Iraqi policies (Rubin, 2001) are responsible for the dire—and often fatal—situation facing many of Iraq's citizens place the Iraq question in the forefront of Canada's overall human security agenda.

Yet the developmental aspects are less central to Bush's political focus than is the threat of weapons of mass destruction that Saddam may pose to the West, particularly if he were to acquire the ability to launch nuclear weapons intercontinentally. As part of its attempt to manage a sustained global campaign against terrorism in the wake of the 11 September attacks, the Bush administration has professed the need to bring about what the US is calling 'regime change' in Iraq. To this end, the US has been attempting to achieve a UN Security Council resolution authorizing the use of force if Iraq fails to comply with UN inspections, despite the fact, as critics have pointed out, that the Bush administration has not generally appeared to be constrained by global institutional norms (Ikenberry, 2002). Thus, in its unilateral—and arguably revisionist—approach to global security, the Bush administration's policies do not necessarily coincide with Canada's own multilateralist and status quo tendencies.

To achieve a balance between Canada's multilateralist ethic and its desire to maintain positive relations with the United States, Prime Minister Jean Chrétien stated in October that Canada would be willing to commit up to 2,000 troops to a war against Iraq if the UN sanctions such an operation.[2] Yet recently Chrétien has been more ambiguous about Canada's potential involvement in a war on Iraq outside of a UN-sponsored framework. For instance, in a speech in Ottawa on 10 October, Chrétien did not issue a direct 'no' to a question from the audience on whether Canada would support a unilateral move by the US to invade Iraq.[3] One month later, at a NATO summit in Prague, the Prime Minister, along with his NATO allies, issued a statement demanding that Saddam Hussein 'fully and immediately' comply with the UN resolution calling for him to disarm or else face serious consequences.[4] This has left the option for a military strike open and does not foreclose any particular course of action on the part of Canada or its allies. Moreover, Defence Minister John McCallum has now said that Canada may indeed join a US coalition even in the absence of a UN Security Council resolution (Koring, 2003).

Nor does Canada seem concerned about Bush's explicit verbal threats against Saddam. Foreign Minister Bill Graham has stated, 'We want Saddam Hussein to be nervous because we want him to know there is no wiggle room and he absolutely has to comply' (Sallot, 2002). The Canadian government, while not wanting outwardly to support US attempts to bypass international legal channels in addressing the Iraqi threat, is clearly able to see the benefits in a tough-talking neighbour. Ideally, though by no means necessarily, the threats Bush is issuing to Iraq will compel Saddam to disarm, thus averting war in the short term and neutralizing a potential adversary in the long term.

While Bush has been the most vocal critic of Saddam Hussein's regime, going so far as to declare in his 2002 State of the Union address that Iraq, Iran, and North Korea constitute an 'axis of evil', Canada has also declared its opposition to Iraq's potential chemical and biological weapons capabilities. Indeed, the nuclear issue provides the US its most tenable cause of war. If the US can convince the international community that Saddam has the potential and willingness to launch a nuclear missile at the US or its allies, then the Bush administration can credibly launch a war against Iraq, a type of operation that would fall under the category of preventive war, and which the Bush administration has begun to call, somewhat paradoxically, 'forward deterrence'. This approach fits squarely within an overall US national security strategy that stresses the problematic notion of pre-emption, which, as the editors have suggested in the introduction to this volume, is inappropriately applied to situations that are considerably more ambiguous than the imminence of threat typically implied by the term.

It is far from clear whether Iraq possesses the capabilities to acquire nuclear weapons in the short to medium term. The Canadian government has been more restrained than the US in accusing Iraq of nuclear potential. As the Department of Foreign Affairs policy position states, 'It is believed . . . that Iraq neither possesses a nuclear weapon nor is close to having one, in large measure due to the difficulty of producing or otherwise acquiring the necessary weapons-grade fissile material' (DFAIT, 2002b).

Canada faces a number of conflicting pressures in its decision on whether to support the United States in a non-UN-sanctioned action against Iraq, in the event that Saddam fails to comply with the inspections and if Bush fails to acquire the necessary Security Council backing for the use of force. On the one hand, Canada's commitment to multilateralism as well as its desire not to follow passively the American foreign policy line in matters of war and peace would suggest that the Chrétien government should hold firm to its earlier claim that it will only send troops if military action against Iraq is sanctioned by the UN.

On the other hand, with the disproportionate American contribution to 'homeland security' in the wake of 11 September, and amid accusations within Canadian and American policy circles that Canada's own defence allocation is too small, Canada might not want to be seen to free-ride by refusing to support the initiative on Iraq altogether.[5] Already, Canada has seemed to shun internationalism in recent years, one scholar dubbing Canada's retrenchment from international involvement 'pinchpenny diplomacy' (Nossal, 1998–9). Moreover, the guns-versus-butter debate in Canada will likely not be resolved anytime soon, and may indeed be leaning towards the latter, as evidenced by the November 2002 Romanow Report on health care, which calls for Ottawa to increase its targeted health spending by $15 billion over the next three years (Curry et al., 2002).

To the degree that Saddam Hussein is responsible for the grave humanitarian situation in his country, Canada should be expected to support intervention in order to remain true to its ethical and strategic preferences. One can argue that Saddam bears much responsibility for both the culture of fear under which his population lives (stemming from, among other things, his record of using non-conventional weapons against the Kurds) and for the dire economic situation in Iraq, which, in addition to the effects of Western sanctions, was greatly exacerbated by Saddam's initial refusal, until 1996, to participate in the UN oil-for-food program. Nevertheless, the question remains whether third parties have the legal and/or moral right to violate the sovereignty of a state—even one led by as ruthless a leader as Saddam Hussein—for the purpose of humanitarian intervention.

The normative relationship between these two values—sovereignty and humanitarianism—has plagued international relations scholars and policy-makers for decades, and has constituted a legal and ethical quandary that led Canada, in September 2000, to take up UN Secretary-General Kofi Annan's call to the international community to grapple with this issue. In response, the Canadian government convened an international commission to discuss this question. The result was a December 2001 report, compiled by an international team of academics and practitioners, entitled *The Responsibility to Protect: Report of the International Commission on Intervention and State Sovereignty* (DFAIT, 2001). The group, advised by former Canadian Foreign Minister Lloyd Axworthy, concluded that the duty to intervene on behalf of civilians in danger ethically and legally overrides the right of state sovereignty, an argument put forth by replacing the traditional 'right to intervene' logic with the notion that states have a 'responsibility to protect' (ibid., paragraph 2.4). While the principle of state sovereignty clearly has legal standing—and certainly constitutes the *sine qua non* of what it means to be a member of the international state system (and a member of the UN, at that)— the report brings to light a number of other legal issues from which the writers conclude that the responsibility to protect can supersede even the enshrined right of states not to have their borders violated (paragraph 2.26).

In its emphasis on the protection of the individual, the conclusions reached in the report are clearly consonant with Canadian human security ideals, stressing a shift away from traditional, state-centric approaches to security towards evaluation of military or other policies based on their impact on the lives of individuals (paragraphs 1.33 and 2.21-2.23). However, because of Canada's tradition of wanting to uphold the rule of law, as well as a desire to privilege consensual, multilateral policy channels over unilateral ones, the report raises some challenging questions for Canada's position on the war in Iraq. It is widely known that Saddam Hussein has flouted moral and ethical principles in maintaining his repressive regime, where women and the Kurdish minority have been the prime targets of his brutal policies. Canada should, therefore, automatically support a military intervention—whether or not it is sanctioned by the UN. On the other hand, the report stresses the importance of 'right intention' in evaluating the justness of a given intervention. One of the main criteria of 'just war theory', right intention is of course difficult to ascertain, especially with the policy rhetoric surrounding most international actions. Nevertheless, Bush's declared aim of 'regime change' in Iraq would itself not fall under right intention, although the report is suitably ambiguous on this point, given the potential need to topple a leadership in order to protect the citizens under it (chapter 4.33–4.34). Neither, typically, would the attempt to maintain access to oil, notwithstanding Michael Ignatieff's recent remarks regarding the ethical importance of protecting the world's oil supply in the context of a potential war on Iraq (Ignatieff, 2002). Moreover, the report stresses the importance of collective or multilateral action, and Canada indeed wants to uphold the international institutional principles enshrined in the UN Charter. This is a similar dilemma faced by human rights groups, including Amnesty International, in their dual policy of denouncing repressive regimes while opposing a war on Baghdad, particularly in the aftermath of the British government's recent report showing the dire human rights situation in Iraq (Freeman, 2002).

Overlying the debate, of course, is the degree to which Canada can and should voice its displeasure with US policies, and whether policy divergence, including open critique, represents a peculiarly Canadian strain of anti-Americanism (Knox, 2002). This issue has become increasingly salient since 11 September, when the attacks on New York and Washington led scholars and others to ask whether US policies—ignoring the 'failed state' of Afghanistan, allowing the Israeli-Palestinian conflict to fester, propping up conservative Arab regimes—contributed to the attacks, or at least to the overt or tacit support they received in many corners of the Arab world and even in Europe (Walt, 2001–2).

CONCLUSION

Canada's Middle East policies are informed by a spirit of multilateralism that shapes much of Canadian foreign-policy making. In the cases of Iraq and the Israeli–Palestinian nexus, this commitment has meant that Canada has largely been limited in its actions, either by existing multilateral channels (the multilateral working groups) that are themselves dependent on the willingness of the regional parties to participate, or by the broader consensus of the international community, embodied in the UN, to decide whether to use military force against what the sole remaining superpower has identified as the primary state-based threat to global peace and stability. However, to remain true to Canada's human security outlook, the government must remain engaged in the Middle East, particularly with regard to improving the socio-economic conditions in the West Bank and Gaza Strip as a hopeful prelude to rebuilding a critical mass of Palestinians supportive of a peace process with Israel. On the Iraq front, Canada needs to grapple with the pressing questions raised by its own commission convened to investigate the relationship between sovereignty and intervention. The Bush administration clearly favours the latter over the former, though possibly for different reasons than might some intervention-minded Canadians. Canada may decide that multilateralism is worth forgoing, not for particular strategic exigencies, i.e., maintaining close ties with the US, but because the ethic of protecting individuals is stronger than a commitment to formal institutional principles.

NOTES

For helpful comments and discussions, I thank John Higginbotham, the participants at the December 2002 *Canada Among Nations 2003* workshop, and one anonymous senior official at DFAIT.

1. Bush issued this pronouncement soon after 11 September, stating that, as long as Israel's right to exist was guaranteed, a Palestinian state has always been 'part of a vision' for a peace settlement. See <http://www.cnn.com/2001/US/10/02/gen.mideast.us/>.
2. Chrétien made this remark at an Ottawa high school on 10 October 2002. See <http://www.ctv.ca/servlet/ArticleNews/story/CTVNews/1034268958333_29678158/>. Accessed 29 Nov. 2002.
3. 'Canada Would Participate in UN Mission in Iraq: PM', CBC News (Internet edition), 10 Oct. 2002. Available at: <http://www.cbc.ca/stories/2002/10/10/Chretieniraq_021010>.> Accessed 29 Nov. 2002.
4. 'NATO "stands united" with Bush on Iraq', *National Post,* 22 Nov. 2002, Internet edition.
5. One of the most dominant Canadian voices on this issue is the Council for Canadian Security in the 21st Century, headed by historian Jack Granatstein.

REFERENCES

Adams, Paul. 2002. 'Mideast Officials to Get Look at Peacekeeping', *Globe and Mail,* 4 Dec., A19.

Amir, Wafa. 2002. 'Deploy Peacekeepers in Mideast, Ottawa Urges', *Globe and Mail,* 18 Dec., A15.

Axworthy, Lloyd. 1999. 'Notes prepared for an address by the Honourable Lloyd Axworthy, Minister of Foreign Affairs to the Partners in Peace Meeting', New York, 24 Sept. Available at: <http://www.dfait-maeci.gc.ca/peaceprocess/speech-2-en.asp>. Accessed 4 Dec. 2002.

Bumiller, Elisabeth, and David E. Sanger. 2002. 'Mideast Turmoil: The White House; Bush Demands Arafat's Ouster Before U.S. Backs a New State', *New York Times,* 25 June, A1.

Canadian International Development Agency (CIDA). 2002. West Bank and Gaza: Facts at a Glance. Available at: <http://www.acdi-cida.gc.ca/CIDAWEB/webcountry.nsf/VLUDocEn/WestBankandGaza-Factsataglance>.

Centre for Security and Defence Studies (CSDS). 2002. 'Canadian Defence and the Canada–US Strategic Partnership', NPSIA Occasional Paper No. 29, Nov.

Cohen, Andrew. 2002. 'Does Canada Matter in Washington? Does It Matter If Canada Doesn't Matter?', in Norman Hillmer and Maureen Appel Molot, eds, *Canada Among Nations 2002: A Fading Power.* Toronto: Oxford University Press, 34–48.

Curry, Bill, Tom Arnold, and Robert Fife. 2002. 'Romanow Wants $15b Infusion', *National Post*, 29 Nov.

Department of Foreign Affairs and International Trade (DFAIT). 2001. *The Responsibility to Protect: Report of the International Commission on Intervention and State Sovereignty.* Available at: <http://www.dfait-maeci.gc.ca/iciss-ciise/report-en.asp>.

————. 2002a. Web site of the Office of the Special Co-ordinator, Middle East Peace Process. Available at: <http://www.dev.dfait-maeci.gc.ca/demo/peaceprocess/office-e.asp>.

————. 2002b. 'Iraq: Weapons of Mass Destruction', policy statement. Available at: <http://www.dfait-maeci.gc.ca/middle_east/iraq_weapons-en.asp>.

————. 2002c. Author's interview with an anonymous senior official at DFAIT.

European Union (EU). 2002. 'The Mediterranean and Middle East Policy of the European Union'. Available at: <http://www.euromed.net/eu/mepp.html>.

Freeman, Alan. 2002. 'The Activist's Dilemma: What to do about Iraq?', *Globe and Mail*, 4 Dec., A1.

Friedman, Thomas L. 2002. 'Bush's Shame', *New York Times*, 4 Aug., A13.

Gordon, Joy. 2002. 'Cool War: Economic Sanctions as Weapons of Mass Destruction', *Harper's* (Nov.).

Hamas. 2002. Web site. Available at: <http://www.palestine-info.co.uk/hamas/>.

Ignatieff, Michael. 2002. Roundtable remarks, Carleton University, Ottawa, 8 Nov.

Ikenberry, G. John. 2002. 'America's Imperial Ambition', *Foreign Affairs* (Sept.–Oct.).

Kaye, Dalia Dassa. 2001. *Beyond the Handshake: Multilateral Cooperation in the Arab-Israeli Peace Process, 1991–1996.* New York: Columbia University Press.

Knox, Paul. 2002. 'The Rise of Anti-Anti-Americanism', *Globe and Mail*, 4 Dec., A25.

Koring, Paul. 2003. 'Canada May Fight without UN Support', *Globe and Mail*, 10 Jan., A1.

Kupchan, Charles A. 2002. 'The End of the West', *Atlantic Monthly* (Nov.).

Makovsky, David. 2001. 'Middle East Peace Through Partition', *Foreign Affairs* (Mar.–Apr.).

Molot, Maureen Appel, and Norman Hillmer. 2002. 'The Diplomacy of Decline', in Hillmer and Molot, eds, *Canada Among Nations 2002: A Fading Power.* Toronto: Oxford University Press.

Nossal, Kim Richard. 1998-9. 'Pinchpenny Diplomacy: The Decline of "Good International Citizenship" in Canadian Foreign Policy', *International Journal* (Winter).

Paris, Roland. 2001. 'Human Security: Paradigm Shift or Hot Air?', *International Security* 26, 2 (Fall).

Peters, Joel. 1999. 'Can the Multilateral Middle East Talks Be Revived?', *Middle East Review of International Affairs* 3, 4 (Dec.) (Internet edition).

Pratt, Cranford. 2001. 'The Impact of Ethical Values on Canadian Foreign Aid Policy', *Canadian Foreign Policy* 9, 1 (Fall).

Prime Minister of Canada (PM). 2002. 'Welcome to Canada's Future', key initiatives of the Prime Minister's Office. Available at: <http://pm.gc.ca/default.asp?Language=E&Page=keyinitiatives>.

Rubin, Michael. 2001. 'Sanctions on Iraq: A Valid Anti-American Grievance?', *Middle East Review of International Affairs* 5, 4 (Dec.).

Ruggie, John Gerard. 1993. 'Multilateralism: The Anatomy of an Institution', in Ruggie, ed., *Multilateralism Matters: The Theory and Praxis of an Institutional Form*. New York: Columbia University Press.

Sallot, Jeff. 2002. 'Hostile US Tone Toward Iraq Not Troubling, Canada Says', *Globe and Mail*, 4 Dec., A21.

Sanger, David E. 2002. 'Mideast Turmoil: Group of 8; Bush, in Canada, Is Facing Skepticism on Arafat's Role', *New York Times*, 26 June, A14.

Thomas, Ward. 2001. *The Ethics of Destruction: Norms and Force in International Affairs*. Ithaca, NY: Cornell University Press.

United States Department of State. 2001. 'Powell Addresses Regional Business Leaders in Shanghai', International Information Programs, 18 Oct. Available at: <http://usinfo.state.gov/topical/pol/terror/01101822.htm>.

Walt, Stephen M. 2001–2. 'Beyond bin Laden: Reshaping U.S. Foreign Policy', *International Security* 26, 3 (Winter).

17

Soft Power Meets Hard: The Ideological Consequences of Weakness

MARK F. PROUDMAN

European leaders are now finding themselves in a position familiar to Canadians: apparent irrelevance in the face of American power. European reactions will also be familiar to Canadians. Formal alignment, protestations of support, and tangible co-operation on the one hand are combined on the other with a desire to restrain American power, the rhetoric of multilateralism, and an undertone of querulous resentment. The American response to Europe is equally familiar to Canadians. In a mirror image of European and Canadian attitudes, the Americans manifest a willingness to co-operate with allies on concrete issues, but it is an attitude that oscillates between dismissal and contempt.

The United States is the only Western country that retains a truly independent capacity to make war. It is the only remaining superpower, a situation without historic parallel (a century ago, there were no non-Western great powers, with the arguable exception of Japan).

Britain and France retain the ability to project power almost globally, but only with the effective assent of the United States and only against relatively minor adversaries—whether African rebels (as with the recent British action in Sierra Leone and the French intervention in the Ivory Coast) or South American dictators (as in the Falklands War of 1982). Even closer to home in the Balkans, the European powers have had to rely on US air power and the threat of US land forces to provide the military backbone of peacemaking and peacekeeping efforts. No doubt the British, French, or German armies could have defeated the Serbs, but the prospect of doing so without US support was unimaginable. Though the US is often criticized for its sensitivity to casualties, in the 1990s the prospect of a ground war between conventional armies deterred any thought of independent European intervention, even on Europe's Balkan doorstep.

NATO has never been an alliance of equals. For a long time the European contribution, especially in ground forces on the central front, was large enough to create a rough balance between the military power of Europe as a whole and that of the United States. In addition, it was the Europeans who required US military assistance against an obvious Soviet threat on their doorstep. If the United States was a hegemon, it was a case of 'empire by invitation', in the much-cited phrase of the Norwegian scholar Geir Lundestad (Lundestad, 1990). There was, at least in some European circles, a sense of obligation to the US—or at least of shared benefit. On the other side of the relationship, though the Americans put themselves in potential harm's way, the Europeans actually lived on the central front; no one could pretend that dangers were not shared. These conditions have changed. The central front in Germany no longer exists. Europe's conventional armies are largely useless for deployment elsewhere. There is no longer a sense of European obligation to the United States. It can even be asserted in mainstream European newspapers that the United States is 'our foremost enemy' (Monbiot, 2002), that the American flag is flown for 'hate' (Kennedy, 2002), and that America, in the words of the German Nobel Prize winner Gunter Grass, is 'dangerous to the rest of the world' (Grass, 2003). Wars in Afghanistan and Iraq are perceived by many Europeans to be American wars, and to be the results of American incompetence or worse. In the wars of the present, US allies are both militarily irrelevant and not possessed of any great sense that they have themselves a direct stake, moral or material, in the outcome.

With the disappearance of the European central front, effective military power must now be deployable to remote regions, and only the United States has the requisite airlift capacity, the European attempt to develop a similar capability in the form of the Airbus A400 having (quite literally) not yet left the ground. The disproportion between allied military capabilities has been increased by the so-called 'revolution in military affairs', the current buzz-phrase for the rapid technological obsolescence of conventionally equipped armies. The Gulf War of 1991 showed that the Reagan buildup of the 1980s had moved the US military a technological generation beyond all others. Encouraged by the example of the Gulf War, US forces leapt forward once again in the 1990s, greatly increasing their use of precision weapons in the recent Afghan war. In the words of one prominent strategic theorist, a 'revolution in military affairs' can be defined as 'a discontinuous increase in military capability' (Gray, 2002), and today, almost solely, the power of American forces has increased. With the exception of such specialized forces as the British Special Air Service and the French Foreign Legion (and perhaps the Canadian JTF2), the United States now considers the military forces of most allies to be an inconvenience—as was demonstrated during the Afghan war. There was talk during the November 2002 NATO summit of the 'boutique skills' of allied militaries, most of whom are reduced to providing small contingents of specialist troops rather than self-supporting fighting formations of their own (Horrock, 2002). European powers now deploy these 'boutique' forces alongside the Americans primarily to impress the latter and to gain a claim to be consulted.

This chapter will focus on the reactions to the new military realities of the three leading European powers: Great Britain, France, and Germany. It will argue that though differing national experiences initially determined different reactions to each country's post-war fall from great power status, the current situation of feared irrelevance has led to similar attitudes to US power on the part of governing intelligentsias. Chief among these attitudes is a widespread derision of perceived US foreign policy, an attitude that is particularly acute when there is a Texas Republican in the White House. American moralism (as in the much-derided 'axis of evil') and the associated willingness to use military power are disturbing to European elites who have little military power and that have long viewed moral imperatives with suspicion.

British Prime Minister Tony Blair is the great apparent exception to European distaste for the newly assertive United States. But Blair holds his Labour Party together with difficulty, and he does it only by deploying the argument that he can better restrain the US if he is seen to be a good ally. This latter argument will be familiar to Canadians who have often been told of the merits of quiet diplomacy. And Blair's pro-Americanism has earned him much obloquy, also of a kind that would not be unfamiliar to Canadian prime ministers, from King to Mulroney, perceived to be too close to the US. The newly demoted middle powers of Europe necessarily focus on the use of institutional, cultural, and multilateral 'soft power' in a way that will be familiar to the citizens of a country that has never been more than a self-advertised 'middle power'.

SOFT POWER AND HARD CONFLICT

An emphasis on the importance of military power to international relations is thought in many circles to be unsophisticated, even simplistic. This is particularly true in Ottawa, where the doctrine of 'soft power' was elevated to something of a state religion. The term first assumed prominence under former Minister of Foreign Affairs Lloyd Axworthy, who deployed the rhetoric of 'soft power' to exalt multilateral projects, such as the anti-personnel landmine treaty, to emphasize the moral claims of Canadian diplomacy, and to do so in contradistinction to the 'simple-minded' militarism of the Americans. Imprecision is not necessarily a disadvantage in a political slogan. In 'soft power' imprecision is combined with a general air of broad-minded progressivism, and, to be sure, these atmospherics further reinforce some of Ottawa's favourite stereotypes. Notions associated with 'soft power' now find a ready home in Europe, as do their polemical, nationalist, and specifically anti-American uses.

Ironically, 'soft power' was originally an American idea, conceived in the 1970s when the United States was militarily paralyzed by defeat in Vietnam and also appeared to be in irreversible economic decline. A conception of 'interdependence', wherein states are not seen as unitary actors with unified interests and in which power takes cultural, political, and institutional forms that could not be reduced to calculations of military and economic strength, was advanced by American scholars Robert O. Keohane and Joseph Nye (Keohane and Nye, 1977). 'Interdependence directly implied that states' true interests were not necessarily or even normally in conflict. These ideas rapidly became a kind of counter-orthodoxy, and were often advanced against the traditional or 'realist' description of international politics as a Hobbesian competition between unitary and adversarial states. Nye has continued to develop his ideas, which have become both an ideological foundation and a source of intellectual respectability for the 'soft power' language and ideas popular in Ottawa. But soft power has its own difficulties of application. 'Power conversion is a basic problem', writes Nye (1990), who later added, in directly addressing former Foreign Minister Axworthy's 'soft power' diplomacy, that hard power can only be ignored at the risk of irritating its sole remaining Western possessor—the United States (Nye, 1999). If counting divisions and aircraft carriers does not provide a reliable measure of state (let alone non-state) power, those qualities of culture and ideology that constitute soft power are even more difficult to measure. Soft power is only with difficulty converted into hard power, as allied blandishments against unilateral US action in Iraq have made clear. The use of soft power to restrain hard power has costs of its own, as increasing American impatience with various allies shows.

The ideology of soft power is as susceptible to vulgarization as the older, self-consciously hard-nosed, 'realist' understanding of international power. Just as hard power, and in particular military power, is most effective in a world where definite lines can be drawn between 'us' and 'them', possessors of soft power are notably ineffective in the face of such boundaries. Soft power is useless—it is not power at all—where shared interests—what is called 'interdependence'—do not exist and are difficult or impossible to construct. Just as those who possess armoured divisions and air wings can be contemptuous of the real uses of soft power, too dogmatic a commitment to soft power can result in a kind of ideologically induced blindness to the existence of real and intractable conflict. The de-emphasis of conflict is one reason why notions of soft power are particularly congenial to modern liberals. An emphasis on rationality and consent has always been at the core of that large but central body of thought and feeling that goes by the name of 'liberalism'. Implicit in such ideas, going back to John Stuart Mill and his utilitarian predecessors, is an assertion of the ultimate compatibility of the rational interests of different individuals and of different groups (Freeden, 1996). Soft power, with its aversion to direct coercion, often relies on an appeal to, and an emphasis on, such implicitly compatible and hence interdependent interests. If conservative realists are sometimes inclined to construct conflict where it need not exist, liberal advocates and employers of soft power are equally prone to a defensive denial of the kind of intractable conflict with which they are ideologically ill-equipped to deal.

This kind of not quite inadvertent inability to perceive profound and radical conflict was displayed by the Canadian government's pre-11 September unwillingness to take Islamic terrorism seriously. In pursuing a soft power strategy towards the Islamist regime in Sudan and towards that regime's Iraqi allies, Axworthy expressed great impatience with the Americans, who were 'simply interested in trying to find [pause] . . . um [pause] . . . the [pause] . . . what they consider to be bin Laden. We think that there's a broader objective, and that is to get a peace process' (Axworthy, 1999). This rhetoric reveals its blind spots: it was difficult for the apostle of soft power to recognize, or even to name, the existence of enmity. There had to have been, as a matter of dogmatic necessity, the possibility of peace. The liberal mind was singularly impatient with those (Americans) who did not consider it possible 'to get a peace process', and hostility therefore focused not upon the underlying problem of Islamic extremism but rather upon those (Americans) who did not accept the liberal denial of enmity. Enmity—radical conflict—had to be represented as nothing more than a simple-minded American construct. An ethereal 'broader objective' could be directly named, while the reality of a concrete enemy had to be buried in the hastily constructed, stumbling conditional phraseology of 'um . . . the . . . what they consider to be'.

Any doctrinal approach to international affairs has blind spots. That liberal blind spots should consist of unmentionable regions of advertent ignorance—of names that cannot directly be named—is particularly ironic given the self-conscious sophistication of the acolytes of soft power, given their readiness to trumpet knowledge as a source of such power, and given their willingness to attribute ignorance to those (Americans) who insist on the need for hard power. In very human ways, international actors emphasize those types of power that they have the ability to exercise, and simultaneously deny those problems with which they are ill-equipped, materially or ideologically, to manage.

The need to deny conflict, and consequently to avert the gaze from evident realities, also afflicts Europeans. Many Europeans, most especially among those dominant intelligentsias that staff state agencies, write newspapers, create legitimacy, and distribute tax money, have been keen to dismiss the American use of the term 'war' to describe the conflict with Islamic terrorism. The use of that unpleasant monosyllable is attributed either to the 'idiocy' of President George W. Bush or to the propagandistic aims of his advisers. One particularly absurd instance of this kind of blindness was presented by the prominent intellectual Slavoj Zizek in the prestigious house organ of the British intelligentsia, the *London Review of Books*. The West does not really have enemies, he contended; they are (of course) mere discursive constructs. Conflating words in order to confuse ideas, he wrote that we merely 'identify/construct' enemies in accordance with (America's) pathological social needs (Zizek, 2002). Along the way, Bush is compared to Hitler and to former Paraguayan dictator Alfredo Stroessner, and the whole is armoured with references to Kantian metaphysics, to Carl Schmitt's binary friend/enemy distinction, and to Lacanian psychoanalysis.

Intellectuals have been writing nonsense for a long time, but this is a particularly thick variety of nonsense, laden with advertent imputations, consciously alluding to as many difficult philosophers as possible, and at the same time trumpeting its ideologically anti-American intent. It is an ideological stance increasingly associated with sophistication, and increasingly adopted by those who only wish to appear sophisticated. Zizek's obtuse rhetorical tactics serve to provide intellectual reputability to the refusal to recognize the reality of conflict that is inherent in the practice of the *Guardian* and the *Observer*. They refer in derisive quotation marks to the 'war on terror', as though the reality of conflict was too frightening—or too ideologically uncongenial—to be directly named. It is an ironic variety of advertent ignorance, given that it is practised by those who place worldliness, knowledge, and sophistication at the centre of their self-constructed identities. If what former French Foreign Minister Hubert Vedrine called 'simplisme' (de Barochez, 2002a) can lead American conservatives to overlook certain complexities, Zizek's kind of discursive fog serves equally to obscure ideologically uncongenial realities. Apparently overwhelming power allows some Americans to be too Manichaean in their perception of the world, but the lack of power also has ideological consequences. It leads many Europeans, like many Canadians, to a defensively dismissive response to the reality of conflict and to a consequent refusal to think seriously about strategic problems. Each ideological distortion adopts its own discursive camouflage. The laconic language of a Western ('smoke 'em out') serves one purpose; the polysyllabic chatter of the Left Bank serves the other.

'THE GERMAN WAY'

World War II permanently ended the independent great power status of Great Britain, France, and Germany. Each reacted differently. Germany had not merely been beaten, it had been reduced to rubble. The depth of defeat was so obvious that, unlike 1918, there could be no room for doubt about the result, no room for 'stab in the back' conspiracy theories, and hence no room for what in a related context had been called *revanchisme*. Germans reacted by accepting their demotion from great power status by becoming the economic powerhouse of Europe—and all under the protection of American troops and American bombs. But man does not live by bread alone: a parallel and less happy reaction to prosperity in a world whose basic but ominous political shape was determined in Moscow and Washington was the development of a widely remarked culture of *angst*, of self-doubt, and even of self-hatred. It was a culture based on obsessive questioning both of the Nazi past and of the prosperous and democratic present. This culture of paralytic self-doubt is led by, but by no means restricted to, the country's large and powerful intelligentsia. It is a culture, and an intelligentsia, that was formed in large part during the anti-American demonstrations of the 1960s and the similar anti-nuclear demonstrations of the 1980s. During the latter period the Green Party, now Germany's third party, which holds the balance of power in German politics, became prominent. These periods were formative for Germany's current rulers, including the retired Marxist and present Chancellor Gerhard Schroeder and the former 'terrorist associate' and present Foreign Minister Joschka Fischer (Berman, 2001). It is not surprising that they have little in common with President Bush or Defense Secretary Donald Rumsfeld. Even those who claim to be pro-American, and who might have had a genuine liking for Bill Clinton, feel a vast emotional distance between themselves and the exuberant nationalism of the Bush White House: 'Never has a President of the United States been so foreign to us and never have German citizens been so sceptical about the policies of their most powerful of allies', said an influential newspaper on the occasion of Bush's May 2002 visit to Berlin (Kupchan, 2002).

The influential Frankfurt Group intellectual Jürgen Habermas echoed these perceptions when he observed to the sympathetic left-wing American magazine, *The Nation*, that:

> Many Americans do not yet realize the extent and the character of the grow-ing rejection of, if not resentment against, the policy of the present American Administration throughout Europe, including in Great Britain. The emotional gap may well become deeper than it has ever been since the end of World War II. For people like me, who always sided with a pro-American left, it is important to draw a visible boundary between criticizing the policy of the American Administration, on one hand, and the muddy stream of anti-American prejudices on the other. (Habermas, 2002)

Habermas is correct about the distance between left-wing Europeans and right-wing Americans. But the administration's 'policy' of which he speaks, often subsumed under the label 'unilateralism', is less a pol-icy than a set of policies and a supporting culture of attitudes and iden-tities. The Bush administration is convinced that America has been attacked because of its virtues rather than its faults, and is equally con-vinced of its right and duty to strike back with the full force that the Republic can muster, and it expresses itself in just that kind of sim-plistic language. Such nationalism expresses itself in direct and unem-barrassed language that offends many in a German culture where clarity is all too easily equated with simple-mindedness. The Bush sen-sibility resonates in America, as the campaign and the results of the 2002 mid-term elections showed. It is a sensibility at radical variance with the pacific and self-doubting culture dominant in Germany.

Not all Germans are pacifist, though a striking number are. Oxford scholar Martin Ceadel argues that 'pacificism' is dominant in Germany. It is an attitude that rejects any notion that war can be a rational instrument of policy, though it may not go so far as to reject in all cases the use of armed force by the state and may accept the legitimacy of self-defence in some cases (Ceadel, 1987). American political culture, by contrast, either accepts war as an inevitable evil or sees it as a necessity for the triumph of right. The former view is a minority position in Germany, and the latter is completely outside mainstream German culture. These differing views, of course, have roots in differing historical experiences. With the exception of the trauma in Vietnam, most American wars have been successful, and all since the nineteenth century have, until now, been fought outside what is now called 'the Homeland'. By contrast, pacifism has become an integral part of German politics and even of the German self-image. In Germany, even the deployment of peacekeeping forces to the Balkans was controversial. Following the 11 September attacks, the German government was able to win approval for the deployment of German peacekeeping forces to Afghanistan only by the narrowest of margins, and in opposition to the governing coalition's Green Party supporters.

By 2002, it was possible for Chancellor Schroeder to win an election by appealing to pacifist and anti-American sentiment. Initially behind in the polls, with an economy in difficulties and questions about Islamic immigration troubling the country, Schroeder was able to win an election by opposing Bush's proposal to forcibly remove Saddam Hussein from power. Though defending Saddam on social democratic principle would be problematic, it was the frank use of American military power that offended many Germans more than the prospect of continued despotism or fearsome weapons in Iraq. Schroeder was able to turn the German election of 22 September 2002 around by focusing on foreign policy and by speaking of a 'German way' in international affairs. This assertion of a characteristic 'German way' was sufficiently popular that the opposition Christian Democratic Union 'did not dare refute the attack in substance', as Henry Kissinger pointed out (Kissinger, 2002). A cabinet minister's spurious comparison of Bush's political tactics to those of Hitler expressed a widespread feeling among Germans, even if, in a scenario repeated in Ottawa's Ducros affair two months later, the offending official had to be sacrificed for the sake of diplomatic relations. The 'German way' emphasized the centrality of multilateral institutions like the United Nations and insisted that the moral use of force required UN approval.

But the 'German way' was also a way that refused to think systematically about the possible existence of elemental conflict and about the use of force in world affairs. The 'German way' has a great deal in common with Governor-General Adrienne Clarkson's and Prime Minister Jean Chretien's talk of Canadian values. Core to these 'ways' or 'values' is a pacificist concern for peace that becomes so intellectually and morally imperative that it overwhelms the possibility of serious strategic thought. The American reaction to talk of the

'German way' would also be familiar to Canadians: Germany was branded 'the angry adolescent of Europe' by the conservative *Weekly Standard*, a political magazine known to be read in the White House and the Pentagon (Caldwell, 2002), and a German-American estrangement remains at this writing. American frustration with pusillanimous and disloyal Germans is strikingly similar to the attitude of American conservatives to Canada, as exemplified by the *National Review* cover showing Mounties with the label 'Wimps!' (Goldberg, 2002).

THE GAULLIST ATTEMPT AT RELEVANCE

If the Germans accepted their forcible demotion from great power status after 1945, the French resisted it—and in some ways continue to do so. A 20-year attempt to preserve their colonial empire as a source of power and status was followed by the Gaullist attempt to steer an independent path between the Russians and the Americans, with the aide of the nuclear *force de frappe*. Though Charles de Gaulle's 1966 withdrawal from the NATO military structure was mollified by a continued adhesion to the political aspects of NATO's founding Washington Treaty of 1949, French prickliness continues to rankle some Americans. George F. Will writes with disgust that France has only two aircraft carriers (in fact, it has one serviceable) and therefore does not deserve a UN Security Council seat (Will, 2002). Many Americans, however, write off the French pretense of power as a national eccentricity of no great importance. As the influential *New York Times* columnist Thomas Friedman wrote, the French are 'bad-weather friends' and their military forces (whose presence in many African countries is regarded as a good thing by Washington) are renowned for their 'attitude', which is meant in its popular and positive sense of aggressiveness. Friedman even gives them honorary 'English-speaking' status (Friedman, 2002). The French were keen that the Americans should notice these qualities—if not their imputed linguistic affinity—during Operation Anaconda in Afghanistan, sending the aircraft carrier *Charles de Gaulle* to launch air strikes under overall American command against Al-Qaeda targets.

It was precisely because the French were reputed to be essentially anti-American that the famous post-11 September headline in *Le Monde* 'Nous sommes tous Américains' attracted such notice: Hubert Beuve Marie's creation had never before (or since) been so enthusiastic about America (Colombani, 2001). But that frame of mind lasted about 48 hours. The French intelligentsia were back on form by the end of the week, one writer (who was also an employee of the French government) writing that Al-Qaeda was a 'civil society organization' expressing the grievances of the 'countries of the [global] South'; it was the voice of Frantz Fanon's 'wretched of the earth' (Khouri-Dagher, 2001). The mood of full support for the United States did not outlast the beginning of the American counterattack in Afghanistan a month later.

The American desire to extend the war on terror to Iraq has attracted particular opposition from the French, who have long valued their close relations with the Arab world, who have a troublesome Islamic immigrant population, and who hold significant amounts of Iraqi debt. Lionel Jospin and his Socialist government of France were particularly supportive of Iraq but were doomed by the success of the nativist leader Jean-Marie Le Pen in winning second place in the presidential election of 21 April 2002. From that point forward, it was obvious that the conservative Gaullist, Jacques Chirac, would retain the presidency and that his party would be well placed to win the parliamentary elections—as they went on to do. But though the anti-American Socialist Foreign Minister Hubert Vedrine was gone, Chirac—now fully in control of foreign policy—was just as eager to assert his independence from the United States as any Socialist. Chirac was keen to accept praise for constraining the United States to act against Iraq only through the UN and for preventing the passage of a Security Council resolution that could automatically trigger war—praise that was lavished on him by the conservative paper *Le Figaro* and the leftist *Le Monde* (de Barochez, 2002b; Girard, 2002; Trean, 2002). But Chirac was careful not to stray too far from the Americans. The pragmatic nature of French policy stops short of ever being the only obstacle to Washington's desires (on the subject of Iraq, the Russians and Chinese also must be appeased), and French exceptionalism is accepted by the US with less fuss than the more moralistic German variety, perhaps because it is perceived as cynical rather than principled, and is almost expected (Mevel, 2002a, 2002b; Vulliamy, et al., 2002).

THE SPECIAL RELATIONSHIP

Of all allied leaders, British Prime Minister Tony Blair stands out as being exceptionally loyal to the United States and its purposes. This is true not only for the war on terror, where British troops and air-craft were involved from the beginning of the allied counterattack in Afghanistan, but also on the Iraqi issue, where the British have long been alone among the allies in helping to enforce the so-called 'no-fly' zones set up to protect civilian populations in northern and southern Iraq. Blair's strong and instinctive stand with the Americans reflects an old and somewhat mythologized British tradition, going back to the era of the world wars. But aspirations to grandeur have proved easy for many to mock. The parallel wars against terror and against Saddam have not proven popular with Blair's Labour Party, and if leading left-wing opinion-makers get their way this may well become the last time that Britain acts with spontaneous loyalty to the Atlantic alliance (Hutton, 2002b). But, for the present, while the Germans insist on their pacifist 'German way' in international affairs and the French on their Gaullist pretensions of great powerdom, the British persist in acting the loyal member of Winston Churchill's World War II 'Grand Alliance', often referred to (with a bit less grandiloquence) as the 'Special Relationship'. It is an appeal that still commands popular support from centrist and middle-class Britons—whose loyalty to Blair is as important as it was to Thatcher—and it does allow Britain to act as Europe's interpreter to the Americans. Blair has been widely credited with persuading Bush to take his quarrel with Iraq to the UN Security Council, although this credit has been notably more grudging in some quarters of the British press than in Washington (Young, 2002a).

The persistence of British Atlanticism is due in part to the Atlantic alliance's undeniable record of success, first against the Nazis and then against the Soviets. Hardly anyone in Britain can remember a time when the American alliance was not at the core of British for-eign policy. The only deviation from a close and co-operative alliance with the United States was the long and bitterly remembered Suez expedition, when Britain attempted independently to act the part of a great power, and Suez is remembered (correctly) as a disaster whose lesson was never to be separated from the Americans. But a factor more fundamental than lessons drawn from any one episode is the fact that Britain emerged from World War II with the illusion of victory. It was an illusion that had some baleful consequences, arguably leading to an economically ruinous sense of 'British is best' complacency, at least in the accounts of such 'declinist' historians as Correlli Barnett (Barnett, 2001). But the illusion of greatness also allowed the British to disband their empire with relatively little trauma: unlike the French, there was little need and hence little attempt to reassert a vanished great power status through continued colonialism, precisely because in the enduringly mythologized afterglow of 1940 the British felt no need to assert a greatness whose absence many were slow to perceive.

The British entered the Grand Alliance with the presumption of equality (though Churchill privately knew better), and it was easy, with the balm of remembered or imagined glory, to preserve long after the war a vision if not of equality with the United States then at least of moral and military primacy among the European allies. And it is a vision that has proved so enduring in part because it is rooted, like most enduring visions, in an aspect of reality. The British military is exceptionally capable for a force of its size. Long and glorious traditions may not be economically useful, but they can be militarily beneficial. In part because of its sterling military record, Britain is probably the only foreign country (aside from Australia) that is regarded as fully and dependably loyal in Washington, and it is a nation whose military is in some respects regarded as a model by the Americans (especially in counter-insurgency and special forces). This fact, of course, is also rooted in the linguistic and cultural community sometimes called (most famously but not originally by Churchill) 'the English-speaking peoples'; even if the British are not Americans, shear familiarity does much to break down the American skepticism of foreigners.

Though Blair is the only foreign leader who is really respected in Washington, and specifically in the White House, it is a status that has cost him dearly at home, and most particularly within his own party. Blair himself put his finger on a spirit of anti-Americanism widespread in the Labour Party with his much quoted remarks to a Labour Party conference shortly after 11 September:

> It is time also for parts of Islam to confront prejudice against America and not only Islam but parts of western societies too. America has its faults as a society, as we have ours. . . . I think of a black man, born in poverty, who became chief of their armed forces and is now Secretary of State Colin Powell and I wonder frankly whether such a thing could have happened here. . . . America has its faults, but it is a free country, a democracy, it is our ally and some of the reaction to September 11 betrays a hatred of America that shames those that feel it. (Blair, 2001)

Here, Blair tenderly hinted at and shamed 'parts of western societies', by which he meant the activists sitting before him; his questioning whether a Colin Powell 'could have happened here' appealed not only to the egalitarianism but also to the guilt of left-wing Britons; the 'shames those that feel it' description of anti-Americanism was a brilliant display of Blair's ability simultaneously to recognize and to silence a feeling that he does not like. But the feeling remains, as does Blair's own distaste for it. Blair holds his party together on war issues with some difficulty, and only by appealing to the widely accepted moral authority of the United Nations.

Much of the British left is enamoured of the European Union and would like to set up Europe as a parallel, competing superpower to the 'reactionary' and 'intolerant' America that they despise (Hutton, 2002a). To their frustration, Blair is being very cautious on the issue of adopting the euro (and therefore abolishing the beloved pound), and is at the same time taking significant risks by attempting to bridge the growing transatlantic gap (Toynbee, 2002). Even relatively moderate parts of his party see Blair's Atlanticism as 'outdated' (Mepham, 2002). 'The English-speaking peoples' is an idea increasingly unfashionable in Britain, and particularly so in the Labour Party. As I have argued elsewhere (Proudman, 2002b), two key groups within the Labour Party are particularly hostile to these transatlantic links: the activist left and the rapidly growing Muslim and developing world immigrant communities. Labour's left wing grew up demonstrating against American intervention in Vietnam and America's nuclear rearmament in the 1980s. The former Labour Party chairman, Charles Clarke, was forced to argue during the war against the Taliban in Afghanistan that while the Americans had been wrong back then they were (paradoxically, it was implied) 'the good guys now' (Clarke, 2001). Immigrants and racial minorities are a second key element of the Labour Party's support, and they are more likely to regard the United States as a hostile power than are native Britons, many of whom are related to Americans, whom they see as kin, albeit kin with funny accents and crass manners.

There have been large demonstrations in British cities against Anglo-American war plans and Muslims have made up a significant proportion of the anti-war demonstrators. Islam is now the second largest religion in the country, and the number of adherents is increasing rapidly. It is notable that no voices are raised to demand that recent immigrants should be loyal to their new country. If

German or Austrian immigrants in the 1930s had demonstrated against the British government, the result would have been very different. In today's exquisitely egalitarian cultural context any such demand for loyalty would be immediately and effectively dismissed as racist. There has been a loss of confidence in the old Union Jack-waving nationalism that, as recently as Mrs Thatcher's Falklands victory, was such a fixed fact in British politics. 'UK values' are often described as being those of a tolerant, multiracial, and multicultural society. Such 'values' can serve many masters; the only use to which they cannot be put is to demand loyalty to a self-confident and assimilationist nationalism, though they can certainly be used to silence those old-fashioned figures who might hanker for such a unified and unifying sense of national identity.

The old British identity is challenged from below by an influx of immigrants, many of whom openly profess a supervening extra-British (or even anti-British) loyalty to a global Islamic community or 'Ummah' (Khan, 2002). It is simultaneously assaulted from above by an intelligentsia that triumphantly predicts 'the break-up of Britain', in Tom Nairn's famous phrase (Nairn, 1981). This eagerly anticipated disintegration has so far failed to materialize, but when leading intellectuals write of the 'England-dominated, war-obsessed, Eurosceptical and racist English identity', a prospective war leader like Blair has little in the way of positive loyalty to which to appeal—which, of course, is precisely the disloyal intelligentsia's intent (Laity, 2002).

Blair has so far been able to keep his party united behind him with the aid of all those tools of patronage and party discipline available to a Prime Minister with a large majority. He has also been able to exploit the Labour Party's regard for the UN, arguing that he was leading Bush away from unilateral wars and towards multilateralism. As Bush went to the UN in September 2002 over the Iraq dispute, this argument gained credibility. The UN is well regarded in some conservative British circles because Britain has a permanent seat on the Security Council, a continuing token of former greatness. But in the Labour Party, UN internationalism is as much a matter of anti-national faith as it is in other European countries. When arguing for an innocuous House of Commons resolution supporting UN Security Council Resolution 1441 on the disarmament of Iraq, British Foreign Secretary Jack Straw was reduced to seeking moral support from the fact that the Security Council had passed the resolution unanimously, with the support not only of the US and other permanent members, but also of such international stray dogs as Cameroon, Mexico, and Syria (Straw, 2002). One might think Syria a particularly absurd source of moral authority, but when wrapped in the blue and white of the UN, Syria's hereditary dictatorship commands the unthinking respect of the Labour backbenches. Skepticism of the UN is as much reviled in Labour circles as is hostility to Brussels. His success in reconciling the Bush administration to a UN-centred approach to the Iraqi problem has done much to solidify Blair's position with his own party and has been welcomed by influential left-wing commentators—though they make it pretty clear that they regard Britain's traditional transatlantic alliance as a distasteful price to pay for such influence (Young, 2002b; Toynbee, 2002).

CONCLUSION: SOFT POWER DEPENDS ON HARD POWER

Significant parallels exist between Canadian and European attitudes to the United States, to its counter-offensive against terror, and to its campaign against Iraq. These parallels are rooted in a lack of military independence, a lack carried to the point of perceived impotence in the Canadian and German cases. The lack of military power leads to a tendency to emphasize other types of power. In one recent European case, anger at steel tariffs led to an attempt to use economic sanctions targeted against US states where Bush was thought to be electorally vulnerable: 'we have to retaliate in ways that will get Mr Rove's attention', said a European official, referring to the White House political campaign manager (Berke and Sanger, 2002). But the mid-term elections in the US were a great success for Bush, and any further attempt to use economic levers would risk a trade war, which would be to no one's benefit.

Multilateralism has been a common middle-power response to American strength. As Jeffrey Simpson has written in the *Globe and Mail*, the standard Canadian approach to the Americans has been to try to engage them in multilateral forums, where potential partners are available (Simpson, 2002). The US is more skeptical of multilateralism, and one reason is the obvious one that in bilateral negotiations the most powerful partner will achieve its goals. Over these considerations of direct negotiating advantage, Canada and other lesser powers have constructed a claim to moral advantage on the part of multilateral institutions, and a part of this claim has been an increasingly moralistic denunciation of perceived US unilateralism.

These claims are often supported by arguments that make an appeal to international law, and that wish to use international law to undermine state sovereignty, though of course state sovereignty is itself at the core of customary international law (Axworthy, 2000). The attractive rhetoric of legality is deployed as a weapon against the core legal idea of national sovereignty, and specifically as a weapon against American national sovereignty. Though moral language from American sources is often denounced as simplistic by Europeans and Canadians, claims of morality (and of others' immorality) are frequently implied within the European and Canadian rhetoric of multilateral legality, and such claims can themselves be effective tools of power, as proponents of soft power will of course point out.

There are a number of other advantages to multilateral institutions, from the viewpoint of the non-great powers: smaller powers have formally the same status and prominence in most multilateral institutions as great powers; in such institutions, alliances of convenience can be made with varied coalitions on disparate issues; a single large power has difficulty coercing an assembly of smaller states, who thereby gain much-valued autonomy. Risks and responsibilities are spread. Even in the event of disaster—and the UN has superintended more than one disaster—responsibility is hard to pin on any one country or statesman. The inherent (and intended) tendency of multilateral institutions is to conceal conflict, and this is regarded as a desirable feature by nations not eager, or not strong enough, for confrontation. On the other hand, multilateral institutions will be frustrating to powers that do feel themselves strong enough to confront and resolve conflict: that is, they are frustrating to the power that thinks it can emerge victorious from conflict. This is particularly true now that the United States considers itself to be at war, while the European powers and Canada by and large do not.

In response to their own individual histories, each of the three major European powers has found a central place for the UN in their diplomacy, as has Canada. The United States remains skeptical of the value of the organization, for reasons equally rooted in its own historical memory. The Americans can certainly argue that for much of the Cold War, the UN was at best useless from their point of view. Since about 1970, various UN bodies have become fecund sources of anti-American invective, a fact that has led to the effective dismissal by the US of the importance of General Assembly resolutions and precipitated the (just ended) US withdrawal from UNESCO. American skepticism of the UN is particularly pronounced under Republican administrations, and there is no shortage of voices in the current administration that would like to circumvent the UN on Iraq and other issues. At the same time, Germany, Britain, and Canada have left-liberal governments ideologically committed to the UN. Ongoing disagreements can therefore be expected regarding not only the UN itself, but, as recent events have shown, regarding attempts to create parallel international and even supranational institutions such as the International Criminal Court, the Comprehensive Test Ban Treaty Organization, and prospective institutions related to chemical and biological weapons. Differing histories combine with differing ideologies to reinforce differing perceptions of national interests, and international institutions with universal pretenses have recently become a site of consequent inter-allied and intra-occidental dissention. These divisions are themselves a powerful argument against such universally pretentious institutions, at least to anyone who values Western unity.

To these ideological and historical sources of inter-allied dissension are added the workings of competing nationalisms. Every nationalism imagines what existentialist jargon calls an 'other', and for American nationalists this image of what they are not (and most certainly do not want to be) can be the UN itself, which is often seen as a self-aggrandizing bureaucracy of scheming foreign socialists. On the other hand, a large and probably increasing number of Europeans, like many Canadians, take the United States as their national opposite—as Habermas and the Oxford scholar Timothy Garton Ash have pointed out (Habermas, 2002; Garton Ash, 2001). This is even truer of those Europeans who wish to create a pan-European nationalism than it is of those content with the nationalisms of the traditional nation-states. These multiple, interrelated, and mutually reinforcing causes of inter-allied dissention run deep and are not about to disappear.

Orthodox advocates of hard power have been wont to speak carelessly of the 'balance of power'—a usage that goes back to William III, whose annual Mutiny (i.e., Military) Acts referred to the importance of maintaining a 'balance of power' against the aggressive French King Louis XIV, and it is a usage that has attracted almost as venerable a critique (Cobden, 1995 [1835]). Nye disdains this formulation, pointing out that there has often been an imbalance of power in international affairs; he prefers the less ambitious term 'distribution of power' (Nye, 1990). In the various global distributions of different kinds of power, international actors of course emphasize those varieties of power that they can most effectively deploy, as proponents of soft power quite rightly argue. But the latter often forget that different types of power are effective in different situations: Saddam Hussein is notoriously unimpressed by moral force. The North Koreans have not been diverted from their nuclear program by diplomatic skill, even when combined with significant technical and economic resources. Whether Iran can be dissuaded from adding to the hard military power of the quasi-state organization Hezbollah by means of soft power alone is very much in dispute.

Though soft power may prove effective in intra-Western disputes, it seems less effective when the West faces conflict across what Samuel Huntington has famously identified as civilizational barriers (Huntington, 1993). If conflict arises outside the West—and extra-Western conflicts often become wars—the issue becomes in the first instance an American problem. Other Western powers usually have the option of being involved or not as their interests, capabilities, and domestic politics dictate. The recent war in Afghanistan has displayed Canadian policy acting in just this way: Canada became involved militarily largely in response to internal political criticism of the Chrétien government's initially pusillanimous response to 11 September, and was then free to withdraw when the political dividends decreased (Proudman, 2002a). The Canadians came and went, and notwithstanding the heroic efforts of a small number of Canadian soldiers, neither the coming nor the going had much impact on the overall distribution of power in Central Asia.

The United States enjoys no such liberties. An American withdrawal would precipitate the collapse of the entire Western stake in Afghanistan, just as an American withdrawal from the frontiers of Iraq would cause a collapse of the Western position in the Persian Gulf. The American presence in or near either country is a major determinant of the global power distribution, while a minor power's presence (or non-presence) is not. The lesser power thereby acquires the freedom of irresponsibility. The United States, which is the ultimate guarantor of the West's having a position at all, has no such freedom. With power comes responsibility, and with irrelevance comes freedom from responsibility. It is a freedom that some lesser powers use for narrowly self-regarding purposes—and that can also be used (with a large element of self-contradiction) to strike moral attitudes.

It is entirely possible that lesser powers acting to maximize their own power may end up increasing aggregate Western power. Arguably, German and other allied forces on peacekeeping duty in Afghanistan were sent there for narrowly self-regarding reasons—in order to establish a claim to be consulted on future policy, for instance—but nevertheless they serve to enhance the Western position generally. But such self-regarding behaviour does not necessarily strengthen the whole: the self-interested post 1991 behaviour of the French in the Persian Gulf has worked precisely to undermine the overall Western position by convincing Saddam that obduracy could eventually be rewarding. And simultaneously, of course, French diplomacy has preened itself on its moral scruples about the effects of economic sanctions. It is therefore quite possible that Canada and Europe may wield soft power in ways that effectively maximize their own power at the expense of an increasingly despised United States. But the power of the West is ultimately rooted in the hard power of the United States. Narrowly self-interested uses of soft power are weakened by undermining the American willingness or capability to employ that essential hard power. Increasingly rancorous inter-allied disputes stimulated by radically differing levels of military power and consequent differences of perception regarding the nature of international politics have led and could continue to lead to situations in which divisions between the United States and its lesser allies are accentuated.

The omens are not good. It would be a bitter vindication for the apostles of soft power were soft power to show itself primarily effective as a solvent of the real, hard power that establishes the very conditions of existence of soft power and its liberal advocates.

REFERENCES

[Axworthy, Lloyd]. 1999. *The World at Six*, CBC Radio, 19 Nov.

———. 2000. 'Notes for an Address . . . to the 55th Session of the United Nations General Assembly', 14 Sept. Available at: <http://www.un.org/Ga/55/Webcast/Statements/Canada.htm>.

Barnett, Correlli. 2001 *The Verdict of Peace: Britain between Her Yesterday and the Future*, London: Macmillan.

Berke, Richard L., and David E. Sanger. 2002. 'Some in Administration Grumble As Aide's Role Seems to Expand', *New York Times*, 11 May.

[Blair, Tony]. 2001. 'Full Text: Tony Blair's Speech', *The Guardian*, 2 Oct.

Berman, Paul. 2001. 'From the radicalism of the '60s to the interventionism of the '90s: The Passion of Joschka Fischer', *New Republic*, 27 Aug.

Caldwell, Christopher. 2002. 'The Angry Adolescent of Europe: Irresponsibility as the German Way', *Weekly Standard*, 7 Oct.

Ceadel, Martin. 1987. *Thinking about War and Peace*. Oxford: Oxford University Press.

Clarke, Charles. 2001. 'Americans are the good guys now: Why I've left behind my old hostility to US foreign policy', *The Guardian*, 4 Dec.

Cobden, Richard. 1995. 'Russia' [1835], in *The Collected Works of Richard Cobden*, vol. 1, ed. Peter Cain. London: Routledge, 256-7.

Colombani, Jean-Marie. 2001. 'Nous sommes tous Américains', *Le Monde*, 13 Sept.

de Barochez, Luc. 2002a.'Etats-Unis, Jospin et Vedrine', *Le Figaro*, 9 Feb.

———. 2002b. 'Retrouvant une influence oubliée', *Le Figaro*, 11 Nov.

Freeden, Michael. 1996. *Ideologies and Political Theory*. Oxford: Clarendon Press.

Friedman, Thomas. 2002. 'The New Club NATO', *New York Times*, 17 Nov., 4:11.

Garton Ash, Timothy. 2001. 'Europe at War', *New York Review of Books*, 20 Dec.

Girard, Renaud. 2002. 'La victoire de la raison', *Le Figaro*, 15 Nov.

Goldberg, Jonah. 2002. 'Wimps', *National Review*, 11 Nov.

Grass, Gunter. 2003. 'No Beginning or End to War', *The Guardian*, 29 Jan.

Gray, Colin S. 2002. *Strategy for Chaos: Revolutions in Military Affairs and the Evidence of History*. London: Frank Cass.

Habermas, Jürgen. 2002. 'Letter to America', *The Nation*, 16 Dec.

Horrock, Nicholas M. 2002. 'Bush: NATO's guest of honor', *Washington Times*, 19 Nov.

Huntington, Samuel P. 1993. 'The Clash of Civilizations?', *Foreign Affairs* (Summer).

Hutton, Will. 2002a. *The World We're In*. London: Little, Brown.

———. 2002b. 'Time to stop being America's lap-dog', *The Observer*, 17 Feb.

Kennedy, A.L. 2002. 'Flying the Flag for Hate', *The Guardian*, 29 Mar.

Keohane, Robert O., and Joseph S. Nye. 1977. *Power and Interdependence: World Politics in Transition*. Boston: Little, Brown.

Kissinger, Henry. 2002. 'Why U.S.–German Rift Could Set Europe Back 100 Years', *Scotland on Sunday*, 20 Oct.

Khan, Aisha. 2002. 'The Veil in My Handbag', *The Guardian*, 18 June.

Khouri-Dagher, Nadia. 2001. 'Une guerre du IIIe millénaire' *Le Monde*, 13 Sept.

Kupchan, Charles A. 2002. 'The End of the West', *Atlantic Monthly* (Nov.).

Laity, Paul. 2002. 'Are the English Human?', *London Review of Books*, 28 Nov.

Lundestad, Geir. 1990. *The American 'Empire'*. Oxford and Oslo: Oxford University Press and Norwegian University Press.

Mepham, David. 2002. 'We've given in to the arms lobby', *The Guardian*, 24 July.

Mevel, Jean-Jacques. 2002a. 'Raffarin dénonce la "vision simpliste" américaine', *Le Figaro,* 9 Oct.

———. 2002b. 'Malgré le dossier irakien, les relations franco-americaines se sont améliorées', *Le Figaro*, 18 Oct.

Monbiot, George. 2002. 'The Logic of Empire', *The Guardian*, 6 Aug.

Nairn, Tom. 1981. *The Breakup of Britain: Crisis and Neo-Nationalism*, London: NLB.

Nye, Joseph S. 1990. 'The Changing Nature of World Power', *Political Science Quarterly* 105, 2 (Summer): 177–92.

———. 1999. 'The Challenge of Soft Power: The Propounder of This Novel Concept Looks at Lloyd Axworthy's Diplomacy', *Time*, 22 Feb.

Proudman, Mark F. 2002a. 'Peacekeeping if Necessary', *National Post*, 27 July.

———. 2002b. 'Blair Faces Party Revolt', *National Post*, 10 Aug.

Simpson, Jeffrey. 2002. 'How to Engage the Bushites?', *Globe and Mail*, 8 Apr.

Straw, Jack. 2002. 'Be cautious over Iraq's Somersault', *The Guardian*, 14 Nov.

Toynbee, Polly. 2002. 'Barrister Blair fights his most difficult case', *The Guardian*, 25 Sept.

Trean, Claire. 2002. 'Diplomatie: la France reprend des couleurs', *Le Monde*, 13 Nov.

Vulliamy, Ed, Paul Webster, and Nick Paton Walsh. 2002. 'Scramble to carve up Iraqi oil reserves lies behind US diplomacy', *The Observer*, 6 Oct.

Will, George F. 2002. 'Fowl Cries From the U.N.', *Washington Post*, 29 Oct.

Young, Hugo. 2002a 'This good cop, bad cop routine is working—so far', *The Guardian*, 22 Oct.

———. 2002b. 'Bush now seems to accept that this must be a UN war', *The Guardian*, 19 Nov.

Zizek, Slavoj. 2002. 'Are we in a war? Do we have an enemy?', *London Review of Books*, 23 May.

The Canada Among Nations Series

Canada Among Nations 1998: Leadership and Dialogue, edited by
Fen Osler Hampson and Maureen Appel Molot
019-541406-3

Canada Among Nations 1999: A Big League Player?, edited by
Fen Osler Hampson, Michael Hart, and Martin Rudner
019-541458-6

Canada Among Nations 2000: Vanishing Borders, edited by
Maureen Appel Molot and Fen Osler Hampson
019-541540-X

Canada Among Nations 2001: The Axworthy Legacy, edited by
Fen Osler Hampson, Norman Hillmer, and Maureen Appel Molot
019-541677-8

Canada Among Nations 2002: A Fading Power, edited by
Norman Hillmer and Maureen Appel Molot
019-541791-7

Canada Among Nations 2003: Coping with the American Colossus,
edited by David Carment, Fen Osler Hampson, Norman Hillmer
0-19-541924-3